baldrige user's guide^{SM}

Organization Diagnosis, Design, and Transformation

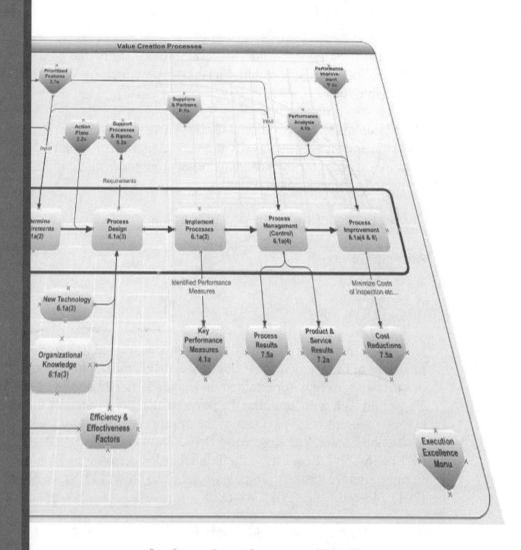

John Latham, PhD
and
John Vinyard

WILEY
Publishers Since 1807

This custom textbook includes materials submitted by the Author for publication by John Wiley & Sons, Inc. The material has not been edited by Wiley and the Author is solely responsible for its content.

The Malcolm Baldrige National Quality Award was created by Public Law 100-107, and signed into law by the U.S. Congress on August 20, 1987. Principal support for the program comes from the Foundation for the Malcolm Baldrige National Quality Award.

To order books or for customer service, please call 1(800)-CALL-WILEY (225-5945).

Printed in the United States of America.

ISBN 0-471-69777-X

10 9 8 7 6 5 4 3 2 1

Dedication

*This book is dedicated to our wives, Kathy Vinyard and Penny Latham,
and our families, John and Ryan Vinyard and Courtney, Chuck, and Dirk Latham,
who have supported and tolerated us while we were away learning many of the lessons presented
in this book and while we were distracted writing this book.*

They are the ones who ultimately paid the price and we are forever grateful!

Contents

Foreword

Fifteen years after the initiation of the Malcolm Baldrige National Quality Award (Baldrige) it is clear that using its attendant criteria helps to dramatically improve performance for any organization. In the early years, however, there was no readily available source of best practices, practitioners or criteria experts to help the pioneer companies.

By the early 1990's companies began to win who had been using the criteria since its introduction. Since that time, businesses worldwide have recognized the impact of using the Baldrige Framework to drive their competitiveness. Hundreds of US and international companies (who are not even eligible to apply for the Baldrige Award) systematically assess themselves against the criteria because they understand its impact on improving results. This has resulted in an extensive source of best practices, documented for example in the "Quest for Excellence" conference proceedings.

For the novice, however, a comprehensive understanding of the criteria can still be elusive. This book fills that void. John Vinyard and John Latham have taken the Baldrige criteria and made them understandable to the novice. At the same time they provide a breakdown of the same criteria to help the most experienced Baldrige user make connections that previously were not obvious.

I would have very much appreciated this book during our Baldrige journey. I encourage you to use it to accelerate your journey. You will find it incredibly rewarding!

Good Luck in your journey to business excellence,

David Spong

President (retired)	Vice President and General Manager (retired)
Boeing Aerospace Support	Boeing Airlift and Tanker
Baldrige Recipient - Service Sector - 2003	Baldrige Recipient - Manufacturing Sector – 1998

David Spong is a self-proclaimed Baldrige zealot! He is the first two-time recipient of the Baldrige Award in two different businesses in two different sectors and he is on the Malcolm Baldrige National Quality Award Board of Overseers.

David has traveled the Baldrige journey three times, winning twice, and "**knows** that Baldrige works! The process helps drive organizations to be more competitive and serves to 'turn up the heat' on performance excellence." In the beginning, David was a skeptic and has been quoted saying, "Who has time for all this extra stuff?" "I have a business to run." However, he started believing in Baldrige when he saw his business results improve and the culture of his organizations become more collaborative. As the journey progressed he became a zealot. To other skeptical leaders he would say "sure you can run a decent or even a great business, but is that what you want? Why not strive for being the best? Start the journey and as you begin to understand the Baldrige process and see improved business results with a cultural transformation you too will become zealots."

Acknowledgements

This book is the product of the thousands of "person years" (not from the authors) that have gone into the development of the Baldrige model and process. The Malcolm Baldrige National Quality Award (Baldrige) began with a dream in the mid 1980's and ultimately resulted in legislation in 1987. Baldrige was designed to make United States organizations more competitive, but its impact has been worldwide. It has been more widely accepted than any of the original authors could have predicted. Since 1988 organizations of all kinds have discovered the power of using the Baldrige Criteria to dramatically improve their performance. For example, we work with clients around the world who use the Baldrige criteria to be more competitive, even though many of them are not U.S. organizations and are not even eligible for the award. They use the Baldrige Criteria to drive the improvement of their organizational performance. We hope each of them will use this book to continue to advance their competitiveness.

For almost two decades the Baldrige Process has been a dynamic force in world competitiveness. We thank those who have been involved to design and improve this process over the years. Without the thousands of people who have written the criteria, revised the criteria, used the criteria and shared their successes (and shared their failures), the knowledge in this book could not have been compiled.

The authors are indebted to a number of key people who helped make this book possible. Putting a book like this together reminds you of all the people who have really made a difference in your world. This list of contributors starts with Harry Hertz, Barry Diamondstone, Curt Reimann and the entire Baldrige Team. These are some of the most professional and dedicated government employees in our country and they are making a difference! Those of us who have been fortunate enough to have worked closely with them have benefited from every day of that association. Not only are they gifted professionals, but they share their knowledge and experience to help others.

An effort like this was not achieved by the authors alone; we had the help of many others. We appreciate David Spong who wrote the Forward and continues to inspire and be a role model leader for the rest of us to follow. Joe Musikowski who was one of our most zealous task masters, and made numerous suggestions most of which we used to improve this edition and the ones we could not implement we noted for the next edition. For example, the accompanying CD (and the software to link the various parts of the criteria) was one of Joe's suggestions. We heard you Joe and you took us to a higher level – Thanks! Other reviewers who gave us great suggestions and actionable feedback included David Branch, Steve Hoisington, Curt Reimann, Richard Schuttler, Jack Swaim, Tina Sung, Marlene Yanovsky and Jim Zurn. To each of them we owe a debt of gratitude for their support, time, talent, insights and best wishes.

We are also very grateful for the award winning practice examples that were generously provided by 14 Baldrige recipient organizations including: BI, Boeing Airlift and Tanker, Branch-Smith Printing, Chugach School District, Clarke American, Dana Spicer Driveshaft, KARLEE, Motorola CGISS, Pearl River School District, Ritz-Carlton Hotels, SSM Healthcare, ST Microelectronics, Texas Nameplate, and The University of Wisconsin Stout. These examples help make the criteria "come alive" for new users and they also provide excellent examples for the more advanced users tasked with the design/redesign of the organization's processes.

Quest for Excellence XVI (March 2004) was a key milestone for us in many respects. The conference was the first time we showed the book and software to anyone outside of our team of expert reviewers. At the Conference we previewed the book and software to a small group who also gave us very constructive and actionable feedback. Many of their comments are reflected in this edition of the book and many are slated for inclusion in future editions. These "Baldrige-savvy" professionals included Jim Beckham, Bettye Bradley, David Branch, Hank Grimmick, Harry Hertz, Marti Jackson, Margaret Johanning, Paige Lillard, Vince Morgillo, Sheryl Morris Meyer, Joe Musikowski, Brad Nelson, Thom Schamberger, Dee Springer, Tina Sung, Roger Triplett, and Marlene Yanovsky.

The Quest for Excellence Conference also gave us the opportunity to preview the product 1-on-1 and gain the suggestions and insights of other leaders, including: Adam Cohen, Debbie Collard, Frank D'Agosta, Ray Emery, Bob Haase, Maureen Greenwood-Hamilton, Charles Korbell, Brad Lovik, Marty Nischi, Sheila Nix, Steve Randol, Rick Roberts, Ed Schaniel, and a group from several TATA Divisions

(India). Each of them made comments and provided perspectives that were helpful to our understanding of the book, the software, and their potential uses.

Last, but certainly not least, we thank our wives Penny Latham and Kathy Vinyard, and our office support staff – Pam Eldredge and Suzie McLaughlin. The time spent on this project was significant and without their support, the book would not have come to pass. Many times this was an active role of reading, rereading, rereading, rereading... and other times it was simply showing heroic tolerance as the authors spent hours on the phone with each other, hours on the computer, or hours sending emails.

Special thanks goes to Landon Cox of MindFab, our technology partner, for his heroic efforts (usually on short notice) and outstanding design work on the CD-ROM. Landon's tolerance for our ever changing requirements and short lead times was above and beyond the "call of duty" and we are forever grateful.

Finally, as with any list of acknowledgements, we know our list has the risk of not mentioning someone who has been key to the development of our thoughts. In that vein, we thank all those who have worked with us over the years and have shared their lessons learned, knowledge, and wisdom.

We feel those clients, coworkers and friends are some of the most talented individuals in the world.

From our hearts -- Thank you! We could not have written this without your help.

About the Authors

John Latham, PhD.

Dr. Latham is a Senior Partner and Founder of GENITECT, LLC an organization diagnosis, design, and transformation firm with offices in Atlanta and Colorado Springs. An international management consultant and organization architect he specializes in the assessment and redesign of business systems to achieve sustainable results for multiple stakeholders. His work focuses on helping senior executives design and lead strategic change initiatives from strategy to results including: strategic leadership, execution excellence, and organizational learning.

John has over 26 years experience working in and with a variety of commercial, non-profit, and government organizations from Asia to Europe. He has had a wide variety of work experiences from his first job as a Jet Engine Mechanic for the U.S. Air Force to Vice President of Corporate Quality and Business Excellence for Dade Behring a $1.3 billion *in vitro* diagnostics manufacturer with operations in 40 countries. Some of his clients have included Boeing Commercial Airplanes, Boeing Airlift & Tanker, Kawasaki Robotics, British Airways, Lockheed Martin, Motorola, and ASTD.

John has served on the Malcolm Baldrige National Quality Award Board of Examiners since 1996. He served as an Examiner in 1996, a Senior Examiner from 1997 to 2001, and an Alumni examiner in 2003 and 2004. As a senior examiner and leader for the program he led the evaluations of some of the nation's highest performing companies including leading site visits in 2000 and 2001. John served as the Chair of the Judges Panel and Lead Judge for the U.S. Army Communities of Excellence (ACOE) Award, a Baldrige-based installation improvement program, in 2003 and 2004. As a member of the Hawaii State Award of Excellence Executive Committee from 1994 to 1997, John helped lead the design and development of the award evaluation and judging processes and personally trained and coached the Board of Examiners.

John Vinyard

John is a Senior Partner and Founder of GENITECT, LLC an organization diagnosis, design, and transformation firm with offices in Atlanta and Colorado Springs. Genitect is passionately dedicated to helping client organizations improve. This is achieved through effectively assessing organizations, and working with leadership to design and implement change.

John has worked with numerous international firms in Europe, the Middle East, India, and the Pacific Rim. He specializes in working with leadership teams to help transform their organizations. John has worked with five Baldrige winners throughout their journey, and has helped them use the Baldrige Model to significantly impact their bottom-line results. John has over 35 years experience working with improvement at all levels. He focuses on helping executives design and lead strategic change initiatives from strategy to results including: strategic leadership, execution excellence, and organizational learning.

John has experience with commercial, nonprofit, education and government organizations including Boeing Aerospace (2003 Baldrige Winner), Clarke American (2001 Baldrige Winner), Ritz Carlton Hotel Company (1999 Baldrige Winner), Boeing Airlift & Tanker (1998 Baldrige Winner) and Corning Telecommunications Products Division (1995 Baldrige Winner). Other clients have included the U.S. Army, the U.S. Air Force, Eaton Corporation, Lanier Worldwide, Cessna Aircraft, Shorts Brothers, LLD, TATA Corporation (India), InfoSys (India), Bekaert Corporation (Belgium – the first winner of the European Foundation for Quality Management (EFQM) Award), and many others.

His first job was as a Quality Engineer for Pratt & Whitney Aircraft. He has held positions as: Director, Engine Maintenance, United Airlines; VP Quality and Manufacturing Operations, GenCorp Polymer Products; and Group VP, Manufacturing, Cadmus Communications.

Introduction

Overview

The Path to Performance Excellence consists of one prerequisite, three competencies, and a journey. The **prerequisite** is a solid foundation that **focuses** on the unique context of the organization including the organization as a system, the core values and concepts underlying the system (a.k.a. design principles), the key internal and external factors the organization must work within (these are called the Organizational Factors), and finally a maturity model that depicts the developmental path to performance excellence.

These prerequisites provide the foundation for developing the three competencies of performance excellence:

- **strategic leadership** *(lead the organization)*
- **execution excellence** *(manage the organization)*
- **organizational learning** *(improve the organization)*.

While some organizations have developed strengths in one competency, the path to performance excellence requires competency in all three. Otherwise the organization will not be able to achieve and sustain excellence. Finally, the path to performance excellence is a **journey** of transformation which must be led.

The Performance Excellence journey has been key to the competitiveness of many organizations. Nevertheless, preparing an assessment document (or an Application for the Malcolm Baldrige National Quality Award or other Baldrige – Based Award) can be a daunting task.

Reading the criteria is difficult; many people have difficulty understanding what all the elements mean on their first reading. For those who become Baldrige Examiners, it is frequently in the third year as an Examiner before the criteria really "come alive." In that third year the flow becomes clearer, the linkages make more sense, and the overall process is clearer. The problem is, however, most people do not have three years to wait. In addition, people entering this process need tools which can help them understand the process more quickly.

This guide is focused on making the process of writing, evaluating, and improving easier. This guide reorganizes the Baldrige criteria to emphasize the three competencies of performance excellence. The actual criteria questions are presented verbatim from the NIST Criteria Booklet. In addition, the format of the document has been designed to help the users to structure their thoughts and eventually their improvement program, so they address the criteria more completely and more effectively as an integrated system.

This guide will:

- Increase your understanding of the individual criteria elements
- Increase your understanding of the criteria system by increasing your knowledge of the linkages between criteria elements
- Increase your ability to explain the criteria to others at all levels of the organization
- Increase your understanding of the three competencies of performance excellence: strategic leadership, execution excellence, and organziational learning
- Help you document your approaches and write an application
- Help you evaluate/diagnose your processes and results
- Help you assess your organization's overall performance
- Help you custom design/redesign your processes to achieve higher performance
- Help you transform your organization to achieve and sustain performance excellence

In addition, this book is also helpful for examiners assessing an organization (the workbook portion of this book can be used to take notes on a site visit).

Book and CD Key Features

This book was written to not only provide a 3-dimensional systems view of the criteria beyond anything currently available but also provides an accompanying CD-ROM that features electronic versions of the criteria "blueprints" with live links between the Areas to Address. This software program allows the user to navigate quickly through the linkages in the criteria and follow their own logical flow of interrogation. This allows the individual to fully understand the answers to their unique questions or concerns. This approach and capability facilitates a 3-dimensional view of the criteria as a system.

A key feature of this book is that it addresses the criteria in a greater level of detail than most other books. This book does not stop at the Category level (7 Categories) or the Item level (19 Items), but addresses all **37 *areas to address***. There are three types of areas to address: (a) 5 key factor areas in the Organizational Profile; (b) 26 process areas in the leadership, strategy, customer, people, process management and information categories; and (c) 6 results areas in Category 7 the Results Category.

Each of the 37 sections in the book follow a similar pattern of: (a) foundation; (b) examples from Baldrige recipients; (c) criteria questions; (d) worksheets (a tool to help organize your own organization's information to respond to the questions); (e) diagnostic questions (these are simple questions which can be asked within an organization to determine whether the organization is addressing the processes or results required by the Baldrige Criteria); (f) blueprints (diagrams of each area showing the key inter-relationships); (g) systems integration (a.k.a. linkages); and finally (h) thoughts for leaders (for some areas).

How to Use This Guide

This guide is designed for the organization architect to help them diagnose, design/redesign, and transform the organization to achieve and sustain performance excellence. Organization architects have varying levels of experience and often different roles and responsibilities in the organization transformation process. This guide is written for several levels of experience with the Baldrige Criteria (Criteria for Performance Excellence) as a business framework:

- The beginning architect can use the workbook to understand the basics of the Baldrige Model and Process – Study: foundation (introduction) sections, examples, questions and the actual criteria on the CD-ROM.

- The award application writer can be used as a workbook to organize the data and write an assessment for an organization. Study: the tools sections and the worksheets on the CD-ROM.

- The examiner or internal assessor can use the guide as a workbook to take notes as they perform an assessment of an organization. Study: tools sections, CD-ROM worksheets and the CD-ROM scoring workbook.

- The more advanced architect can use the workbook to advance their knowledge in areas of criteria linkages and relationships. Study: blueprints, system integration, and "fly the blueprints" on the CD-ROM.

- The designer can use the examples in the guide to inspire creative designs that are a custom fit for the unique organization. Study the examples, blueprints, and linkages.

Navigating Using the Icons

Orientation

The first sub-section in each Area to Address section gives the new user of the Baldrige Framework simple explanations of what the criteria mean and examples of what how organizations approach this area (e.g., example factors, practices, or results).

 FOUNDATION

Introduction - The introduction is a common sense description of what the criteria in this Area to Address mean and are trying to achieve. The introduction focuses on what the criteria are trying to get at and not just the words in the criteria. This will help new and experienced users gain a better understanding of the criteria, their background and their meaning.

 EXAMPLE

Example Factors, Practices, and Results – Examples respond to the key elements of the particular Areas to Address. These live demonstrations of the Area to Address are included courtesy of the Baldrige Award recipients. Typically these include both graphics (in some cases), and descriptions of the Best Practices Examples from Baldrige winning organizations.

Diagnosis

The second sub-section is designed for those actually tasked with assessing and diagnosing the organization. Included in this sub-section are: the actual Baldrige Criteria questions, "fill-in-the-blank" worksheets, and diagnostic questions. The worksheets restructure the criteria into a format that facilitates the documentation of the current factors, processes, and results.

 QUESTIONS

> ***Baldrige Criteria Questions*** *- The actual Malcolm Baldrige National Quality Award Criteria is presented verbatim in the boxed area labeled Questions. Included are the actual questions and the notes (explanations) from the Malcolm Baldrige National Quality Award Criteria.*

WORKSHEETS

Worksheets – The "fill-in-the-blank" worksheets help the assessors organize information about the organization's key factors, processes, and results. Completing these worksheets will help an organization to eventually write responses in the form of an award application. The worksheets are structured and aligned in a manner that will help the user understand the breadth and depth of what the criteria are trying to address. The worksheets presented in the book are condensed to save space. The full-size (landscape) format worksheets are available on the CD-ROM.

 ASSESSMENT

Diagnostic Questions – These questions help the assessor quickly take the "temperature" of the organization. Included in this part is a list of questions that can help the user develop a rough estimate score for their organization. This portion of the book can also be used as a survey across different groups to understand how they feel the organization is currently performing.

Design	**Advanced Users**

The third sub-section is focused on helping the more advanced Baldrige user to understand the criteria system in greater depth and detail than the previous sub-sections. The diagrams which show the flow in and out of an Area to Address help to make the Baldrige Criteria more dynamic than reading the criteria as isolated "stand alone" components. In addition, this section describes the inputs and outputs to the Area to Address in terms of system integration linkages.

 BLUEPRINT

Blueprint – These are flowchart type diagrams that depict the logic flow and relationships of the elements found in the particular area to address and the linkages to other areas to address (factors, processes, and results). Together these blueprints provide a "visual version" of the criteria. Accompanying the blueprint is a brief description of the key elements and their relationships.

SYSTEM INTEGRATION

System Integration (a.k.a. Linkages) – These support the blueprints by describing the nature of the relationships (linkages) to other areas to address. A description of the linkages depicted in the blueprint and their relationships to other criteria factors, processes, and results both inputs and outputs are presented for the advanced user. These linkages help the advanced user design processes that are integrated with other processes throughout the organization. The CD-ROM versions of the blueprints allow the reader to "fly" around the criteria at light speed by simply pointing and clicking on the linkage symbols.

Transformation | **Leaders**

The final sub-section is focused on helping the user to understand some of the lessons learned from (and for) leaders. These are aimed at helping leaders understand how their actions impact the organization and its ability to succeed and improve.

THOUGHTS FOR LEADERS

Thoughts for Leaders - Thoughts for leaders are included for many areas to address and are focused on bringing the concepts within the area to address alive for the leaders of the organization. This is typically accomplished through brief anecdotes.

RESEARCH SAYS

Research Findings - Occasionally there is a sub-section that describes the research findings on a particular topic. This section can show up anywhere in the sequence.

DDT – Core Competencies of the Organizational Architect

This book supports and facilitates the three core activities of the organization architect – organization diagnosis, design/redesign, and transformation.

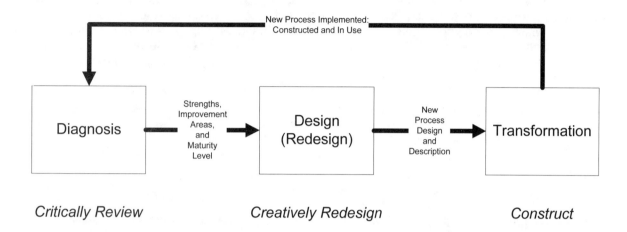

Critically Review   *Creatively Redesign*   *Construct*

Using this guide can help organizations understand and critically review their current practices and processes, analyze those practices, compare them to world-class practices, and significantly change their overall performance and competitiveness. To do this the user needs to understand the diagnosis, design and transformation (DDT) sequence.

Diagnosis – How do we know where we are?

To plot a course for improvement requires two points of reference – the organization's current position and the desired position. The user of this book can diagnose where the organization has significant (or even subtle) Opportunities for Improvement (or what examiners call OFIs). This process will give the leaders of any organization a large supply of ideas on how to improve. It also helps the organization establish a common language with which they can communicate with other organizations, divisions, departments, functions, etc. A common language enables sharing between organizations. This sharing is one of the reasons many organizations use the Baldrige Assessment process. There are three key elements of diagnosis:

- qualitative descriptions of the process or results
- evaluation of those descriptions formatted as strengths and opportunities for improvement
- identified levels on the maturity scale which is also known as scoring based on the evaluation comments

Design – What should we do?

This book includes examples of what other organizations have done to respond to the criteria. While these approaches will not perfectly fit any organization except the one for which they were designed, the generic concepts described may be creatively adapted for use in other organizations. This means the learning gained from others can be revised to fit your organization. Additionally, the "common sense" descriptions of what the criteria are addressing (the first portion or each section) can be used to guide the tailoring of the benchmarked process. The output of this phase is a new process design and description. This phase also has three main steps or elements:

- evaluate the examples
- synthesize various examples into a new model
- apply or custom fit the new model to your unique organization

Transformation – Are we learning and improving?

The process of transformation is a process of learning. By tracking the performance trends the organization can determine whether the Diagnosis and Design processes were effective.

The only valid reason that we can think of for using the Baldrige Criteria for Performance Excellence is to improve the performance of the organization. If this does not occur, then changes to the approaches need to be made. Each change implemented should be monitored and the approach improved if the changes which were anticipated are not achieved. One way to improve the success rate of implementation and actually get people to use the new process is to involve them in the design/redesign of the process. There are again three key elements of the transformation phase:

- implementation of the new design/redesign
- measure and stabilize the performance of the new design
- evaluate and improve the new design

The Performance Excellence Framework

The framework provides a high-level or "category" view of the Criteria for Performance Excellence. There are seven categories as shown in the diagram below. Within the seven Categories are 19 more specific "Items" and within the items there are 32 Areas to Address, plus the 5 areas in the Organizational Profile. This book is written to address the most detailed level of the criteria – the 37 Areas to Address.

Organizational Profile:

Environment, Relationships, Challenges

Measurement, Analysis, and Knowledge Management

The book is divided into 5 major parts that organize and address the 37 areas to address that make up the performance excellence model. The first four "core" sections cover the performance excellence model in detail and the last part covers the process of using the model for improvement.

Part 1 - Focus is composed of the Organizational Profile (the umbrella at the top of the figure above) that sets the context for the way an organization operates. The environment, key working relationships, and strategic challenges serve as an overarching guide for an organizational performance management system.

Part 2 - Strategic Leadership is composed of leadership, strategic planning, and the customer and market knowledge half of the customer and market focus category. Baldrige examiners call this the leadership triad. Some call this the 'driver' of the other areas because it sets the direction and establishes the priorities.

Part 3 - Execution Excellence is composed of process management, human resource focus and the customer relationship and satisfaction determination half of the customer focus category. Baldrige examiners often include the results in this grouping and call it the results triad. Some call this grouping the enablers because developing the capacity of the people and processes is key to accomplishing the overall strategy.

Part 4 - Organizational Learning is composed of the information and analysis and results categories. While all the categories point toward business results, these results are most useful for validating the improvements and supporting the learning process by providing insight into what works and what doesn't work in the overall system.

Part 5 – The Journey is a brief look at the diagnosis, design, and transformation sequence as a learning process. Helpful hints on conducting assessments are discussed along with techniques for leading change.

Systematic Processes

What is a Process?

Of the 37 areas to address, 26 are focused on processes. NIST (2004) defines a process (in the Glossary of Terms at the back of this book) as :

> *linked activities with the purpose of producing a product or service for a customer (user) within or outside the organization. Generally, processes involve combinations of people, machines, tools, techniques, and materials in a defined series of steps or actions. In some situations, processes might require adherence to a specific sequence of steps, with documentation (sometimes formal) of procedures and requirements, including well-defined measurement and control steps. (p. 34)*

In many service situations, particularly when customers are directly involved in the service, the term 'process' is used in a more general way, i.e., to spell out what must be done, possibly including a preferred or expected sequence. If a sequence is critical, the service needs to include information to help customers understand and follow the sequence. Service processes involving customers also require guidance to the providers of those services on handling contingencies related to customers' likely or possible actions or behaviors.

In knowledge work such as strategic planning, research, development, and analysis, process does not necessarily imply formal sequences of steps or procedures. Rather, process implies general understandings regarding competent performance such as timing, options to be included, evaluation, and reporting – more flexible frameworks in the end. Sequences for knowledge work might arise as part of these understandings but the knowledge work approaches seldom benefit from strict procedures.

Generic Process Model

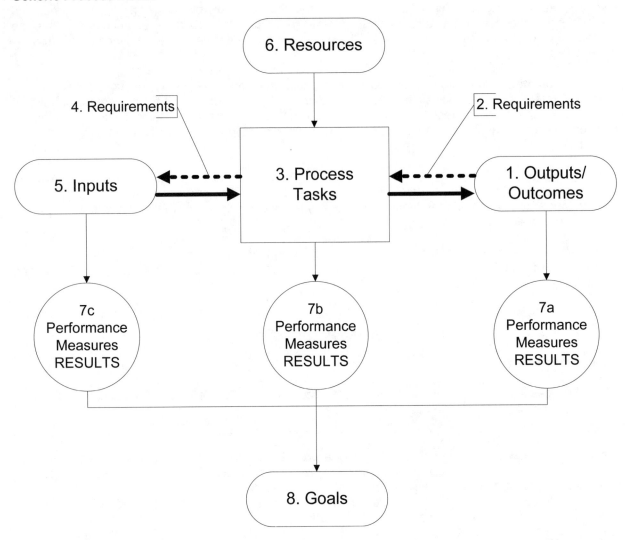

The authors define a "Systematic Process" as one which has the following characteristics:

1. Outputs and Outcomes are clearly defined. These are also often called "deliverables."
2. Requirements for the outputs or deliverables are clear and explicit and drive the design of the process.
3. Process - Clearly defined and understood (activities and their internal and external relationships described)
4. Requirements for the inputs or the process activities are clear and explicit.
5. Inputs are clearly defined – these are the deliverables for the processes suppliers and partners which may be internal or external.
6. Resources are allocated (people, capital, technology, etc.) to make the process work.
7. Measurements/Results levels, trends and comparisons are measured at several places along the value chain or process: at the end of the process (outputs), in-process, and inputs to the process.
8. Goals - are set for improved performance

What is Systematic?

NIST (2004) defines systematic (in the Glossary of Terms at the back of this document) as :

> *approaches that are repeatable and use data and information so that learning is possible. In other words, approaches are systematic if they build in the opportunity for evaluation, improvement, and sharing, thereby permitting a gain in maturity.* (p. 35)

A Systematic Process Continually Improves:

An organizational learning cycle is a key aspect of a systematic process. A typical learning cycle is presented below.

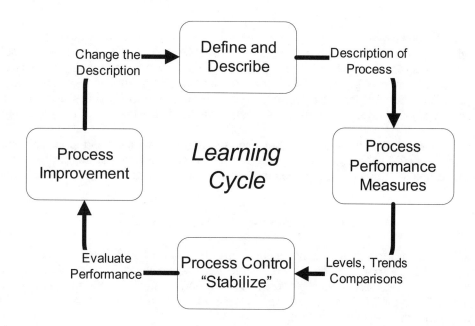

An organization as a system is not really a new idea. It has been around for as long as 2500 years.

"Whoever pursues a business in this world must have a system. A business which has attained success without a system does not exist. From ministers and generals down to the hundreds of craftsmen, every one of them has a system. The craftsmen employ the ruler to make a square and the compass to make a circle. All of them, both skilled and unskilled, use this system. The skilled may at times accomplish a circle and a square by their own dexterity. But with a system, even the unskilled may achieve the same result, though dexterity they have none. Hence, every craftsman possesses a system as a model. Now, if we govern the empire, or a large state, without a system as a model, are we not even less intelligent than a common craftsman?"

Mo-Tze (a.k.a. Micius) approximately 500 B.C. (Wu, 1928, p. 226)

A final note - Organization systems are custom designs based on the key organizational factors. These are unique for every organization, as identified in the Focus section of this book. There are no commercial off-the-shelf (COTS) solutions!

THOUGHTS FOR LEADERS

A lot of leaders ask, "Why should I embrace processes, wouldn't they restrict the way I lead?"

A leader's presence in an organization is like sticking your hand in a bucket of water. It takes up a lot of room, you can make a big difference when you splash, you can make waves, you can splash water out of the bucket, but when you pull your hand out of the water, there is no evidence that you were ever there. Putting processes into organizations is like putting cement in the water, you put your hand in – you pull your hand out and the impression stays. Those processes are the legacy a leader leaves behind.

As you reflect on your career, you may remember some extremely dominant leaders who lead with their own style. The day they left the organization, it was like they were never there. You may also remember other leaders who really 'built the roads.' Leaders can be 2 types: one conquers the empire, the other builds the roads (e.g., establishes the processes). The leader who builds the roads (and leaves the processes behind) leaves a legacy. You may find years and years after they leave, that those processes still exist. The culture they built lasts and stands the test of time.

Very few leaders can point to buildings or other concrete things they are going to leave behind. Every leader, however, should be able to leave processes and a culture which is supportive of the people, focused on customers and has mature processes which will improve and keep the organization viable.

Anchor Systems and Linkages

At first glance the 5 key factors areas, the 26 process areas, and the 6 results areas may seem a bit overwhelming. We have organized the 37 areas into what we call the competencies for performance excellence. However, there are many other ways to organize the components of the performance excellence model. To help think about these many elements you may want to organize them into what we call the six key anchor systems and the 17 critical systems.

Six Key Anchor Systems

Similar to the shopping mall, Baldrige has "Anchor Stores" which are the focal points of the overall experience. For Baldrige they are the "Anchor Systems" for each of the Process Categories (Categories 1 through 6). This is the key system for the Category, and is what the examiners will remember.

Typically this Anchor System is shown on the first page of the Category, and addresses the overall essence of the criteria for that Category. For Example, Anchor System for an application could include:

- Category 1 – Leadership System
- Category 2 – Planning System
- Category 3 – Customer Relationship System
- Category 4 – Measurement Selection & Deployment System
- Category 5 – People System
- Category 6 – Process Development (and management) System

17 Critical Systems

The Baldrige Criteria use the word "How" approximately 120 times throughout the Approach and Deployment Categories (Categories 1 through 6). Since in Baldrige terms, "How" means "describe your process," this means there need to be 120 places in your response where you describe your use of a process approach.

Although all 120 processes or activities are required, a smaller number of processes are key to an organization's ability to begin to manage through processes. Also, several of these smaller "How" processes can be within a larger process which accomplishes several things.

The 17 systems (shown as Item Numbers under the left column of the chart below) can accommodate most of what the Baldrige criteria requires in Categories 1 through 6. If the specific systems used by an organization, however, are not as robust as necessary, some of the areas shown as bullets (●) in the listing will need to be systems of their own. This would increase the total number of systems for the organization to develop and use.

These Critical Systems do not correspond with the 26 Approach and Deployment Areas to Address on a one-for-one basis. For example, Area to Address 3.2a has two critical systems – the Customer Relationship System and the Complaint Management System. Other Areas to Address may have Critical Systems which are typically addressed within a Critical System described for a different Area to Address. For example, Area to Address 1.1c requires a review of organizational performance. This is typically addressed within the organization's Leadership System. The Leadership System, however, is normally addressed under Area to Address 1.1a and not Area to Address 1.1c.

These Critical Systems include (but are not necessarily limited to) the large processes (or systems) listed on the next page.

 THOUGHTS FOR LEADERS

People often ask if a process has to be documented to be effective.

The question really becomes, *does everyone who needs to know about the details and the sequence of that process really understand it?*

Even a sports team that may only have eleven players on the field has clearly documented processes. They have plays, they study the playbook, and if the leader of the team wants to make a change, the players cannot understand the change unless they understand the playbook.

Even on teams as small as eleven, documented processes make the organization more flexible.

Different Ways to Organizes the Criteria Elements:

6 Anchor Systems	17 Critical Systems	Areas to Address
1. Leadership System	1.1 Leadership System • Set Direction • Organizational Performance Review • Responsibilities to the Public • Ethical Behavior • Support to Key Communities	1.1a 1.1c 1.2a 1.2b 1.2c
	1.1 Organizational Governance System	1.1b
2. Planning System	2.1 Strategy Development System	2.1a
	2.2 Strategy Deployment System	2.2a
3. Customer Relationship System	3.1 Customer and Market Knowledge System	3.1a
	3.2 Customer Relationship System	3.2a
	3.2 Complaint Management System	3.2a
	3.2 Customer Satisfaction Determination System	3.2b
4. Measurement Selection and Deployment System	4.1 Data Selection and Use System • Select • Gather • Align • Comparative Data Selection & Use System • Analyze • Act • Communicate	4.1a 4.1b
	4.2 Data Availability and Quality System • Availability • Friendly • Currency	4.2a
	4.2 Organizational Knowledge System • Manage Knowledge • Ensure the key properties of data, information, and organizational knowledge	4.2b P.2c
5. People System	5.1 Work Enablement System • Indentify Employee characteristics • Get Employees • Organize Work and Jobs • Enable Full Potential • Track Performance • Communicate • Plan for Succession	5.1a 5.1b 5.1c
	5.2 Employee Education, Training, and development System	5.2a 5.2b
	5.3 Employee Well-being • Work Environment • Employee Support • Employee Satisfaction	5.3a 5.3b
6. Process System	6.1 and 6.2 Process Design System	6.1a, 6.2a
	6.1 and 6.2 Process Management System	6.1a, 6.2a
	P.2, 6.1, and 6.2 Process Improvement System	P.2c, 6.1a, 6.2a

Focus

Overview

The first step is to build a solid foundation for the three competencies by focusing on the organization system, the core values and concepts, the key organization factors, and the maturity model. The organization is an interdependent system of activities that make up the three competencies – strategic leadership, execution excellence, and organizational learning. This system is characterized by 11 core values and concepts that provide the basis for performance excellence. These core values and concepts are the characteristics of a high performing organization. The key organizational factors establish the unique context of the specific organization. They are necessary to determine what is relevant and important to the organization. Finally, the maturity model helps to define where the organization is currently on the performance excellence journey and helps identify the next stages of development.

The focus on the key organizational factors provides a design "guidance system" by establishing requirements and priorities for the three performance excellence competencies. The focus phase consists of three steps: an understanding of the organization as a system, the organization characteristics essential for future success (design principles), and the organization's specific context (key organization factors).

- How can your organization work as an integrated high performance system?
- What organization characteristics are most important to the future success of your organization?
- How can you avoid "book of the month club" management fads?

The answers to these questions create a foundation on which you can critically review, creatively re-design, construct, and continuously improve your strategic leadership, execution management, and organizational learning systems.

Organization System

In the last few decades there has been an increasing interest in "the systems" perspective and approach to understanding organizations. This seems to have been largely driven by our dissatisfaction with the progress and ability to create the desired overall results and outcomes by focusing on improving the pieces (individual functional aspects) of the organization. The frustration is compounded by the unintended consequences and outcomes that are a result of changing the individual pieces of an organization. Key contributors (such as Forrester, 1975; Senge, 1990; and Deming 1994) have proposed that the organization, when viewed as a system, is a powerful lens to understand, diagnose, improve, and sustain the performance results most important to the key stakeholders (customers, employees, investors, supplier/partners, and the public at large).

The systems perspective has allowed some organizations to look beyond the direct goal or desired outcome and find key leverage points in the organization to achieve their objectives. For example, we are familiar with an organization that did not have any explicit financial goals. No financial goals are unheard of in business – right? Instead they had employee satisfaction and customer satisfaction goals. The notion was that if they focused on attracting, developing, and retaining a turned on and empowered workforce - a workforce that is focused on creating happy customers then the money would follow. As the president of the company used to say "you don't make many baskets while looking at the scoreboard." While money was critical to survival and was the "life blood" of the organization, it was not the *only* reason the organization existed. Just like a basketball team – they focused on how the team worked together to move the ball and put the ball through the customer's hoop – time after time. The more they put the ball through the hoop the more satisfied the customers were and consequently the more they requested their services (repeat business) and the more that they told their friends (referral business). The result was exponential growth in revenue and profits without a marketing or sales department. The ultimate goal of profitability and growth was accomplished not by focusing on the money, but rather by focusing on the key leverage points in the organization; people and customer in this case, that created sustainable results.

Design Principles

The design principles are the underlying core values and concepts of performance excellence. They are cross cutting through the organization and define performance excellence for the organization. Not all design principles are equally relevant and important to all organizations. Consequently, each organization should consciously examine and prioritize the principles prior to designing or redesigning the business systems.

Key Organization Factors

The key organization factors include: organizational environment and relationships, competitive environment and strategic challenges, and the organization's performance improvement system. These factors define what is **relevant** and **important** for the custom design of the strategic leadership, execution excellence, and organizational learning systems. For example, the appropriate design of the strategic planning system might be quite different for the "Mom and Pop" grocery store down the street than it is for a multi-national Fortune 500 corporation spread over 40 countries. Understanding these factors helps the organization avoid management fads and what have come to be called "book of the month club management."

Key Organization Factor Areas to Address:

> P.1a – Organizational Environment
> P.1b – Organizational Relationships
> P.2a – Competitive Environment
> P.2b – Strategic Challenges
> P.2c – Performance Improvement System

The Maturity Model

There are two maturity models used with the performance excellence criteria – one for processes and one for results.

The process maturity model consists of four dimensions:
- approach,
- deployment,
- learning, and
- integration.

The results maturity model also has four dimensions:
- level of performance,
- trend over time,
- comparison of performance to others, and
- the importance of the results.

Each dimension has six levels – level 0 through level 5. While all four dimensions are evaluated for a given process, the level of "best fit" is determined by considering all four dimensions together. Knowing the maturity level if helpful in two ways. First, it establishes the current status of the process or results. Second, it provides a description of the next steps on the performance excellence journey. Armed with these two pieces of information a plan for improvement can be developed.

Path to Performance Excellence

The path to performance excellence is a journey of improvement up the maturity model. Building on the work by Tang and Bauer (1995) the journey can be plotted on a matrix with three dimensions – strategic leadership, execution excellence, and organizational learning.

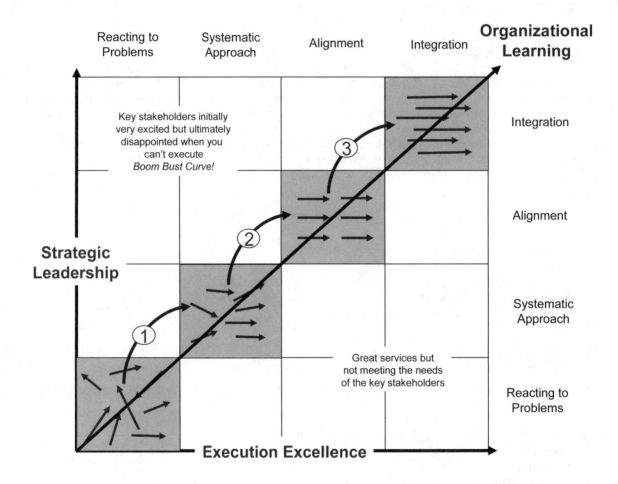

Adapted from: Tang, V. & Bauer, R. (1995). *Competitive Dominance: Beyond Strategic Advantage and Total Quality Management,* p. 9

According to Tang and Bauer an organization has to develop strategic and operational aspects to achieve and sustain performance excellence. The concept above builds on this notion and adds the competency of organizational learning as an enabler for the development of both strategic leadership and execution excellence. The three competencies address all performance excellence criteria areas. In addition, the maturity scale is based on the performance excellence scoring scale.

Criteria System	**The Organization as a System**

It is the belief of the authors that leaders: 1) must have a strategic direction; 2) must be excellent at executing that direction, and 3) must have learning cycles. Although this does not follow the Baldrige criteria in a numerical sequence order (Categories 1 through 7), it does follow a logical flow. The authors feel this logic flow helps the reader understand the Baldrige Framework as a complete business model.

For **Strategic Leadership** organizational leaders must determine what is important in the company, the overall company direction, the company beliefs and values, what governance will be embraced, and they must review performance. Leaders must also establish the legal, ethical, and regulatory guidelines for the organization. All of these have to be well established in the strategy development phase and in the deployment of the strategy. To ensure the strategy is deployed down to individual goals, and to ensure that the organization stays on track, leaders must review performance. One of the key inputs to the overall strategy is customer and market knowledge. This is what the external customers need and expect from the organization, and what they are willing to pay for.

For **Execution Excellence** organizational leaders must execute the overall direction of the organization. Everything which occurs happens through people or processes. Work systems must be designed. They are fed by the employees' knowledge levels and the employees' wellbeing. Through the delivery of products and services the customer relationships are built over both the short- and longer-term.

In a fast changing unpredictable environment, all organizations need to be competent at **Organizational Learning**. An organization cannot improve any more rapidly than their leaders can learn and improve. Those improvements are driven by *Execution Excellence* which is tracked through measurement and analysis.

Organizational Learning places a responsibility on Category 7 (the results portion of Baldrige) to not only effectively track performance, but to provide feedback to the organization (in the form of data which can be analyzed to drive improvement actions) as to how performance can be improved. This occurs through the knowledge management systems of the organization as well as through the measurement and analysis channels.

The figure below depicts the 19 essential elements of the organizational system. None of these are new, they are time tested concepts that all seem to make sense. What might be new is the system perspective of the elements – how they interact. That figure identifies only a few of the many linkages or interactions among the activities. Later we will show how each of the areas to address link to other areas to address to form an integrated system. As the organization develops the systematic approaches that address these areas they begin to evolve from a primarily reactive process to a more proactive one and then eventually to an aligned and integrated system of processes. The system perspective is required for the purposeful alignment and integration of the individual processes. As you can see by the shading, these 19 elements can be grouped into the three major competencies.

The group on the left is composed of the strategic leadership elements including – organizational leadership, strategy development and deployment, customer and market knowledge, and social responsibility.

In the middle, the execution excellence competency is composed of processes and people - the value creation processes, support processes, and the customer relationship building processes; and the people elements include the work system, employee learning and motivation, and employee well-being and satisfaction.

The development or maturity of the first two competencies is dependent on the third competency of organizational learning. On the right the organizational learning competency is composed of the results or data from a comprehensive performance scorecard (customers, products and services, financial, people, processes, and social responsibility) and the analysis and management of that information to support learning. How an organization actually accomplishes these elements varies depending on the core values and concepts and the key organizational factors.

The Organization System

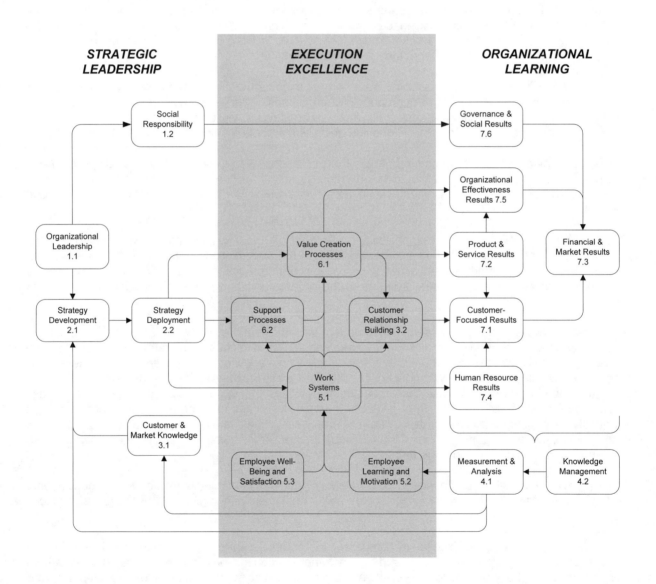

Strategic Leadership

Beginning with a leader who has a vision for an organization and an understanding of customer requirements, strategic leadership is the first component of a performance excellence system. The strategic leadership component is comprised of five of the 19 items: organizational leadership (1.1), customer and market knowledge (3.1), strategy development (2.1) and deployment (2.2) and social responsibility (1.2). These five components work together to set direction for the organization and the other two competencies of execution excellence and organizational learning.

Organizational Leadership (1.1)

It all begins with leadership! Senior leadership comes up again and again as a key factor in the transformation of organizations. Even Jim Collins, although he instructed his research staff to not come back with leadership as an answer, finally admitted, in the end that it was one of seven key factors in organizations that make the leap from what he termed "Good to Great" (Collins 2001). Organizations tend to move in the direction the people perceive as important to the leader. Why such influence? There are probably several key factors not the least of which is the power to compensate and promote. While there are many theories and little agreement on what is good leadership, organizational leadership in this context is both transactional and transformational and is composed of three dimensions - senior leadership direction, governance, and organization performance review.

How does the leadership team design, create, and maintain an organization that is focused on satisfying the key stakeholders? While there are a variety of individual leadership styles, the question becomes what systematic, repeatable approach is in place to ensure the key activities are accomplished regardless of which executives are in what positions. This brings up an important concept or underlying assumption – systems help to enable and support talented leaders – systems do not replace talented leaders. How do they set and communicate the direction for the organization and how do they create an environment that facilitates empowerment, innovation, agility, learning, and legal and ethical behavior?

With all the recent emphasis on corporate scandals and what appears to be a lack of "adult supervision" in some large firms – there is a new emphasis on ethics and executive oversight. This is somewhat counter to the recent trend toward empowerment. It actually highlights, however, one of the risks of empowerment. "Empowerment is a combination of motivation to act, authority to do the job, and the enablement to get it done. Enablement requires a vivid picture of the destination" (Latham, 1995, p. 66). Part of the vivid picture is the concept of how the organization operates – its values! How does the leadership ensure that the organization is governed in a way that ensures fiscal and ethical behavior in all aspects of the operations?

Finally, how does the leadership team review performance and progress toward the desired organizational performance levels? What leadership or management system does the organization use to implement the strategy? What review methods are used to ensure the action plans are being accomplished? Without periodic review, managers and employees tend to place a low priority on improvement action plans. Some organizations use inter-linked senior leader sub-groups from the top of the organization to the bottom.

The local coffee shop entrepreneur is an example of a catalyst for creating or transforming the organization into a system that serves multiple stakeholders. The coffee entrepreneur started their own business because they thought they had a better way to run a coffee shop. It started with a dream of a coffee shop where the value system was consistent with their own. In the beginning governance largely consisted of the individual and maybe their family. A dream if you will of how it "could be" and the *guts* to make it happen. Once it was up and running and employees were on board and working, there was a need to make the value system explicit and incorporate it into the business practices that enable all the employees. Originally the performance review process was simply counting the revenue each evening and comparing that to the budget to see how the shop was doing. But as the business develops there is also a need for more formal periodic reviews of how well the business is doing in serving its multiple stakeholders and progressing toward the strategic goals.

Customer and Market Knowledge (3.1)

One of the first questions for the entrepreneur and the large organization leader is what do the customers want? Or, maybe more importantly, what will they pay for? And, what will it take for them to come back (repeat business) and tell their friends about us (referral business)? These are the questions of exponential growth. When customers are satisfied with the experience of doing business with the organization, unless there is a competing offering to entice them away they tend to keep coming back. It may be stating the obvious, but if you can keep the customers that you have, and continue to attract more, the business will grow. If the experience is remarkable then customers will be inclined to tell their friends and the growth will be exponential which means that it will grow at an increasing pace just like compound interest in your retirement account. So, what do you need to know to create a remarkable experience?

There are three key dimensions to customer and market knowledge: the determination of customer groups, an approach to listen and learn to determine key customer requirements, and a method to translate those requirements into features and functions and identify their relative importance. How can we know the answers to these questions? The menu is large, of course, with many options to determine customer needs, wants, and desires.

Why segment customers into groups? At the core of this concept is the notion that there are groups of customers with different needs, wants, and desires. How do we segment our customers into groups that have similar needs, wants, and desires? Some organizations segment their customers based on products, regions, type of business, and profitability just to name a few. Regardless of the scheme the fundamental premise is that these groups are defined by their common needs, wants, and desires. So, while the organization might serve two very different industries, if their requirements are the same then for all practical purposes they can often be grouped together in the same customer group. Why the focus on needs, wants, and desires? Those drive the offerings – market strategies, products and services and their features, relationship building approaches, and listening and learning approaches.

How do you know what the customers want? How do you know what they will pay for? Listening and learning strategies are critical to a fact-based approach to customer knowledge. These vary from the small shop owner's approach of talking with their customers on a daily basis to sophisticated research on customer requirements and their behaviors. The specific strategies or approach should fit the individual customer group. The requirements (needs, wants, and desires) drive product and service offerings and features.

By definition the entrepreneur thinks that they have some sort of *sixth sense* and know what will succeed in the market. Even this sixth sense, however, can be "turbo-charged" and more informed by fact-based approaches to understanding customers and markets.

In the case of the local coffee shop the customers' generic requirements might be: reasonable price, good taste, temperature just right, convenient, atmosphere, and free wireless internet. But how does the entrepreneur know these things? What techniques can they use to determine the requirements, their priority, and what makes the difference in the customer's purchase decision? Will free wireless internet make the difference in anyone's purchase decision?

Strategy Development (2.1)

Once the leadership has a direction (purpose, mission, vision, values) and knows what the customers want – they are ready to develop a strategy to serve those markets and customer groups. A strategy provides the organization with a roadmap to help navigate the changing environment in which they operate. There has been a lot of discussion in recent years on the topic of strategic planning and how it is often ineffective. While detailed voluminous plans created by the "staff" have proven to be of little value - strategies, objectives, action plans, and measures developed and monitored by the leadership team and other key participants have proven to be useful in guiding organizations. Drucker may have summed it up best back in 1973 when he wrote that strategic planning "is the continuous process of making present entrepreneurial *(risk-taking) decisions* systematically and with the greatest knowledge of their futurity; organizing systematically the *efforts* needed to carry out these decisions; and measuring the results of these decisions against the expectations through organized, *systematic feedback*" (p. 125). Strategic planning answers four fundamental questions.

1. Where are we now?
2. Where do we want to be?
3. How will we get there?
4. How will we know how we are progressing and when we get there?

What framework and method is best for developing strategy? There are many books and articles written to answer this question and each one in its own way has some redeeming qualities. One thing that we are pretty sure of is that strategy creation is a creative process and consequently needs some structure to facilitate the process but not so much that the creativity is inhibited. We have yet to devise a mechanistic process where the leadership team can simply "turn a crank" and a viable strategy emerges. A systematic planning process, however, takes into consideration several key inputs, involves key players, has a defined process, and produces short and long-term objectives and a timeline for accomplishing them.

For our coffee entrepreneur a strategy must address two basic issues, one external and one internal. First, how can our entrepreneur capture and hold the external market when the national chain competitors are knocking at the door? Second, how can the coffee shop, the offerings, and the operations be designed and developed to best serve this market?

Strategy Deployment (2.2)

How does the organization make the plan a reality? Just like in golf – follow through is the key to success. It seems obvious that a strategy that is not implemented is just a fantasy. Translating the short- and long-term strategic objectives into specific initiatives and actions is a key success factor to making the strategy a reality. The key elements of a strategy deployment approach are: action plans, measures or indicators to track progress, and performance projections for both short and longer-term planning time horizons.

The first step is to identify the actions and initiatives that will accomplish the strategic objectives. Second, identify the organization's human resource plans to support the strategic objectives. Third, identify the measures to track progress of the initiatives and to measure the impact that the changes have on performance. The last step is to establish targets for performance improvement which are predictions based on the logical changes in performance if the action plans are implemented successfully.

Social Responsibility (1.2)

To be sustainable the direction and strategy of the organization need to be compatible with the larger community and public interest. Part of the overall direction is how to implement that strategy and at the same time address the social responsibilities or "win-win." How does the organization include its community responsibilities in its policies, improvement plans, and practices? In addition to building houses, how does the organization systematically fulfill their responsibilities as a citizen in the community?

This is much more than simply giving to the local charity. Social responsibility includes proactively addressing the organization's responsibilities to the public, ethical behavior in all transactions, and support to key communities. To address each of these areas proactively requires that the organization have a process to determine the requirements and expectation of the key stakeholders, a process to address those requirements, measures to track performance and identify areas for improvement, and goals and targets for improving the performance.

For the local coffee shop the processes to address these areas might be fairly simple. For example, the approach to dealing with ethical interactions may only need to reach 10 – 20 employees who all work in the same location under the supervision of the owner or supervisor. However, the ethical expectations still need to be explicitly defined, communicated, and reinforced to ensure the desired behavior. Finally, how should the coffee shop support the local community?

Strategic leadership without excellent execution results in a "boom and bust" experience. The customers and potential customers get excited as expectations are raised but then leave when the organization fails to deliver. With a clear direction and systematic approach to strategic leadership in place, the next step is to develop the processes and people to execute the strategy. According to Larry Bossidy – "My job at Honeywell International these days is to restore the discipline of execution to a company that had lost it. Many people regard execution as detail work that's beneath the dignity of a business leader. That's wrong. To the contrary, it's a leader's most important job" (Bossidy and Charan, 2002, p. 1). Execution excellence depends on the capabilities of the processes and the people.

Execution Excellence

Execution excellence is the result of a well designed and implemented system of processes and people that are integrated and aligned with the goals of the organization. The process component of execution is composed of the value creation process, the support processes, and the customer relationship building processes. This collection of processes forms what Porter (1995) called the "Value Chain." Since the processes are executed by people, the second major component of execution excellence is the workforce and how they are organized, developed, and cared for.

Value Creation Processes (6.1)

How does the organization create value for the customers? The value chain consists of the main sequence of events that occur to transform the inputs into a product or service that can be sold for a profit. The first step is to identify and describe the organization's value creation processes.

For each value creation process identified there are five elements to creating, controlling, and improving the processes.

1. How do you determine the requirements of the process and the products and services that it produces?
2. How do you design the processes to meet or exceed those requirements?
3. How do you implement the process to ensure that it meets performance expectations right away?
4. How do you measure and control the process to ensure performance?
5. How do you continuously evaluate and improve the process?

For the local coffee shop, one of the value creation processes might be the brewing and delivery of coffee of all types (e.g., Latte). The requirements are likely to include – taste, temperature, no spillage, and a thermal hand protector. The process is then designed to deliver good tasting coffee (bean selection and grinding processes) at the right temperature (measured with a thermometer) while the milk for the Latte is being frothed and poured with the right technique to prevent spillages and then a thermal hand protector is installed to help insulate the customers' hands from the heat that is radiating from the cup.

How then could the coffee shop evaluate and improve their process? They would need customer feedback along with the participation of the key players in the coffee creation process to systematically evaluate and develop changes to the process. Of course if there are several customer groups with varying needs as discussed in the Focus section then there are other requirements that also influence overall satisfaction.

Support Processes (6.2)

What are the key processes that support the value creation processes? Support processes are all those processes that are essential for running the organization and operating the value creation processes but are not in the primary chain of events that determine the value that is created for the customer. This does not mean that they are not important. The organization is a system and only as strong as its weakest link. The billing process might be a support process but it can have a big impact on the satisfaction of the customer. Just ask about our friend's wireless bill that has yet to be correct. Our friend wastes an hour of her time each month trying to get the wireless company to make it right. What do you think this adds to her total cost of the service?

Identify the key support and business processes that make the key products and services possible. Building on our coffee shop example, some of the support processes might include bookkeeping, facilities maintenance, and the supplies acquisition processes.

It may seem obvious but a support process is a process and as such requires the same generic components. Consequently, the support processes need the same steps that the value creation processes used.

1. How do you determine the requirements of the process and the products and services that it produces?
2. How do you design the processes to meet or exceed those requirements?
3. How do you implement the process to ensure that it meets performance expectations right away?
4. How do you measure and control the process to ensure performance?
5. How do you continuously evaluate and improve the processes?

Support processes that, depending on the business, can have a big impact on the value creation processes are the supplier management processes. Some including Deming (1994) and Crosby (1994) both have proposed that it is in the organization's best interest to help their external suppliers be successful and provide quality products and services. Since the value-added chain simply increases the quality of the input, as computer programmers say, "garbage in, garbage out."

Identify the key external suppliers. How does the organization ensure their suppliers deliver quality products and services? This might include everything from the most rudimentary method of acceptance inspection to the more sophisticated method of supplier certification. They must identify the quality indicators for the incoming materials and services, these are the same indicators that are the suppliers' proxies for customer satisfaction. The suppliers need the same information from the organization that the organization needed from its customers when they were addressing their value creation processes.

There are at least two critical suppliers for the modern coffee experience – the provider of the beans and the internet service provider. The bean supplier has a rather large impact on the taste of the coffee. For instance, there is an old saying – "you can't make a silk purse out of a sow's ear." In addition, the internet service provider has a large impact on the information exchange experience.

Customer Relationship Building and Satisfaction Determination (3.2)

There are additional processes that connect the customer with the value creation and support processes. These processes are linked to the value chain at key interaction points along the processes. The three main paths for building customer relationships are access mechanisms to facilitate the customers' experience when they seek information about your products, services, or company; conduct business such as ordering, paying invoices, returning merchandise; and when they have a problem with the products or services, complain about the products, services, or company.

Doing it right the first time is important but until the products and services are perfect, a responsive method to fix the mistakes is important to building a strong relationship with your customer. In fact, when it comes to customer relationships, how an organization fixes things that go wrong can be more important than getting it right the first time. How do you provide access to customers to accomplish these three key types of interactions? What are the service standards for building and maintaining a good relationship? How do you systematically recover when things go wrong?

In addition to building a relationship there is the issue of knowing how well you are doing. How does the organization measure customer satisfaction? The customers' satisfaction results should correlate to the other key levels and trends of organization performance. Examples might include: surveys, repeat business, and referred business just to name a few.

At the local coffee shop, getting objective unfiltered customer feedback might be more difficult than you might think. First is the issue of personal relationships especially in smaller towns. The customers may be reluctant to give honest and unvarnished feedback to the owner if they are personal friends or have built a relationship at the coffee shop. In this case anonymous surveys might be the best method to gather this information.

Work Systems (5.1)

Now that the organization has sound systematic processes, someone has to do the work. How do you get the right people on board, organize and manage the work to ensure they reach their potential, and how do you evaluate their performance and provide feedback and incentives to improve? How do the hiring and career progression, and succession planning and manage career progression processes ensure that the organization has the right people in the organization? How is the work organized and managed to promote cooperation, initiative, and empowerment? How does the employee performance management system (evaluation, feedback, compensation, recognition, and incentives) ensure a customer focus?

How does the organization involve the people and create high performance teams? Although suggestion programs provide the opportunity to be involved and are appropriate for this item, they do little to proactively promote involvement of all the workers to work together as a synergistic team. Other options include, but are not limited to, cross functional improvement teams and functional or process oriented natural working groups. Once involved, how does the organization ensure the people repeat the "role model" behavior and performance? There is an old saying, "What gets measured gets done--what gets rewarded gets repeated!" Does the reward and recognition system reinforce team behavior that helps accomplish the organization's goals and objectives? To be effective team members, individuals must know their job and how to contribute to the team effectively.

All of these are issues for the local coffee shop. The local coffee shop has to attract the right employees that have the knowledge, skills, and abilities to succeed. They have to organize the work and assign people to jobs and shifts. Finally, they have to evaluate the performance of the individuals and provide feedback and incentives to improve.

Employee Learning and Motivation (5.2)

How does the organization systematically educate and train the people to do their jobs, lead the organization, and improve their products, services, and processes? The approaches to employee development might include on-the-job training program, professional development, quality education and training efforts, and so forth. Finally, how effective are the training programs and how many people are involved in each type of training?

The amount of training and development that is needed will vary significantly depending on the key organizational factors. However, even the local coffee shop needs to develop the employees to make great coffee, provide service with a smile, and create an atmosphere for an outstanding customer experience.

Employee Well-Being and Satisfaction (5.3)

Now that the employees are systematically involved, trained and motivated, how does the organization make sure their health and well-being needs are taken care of? How do you know that their needs are being taken care of? Why worry about employee well-being and satisfaction? There are three compelling reasons: attract and retain a first class workforce; reduce unproductive time due to illness, accidents, and so forth; and finally take care of the families so that the worker can focus on work instead of worrying about the doctor bill for little Jimmy.

Measures might include: work environment (health, safety, security, ergonomics, measures, employee input, emergencies or disasters); employee support and satisfaction: determine key factors that affect employee well-being, satisfaction, and motivation; services, benefits, policies; measures to determine employee satisfaction and improvement.

Organizational Learning

Finally, the world stands still for no organization. To keep the organization on the cutting edge, the organization must learn how to learn, and, continuously get better at learning. Regardless whether you are a coffee shop entrepreneur or an executive for a global billion dollar business, continuous and breakthrough improvement are prerequisites for thriving in a constantly changing and increasingly competitive environment.

This competency is focused on identifying the information system, scope and management of quality and performance data, comparison and benchmarking, and analysis and uses of organizational-level data. This is the neural network that connects the organization's process and systematic approaches and feedback results.

According to Deming (1994 (p. 93)) profound knowledge about an organization requires knowledge of four key elements:

- appreciation for a system,
- knowledge about variation,
- theory of knowledge,
- psychology.

We have already discussed how a systems' perspective is essential to developing the three competencies. An understanding of the system is essential to selecting and using measurement to understand the interrelationships in the system and diagnose causes and identify leverage points. Knowledge of variation and historical trends are essential for understanding the difference between performance that is normal given the current system design and performance that needs intervention. In other words, how to interpret the changing performance results when the changes to the processes are implemented. A theory of knowledge is a concept or understanding that allows prediction. Deming proposed that "management is prediction" and prediction is based on a theory. Without a theory there is nothing to revise and no way to capture learning. Finally, profound knowledge requires an understanding of psychology. Although many have tried to make organizations rational, this approach taken to excess has proven disappointing. Organizations are not often very rational because they are composed of people. Understanding how people behave and interact with one another (customers, other functions, suppliers, etc.) is necessary for understanding organizations. In other words, a theory of the organization that excludes people cannot possibly be a useful theory unless of course you do not have any people in your organization. This concept of profound knowledge is supported by the measurement and analysis of the organization's performance, knowledge management and a comprehensive scorecard.

Measurement and Analysis (4.1)

How can measurement and analysis support organizational learning? The first question centers on what to measure? Here is where a systems perspective and theory of the business come in handy. Measures need to be sufficient to understand the key components of the organization system and their relationships to one another. Measures need to support both the strategic leadership and execution excellence perspectives, activities, decisions. Or, as Clarke American puts it – "run the business and improve the business."

This item should connect the systematic approaches with their deployment and the results. For example, the key products, services, and processes identified should correspond to the indicators of progress in part of the database which should correspond to the results graphs depicted in the results items.

Why compare? The purpose behind comparisons is twofold. First, when analyzing the level of organizational performance it provides a level and trend to compare with to better understand the meaning of the organization's performance and the rate of improvement. Second, for important processes in need of significant improvement the information enables the organization to select someone to benchmark who is world-class (really good) in that specific process.

How do you convert the data into information that can be used to manage and improve the organization's performance? How does the organization compile, correlate, and validate their data into actionable information?

Knowledge Management (4.2)

The Key Elements of this are: (1) data and information availability – available and access for employees, customers, suppliers, etc. and (2) hardware and software are reliable, secure, and user friendly. This helps the organization keep current with changing business needs.

Organizational Knowledge – Is the collection and transfer of knowledge of all types including employees, customers, suppliers, etc. It includes the identification and sharing of best practices. A key question is how do you ensure the following properties of data, information, and organizational knowledge? This includes how you ensure data integrity, timeliness, reliability, security, accuracy, and confidentiality.

A comprehensive scorecard is needed to understand the system and test theories of the business. The performance excellence model contains a six perspective interrelated scorecard that is composed of six key areas – customer, product and services, human resources, organization effectiveness, financial and market results, and governance and social responsibility results.

Customer Satisfaction Results (7.1)

How satisfied are your customers? Are they more satisfied today than they were yesterday? How satisfied are your competitors' customers? These three questions are the validation question for how well your organization is creating and delivering products and services that meet and exceed customer expectations. It is often impractical, however, to have the customer stand over the employees shoulder and smile or frown when they are satisfied or dissatisfied.

Product and Service Results (7.2)

Product and service results are the "proxies for customer satisfaction. Since customer satisfaction measures are often lagging, these measures provide timely feedback to help manage the processes. Considering the requirements identified in the customer knowledge item, what are the product and service characteristics that (if you do well) will result in a happy customer? For the example, the customer might define quality and on-time delivery with no defects. This might translate into percentage delivered on-time, average variance of delivery times, and number of defects per product found during final inspection, all measurable by the organization. The product and service results should directly correlate with the customer's satisfaction results.

Organizational Effectiveness Results (7.5)

Identify the internal indicators used to control and improve the key product and service processes. These are the internal efficiency and process performance type indicators that are important to the organization but the customer could not care less about. To build on our example, this might be the completion time for the foundation or the frame. The customer doesn't care if you finish the foundation on time. They only want the house ready to move into when predicted. The builder knows, however, that the probability of the house being ready to move into on-time is dramatically increased by finishing the foundation on-time. So this would be an in-process measure that the builder might use to ensure they meet the end of process measures that are important to the customer. Now that you have identified: what the customers want; the design process; the key products, services, processes, and indicators; the next question is what are the necessary internal support products, services, and processes needed to enable the key processes.

Human Resource Results (7.4)

Process performance is important but seldom works without the involvement of people. People measures are an important input and predictor of process performance. Included in this area might be indicators of employee satisfaction, learning, and performance. Are the employee results good? Are they getting better? How does this organization's employee results compare to its competitors or organizations in the same business? Are their employees more or less satisfied? Who is getting better faster?

Governance and Social Responsibility Results (7.6)

While it is critically important to satisfy the customers and to have a turned-on empowered workforce these measures are incomplete. Performance excellence is only sustainable if the organization is operating in a way that is consistent and in the interests of the communities in which it operates and the public at large. Take for instance the company that pollutes the town's water supply. It won't be long before the reaction from the local community makes it difficult for the business to profitably operate in that community. If the executives act unethically then at some point the trust is destroyed with the employees, customers, partners, and investors. Without the trust and support of these key stakeholders the processes, no matter how fancy will not produce sustainable results.

Financial and Market Results (7.3)

The financial and market results, when considered over the long-term, provide a reasonably good overall indication of the organization's performance – at least for the for profit companies. These results include: levels, trends, comparisons for financial performance including aggregate measures of financial return and economic value. Also, for marketplace performance including market share or position, business growth, and new markets entered as appropriate. The financials combine the effectiveness of the value creation processes (revenue) with the efficiency of the processes (expenses). Together they provide useful insight into the workings of the organization system.

Design Principles	**Core Values and Concepts**

The performance excellence system is based on 11 core values and concepts. Think of these as design principles or the desired characteristics of the systems and processes identified. While Collins (2001) for practical reasons limited the definition of "great" to financial performance, specifically sustained stock price improvement, the performance excellence model proposes a more comprehensive definition that includes multiple stakeholders.

A great company according to the performance excellence model demonstrates the 11 characteristics found in the table below.

Design Principles

Good Organization	Great Organization
• Directive Leadership	• Visionary Leadership
• Product/Service-Driven	• Customer-Driven Excellence
• Meet Standards or "*status quo*"	• Organizational and Personal Learning
• Suppliers and Unions as Adversaries	• Valuing Employees & Partners
• Respond in Time Allotted	• Agility
• Focus on Next Quarter's Results	• Focus on the Future
• Employees Follow Procedures	• Managing for Innovation
• Management by Intuition	• Management by Fact
• Compliance with Regulation	• Social Responsibility
• Focus on $ "*bottom-line*" Exclusively	• Focus on Results and Creating Value
• Functional Perspective	• Systems Perspective

A key point to keep in mind is that the design principles of a "Great" organization do not necessarily replace those of a "Good" organization. Rather they build upon them and in some cases transform them. While the performance excellence model would propose that all 11 are important, depending on your situation and vision some of these principles might be more important than others.

Design Principles

While the values can apply to all parts of the system, there are parts that seem to be more important to some areas than others. As with the Organization System, the core values of Baldrige can be divided into Strategic Leadership, Execution Excellence, and Organizational Learning. In Strategic Leadership an organization must have visionary leaders who can focus on the future. Within that visionary leadership, leaders must understand the integrated systems of the company and show a responsibility for social issues. Within Execution Excellence, the organization's overall performance must be driven by what customers need and expect (and are willing to pay for). This is achieved by employees who are agile and focused on the results customers expect. Organizational Learning cycles need to be driven from organizational and personal learning, managing by fact, and being innovative to drive the competitive advantage.

Design Principles Organized by Competency

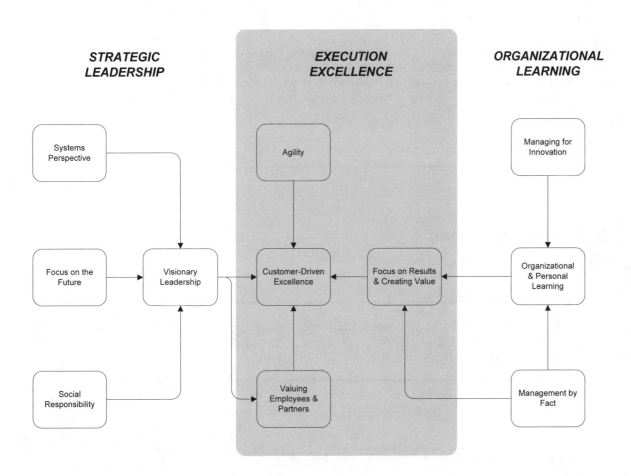

Visionary Leadership

 FOUNDATION

Visionary Leadership – Baldrige Core Value

Your organization's senior leaders should set directions and create a customer focus, clear and visible values, and high expectations. The directions, values, and expectations should balance the needs of all your stakeholders. Your leaders should ensure the creation of strategies, systems, and methods for achieving excellence, stimulating innovation, and building knowledge and capabilities. The values and strategies should help guide all activities and decisions of your organization. Senior leaders should inspire and motivate your entire workforce and should encourage all employees to contribute, to develop and learn, to be innovative, and to be creative. Senior leaders should be responsible to your organization's governance body for their actions and performance. The governance body should be responsible ultimately to all your stakeholders for the ethics, vision, actions, and performance of your organization and its senior leaders.

Senior leaders should serve as role models through their ethical behavior and their personal involvement in planning, communications, coaching, development of future leaders, review of organizational performance, and employee recognition. As role models, they can reinforce ethics, values, and expectations while building leadership, commitment, and initiative throughout your organization.

NIST (2004) p. 1

 RESEARCH SAYS

Evans and Ford (1997) found that the leadership value had a high or medium importance to two categories – leadership and strategic planning. Confirming the notion that this value is more important to strategic leadership than the other competencies (p. 26).

WORKSHEETS

Visionary Leadership - Work Sheet

Core Value - Visionary Leadership

Three ways the organization demonstrates this value:	Barriers that need to be overcome to fully implement this value throughout the organization:
1.	1.
2.	2.
3.	3.

Actions we need to take to achieve excellence in this core value:

1

2

3

4

Organizations you can learn from:

- Clarke American
- Medrad
- Boeing Aerospace Support

Systems Perspective

 FOUNDATION

Systems Perspective - Baldrige Core Value

The Baldrige Criteria provide a systems perspective for managing your organization and its key processes to achieve results—performance excellence. The seven Baldrige Categories and the Core Values form the building blocks and the integrating mechanism for the system. However, successful management of overall performance requires organization specific synthesis, alignment, and integration. Synthesis means looking at your organization as a whole and builds upon key business requirements, including your strategic objectives and action plans. Alignment means using the key linkages among requirements given in the Baldrige Categories to ensure consistency of plans, processes, measures, and actions. Integration builds on alignment so that the individual components of your performance management system operate in a fully interconnected manner.

These concepts are depicted in the Baldrige framework on page 5. A systems perspective includes your senior leaders' focus on strategic directions and on your customers. It means that your senior leaders monitor, respond to, and manage performance based on your business results. A systems perspective also includes using your measures, indicators, and organizational knowledge to build your key strategies. It means linking these strategies with your key processes and aligning your resources to improve overall performance and satisfy customers. Thus, a systems perspective means managing your whole organization, as well as its components, to achieve success.

NIST (2004) p. 4

WORKSHEETS

Systems Perspective – Work Sheet

Core Value - Systems Perspective

Three ways the organization demonstrates this value:	Barriers that need to be overcome to fully implement this value throughout the organization:
1.	1.
2.	2.
3.	3.

Actions we need to take to achieve excellence in this core value:

1

2

3

4

Organizations you can learn from:

- Boeing Aerospace Support
- Motorola CGISS
- Boeing Airlift and Tanker

Focus on the Future

 FOUNDATION

Focus on the Future - Baldrige Core Value

In today's competitive environment, a focus on the future requires understanding the short- and longer-term factors that affect your business and marketplace. Pursuit of sustainable growth and market leadership requires a strong future orientation and a willingness to make long-term commitments to key stakeholders—your customers, employees, suppliers and partners, stockholders, the public, and your community. Your organization's planning should anticipate many factors, such as customers' expectations, new business and partnering opportunities, employee development and hiring needs, the increasingly global marketplace, technological developments, the evolving e-business environment, new customer and market segments, evolving regulatory requirements, community and societal expectations, and strategic moves by competitors. Strategic objectives and resource allocations need to accommodate these influences. A focus on the future includes developing employees and suppliers, doing effective succession planning, creating opportunities for innovation, and anticipating public responsibilities.

NIST (2004) p. 3

 RESEARCH SAYS

Evans and Ford (1997) found that the **long-range view** (as it was called in 1996) value was of medium importance to the strategic planning category. It was of low importance to all other categories. Again, confirming the notion that it is important to strategic leadership (p. 26).

WORKSHEETS

Focus on the Future – Work Sheet

Core Value - Focus on the Future

Three ways the organization demonstrates this value:	Barriers that need to be overcome to fully implement this value throughout the organization:
1.	1.
2.	2.
3.	3.

Actions we need to take to achieve excellence in this core value:

1

2

3

4

Organizations you can learn from:

- SSM Health Care
- Clarke American
- Motorola CGISS

Social Responsibility

 FOUNDATION

Social Responsibility - Baldrige Core Value

An organization's leaders should stress responsibilities to the public, ethical behavior, and the need to practice good citizenship. Leaders should be role models for your organization in focusing on business ethics and protection of public health, safety, and the environment. Protection of health, safety, and the environment includes your organization's operations, as well as the life cycles of your products and services. Also, organizations should emphasize resource conservation and waste reduction at the source. Planning should anticipate adverse impacts from production, distribution, transportation, use, and disposal of your products. Effective planning should prevent problems, provide for a forthright response if problems occur, and make available information and support needed to maintain public awareness, safety, and confidence.

For many organizations, the product design stage is critical from the point of view of public responsibility. Design decisions impact your production processes and often the content of municipal and industrial waste. Effective design strategies should anticipate growing environmental concerns and responsibilities.

Organizations should not only meet all local, state, and federal laws and regulatory requirements, but they should treat these and related requirements as opportunities for improvement "beyond mere compliance." Organizations should stress ethical behavior in all stakeholder transactions and interactions. Highly ethical conduct should be a requirement of and should be monitored by the organization's governance body.

Practicing good citizenship refers to leadership and support—within the limits of an organization's resources—of publicly important purposes. Such purposes might include improving education and health care in your community, environmental excellence, resource conservation, community service, improving industry and business practices, and sharing nonproprietary information. Leadership as a corporate citizen also entails influencing other organizations, private and public, to partner for these purposes. For example, your organization might lead or participate in efforts to help define the obligations of your industry to its communities. Managing social responsibility requires the use of appropriate measures and leadership responsibility for those measures.

NIST (2004) pp. 3 - 4

 RESEARCH SAYS

Evans and Ford (1997) found that the **corporate responsibility** (as it was called in 1996) value was of medium importance to the leadership category. It was of low importance to all other categories. This is an interesting finding and would be interesting to see what the results would be if the survey was repeated today. Again, the notion that this value is most important to the strategic leadership competency is supported by the findings (p. 26).

WORKSHEETS

Social Responsibility – Work Sheet

Core Value - Social Responsibility

Three ways the organization demonstrates this value:	Barriers that need to be overcome to fully implement this value throughout the organization:
1.	1.
2.	2.
3.	3.

Actions we need to take to achieve excellence in this core value:

1

2

3

4

Organizations you can learn from:

- Los Alamos National Bank
- Boeing Aerospace Support
- All Baldrige Winners

Customer-Driven Excellence

FOUNDATION

Customer-Driven Excellence - Baldrige Core Value

Quality and performance are judged by an organization's customers. Thus, your organization must take into account all product and service features and characteristics and all modes of customer access that contribute value to your customers. Such behavior leads to customer acquisition, satisfaction, preference, referral, retention and loyalty, and business expansion. Customer-driven excellence has both current and future components: understanding today's customer desires and anticipating future customer desires and marketplace potential.

Value and satisfaction may be influenced by many factors throughout your customers' overall purchase, ownership, and service experiences. These factors include your organization's relationships with customers, which help to build trust, confidence, and loyalty.

Customer-driven excellence means much more than reducing defects and errors, merely meeting specifications, or reducing complaints. Nevertheless, reducing defects and errors and eliminating causes of dissatisfaction contribute to your customers' view of your organization and thus also are important parts of customer-driven excellence. In addition, your organization's success in recovering from defects and mistakes ("making things right for your customer") is crucial to retaining customers and building customer relationships.

Customer-driven organizations address not only the product and service characteristics that meet basic customer requirements but also those features and characteristics that differentiate products and services from competing offerings. Such differentiation may be based upon new or modified offerings, combinations of product and service offerings, customization of offerings, multiple access mechanisms, rapid response, or special relationships.

Customer-driven excellence is thus a strategic concept. It is directed toward customer retention and loyalty, market share gain, and growth. It demands constant sensitivity to changing and emerging customer and market requirements and to the factors that drive customer satisfaction and loyalty. It demands listening to your customers. It demands anticipating changes in the marketplace. Therefore, customer-driven excellence demands awareness of developments in technology and competitors' offerings, as well as rapid and flexible response to customer and market changes.

NIST (2004) pp. 1 - 2

RESEARCH SAYS

Evans and Ford (1997) found that the **customer-driven quality** (as it was called in 1996) value was of high or medium importance to four categories including: Customer and Market Focus, Strategic Planning, Process Management and Measurement, Analysis, and Knowledge Management (p. 26). This is not surprising since this value ideally creates a thread of excellence and permeates the entire enterprise system and culture.

WORKSHEETS

Customer-Driven Excellence – Work Sheet

Core Value - Customer Driven Excellence

Three ways the organization demonstrates this value:	Barriers that need to be overcome to fully implement this value throughout the organization:
1.	1.
2.	2.
3.	3.

Actions we need to take to achieve excellence in this core value:

1

2

3

4

Organizations you can learn from:

- **All Baldrige Winners**

Agility

FOUNDATION

Agility - Baldrige Core Value

Success in globally competitive markets demands agility—a capacity for rapid change and flexibility. E-business requires and enables more rapid, flexible, and customized responses. Businesses face ever-shorter cycles for the introduction of new/improved products and services, as well as for faster and more flexible response to customers. Major improvements in response time often require simplification of work units and processes and/or the ability for rapid changeover from one process to another. Cross-trained and empowered employees are vital assets in such a demanding environment.

A major success factor in meeting competitive challenges is the design-to-introduction (product or service initiation) or innovation cycle time. To meet the demands of rapidly changing global markets, organizations need to carry out stage-to-stage integration (such as concurrent engineering) of activities from research or concept to commercialization.

All aspects of time performance now are more critical, and cycle time has become a key process measure. Other important benefits can be derived from this focus on time; time improvements often drive simultaneous improvements in organization, quality, cost, and productivity.

NIST (2004) pp. 2 - 3

RESEARCH SAYS

Evans and Ford (1997) found that **fast response** (as it was called in 1996) value was of medium importance to the Process Management category and low importance to all other categories which supports the placement of this value in the execution excellence competency area (p. 26)

At the time of writing this book, agility is an important attribute for many organizations. It seems to us that agility is important not only to process, but at a minimum - strategy (agile v. fixed plan) and customer focus (respond to changing needs quickly).

WORKSHEETS

Agility – Work Sheet

Core Value – Agility

Three ways the organization demonstrates this value:	Barriers that need to be overcome to fully implement this value throughout the organization:
1.	1.
2.	2.
3.	3.

Actions we need to take to achieve excellence in this core value:

1

2

3

4

Organizations you can learn from:

- **Clarke American**
- **3M Dental**
- **Motorola CGISS**

Focus on Results and Creating Value

 FOUNDATION

Focus on Results and Creating Value - Baldrige Core Value

An organization's performance measurements need to focus on key results. Results should be used to create and balance value for your key stakeholders—customers, employees, stockholders, suppliers and partners, the public, and the community. By creating value for your key stakeholders, your organization builds loyalty and contributes to growing the economy. To meet the sometimes conflicting and changing aims that balancing value implies, organizational strategy should explicitly include key stakeholder requirements. This will help ensure that plans and actions meet differing stakeholder needs and avoid adverse impacts on any stakeholders. The use of a balanced composite of leading and lagging performance measures offers an effective means to communicate short- and longer-term priorities, monitor actual performance, and provide a clear basis for improving results.

NIST (2004) p. 4

 RESEARCH SAYS

Evans and Ford (1997) found that the importance of **results orientation** (as it was called in 1996) value was of medium importance to five categories including: Strategic Planning; Customer and Market Focus; Process Management; Human Resource Focus; and Measurement, Analysis, and Knowledge Management, placing it in a similar situation with customer-focus as a cross-cutting value that should ideally permeate the entire enterprise (p. 26).

WORKSHEETS

Focus on Results and Creating Value - Work Sheet

Core Value - Focus on Results and Creating Value

Three ways the organization demonstrates this value:	Barriers that need to be overcome to fully implement this value throughout the organization:
1.	1.
2.	2.
3.	3.

Actions we need to take to achieve excellence in this core value:

1

2

3

4

Organizations you can learn from:

- Ritz Carlton
- Clarke American
- Pals Sudden Service

Valuing Employees and Partners

 FOUNDATION

Valuing Employees and Partners - Baldrige Core Value

An organization's success depends increasingly on the diverse knowledge, skills, creativity, and motivation of all its employees and partners.

Valuing employees means committing to their satisfaction, development, and well-being. Increasingly, this involves more flexible, high-performance work practices tailored to employees with diverse workplace and home life needs. Major challenges in the area of valuing employees include (1) demonstrating your leaders' commitment to your employees' success, (2) recognition that goes beyond the regular compensation system, (3) development and progression within your organization, (4) sharing your organization's knowledge so your employees can better serve your customers and contribute to achieving your strategic objectives, and (5) creating an environment that encourages risk taking and innovation.

Organizations need to build internal and external partnerships to better accomplish overall goals. Internal partnerships might include labor-management cooperation, such as agreements with unions. Partnerships with employees might entail employee development, cross-training, or new work organizations, such as high-performance work teams. Internal partnerships also might involve creating network relationships among your work units to improve flexibility, responsiveness, and knowledge sharing.

External partnerships might be with customers, suppliers, and education organizations. Strategic partnerships or alliances are increasingly important kinds of external partnerships. Such partnerships might offer entry into new markets or a basis for new products or services. Also, partnerships might permit the blending of your organization's core competencies or leadership capabilities with the complementary strengths and capabilities of partners.

Successful internal and external partnerships develop longer-term objectives, thereby creating a basis for mutual investments and respect. Partners should address the key requirements for success, means for regular communication, approaches to evaluating progress, and means for adapting to changing conditions. In some cases, joint education and training could offer a cost-effective method for employee development.

NIST (2004) p. 2

 RESEARCH SAYS

Evans and Ford (1997) found that the importance of the employee participation and partnership development value (as it was called in 1996) was of high importance to the human resource focus category and of medium importance to the process management category (p. 26).

WORKSHEETS

Valuing Employees and Partners – Work Sheet

Core Value - Valuing Employees and Partners

Three ways the organization demonstrates this value:	Barriers that need to be overcome to fully implement this value throughout the organization:
1.	1.
2.	2.
3.	3.

Actions we need to take to achieve excellence in this core value:

1

2

3

4

Organizations you can learn from:

- SSM Health Care
- Clarke American
- Boeing Aerospace Support

Organizational and Personal Learning

 FOUNDATION

Organizational and Personal Learning - Baldrige Core Value

Achieving the highest levels of business performance requires a well-executed approach to organizational and personal learning. Organizational learning includes both continuous improvement of existing approaches and adaptation to change, leading to new goals and/or approaches. Learning needs to be embedded in the way your organization operates. This means that learning (1) is a regular part of daily work; (2) is practiced at personal, work unit, and organizational levels; (3) results in solving problems at their source ("root cause"); (4) is focused on building and sharing knowledge throughout your organization; and (5) is driven by opportunities to effect significant, meaningful change. Sources for learning include employees' ideas, research and development (R&D), customers' input, best practice sharing, and benchmarking.

Organizational learning can result in (1) enhancing value to customers through new and improved products and services; (2) developing new business opportunities; (3) reducing errors, defects, waste, and related costs; (4) improving responsiveness and cycle time performance; (5) increasing productivity and effectiveness in the use of all resources throughout your organization; and (6) enhancing your organization's performance in fulfilling its societal responsibilities and its service to your community as a good citizen.

Employees' success depends increasingly on having opportunities for personal learning and practicing new skills. Organizations invest in employees' personal learning through education, training, and other opportunities for continuing growth. Such opportunities might include job rotation and increased pay for demonstrated knowledge and skills. On-the-job training offers a cost-effective way to train and to better link training to your organizational needs and priorities. Education and training programs may benefit from advanced technologies, such as computer- and Internet-based learning and satellite broadcasts.

Personal learning can result in (1) more satisfied and versatile employees who stay with your organization, (2) organizational cross-functional learning, (3) building the knowledge assets of your organization, and (4) an improved environment for innovation.

Thus, learning is directed not only toward better products and services but also toward being more responsive, adaptive, innovative, and efficient—giving your organization marketplace sustainability and performance advantages and giving your employees satisfaction and motivation to excel.

NIST (2004) p. 2

RESEARCH SAYS

Evans and Ford (1997) found the importance of the continuous improvement value (as it was called in 1996) of high or medium importance to four categories including: Customer and Market Focus; Process Management; Measurement, Analysis, and Knowledge Management; Human Resource Management (p. 26).

 WORKSHEETS

Organizational and Personal Learning – Work Sheet

Core Value - Organizational and Personal Learning

Three ways the organization demonstrates this value:	Barriers that need to be overcome to fully implement this value throughout the organization:
1.	1.
2.	2.
3.	3.

Actions we need to take to achieve excellence in this core value:

1

2

3

4

Organizations you can learn from:

- Boeing Aerospace Support
- Clarke American
- Pals Sudden Service

Management by Fact

 FOUNDATION

Management by Fact - Baldrige Core Value

Organizations depend on the measurement and analysis of performance. Such measurements should derive from business needs and strategy, and they should provide critical data and information about key processes, outputs, and results. Many types of data and information are needed for performance management. Performance measurement should include customer, product, and service performance; comparisons of operational, market, and competitive performance; and supplier, employee, and cost and financial performance. Data should be segmented by, for example, markets, product lines, and employee groups to facilitate analysis.

Analysis refers to extracting larger meaning from data and information to support evaluation, decision making, and improvement. Analysis entails using data to determine trends, projections, and cause and effect that might not otherwise be evident. Analysis supports a variety of purposes, such as planning, reviewing your overall performance, improving operations, change management, and comparing your performance with competitors' or with "best practices" benchmarks.

A major consideration in performance improvement and change management involves the selection and use of performance measures or indicators. The measures or indicators you select should best represent the factors that lead to improved customer, operational, and financial performance. A comprehensive set of measures or indicators tied to customer and/or organizational performance requirements represents a clear basis for aligning all processes with your organization's goals. Through the analysis of data from your tracking processes, your measures or indicators themselves may be evaluated and changed to better support your goals.

NIST (2004) p. 3

 RESEARCH SAYS

Evans and Ford (1997) found that the importance of the **management by fact** value was high or medium for five categories including: Measurement, Analysis, and Knowledge Management; Strategic Planning; Customer and Market Focus; Process Management; Human Resource Focus
(p. 26).

WORKSHEETS

Management by Fact – Work Sheet

Core Value - Management by Fact

Three ways the organization demonstrates this value:	Barriers that need to be overcome to fully implement this value throughout the organization:
1.	1.
2.	2.
3.	3.

Actions we need to take to achieve excellence in this core value:

1

2

3

4

Organizations you can learn from:

- **Pals Sudden Service**
- **Medrad**
- **Catapillar Financial Services**

Managing for Innovation

 FOUNDATION

Managing for Innovation - Baldrige Core Value

Innovation means making meaningful change to improve an organization's products, services, and processes and to create new value for the organization's stakeholders. Innovation should lead your organization to new dimensions of performance. Innovation is no longer strictly the purview of research and development departments; innovation is important for all aspects of your business and all processes. Organizations should be led and managed so that innovation becomes part of the learning culture and is integrated into daily work.

Innovation builds on the accumulated knowledge of your organization and its employees. Therefore, the ability to capitalize on this knowledge is critical to managing for innovation.

NIST (2004) p. 3

 WORKSHEETS

Managing for Innovation – Work Sheet

Core Value - Managing for Innovation

Three ways the organization demonstrates this value:	Barriers that need to be overcome to fully implement this value throughout the organization:
1.	1.
2.	2.
3.	3.
Actions we need to take to achieve excellence in this core value: 1 2…	
Organizations you can learn from: <ul><li>SSM Health Care</li><li>Clarke American</li><li>Sunny Fresh Foods</li></ul>	

Key Factors	**Organizational Profile**

The final component of the Focus is the unique context of the organization. The performance excellence model is a context dependent model. In other words, the appropriate approach to an aspect of the model (e.g., Strategic Planning) is dependent on the unique organization situation. For example the appropriate strategy development and deployment process for the "Mom and Pop" grocery store down the road is likely to be a bit different than a Fortune 100 company with operations in over 40 countries. The key organization factors are organized into two areas – organization description and organizational challenges. The organization description is composed of two main elements – the organizational environment and organizational relationships. The organizational challenges component of the key factors is focused on three areas – the competitive environment, strategic challenges, and the performance improvement system.

The Focus on the organization as a system, the design principles, and the key organizational factors enables the organization to identify what is *relevant* and *important* to future organization development and success. Of course this is only the beginning. The next step is to develop systematic approaches to strategic leadership and start setting the course to performance excellence.

Ask any executive in any organization and chances are they will tell you that their organization is unique. Answering the key organizational profile questions enables you to understand that uniqueness in a way that will be useful to evaluate and improve the performance review system.

"Your Organizational Profile sets the context for the way your organization operates. Your environment, key working relationships, and strategic challenges serve as an overarching guide for your organizational performance management system." (Baldrige)

The design of a custom performance review system requires a clear understanding of the context of the organization. This context will help to design the processes in a way that reflects those elements that are most relevant and important.

The first question is, who is the organization? What are its key characteristics, including what it does (products/services), why it does it (culture & purpose), who does it (employee demographics), what tools do they have to do it (technology, equipment, facilities), and finally what kind of regulatory environment do they work in?

The next question is who is in the fight with them? There are two major types of relationships – those with customers and those with supplier partners. Who are their key customers and what are their requirements? Who are the major supplier partners and what are the key supply chain requirements? What methods does the organization use to build and maintain the relationship and communicate with the supplier partners?

Who is against the organization? Who are the key competitors and how good are they? How does the organization compare to these competitors? What performance factors will make the greatest difference with the customers?

What are the main challenges the organization faces in winning in the marketplace? What are the most significant operations, people, and global challenges?

Finally, what is the system the organization uses to evaluate and improve the organization's processes and approaches and share that knowledge throughout the organization?

These are the five most influential areas in setting the organization's context in order to assess and redesign an organizational performance review system.

A Context Dependent Business Model

Importance of Beginning with Your Organizational Profile

Your Organizational Profile is critically important because

- it is the most appropriate starting point for self-assessment and for writing an application;

- it helps you identify potential gaps in KEY information and focus on KEY PERFORMANCE requirements and business RESULTS;

- it requires the leaders of the organization to decide/finalize/clarify key aspects of the business;

- it is used by the Examiners and Judges in application review, including the site visit, to understand your organization and what you consider important; and

- it also may be used by itself for an initial self-assessment. If you identify topics for which conflicting, little, or no information is available, it is possible that your assessment need go no further, and you can use these topics for action planning.

The Organizational Profile provides your organization with critical insight into the key internal and external factors that shape its operating environment. These factors, such as the mission, vision, values, competitive environment, and strategic challenges, impact the way your organization is run and the decisions you make. As such, the Organizational Profile helps your business understand better the context in which it operates; the key requirements for current and future business success; and the needs, opportunities, and constraints placed upon your organization's performance management system.

This section needs to be completed before the Application Document is written. If that does not happen, then the organization will be writing about factors which have yet to be decided. It would be analogous to playing a sports match and after the match is over deciding what the rules should have been!

The Organizational Profile gives the organization the opportunity to describe the culture.

 THOUGHTS FOR LEADERS

In the 1990's a customer had a serious problem and called the supplier's plant. The night guard at the plant called somebody in accounting, they called somebody in shipping, and a number of hourly employees came in.

They called the trucking line, shipped products to the customer, and cut invoices. Nobody in management even knew it had been done until Monday morning. When the Plant Manager found out Monday Morning, he was so proud he told everyone who would listen,

The culture? In that plant, the level of empowerment and teamwork was clear – do what the customer needs.

Do employees clearly understand their level of empowerment?

P.1a	Organizational Environment

Orientation	New Users

 FOUNDATION

Organizational Environment P.1a - Introduction

The organizational environment is focused on the internal operations of the organization including key products and services; organizational culture; people; major technologies, equipment, and facilities; and the regulatory environment which impacts these factors.

In the example of the local coffee shop entrepreneur, some of the decisions would be what products and services to provide. Some might say that coffee is the central product while others might say that a forum for information exchange is the primary product or service and coffee is an enhancer. If the primary product is the latter the coffee shop might offer free wireless internet along with a variety of coffees and snacks. Which delivery mechanisms to use is another decision. For the local coffee shop the options might be – counter service, drive-up window, and maybe even internet order and mail delivery for coffee beans and accessories.

The culture of the organization is critical to the organization's direction and internal environment. If the culture is characterized by an open collaborative and creative operating style that is known for its innovation then detailed procedures on information sharing might not fit. At the local coffee shop a culture of teamwork focused on creating an environment for information exchange that is personal might be the desired environment. In other words, to steal a line from the theme song for a popular television show, a place "where everybody knows your name."

Now that we know what work is to be accomplished and the culture (norms, values, behaviors) to accomplish it – who is going to actually do the work? What types of employees does the organization use to accomplish the work? For the local coffee shop, the workforce might consist of supervisors who are full-time employees and workers who are most often part-time employees and full-time students. The bigger question, of course, is what do these two groups of employees need to be successful?

After the work, the culture, and the employees are determined, the next question is where are we going to do the work and what kind of equipment do we need? What are the organization's major technologies, equipment, and facilities? This of course varies widely depending on the type of business. A Fortune 100 "high tech" firm with operations around the world will have a very different answer to this question than the local coffee shop. The local coffee shop needs a shop with furniture, some coffee making equipment, and high speed wireless internet.

The last element of the organizational environment is the regulatory environment. What external rules and regulations does the organization have to comply with. This of course is again very different for a nuclear power plant than it is for the "Mom and Pop" grocery store down the street.

The organizational environment is the first major component of the context. It consists of five major elements: products and services; culture and philosophy; employees; technology, equipment, and facilities; and finally the regulatory environment in which the organization operates. A complete understanding of the main products and services is essential to identifying and analyzing the key measures that will provide a comprehensive view of the production and delivery system or value chain.

The culture and purpose of the organization along with the vision and values help establish the areas that are of greatest importance to the organization's success. Take ownership for example. If the owners are the same as the customers, the focus purpose of the firm is different than if the owners are investors in a for profit. The cooperative typically is focused on the greatest benefit to the members at the least expense. In this case the customers are the owners.

The employee demographics will impact the types and methods of measurement needed to acquire, develop, utilize, evaluate, and promote the workforce uniquely suited to your business.

The technology, equipment, and facilities will influence what is important to measure, how best to measure it, and how best to aggregate the data.

The regulatory environment is a key variable to understanding the most important measures that will help the organization anticipate issues and prevent problems with areas of public well-being.

 EXAMPLE

Organizational Environment P.1a - Example Factors

SSM Healthcare - **(Baldrige Recipient 2002)**

Products and Services

- 90% of SSMHC's revenue is derived from health care services provided at its hospitals.
- Primary services include: emergency, medical/surgical, oncology, mental health, obstetric, cardiology, orthopedic, pediatric, and rehabilitative care.
- Delivers health care services in inpatient, outpatient, emergency department, and ambulatory surgery settings associated with 17 acute care hospitals.
- Secondary services, which support SSMHC's core hospital business, include physician practices, skilled nursing (long term) care, home care, and other nonpatient business services.
- SSMHC's networks coordinate the delivery of care; facilitate communication, cooperation, and sharing of knowledge and skills; and provide support services (planning, finance, human resources, physician practice management) for the entities within a specific market. The entities focus on meeting their communities needs and delivering care to their patients.

Culture - Mission, Vision, Values

- Founded 130 years ago by Mother Mary Odilia Berger, who migrated with four other sisters to the United States from Germany.
- Private, not-for-profit health care system.
- Vision – Through our participation in the healing ministry of Jesus Christ, communities, especially those that are economically, physically and socially marginalized, will experience improved health in mind, body, spirit and environment within the financial limits of the system.
- Mission – Through our exceptional health care services, we reveal the healing presence of God.

- Core Values – Compassion, Respect, Excellence, Stewardship, and Community
- Quality Principles –
  - Patients and other customers are our first priority
  - Quality is achieved through people
  - All work is part of a process
  - Decision making by facts
  - Quality requires continuous improvement
- Culture is also characterized by consensus building and decision-making at the level of greatest impact and responsibility.

Employees

- Nearly 5,000 physician partners
- 22,041 employees work together to provide healthcare services
- Physician diagnostic and treatment services are provided through the offices of SSMHC's 209 employed physicians.
- The system's health care staff is diverse and includes nurses (patient care and administrative), physicians, executives and managers/supervisors; support, clinical and technical professionals; lead clinical/technical professionals; allied health; support services; and administrative assistants/coordinators/office clerical.
- Eighty-two percent of the employees are women, and 18 percent represent minority groups. SSMHC has no unionized employee groups. Periodically, contract workers are used to supplement the workforce.
- Special safety requirements for employees include ergonomics, exposure control through sharps alternatives, hazardous and biohazardous material management, life and environmental safety, and emergency preparedness.

Major Technologies, Equipment, and Facilities

- Vast organization with owned facilities totaling more than 11.5 million square feet. These facilities include acute care hospitals, nursing homes, outpatient care buildings, physician and other office buildings, and clinics.
  - SSMHC entities are located in the Midwest in four states--Missouri, Illinois, Wisconsin, and Oklahoma.
  - Sixteen of the hospitals are owned and operated by SSMHC, and one is managed by the system, but jointly owned with another health care system.
- Major medical equipment supports diagnostic and treatment services within its acute care settings. This equipment includes state-of-the-art technology, such as MRI, CT, ultrasound, diagnostic imaging, angiography, and surgical lasers.
- A standardized, systemwide information system supports SSMHC's assessment, measurement, accountability, and e-health activities. The infrastructure initiated in 1992 includes:
  - local area networks (LANS);
  - system-spanning wide-area networks (WANS);
  - access to external, government, and commercial databases;
  - video teleconferencing; tele-radiology; and other services.

Regulatory Environment

- The system operates under the requirements of the federal sector, including:
  - OSHA
  - EEOC
  - EPA (health, safety and environmental)
  - City, state, and county regulations
- While SSMHC is not legally required to meet EEOC regulations, the organization has elected to do so because of its strong commitment to diversity.

- SSMHC is committed to exceeding regulatory requirements, and considers compliance a minimum standard. All hospitals, nursing homes, care sites, and services are fully licensed and accredited by all appropriate federal, state and local agencies.

Source: SSM (2003) pp. xix – xxi

Diagnosis	**Assessors**

QUESTIONS

Organizational Environment P.1a – Baldrige Organizational Profile Questions

Describe your organization's business environment and your KEY relationships with CUSTOMERS, suppliers, and other partners.

Products and Services

(1) What are your organization's main products and services? What are the delivery mechanisms used to provide your products and services to your CUSTOMERS?

Note 1: Product and service delivery to your customers (P.1a[1]) might be direct, or through dealers, distributors, or channel partners.

Culture

(2) What is your organizational culture? What are your stated PURPOSE, VISION, MISSION, and VALUES?

(Further Description) Use of such terms as "purpose," "vision," "mission," and "values" varies depending on the organization, and some organizations may not use one or more of these terms. Nevertheless, you should have a clear understanding of the essence of your business, why it exists, and where your senior leaders want to take the business in the future. This clarity enables you to make strategic decisions affecting the future of your organization and implement these decisions.

Employees

(3) What is your employee profile? What are their educational levels? What are your organization's workforce and job diversity, organized bargaining units, use of contract employees, and special health and safety requirements?

Technologies, Equipment, Facilities

(4) What are your major technologies, equipment, and facilities?

Regulatory Environment

(5) What is the regulatory environment under which your organization operates? What are the applicable occupational health and safety regulations; accreditation, certification, or registration requirements; and environmental, financial, and product regulations?

(Further Description) *The regulatory environment in which you operate places requirements on your organization and impacts how you run your business. Understanding this environment is key to making effective operational and strategic decisions. Further, it allows you to identify whether you are merely complying with the minimum requirements of applicable laws and regulations or exceeding them. Exceeding minimum requirements is a hallmark of leading organizations.*

NIST (2004) pp. 10 - 11

 WORKSHEETS

Organizational Environment P.1a – Work Sheet

P.1a(1) - Product, Services, and Delivery Mechanisms

Main Products and Services	Delivery Mechanisms

P.1a(2) - Purpose, Mission, Vision, Values

Values	Purpose – Mission - Vision	Stakeholders

P.1a(3) – Employees

Job Type	Number and/or %	Special Health and Safety Requirements	Education Level	Number and/or %	Diversity Group	Number and/or %

P.1a(4) - Major Technologies, Equipment, and Facilities

Technology	
Equipment	
Facilities	

P.1a(5) - Regulatory Environment

Regulatory Agency/Body	Requirements, including: • Occupational Safety & Health • Accreditation, Certification, Registration Requirements • Environmental, Financial and Product Regulations	Impact on the Organization – This can include the number of employees impacted, importance to the product or importance to the customer.

	Advanced
Design	**Users**

 BLUEPRINT

The organizational environment is composed of five major components. These five major components are linked to fourteen different Areas throughout the criteria. The organization environment starts with the culture which includes the organization's purpose, vision, mission, and values. This culture determines what it is like to work at this organization and in addition drives the value chain which consists of the main products and services and the delivery mechanisms. The value chain is influenced by three other components: the regulatory environment; the employee profile; and the major technologies, equipment, and facilities.

Two of the most interconnected components are the employee profile and the technologies, equipment, and facilities. The employees are found throughout the criteria and the nature and makeup of your employee base will drive many of the employee processes and practices. For example, if you have a lot of frontline employees who are high school students, the training requirements might be different than if the organization is an established consulting firm with 90% midlevel mid-career experienced professionals. The same goes for the technologies, equipment, and facilities. What works for the mom and pop grocery store chain down the street may not be the same thing that works for a fortune 100 company with locations in 40 countries.

Organizational Environment P.1a – Blueprint

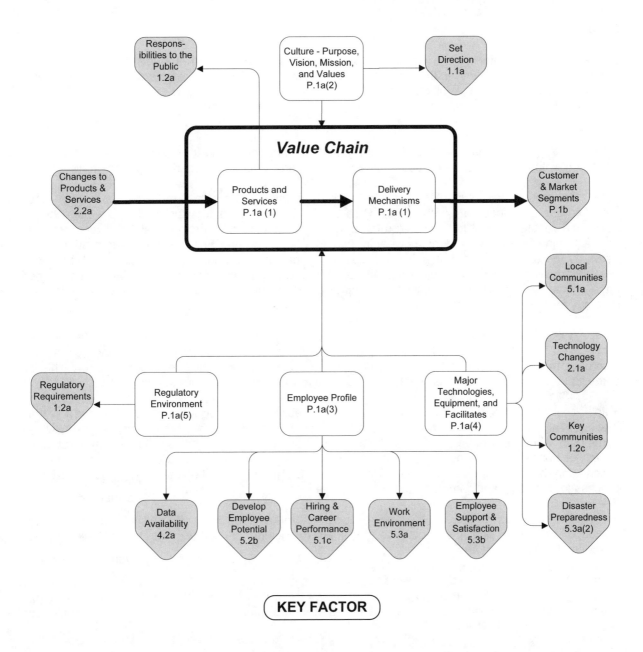

SYSTEM INTEGRATION

Organizational Environment P.1a – Linkages

Inputs

2.2a - Action plans often call for additions, changes, and improvement to products, services, and the processes that create them. In this case the value creation processes are refined or changed to assist in accomplishing the strategic objectives.

Outputs

1.1a – The setting of values and direction including short and long-term expectations should be consistent with and include the purpose, mission, vision, and values described here in the profile.

1.2a – The most important input to area 1.2a is the description and nature of the products and services identified and described here in the profile P.1a(1). Since this area is focused on the public concerns, risks, and regulatory and legal issues related to the firm the type of products and services are the central driving factor that determines what is relevant and important. For example, if the products are eaten by the consumers then the FDA will be part of the regulatory environment. Some of the risks associated will be health risks to consumers, and there are public concerns to deal with, such as the case of Mad Cow disease. The design of the processes to address these areas will likely be different than say for a business consulting firm or an airline.

1.2a – A key input to area 1.2a is the description of the regulatory environment described here in the profile P.1a(5). This environment is largely driven by the products and services but other factors can also drive this environment including the nature of the ownership, the employees, and so forth. This is a key input to the identification of regulatory and legal requirements called for in area 1.2a.

1.2c – The key inputs to the 1.2c area are the major facilities and their locations as described in the profile. While the criteria does not specify that an organization has to be involved and support every community where they have an office, it does expect that the key communities will be determined from the major operating locations and possibly the locations where their products and services are used, which might be different from the production facilities. So, the communities that are considered by the process for status as key communities should include those identified here in P.1a.

2.1a – The analysis of technology changes and key innovations is another key input to strategy development. This analysis should be designed to include or address the major technologies described here in profile area P.1a.

4.2a – The number, type, and nature of the workforce described in the employee profile is a critical input to the design of the process/system that makes the right data available to the right employees. There should be processes to ensure that the appropriate information is available for all employee groups.

5.1a – The location of the facilities as described in the profile determines the nature and make up of the local communities. This make up, in turn, influences the approaches to capitalize on the diverse ideas, cultures, and thinking of the local communities.

5.1c – The employee segments identified in the profile together with the organization's requirements will determine the gaps that need to be filled with new employees. These can be gaps in technical skills, diversity, education and so forth.

5.2b – The employee profile (number, type, characteristics of employees) influences the appropriate design of the motivation and career development approaches.

5.3a – Employee profile is a key input to the nature of employee groups, work units, and work environments which, in turn, influence the design of the processes, measures, and goals to create the desired work environment.

5.3a – The location and type of facilities and the nature of the technology used in the facilities is a direct input to the emergency and disaster preparedness approaches. In other words, the disaster threats differ depending on location and the nature of the technology.

5.3b – The employee profile identifies the number, type, and characteristics of key employee segments. The description of the employees in the profile should correspond to the segments used to determine key factors, processes, and measures for employee support and satisfaction approaches.

P.1b – The delivery mechanisms identified in this profile area should be consistent with the distribution channels and distributors identified in profile area P.1a.

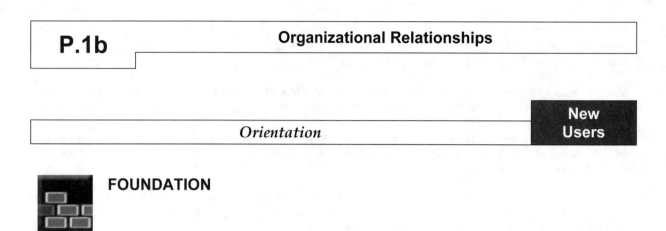

P.1b   **Organizational Relationships**

Orientation   **New Users**

FOUNDATION

Organizational Relationships P.1b – Introduction

The second part of the organizational description looks outside to the key external relationships including governance, customers, and suppliers.

The first question is what is your organizational structure and governance system? In addition, what are the reporting relationships among your board of directors, senior leaders, and parent organization? The bottom-line is who are these people, what do they want, and how do you interact with them? As is probably obvious, the answer to this varies widely depending on size of the organization, ownership model, and the level of autonomy of the organization. For example, single owner Limited Liability Company will have a very different board of directors than say a corporation that is publicly traded.

The second set of relationships are the key customer segments or groups. These are typically determined by the difference in requirements. In other words each segment has different needs, wants, and desires or prioritizes their needs, wants, and desires differently than the other segments. For example, the local coffee shop might have several schemes for segmenting customers including the on the way to work crowd, the traditional conversation crowd, and the technology crowd. The first two segments might not rate the wireless internet as important to their experience but the technology crowd probably would. The traditional conversation crowd might not rate speed of service as important but the "on the way to work crowd" probably would. So, each segment while they all drink coffee and may have similar coffee requirements (temperature, taste, etc.) at the same time may have very different "experience" requirements.

Finally, suppliers are key to the quality of the value chain. There is an old computer programmer saying – "garbage in, garbage out." What role do suppliers and distributors play in your value creation processes? You cannot make good coffee from lousy beans. If the internet works only half the time then the experience for the technology crowd will suffer. Finally, how do you build relationships and communicate with customers and suppliers?

With the environmental context established the next key area to understand is the organization's key relationships. There are two major types of external relationships – those with customers and those with supplier partners.

The relationships with customers are often determined by the segmentation approach the organization uses. For example, some organizations segment their customers by their profitability or contribution to margin. This is the airline approach that often classifies customers into cheap fare infrequent flyer, business full fare flyer, and frequent flyer at various fares. The relationship mechanisms differ for each segment. Access to information, seating, etc. varies with the status of the customer. The airlines spend less time impressing the infrequent supper saver passenger than they do the frequent business passenger. This is simply a matter of allocation of their limited resources to areas that will have the greatest impact on the top line in a highly competitive environment. Service levels are appropriate for what the consumer is willing to pay for.

Supplier partners on the other hand are the key to business in the next decade or so. As organizations get better at focusing on core competencies and outsourcing the rest, the need for relationship management with key supplier partners grows. It is very difficult to successfully outsource key operations using the traditional us v. them procurement processes and relationship techniques. The future of the integrated supply chain network will require close relationships and increased sharing of information. The reality of your supplier partner network will determine what is necessary to measure and how it can be used to improve performance of the entire supply chain system.

 EXAMPLE

Organizational Relationships P.1b – Example Factors

SSM Healthcare **- (Baldrige Recipient 2002)**

Patients and Their Families	Key Requirements
Inpatients	- Responsiveness - Pain management
Outpatients	- Wait Times - Pain Relief
Emergency Department	- Wait Times - Pain Management
Home Care	- Timeliness - Accuracy
Long-term Care	- Technical Skill

SSMHC views patients and their families as its primary customer group. SSMHC further delineates this customer group by five key patient groups: inpatient, outpatient, emergency department, home care and long term care. Surveys have shown that family members, who act in behalf of children or relatives not competent to make decisions, have the same key requirements as patients and as such they are not a separate segment. All patient segments expect accuracy, good communication, and positive health care outcomes.

Source: Figure P.1-5 Key Customer Requirements – SSM (2003) p. xxi)

EXAMPLE

Organizational Relationships P.1b – Example Factors

Clarke American **– (Baldrige Recipient 2001)**

P.1b - Clarke American – Partner Segmentation Builds Loyalty

Defining and Delivering your partners' and customers' individual needs!

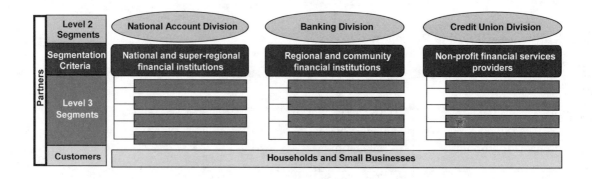

Over 4,000 Financial Institution Partners Serving Over 30 Million Customers.

Clarke American's first echelon of segmentation is to divide the segments (based on different requirements) into customers and partners.

Customers which break down into households and small businesses are not segmented further.

Partners are segmented down to several more levels. The first level of segmentation under Partners (level two segmentation) includes National Accounts, banking and Credit Union Divisions. The third level of partner segmentation (only shown conceptually in the above graphic) divides each level two segment based on the unique segmentation criteria (requirements) for each of the divisions.

Source: Clarke American Quest for Excellence Presentation (2002)

Diagnosis

QUESTIONS

Organizational Relationships P.1b – Baldrige Organizational Profile Questions

Structure and Governance

(1) What is your organizational structure and GOVERNANCE system? What are the reporting relationships among your board of directors, SENIOR LEADERS, and your parent organization, as appropriate?

Authors Note: (Further Description) Leading organizations have well-defined governance systems with clear reporting relationships. It is important to clearly identify which functions are performed by senior leaders and, as applicable, by your board of directors and your parent organization. Board independence and accountability are frequently key considerations in governance structure.

Customers

(2) What are your KEY CUSTOMER groups and market SEGMENTS, as appropriate? What are their KEY requirements and expectations for your products and services? What are the differences in these requirements and expectations among CUSTOMER groups and market SEGMENTS?

Note 2: Market segments (P.1b[2]) might be based on product lines or features, geography, distribution channels, business volume, or other factors that allow your organization to define related market characteristics.

Note 3: Customer group and market segment requirements (P.1b[2]) might include on-time delivery, low defect levels, ongoing price reductions, electronic communication, and after-sales service.

Suppliers and Partners

(3) What role do suppliers and distributors play in your VALUE CREATION PROCESSES? What are your most important types of suppliers and distributors? What are your most important supply chain requirements?

(Further Description) In supplier-dependent organizations, suppliers play critical roles in processes that are important to running the business and to maintaining or achieving a sustainable competitive advantage. Supply chain requirements might include on-time or just-in-time delivery, flexibility, variable staffing, design capability, and customized manufacturing or services.

(4) What are your KEY supplier and CUSTOMER partnering relationships and communication mechanisms?

Note 4: Communication mechanisms (P.1b[4]) should be two-way and might be in person, electronic, by telephone, and/or written. For many organizations, these mechanisms might be changing as marketplace requirements change.

NIST (2004) p. 10 - 11

WORKSHEETS

Organizational Relationships P.1b - Work Sheet

P.1b(1) - Organization Structure

Positions	Roles & Responsibilities	Reporting Relationships

P.1b(2) - Customer and Market Segments

Customer Groups and/or Market Segments	Requirements & Expectations (in priority order)
	1.
	2.
	3.
	1.
	2.
	3.
Note: Performance against the above Segments for Customer Satisfaction, and Dissatisfaction should be reported in Item 7.1	Note: Performance against the above requirements should be reported in Item 7.2.

P.1b(3) - Suppliers and Partners

Key Suppliers & Partners	Most Important Requirements and Expectations

P.1b(4) - Key Supplier and Customer Partnering Relationships and Communication Mechanisms.

Relationship	Communication Mechanisms

Design

BLUEPRINT

Organizational Relationships P.1b – Blueprint

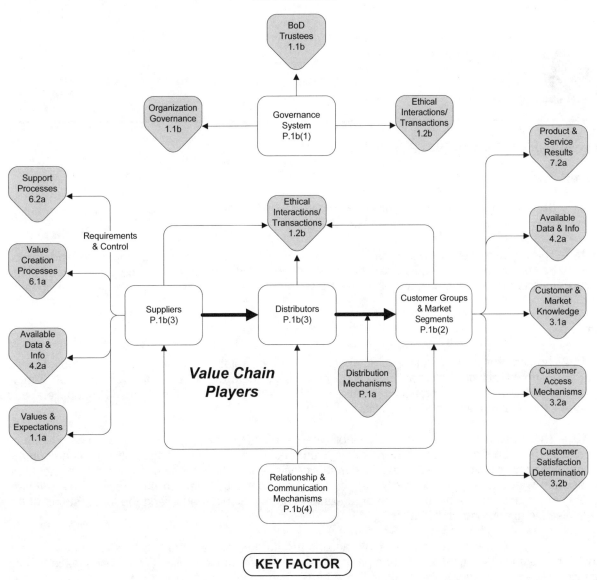

The organizational relationships are categorized into five components or key stakeholder relationships. The first one is the governance system followed by the main players in the value chain. This includes suppliers and partners, distributors, and the ultimate recipients of the products and services - the customer groups and market segments. In addition, the nature and makeup of these groups is a fifth question. What communication and relationship mechanisms are used?

These major components are linked to fourteen different Areas throughout the criteria. For example, the governance system is linked to both Item 1.1 and Item 1.2. The customer groups and market segments are linked to at least five Areas in the criteria. These groups drive the customer access mechanisms and the customer and market knowledge Items.

When an organization is preparing an assessment and writing those two Items they should address the same customer groups' market segments that are identified in the Organizational Profile. In addition, the customer satisfaction determination or measures, product and service results and the information and data analysis should reflect the same customer groups and market segments. The key players in the supply chain, Suppliers and Distributors, will impact the processes in both Item 6.1 and Item 6.2 and data analysis in Item 4.2.

 SYSTEM INTEGRATION

Organizational Relationships P.1b – Linkages

Inputs

P.1a - The delivery mechanisms identified in profile area P.1a should be consistent with the distribution channels and distributors identified here in profile area P.1b.

3.1a – The activities described in area 3.1a to determine customer and market segments and groups should be consistent with the customer and market segments described here in the profile. In addition, if this process modifies the customer and market segments then that should be reflected in an updated profile.

Outputs

1.1a - The communication of the values, directions, and expectations to all employees, suppliers, and partners should include the employees, suppliers and partners described in the profile p.1b. Simply put, the communication approaches should be designed to address the same key suppliers and partners that were described in the profile area P.1b.

1.1b – There are two key factors to consider when evaluating or designing a governance system or process – first the structure and governance system and second the reporting relationships among the board of directors which are both described in this profile area. The approach to governance should be consistent with and appropriate for the specific situation described here in the profile. This will vary widely depending on the history of the organization, the ownership model, and the legal status of the organization (incorporated, 501c, etc.).

1.2b – A key input to ensuring ethical interactions are the key players the organization interacts with, including customers, stakeholders, and partners identified here in the profile. The processes to ensure ethical interactions need to be designed to address interactions with all the categories and types of relationships the organization has.

1.2b – The processes that ensure ethical interactions also need to be designed to work within the governance system described here in P.1b. All too often organizations will create processes and structures that are completely different from the main part of the organization. While this might be appropriate for processes that require "third party" status to be effective (e.g., ombudsman) they should be designed to work within and be consistent with the overall system or structure.

6.1a – The suppliers and partners identified here in the profile are key inputs to both the requirements determination process 6.1a(2) and the process management activities 6.1a(4). First, the suppliers and partners capabilities and needs should be part of the requirements process to ensure that the supply chain works as an integrated system. Second, since suppliers and partners are sometimes working side-by-side or even doing key tasks in the value chain by themselves, they may also need to be part of the process management design and execution activities.

6.2a – Suppliers and partners are often engaged in and an integral part of the support processes. The suppliers and partners are key inputs to both the requirements determination process 6.2a(2) and the process management activities 6.2a(4). First, the suppliers and partners capabilities and needs should be part of the requirements process to ensure that the support network works as an integrated system. Second, since suppliers and partners are sometimes working side-by-side or even doing key tasks in the support network by themselves, they may also need to be part of the process management design and execution activities.

3.2a – The customer relationship building process – seek information, conduct business, and complain – should be designed to serve the key customer and market segments and groups identified here in the profile.

3.2b – The customer satisfaction determination processes should be designed to capture the satisfaction of the key customer and market segments and groups identified here in the profile.

4.2a – The number, type, and nature of the suppliers and partners as described here in the profile is a critical input to the design of the process/system that makes the right data available to the right suppliers and partners. There should be processes to ensure the appropriate information is available for all key suppliers and partners.

4.2a – The number, type, and nature of the customers, groups, and segments described here in the profile are critical inputs to the design of the process/system that makes the right data available to the right customers. There should be processes to ensure the appropriate information is available for all customers.

7.2a – Customer requirements as described here in the profile are key inputs to determining the key product and service results that are "proxies" for customer satisfaction.

P.2a	Competitive Environment

Orientation	New Users

 FOUNDATION

Competitive Environment P.2a – Introduction

Where do you stand in relation to your competitors? How fast are you growing? Who are your competitors? What factors will determine who wins in the marketplace? How are you and your competitors doing on these key factors? How do you know?

Why are these questions important? In the for-profit free marketplace they are critical to developing strategies to ensure continued success and sustainable results. For the local coffee shop the position might be equal head-to-head competitor with the local Starbucks. When Starbucks came to our town the customers loyal to the local coffee shop put bumper stickers on their cars that read "Friends don't let friends drink Starbucks." While Starbucks might make a fine cup of coffee something else was at work here. Of course the *free* wireless internet at the local shop might have had something to do with it, but there were clearly other factors including personal relationships between the customers and the owner of the local coffee shop. The good news - both coffee shops are thriving and I suspect that may be because they serve different markets or customer groups. How would each coffee shop know how they were doing against each other?

Performance measures and competitive comparisons provide evidence to increase the understanding of the competitive environment. The competitive environment is advanced customer knowledge and understanding. It is one thing to understand the customer's stated wants and needs and it is quite another to understand what they will pay for.

The performance measures will be influenced by the competitors and the areas of greatest importance for comparison. Comparison measures provide a relative measure to compare performance levels and trends to. Comparisons help to understand gaps and the degree of the gaps. They also help to set realistic but meaningful targets.

The danger in comparisons is that they can limit the organization's improvement efforts to catching up as opposed to leaping beyond with innovative products, services, and processes. "Comparison, a great teacher once told me, is the cardinal sin of modern life. It traps us in a game that we can't win. Once we define ourselves in terms of others, we lose the freedom to shape our own lives." Jim Collins.

Competitive environment can be critical to future survival. It certainly will impact whether your organization thrives in the future. Tang and Bauer in their book "Competitive Dominance" identify several competitive positions from dead to follower to dominance. Knowledge of the competition and their performance particularly in the customers' eyes is key to developing strategies to overtake their position and dominate the market.

As we will see later, performance relative to competitors can be categorized into four categories. Two of these categories require little to no action while the other two require fundamental shifts in the organizations' methods.

This area is particularly difficult to address for many non-profits and government organizations. For one thing they are not taught to think like a competitive market and second many of their competitors are potential but not actually in the arena today.

 EXAMPLE

Competitive Environment P.2a – Example Factors

Clarke American - **(Baldrige Recipient 2001)**

Market Performance

- *Clarke American has outperformed the market in the FI check supply industry over the past five years.*
- Another source of competition to the FI check industry is direct mail competitors with 20 percent of the US check market. Their growth has come as a result of lower prices and consumer awareness of the variety of check styles offered through mail circulars. Three major players exist in this market.

Growth

- *Our growth is attributable to our refined, consistent FIS strategy of partnering with Financial Institutions (FIs) to provide best-in-class check printing and check-related services and products to enhance their businesses.*
- During the early 1990s, aggressive competitive pricing drove all check providers to significantly reduce costs. Clarke American increased investment in the emerging **FIS** approach to ensure improvement in quality, products and services. This committed strategy of differentiating through **FIS** is the principal factor in determining success.

Source: Clarke (2002) p. 5

 EXAMPLE

Competitive Environment P.2a – Example Factors

University of Wisconsin - Stout - **(Baldrige Recipient 2001)**

- There are two competitive considerations essential to achieving UW-Stout's goals: (1) competition for faculty, and (2) competition for students. Mission-similar universities and business/industry compete for skilled and qualified faculty.
- Competitive differentiators for faculty include: participation in the university decision-making process, quality of laboratory and other facilities, technology infrastructure, peer recognition,

campus atmosphere and image, and opportunities for research and professional and career development.

- Competition for students comes from other UW System universities, public universities and colleges in the State of Minnesota (because of reciprocity agreements), and other national and international private and public universities.

- Business and industry are also competitors for high school and technical college students. Since our primary market is Wisconsin (72 percent of students), the other UW System campuses are the major competition. Twenty-eight percent of students are non-residents and come to UW-Stout because of its unique mission and curriculum. UW-Stout's outreach initiatives with high schools, businesses, alumni, and Friends of Stout are effective methods to compete for students.

- Competitive differentiators for students include: UW-Stout's image and focused mission, career focus and placement success, student services, and active learning facilities.

- In order to achieve leadership in these key competitive factors, UW-Stout compares its performance with the other UW System campuses and with a selected set of nationally recognized universities with similar mission and/or curriculum, including California Polytechnic State University–San Luis Obispo, Ferris State University, and the New Jersey Institute of Technology. These comparisons provide data to assess leadership performance levels within the market of opportunity and for mission differentiation. To build and sustain its reputation and image nationally and internationally, UW-Stout also uses major national university benchmarks to compare its performance in key areas of student satisfaction, diversity, and financial management. This year, the universities selected for comparison are from states attaining A-B scores in the 2000 "Measuring Up" National Education Survey. Wisconsin was one of only three states attaining "A" or "B" scores in all five categories.

Source: U.W. Stout (2002) p. 186

Diagnosis	**Assessors**

 QUESTIONS

Competitive Environment P.2a – Baldrige Organizational Profile Questions

Competitive Position - *(1) What is your competitive position? What is your relative size and growth in your industry or markets served? What are the numbers and types of competitors for your organization?*

Key Success Factors - *(2) What are the principal factors that determine your success relative to your competitors? What are any KEY changes taking place that affect your competitive situation?*

Note 1: Factors (P.2a[2]) might include differentiators such as price, leadership, design services, e-services, geographic proximity, and warranty and product options.

Comparative Data - *(3) What are your KEY available sources of comparative and competitive data from within your industry? What are your KEY available sources of comparative data for analogous PROCESSES outside your industry? What limitations, if any, are there in your ability to obtain these data?*

NIST (2004) p. 12

WORKSHEETS

Competitive Environment P.2a - Work Sheet

P.2a(1) - Competitive Position

Market	Size	Growth	Key Competitors

P.2a(2) - Success Factors

Market Served	Key Success Factors	Changes Taking Place

P.2a(3) - Comparative Data

Sources of Comparative or Competitive Data	Measures	Limitations in Obtaining Data

BLUEPRINT

Competitive Environment P.2a – Blueprint

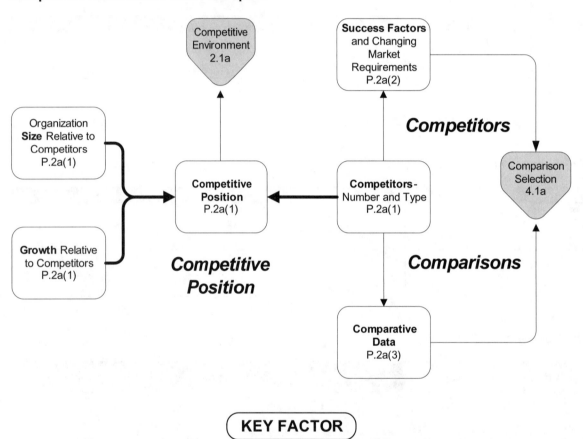

KEY FACTOR

The first two key factors were focused on the organization itself, the remaining three key factors focus on external aspects or the external environment that the organization operates in and the methods the organization uses to continuously learn and improve to meet the challenges of that environment.

The first of these three is the competitive environment. The competitive environment consists of the organization's competitive position, the main competitors, and the comparisons to those competitors. The competitive position is made up of two key elements: the organization's size relative to the competitors'; and the growth of the organization relative to the competitors'.

The competitors' number and type drive the impact the organization's key success factors have in the marketplace. It is these success factors that drive organization strategies and help to set priorities for improvements in the organization. As the blueprint depicts, the success factors and the competitors are both linked to the comparisons selected in Area to Address 4.1a. This is then connected and linked to performance analysis and eventually strategy development and deployment.

SYSTEM INTEGRATION

Competitive Environment P.2a – Linkages

Inputs

There are no significant input linkages to other criteria areas.

Outputs

2.1a – The analysis of the competitive environment is a key input to the strategy development process. This analysis should be designed to analyze the competitive environment described here in the profile.

4.1a – The selection of comparative data and information should be influenced by the key competitors described here in the profile. While direct competitor performance is sometimes difficult to obtain, the process should be designed to select the most appropriate data first and then work the practicality issues as opposed to selecting the easy data then asking if it is appropriate.

P.2b	**Strategic Challenges**

	New Users
Orientation	

 FOUNDATION

Strategic Challenges P.2b – Introduction

This element focuses on three main areas – business challenges, operational challenges, and human resource challenges. The business challenges vary depending on the nature of the organization (for profit, non-profit, government) but often include how to keep the ink black in the books! Local coffee shops are not the most highly capitalized firms in the country. Consequently, sometimes the business challenges are focused on how to keep the cash flowing.

Operational challenges on the other hand generally are focused on the organization's ability to meet the demands of the customers while at the same time doing that efficiently, safely, and meeting or exceeding the regulatory requirements. This can get even more complicated when there are multiple customer groups with varying demands. For example, the on the way to work crowd that needs fast service might be difficult when the line is also filled with the other customer groups that are staying in and often order food to go with their coffee. Finally, there are human resource challenges. How do you keep well trained motivated employees when the industry pay is relatively low and the students and workers graduate and cause turnover on a regular basis?

What are the key challenges and what are the systematic methods used to meet those challenges? The key strategic challenges the organization face in operations, employees, or in global issues should be represented in the organizational performance review system. The Organization Performance Review System (OPRS) is a component of the overall performance improvement system and consequently needs to be designed with the existing system in mind. The idea is to integrate and enhance the existing system and not add another layer of unrelated techniques on the organization's agenda. The essence of custom design is integration as opposed to a veneer layer.

 EXAMPLE

Strategic Challenges P.2b – Example Factors

University of Wisconsin-Stout (Baldrige Recipient 2001)

Guided by its vision, values, and mission, UW-Stout's objective is to be the school of choice for the 21st century. To achieve this objective, campus direction is guided by seven strategic goals with specific action plans deployed through its annual budget planning process involving the entire campus.

This process enables UW-Stout to respond to its strategic challenges with constancy of purpose and consistency of actions, avoiding year-to-year major shifts in direction. UW-Stout's strategic challenges and goals are:

1. *Offer high quality, challenging academic programs that influence and respond to a changing society.* UW-Stout's challenge is to keep its programs continually renewed and refreshed. Strong stakeholder contact processes are employed to keep current on changing requirements. These relationship processes are complemented by Program Directors who use an effective Program Development Process to refine existing programs and to design new programs that cut across the three Colleges and strengthen UW-Stout's mission. Key indicators of success include: (1) curriculum renewal, (2) employer assessment of graduate readiness and job performance, and (3) increased level of academic challenge.

2. *Preserve and enhance our educational processes through the application of active learning principles.* *Hands-on, minds-on* student learning capabilities have differentiated UW-Stout in the marketplace as demonstrated by its superior job placement success. The challenge in maintaining this reputation is to continue to lead in the percent of instruction provided in laboratories and to increase the number of experiential learning opportunities through cooperative relationships with industry. Key success indicators include: (1) increased level of student engagement (collaborative learning, student interactions with faculty, and enriching experiences), (2) targeted computer competencies for students, and (3) job placement success.

3. *Promote excellence in teaching, research, scholarship, and service.* The campus promotes and facilitates research and developmental opportunities to attract, retain, and develop UW-Stout's faculty and staff. Even though UW-Stout is primarily a teaching university, its objective is to be a leader among the UW System comprehensives in federal grants and in budget allocated for professional development. Key indicators of success include (1) faculty engaged in research grants, (2) professional development expenditures, (3) number of sabbaticals and professorships, and (4) distance education offering growth.

4. *Recruit and retain a diverse university population.* To support the increasing requirement for students to operate effectively in a globally diverse environment, UW-Stout deploys initiatives to retain and graduate all student groups, has strengthened multicultural student services, and implements specialized academic support programs and new cultural-specific courses. New study abroad programs and additional foreign language requirements for graduation are also being implemented. Key success indicators include (1) recruitment of minority faculty and staff, (2) freshman retention rate, (3) graduation success, and (4) scholarship growth for diversity recruiting and academic quality.

5. *Foster a collegial, trusting, and tolerant environment.* The challenge in achieving this goal is to make shared governance effective by integrating the Faculty Senate, the Senate of Academic Staff and the Stout Student Association (SSA) in planning and decision-making processes. Success indicators include (1) faculty/staff morale, (2) employee turnover, and (3) student retention and satisfaction.

6. *Provide safe, accessible, effective, efficient, and inviting physical facilities.* UW-Stout implements effective capital and budget planning processes and innovative methods of funding new technology plans to continually improve its physical facilities in an environment of constant budgetary challenges. This commitment to up-to-date, safe facilities and services has enabled UW-Stout to achieve leadership in student morale in national surveys. The Stout Foundation leads universities its size in fund raising, and strong industry partnerships provide additional sources for state-of the art laboratory technology. Key success indicators are (1) student satisfaction with the college environment, (2) safety and security, and (3) Stout Foundation financial growth.

7. ***Provide responsive, efficient, and cost-effective (educational support) programs and services.*** UW-Stout must continuously improve and refine internal capabilities to: (a) strengthen its attraction as a leading academic institution; (b) optimize its support programs and services to best meet the needs of its students and stakeholders; and (c) ensure that budget priorities are allocated to instruction. In order to achieve this goal, UW-Stout systematically evaluates its support process effectiveness, efficiency, and satisfaction as described in P.2 c. Key success indicators include (1) percent of budget allocated to instruction; (2) student evaluation of support programs and services; and (3) energy use.

Source: UW-Stout (2002) pp. 186 - 187

 EXAMPLE

Strategic Challenges P.2b – Example Factors

Branch Smith Printing (Baldrige Recipient 2002)

- Structurally, within competitive markets, the number of printing plants is declining and the size of each increasing. There are fewer small startups and better businesses have grown larger. Small to medium size companies are being squeezed out by small outlet chains and larger competitors. Organizations of this type must find a niche to survive, as did we. Growth is important to create economies of scale and the critical mass to invest in new technologies. The high cost of labor and capital forces a strong focus on productivity, capacity utilization, and automation.
- These factors created a few years of industry consolidation that has since slowed down, as more focus is on strategy rather than financially driven deals. There were three major companies that purchased dozens of smaller companies and attempted to bring economies of scale to their operations with total sales of over $500 million each.
- The Internet is a recent issue on the print supply chain horizon. There are many new startups with different value propositions for major customer companies, printers, or general consumers. These entrants are best suited for commodity orders capable of online proofing and fulfillment and they do not cost-effectively serve the base of customers. The Internet is very beneficial to the strategy to create strong electronic customer communication solutions for large files through the FTP hosted site.
- According to a PIA future market study, the core markets will all grow at a pace exceeding that of the industry average. Even the growth of electronic books and directories will only supplement the traditional growth in these markets. In any event, digitalization is the future and they are strongly positioned to move into a print-on-demand or other scenario as technology develops.

Source: Branch-Smith (2003) p. 4

Diagnosis

QUESTIONS

Strategic Challenges P.2b – Baldrige Organizational Profile Questions

What are your KEY business, operational, and human resource STRATEGIC CHALLENGES?

Note 2: Challenges (P.2b) might include electronic communication with businesses and end-use consumers, reduced cycle times for product introduction, mergers and acquisitions, global marketing and competition, customer retention, staff retention, and value chain integration.

NIST (2004) p. 12

WORKSHEETS

Strategic Challenges P.2b – Work Sheet

P.2b - Strategic BUSINESS Challenges

Strategic BUSINESS Challenges (Typically External Influences on the Organization)	Initiatives to Address the Challenges (linked to Strategic Objectives)

P.2b - Strategic OPERATIONAL Challenges

Strategic OPERATIONAL Challenges (Typically External Influences on the Organization)	Initiatives to Address the Challenges (linked to Strategic Objectives)

P.2b - Strategic HUMAN RESOURCE Challenges

Strategic HUMAN RESOURCE Challenges (Typically External Influences on the Organization)	Initiatives to Address the Challenges (linked to Strategic Objectives)

BLUEPRINT

Strategic Challenges P.2b – Blueprint

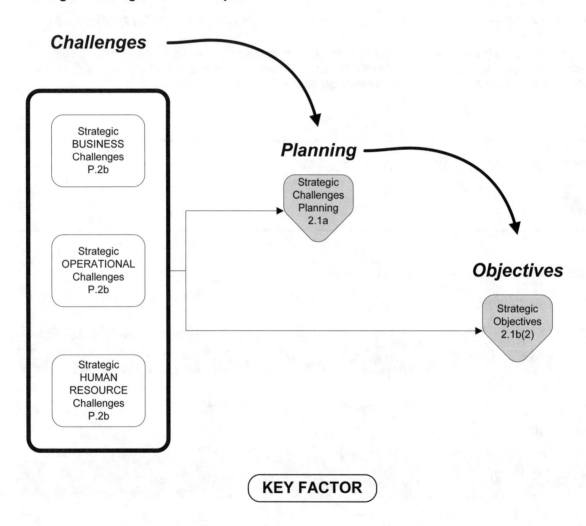

The second of the external key factors is the set of strategic challenges that the organization faces. These challenges can be broken down into three types or categories: business challenges, operational challenges, and human resource challenges. These challenges drive strategic planning and eventually the strategic objectives of the organization. There should be a direct and explicit linkage and alignment between these challenges (the challenges presented in this profile) and those that are described in the strategic planning and strategic objectives Areas to Address.

SYSTEM INTEGRATION

Strategic Challenges P.2b – Linkages

Outputs

2.1a – The strategic challenges identified here in the profile are a direct input to the strategy development process. In addition, the strategic objectives that are developed as an output of this process should reflect and address these challenges.

2.1b(2) – The 2.1b criteria area ask how the strategic objectives address the strategic challenges identified here in the profile P.2b. There should be an explicit linkage and alignment between the challenges and the objectives.

P.2c	Performance Improvement System

	New
Orientation	Users

FOUNDATION

Performance Improvement System P.2c – Introduction

This element focuses on the continuous improvement processes, organizational learning, and knowledge sharing.

How does the organization systematically and continuously improve and stay current with the changing needs of the key stakeholders?

There are at least three key dimensions of this component:

- Process
- Culture
- Information

One of the greatest challenges for organizations is the capture and sharing of knowledge throughout the organization. When the business consists of one coffee shop then you can hold meetings at shift change to pass on the lessons learned. When you have 10 – 20 shops around the state, however, the process becomes more complicated. Of course companies like FedEx that are spread around the world need an even more sophisticated system.

EXAMPLE

Performance Improvement System P.2c – Examples

Branch-Smith Printing - (Baldrige Recipient 2002)

To pursue excellence and satisfy customers, they are committed to continuous improvement of processes and people. The key mechanism to accomplish organizational focus on continuous improvement is through the Innovating Excellence system.

P.2c Branch-Smith – Innovating Excellence System

This approach focuses on building, sharing, and applying information to empower the organization. The model consists of four subsystems, each with its own focus:

- *Strategic Planning* – creating value
- *Leadership Accountability* – developing results
- *Management Review* – driving agility
- *Quality Information* – accessing knowledge

Within this structure, processes and approaches are regularly evaluated and addressed. Employees actively review and improve their approaches through the continuous improvement process, which is taught to employees as a part of the Quality Training. Employees follow this process to determine root causes, solutions, cost/benefit optimization, and plans for implementation.

P.2c Branch-Smith – Innovative Excellence Approach Systems Relationships

As a part of the management review, all inputs relative to quality are considered and acted upon. This includes trends in Price of Non-Conformance (PONC) or complaints, issues with the leadership system, employee suggestions (OFIs), strategic planning initiatives, etc. They maintain exposure to trends through industry peer groups and associations. Beyond the printing industry, they participate in local Performance Excellence roundtables and use input from TAPE and Baldrige applications as invaluable feedback for ongoing strategies for improvement. Changes in technology and the ability to provide for customers' needs demand that they proactively improve their way of doing business. Their approach is to shorten communication links, streamline and enhance processes, actively manage the future, and empower trained and motivated employees to work effectively together for the good of the customer, the company, and themselves.

Source: Branch-Smith (2003) p. 4 - 5

EXAMPLE

Performance Improvement System P.2c – Examples

Boeing Airlift and Tanker - **(Baldrige Recipient 1998)**

P.2c Boeing Airlift and Tanker – Process Based Management (PBM) Structure

PBM STRUCTURE

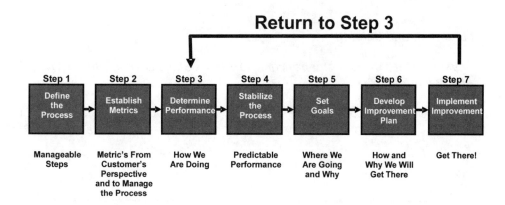

Boeing Airlift and Tanker's approach to improvement across the organization is a seven step tool called Process Based Management (PBM).

PBM helped the organization define processes, and once they were defined improve them continually. Boeing A&T: 1) identified over 700 processes; 2) gave each process an owner, and; 3) trained the owners effectively using the PBM tool.

This constitutes an effective approach to developing systematic processes, and is compatible with the definition of systematic processes used elsewhere in this book (the definition used in this book is where processes are defined, measured, stabilized, and then improved).

Diagnosis

QUESTIONS

Performance Improvement System P.2c – Baldrige Organizational Profile Questions

Performance Improvement

(1) What is the overall APPROACH you use to maintain an organizational focus on PERFORMANCE improvement and to guide SYSTEMATIC evaluation and improvement of KEY PROCESSES?

Note 3: Performance improvement (P.2c) is an assessment dimension used in the Scoring System to evaluate the maturity of organizational approaches and deployment (see pages 55–58). This question is intended to help you and the Baldrige Examiners set a context for your approach to performance improvement.

Organizational Learning and Sharing

(2) What is your overall APPROACH to organizational LEARNING and sharing your KNOWLEDGE ASSETS within the organization?

Note 4: Overall approaches to process improvement (P.2c[1]) might include implementing a Lean Enterprise System, Six Sigma methodology, use of ISO 9000:2000 standards, or other process improvement tools.

NIST (2004) p. 12

WORKSHEETS

Performance Improvement System P.2c – Work Sheets

P.2c(1) – Performance Improvement System

Method used for Process Improvement throughout the organization
Continuous Improvement Methods (e.g., Plan, Do, Check, Act - PDCA)
Focused Audits (internal or external) used to validate improvement:
Larger-scale Self-Assessments used to validate improvement:

P.2c(2) - Overall Approach to Organizational Learning

Approach to Organizational Learning for the entire organization

P.2c(2) - Sharing of knowledge assets within the organization

Sources of Knowledge	Methods Used to Share Knowledge

Design	Advanced Users

BLUEPRINT

Performance Improvement System P.2c – Blueprint

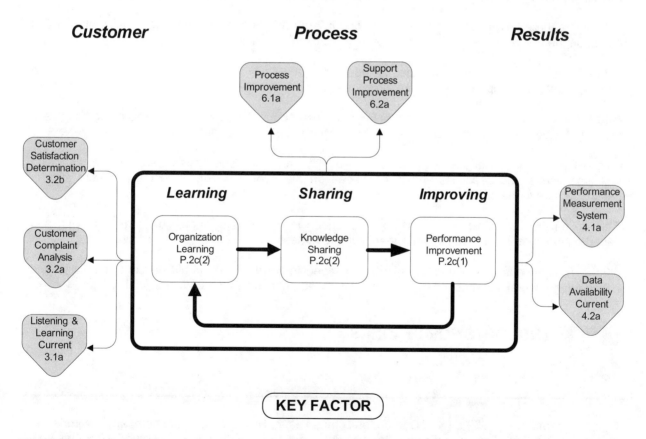

The performance improvement system is the last component in the key factors or Organizational Profile section. Given that throughout the criteria, improvement and refinement is found in the maturity model, every Item in the criteria and every process Item in the criteria is subject to refinement and improvement. There are at least seven key places in the criteria, however, where an improvement system is specifically or explicitly called for. These Areas focus around the customer, the processes, and the measurement and data analysis Areas to Address. The criteria (of course) do not require a specific performance improvement system. They do ask two key questions – 1) how does the organization learn how to sit and share what it has learned? and 2) how does it use that information to improve the overall organization?

The performance improvement system that is described in this part of the profile should also be the system that is described in the other parts of the criteria when asked, how do you keep a certain process current with changing business needs and improve to meet the customer requirements?

 # SYSTEM INTEGRATION

Performance Improvement System P.2c – Linkages

Outputs

3.1a – The marketing and process improvement activities in 3.1a(2) should be consistent with the overall approach to the performance improvement approach described here in the profile.

3.2a – The three improvement activities included in area 3.2a(3 and 4) should be consistent with and based on the performance improvement approaches described here in the profile.

3.2b – The three improvement activities included in area 3.2b(1) should be consistent with and based on the performance improvement approaches described here in the profile.

4.1a – The evaluation and improvement of the performance measurement system should be consistent with and based on the improvement approaches described here in the profile.

4.2a – The processes for keeping the data availability processes and systems current with changing business needs and directions should be based on the overall performance improvement system described here in the profile.

6.1a – The process improvement methods described in 6.1a(4 & 6) should be consistent with and based on the overall approach to performance improvement described here in the profile.

6.2a – The process improvement methods described in 6.2a(4 & 6) should be consistent with and based on the overall approach to performance improvement described here in the profile.

 # THOUGHTS FOR LEADERS

Of the December 30, 1899 top ten Dow Jones companies, only one is still a top company. Number six on the list was GE. They are still an extremely dominant company in the 21st century. What has kept them on top for over one hundred years? GE is passionate about improvement. They are invested in the tools to improve but, more importantly, it is culturally unacceptable to be stagnant in GE. The only sustainable competitive advantage for an organization is the rate of improvement!

Scoring Scales	**Maturity Models**

The performance excellence model uses two maturity frameworks or models to evaluate the organization – one for processes and one for results. The process maturity model is based on four dimensions – approach, deployment, learning, and integration and six levels 0 through 6.

Approach

"Approach" refers to how the process addresses the Item requirements—the method(s) used. The factors used to evaluate approaches include:

- The methods used to accomplish the process
- The appropriateness of the methods to the Item requirements
- The effectiveness of use of the methods
- the degree to which the approach
    - is repeatable, integrated, and consistently applied
    - embodies evaluation/improvement/learning cycles
    - is based on reliable information and data

Deployment

"Deployment" refers to the extent to which your approach is applied to the appropriate area and activities in your organization. The extent to which:

- your approach is applied in addressing Item requirements relevant and important to your organization
- your approach is applied consistently
- your approach is used by all appropriate work units

Learning

- refining your approach through cycles of evaluation and improvement
- encouraging breakthrough change to your approach through innovation
- sharing refinements and innovation with other relevant work units and processes in your organization.

Integration and Alignment

- your approach is aligned (from the top of the organization all the way down) with your organizational needs identified in other Criteria Item requirements
- your measures, information, and improvement systems are complementary across processes and work units (integrated)
- your plans, processes, results, analysis, learning, and actions are harmonized across processes and work units to support organization-wide goals (integrated)

NIST (2004) defines alignment as "consistency of plans, processes, information, resource decisions, actions, results, and analysis to support key organization-wide goals. Effective alignment requires a common understanding of purposes and goals. It also requires the use of complementary measures and information for planning, tracking, analysis, and improvement at three levels: the organizational level, the key process level, and the work unit level" (p. 30).

Alignment of performance review inputs contributes to making decisions that align action with goals. Alignment of action and goals requires that measurements and incentives are also aligned and provide a bridge between vision and behavior.

According to the maturity model, a high degree of alignment is associated with more mature organizations. On the maturity scale "integration" does not appear until level 4 of the maturity model (a very high level). Organizations typically improve the components of the management systems, then bring it together as they move up the upper portion of the maturity scale. It does not have to be this way. Alignment and integration can be introduced earlier using systems integration techniques at every maturity level.

Alignment does conjure up images of an overly mechanistic view of organizations. However, the authors propose that it is the application or misapplication of alignment techniques that determine if it is mechanistic. Creating consistency of guidance across the organization can be accomplished in a way that allows for multiple specific actions appropriate for the specific situations (business units, departments, etc.). Ultimately the goal is to create an organization with a holographic character.

Alignment does not have to involve a high degree of control. If goals, measures, and initiatives are aligned and communicated these priorities will drive decisions and behavior at all levels. If each level is free to act, measure, reflect, and revise, then each will learn the specifics that lead to the greatest contribution to the overall organization system.

Alignment will contribute to the efficiency and effectiveness (impact) of execution and improvement efforts. By aligning the strategy with measurement and action plans early in the journey you can accelerate the development of the organization up the maturity model levels.

Steps toward a Mature Process

Below are the six stages of developing a mature process approach. The beginning stage (Stage 0 – No Systematic Process) is the least mature, and the last stage (Stage 5 – Highly Refined Benchmark) is the most mature.

Level 0 – No Systematic Process

> At this level no systematic process exists so this is in reality a starting point.

Level 1 - Reacting to Problems

> Operations are characterized by activities rather than by processes, and they are largely responsive to immediate needs or problems.

Level 2 - Early Systematic Approach

> The organization is at the beginning stages of conducting operations using processes with repeatability, evaluation and improvement, and some coordination among organizational units.

Level 3 -Aligned Approach

> Operations are characterized by processes that are repeatable and regularly evaluated for improvements, with learnings shared and with coordination among organizational units.

Level 4 - Integrated Approach

> Operations are characterized by processes that are repeatable and regularly evaluated for change and improvement in collaboration with other affected units. Efficiencies across units are sought and achieved.

Level 5 – Benchmark

The final level is reserved for those highly refined processes that are truly benchmarks and have few if any opportunities for improvement.

Process Maturity Model – (a.k.a. Scoring Guidelines)

Points	Approach	Deployment	Learning	Integration
Level 5 90%, 95%, or 100%	An effective, systematic approach, fully responsive to the multiple requirements of the Item, is evident.	The approach is fully deployed without significant weaknesses or gaps in any areas or work units.	Fact-based, systematic evaluation and improvement and organizational learning are key organization-wide tools; refinement and innovation, backed by analysis and sharing, are evident throughout the organization.	The approach is well integrated with your organizational needs identified in response to the other Criteria Items.
Level 4 70%, 75%, 80% or 85%	An effective, systematic approach, responsive to the multiple requirements of the Item, is evident.	The approach is well deployed, with no significant gaps.	Fact-based, systematic evaluation and improvement and organizational learning are key management tools; there is clear evidence of refinement and innovation as a result of organizational-level analysis and sharing.	The approach is integrated with your organizational needs identified in response to the other Criteria Items.
Level 3 50%, 55%, 60%, or 65%	An effective, systematic approach, responsive to the overall requirements of the Item, is evident.	The approach is well deployed, although deployment may vary in some areas or work units.	A fact-based, systematic evaluation and improvement process and some organizational learning are in place for improving the efficiency and effectiveness of key processes.	The approach is aligned with your organizational needs identified in response to the other Criteria Categories.
Level 2 30%, 35%, 40%, or 45%	An effective, systematic approach, responsive to the basic requirements of the Item, is evident.	The approach is deployed, although some areas or work units are in early stages of deployment.	The beginning of a systematic approach to evaluation and improvement of key processes is evident.	The approach is in early stages of alignment with your basic organizational needs identified in response to the other criteria categories.
Level 1 10%, 15%, 20%, or 25%	The beginning of a systematic approach to the basic requirements of the Item is evident.	The approach is in the early stages of deployment in most areas or work units, inhibiting progress in achieving the basic requirements of the Item.	Early stages of a transition from reacting to problems to a general improvement orientation are evident.	The approach is aligned with other areas or work units largely through joint problem solving.
Level 0 0% or 5%	No systematic approach is evident; information is anecdotal.	Little or no deployment of an approach is evident.	No evidence of an improvement orientation; improvement is achieved through reacting to problems.	No organizational alignment is evident; individual areas or work units operate independently.

Assignment of Levels to Your Responses

The following guidelines should be observed in assigning maturity levels (a.k.a. scores) to your processes:

In assigning a score to an Item, first decide which level (a.k.a. scoring range) best fits the overall Item response. Overall "best fit" does not require total agreement with each of the statements (dimensions) for that scoring range. Assigning the actual score within the range requires evaluating whether the Item response is closer to the statements in the next higher or next lower scoring range.

An Approach-Deployment Item score of 50 percent represents an approach that meets the overall objectives of the Item and that is deployed to the principal activities and work units covered in the Item. Higher scores reflect maturity (cycles of improvement), integration, and broader deployment.

A Results Item score of 50 percent represents a clear indication of improvement trends and/or good levels of performance in the principal results areas covered in the Item. Higher scores reflect better improvement rates and/or levels of performance, better comparative performance, and broader coverage and integration with business requirements.

Results

"Results" refers to outcomes in achieving the purposes given in areas 7.1a–7.6a. The factors used to evaluate results include:

- the **current level of performance**
- **rate** (i.e., slope of trend data) and breadth (i.e., how widely deployed and shared) of your **performance improvements**
- your performance **relative to appropriate comparisons** and/or benchmarks
- **linkage** of your results measures (often through segmentation) to **important** customer, product and service, market, process, and action plan **performance requirements** identified in your Organizational Profile and in Process Items

Results areas call for data showing performance levels, relevant comparative data, and improvement trends for key measures/indicators of organizational performance. Results Items also call for data on breadth of performance improvements, i.e., on how widespread your improvement results are. This is directly related to the Deployment dimension; if improvement processes are widely deployed, there should be corresponding results. A score for a Results Item is thus a composite based upon overall performance, taking into account the rate and breadth of improvements and their importance. (See next paragraph.)

For a definition of the following key terms (which are used in the Scoring Guidelines above), see the Glossary which is the last section in this document:

- Anecdotal
- Alignment
- Basic requirements
- Integration
- Multiple requirements
- Overall requirements
- Systematic.

Results Maturity Model (a.k.a. Scoring Guidelines)

Points	Levels	Trends	Comparisons	Importance
Level 5 90%, 95%, or 100%	Current performance is excellent in most areas of importance to the Item requirements.	Excellent improvement trends and/or sustained excellent performance levels are reported in most areas.	Evidence of industry and benchmark leadership is demonstrated in many areas.	Business results fully address key customer, market, process, and action plan requirements.
Level 4 70%, 75%, 80% or 85%	Current performance is good to excellent in most areas of importance to the Item requirements.	Most improvement trends and/or current performance levels are sustained.	Many to most reported trends and/or current performance levels—evaluated against relevant comparisons and/or benchmarks—show areas of leadership and very good relative performance.	Business results address most key customer, market, process, and action plan requirements.
Level 3 50%, 55%, 60%, or 65%	Improvement trends and/or good performance levels are reported for most areas addressed in the Item requirements.	No pattern of adverse trends and no poor performance levels are evident in areas of importance to your organization's key business requirements.	Some trends and/or current performance levels—evaluated against relevant comparisons and/or benchmarks—show areas of good to very good relative performance.	Business results address most key customer, market, and process requirements.
Level 2 30%, 35%, 40%, or 45%	Improvements and/or good performance levels are reported in many areas addressed in the Item requirements.	Early stages of developing trends are evident.	Early stages of obtaining comparative information are evident.	Results are reported for many areas of importance to your organization's key business requirements.
Level 1 10%, 15%, 20%, or 25%	A few business results are reported; there are some improvements and/or early good performance levels in a few areas.	Little or no trend data are reported.	Little or no comparative information is reported.	Results are reported for a few areas of importance to your organization's key business requirements.
Level 0 0% or 5%	There are no business results or poor results in areas reported.	Trend data are either not reported or show mainly adverse trends.	Comparative information is not reported.	Results are not reported for any areas of importance to your organization's key business requirements.

Conclusion

The four focus areas of organization system, design principles, key factors, and maturity model are all used together to diagnose and design/redesign the processes to achieve performance excellence.

Looking through the Four Focus Component Lenses

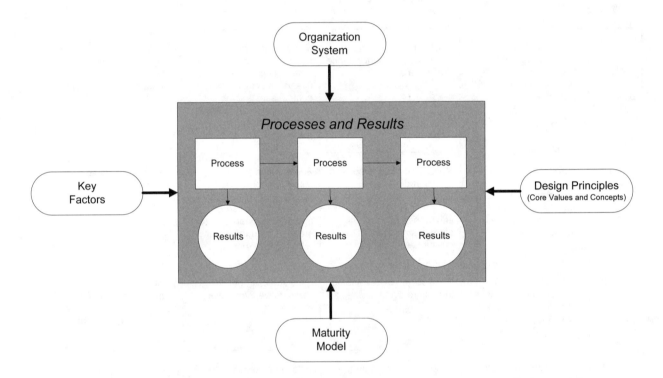

As you assess and diagnose your processes and results use these four "lenses" to help identify the relevant and important strengths, opportunities for improvement, and the appropriate maturity levels.

As you design/redesign your processes and measures use these lenses to help create the design that:

- addresses the most important and relevant key factors,
- incorporates the most important design principles,
- integrates with the other parts of the system (see blueprints), and
- transforms the processes and results to the next maturity level.

Strategic Leadership

Part
2

Overview

The Strategic Leadership competency is composed of leadership, strategic planning, and customer and market knowledge systems. In other words - How do you lead the organization to do the right things that will make it successful today, tomorrow, and in the future?

Leadership System

The Leadership System is composed of six components: senior leader direction, governance, organization performance review, public responsibilities, ethical behavior, and support to key communities. The Leadership System sets the priorities and focuses the organization on the areas that matter most to their overall success.

- How do you set the direction for the organization?
- How does your approach to governance address accountability and protect stakeholder interests?
- How do senior leaders review organizational performance and progress?

Leadership Areas to Address:

> 1.1a – Senior Leadership Direction
> 1.1b – Organizational Governance
> 1.1c – Organization Performance Review
> 1.2a – Responsibilities to the Public
> 1.2b – Ethical Behavior
> 1.2c – Support to Key Communities

Strategic Planning

This system consists of strategy development (development process and strategic objectives) and strategy deployment (action plans and performance projections). The main focus of this system is to develop strategies based on a rich set of inputs from multiple stakeholders and then deploy that strategy systematically throughout the organization.

- Where is the organization going?
- How do you develop strategies for the future?
- How do you develop and implement action plans that make the strategy a reality?

Strategic Planning Areas to Address:

> 2.1a – Strategy Development Process
> 2.1b – Strategic Objectives
> 2.2a – Action Plan Development and Deployment
> 2.2b – Performance Projections

Customer and Market Knowledge

This system is composed of customer and market segmentation, listening and learning approaches, product and service feature determination and their relative importance.

- How do you segment your customers?
- How do you know what the customers in each segment want or more importantly what they will pay for?

Customer Focus Areas to Address:

3.1a – Customer and Market Knowledge

1.1a	Senior Leadership Direction

Orientation	New Users

 FOUNDATION

Senior Leadership Direction 1.1a - Introduction

This Area to Address initiates an entire organization's focus on performance excellence (Baldrige) as an effective business model. Clearly senior leaders must define where the company is headed, what they want the company to be, the values, and what are acceptable behaviors during the journey.

Leaders must set the organizational beliefs, vision, mission, values, purpose or other foundational factors so all employees clearly understand what the company stands for and what the company believes. More importantly, however, all leaders must be role models (100% of the time) for these foundational beliefs.

Once the foundational beliefs are established, leaders must set the direction. Direction must be set for both the short- and longer-term periods. The direction must be clear to all employees. This clarity in direction is the foundation for the organization's ability to deploy the direction from the top of the organization down to every employee. Frequently leaders see that clarity of the communication of direction to be one of their most important roles.

Once the direction is set, leaders must ensure their performance expectations are clear and communicated throughout the organization. This includes clear communication down to every employee, to suppliers, partners, the community, the owners, and other key stakeholders.

In 2003, Baldrige first focused on leaders ensuring two-way communication on each of these topics. Now an applicant needs to report the breadth and depth of their communications, and indicate 1) which are two-way; 2) which are one way; and 3) for the two–way communication, how the leadership ensures that the two-way communication process is effective.

Once leaders have established foundations of beliefs, direction, and expectations, it is then their responsibility to create an environment where people can do their best in achieving the objectives which have been flowed-down. This means leaders need to have specific processes in place to ensure empowerment, ensure that the employees have the opportunity to innovate, and ensure the employees have the opportunity to learn. Finally, leaders must make sure the culture fosters and requires legal and ethical behavior on the part of every employee at all times.

All of Item 1.1 focuses on the responsibilities of senior leaders to establish the right culture in an organization. Frequently, Item 1.1 is viewed as a descriptor of the things a senior leader cannot delegate, but must personally exhibit and ensure are flowed-down throughout the organization. This is true for all of Item 1.1, but is particularly true for Area to Address 1.1a. This is where the leaders establish a foundation for all other leadership responsibilities.

EXAMPLE

Senior Leadership Direction 1.1a – Example Practices

Boeing Airlift and Tanker **– (Baldrige Recipient 1998)**

Boeing Airlift and Tanker (1998 Baldrige Recipient) was one of the first companies to implement a systematic approach to leadership.

Their Leadership System clearly defines the responsibility of leaders. This is not only the responsibility of the top leadership team, but is the responsibility of all leaders at all levels of the organization. All leaders must understand their stakeholder requirements and expectations. Additionally, leaders must exhibit the ability to involve, communicate, and innovate with all stakeholders.

1.1a Boeing A & T - Leadership System

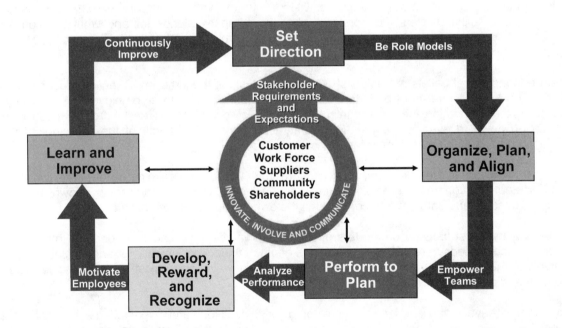

With this background, leaders can set the overall direction for the organization. After setting direction they need to organize, plan and align; ensure the organization performs to plan; and develop reward and recognize employees.

Finally, all leaders must ensure they, and the organization, learn and improve. If the leaders do not improve themselves, then the organization will not learn and grow. The activities in each of the boxes are things that leaders must ensure happen. The activities in the arrows are personal behaviors which every leader must exhibit.

EXAMPLE

Senior Leadership Direction 1.1a – Example Practices

Clarke American **- (Baldrige Recipient 2001)**

Clarke American feels that all leaders must:

- Demonstrate commitment & passion
- Develop associates & teams
- Reward & recognize

Additionally, leaders must understand the mission, vision, values, and core purpose of the organization and effectively role model these beliefs to all associates. With these beliefs and personal characteristics as a foundation, leaders can set direction & plan; communicate & align; perform to plan; review & adjust; and learn & innovate.

The Clarke American Key Leadership Team (KLT) establishes, communicates and deploys values, direction, and performance expectations through the First In Service (FIS) Leadership System. At the heart of the leadership system are the balanced Stakeholder quadrants.

These stakeholders' requirements drive all leadership actions. Leaders address these stakeholder requirements in alignment with the **Vision, Mission, Values and Core Purpose**. These defining statements were originally developed through the systematic Goal Deployment process and are regularly reviewed and, when needed, updated through this same process. These have been completely communicated and deployed across the matrix organization through the ***Linked Review and Communication Process***.

The **Vision** defines the organization's future direction and provides a view of "what we can be." In the drive to satisfy the stakeholders, the **Mission** enhances the Vision and provides clear guidance in identifying and prioritizing business alternatives. **Values** establish the parameters of the work climate and set the standard of ethical personal conduct for associates, with commitment to honesty, fairness and accountability. The values, established in 1993, were first refined and updated in 1995. Most recently, in 1999, the KLT added the value of Knowledge Sharing to demonstrate their commitment to continually learning and improving both individually and as a company. The **Core Purpose**, first expressed in 1995, defines the boundaries of the business activities.

Building on the foundation of the Vision, Mission, Values and Core Purpose, the leaders ***Set Direction and Plan*** with a focus on stakeholder requirements. Evolving from an internally focused process in 1986, today's approach collects multiple internal and external inputs, establishes performance expectations with a long-range view, and creates a balanced strategy addressing all of the stakeholder needs. They ***Communicate & Align*** through a wide range of media and tools to link action plans at all levels of the organization. Leaders develop the Balanced Business Plan (BBP) through the Goal Deployment Process. The BBP defines goals and targets to both deliver on stakeholder requirements and to achieve the Vision, Mission, and Core Purpose. These goals and targets are linked from overall company levels to the individual contributor to ensure complete alignment throughout the organization, flowing from the BBP is the Balanced Scorecard (BSC).

1.1a Clarke American – Leadership Model
Guides all Behaviors, Activities, and Decisions

- The BSC is composed of the vital few *change the business* metrics that set the expectation of breakthrough improvement for each year.
- Through the Goal Deployment Process they also identify *run the business* Key Performance Indicators (KPIs).
- The final step in the Goal Deployment Process is the development of a Business Excellence Agreement (BEA) for each associate to link individual roles and performance to company performance and the bonus plan.

The Goal Deployment process is the primary tool for communicating and aligning the organization. Clarke American uses a variety of mechanisms to communicate values, direction, and expectations to associates. The *Linked Review and Communication Process* drives two-way review and communication. This system ranges from weekly, monthly, quarterly and annual reviews conducted by the KLT, division steering teams, and core and enabling processes to associate "huddles." The system reinforces understanding of the Vision, Mission, Values and Core Purpose, reviews performance and delivers communications throughout the business. The KLT sponsors a scripted "*FIS* Focus" PowerPoint presentation to ensure a common message is delivered to all associates by local leaders.

Linked Review and Communication Process:

- Weekly and Monthly meetings of the Key Leadership Team
- Steering teams (monthly)
- Staff and Process Meetings (monthly)
- All Associates FIS Focus (monthly)
- Associate team "Huddles" (once a week)

1.1a Clarke American   – Communicate and Align

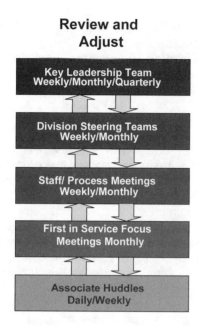

Review and Adjust

Key Leadership Team
Weekly/Monthly/Quarterly

Division Steering Teams
Weekly/Monthly

Staff/ Process Meetings
Weekly/Monthly

First in Service Focus
Meetings Monthly

Associate Huddles
Daily/Weekly

First in Service®
**Common Language
and Tools**

- FIS training for all associates
- Institutionalized FIS team structure and tools
- Monthly meeting with all associates includes company -wide FIS Focus presentation
- Visual workplace (posted charts and graphs, journey boards …)
- Business excellence agreement and common bonus

Clarke American leverages their systematic review processes to increase the flexibility and agility of the organization.   They have the ability to review performance at all levels of the organization during various time frames.

This starts with the Key Leadership Team (KLT) reviewing performance at least weekly. This is also being done at all levels of the organization down to and including associate huddles. At the lowest level, the associates not only review performance weekly, but in certain cases review performance as frequently as daily.

They have the ability to communicate performance, adjustments needed, or adjustments made from the top of the organization down, or from the bottom of the organization up, very quickly. Additionally, every employee has a personal commitment and a financial incentive to achieve the organization's business objectives. All associates have a Business Excellence Agreement which clearly documents their goals.   Each employee can share in the financial rewards when the company achieves its performance targets.

Built around the company's performance in the four quadrants of the BBP, this presentation provides up-to-date status on BSC goals, bonus objectives, and addresses other critical information. Leaders at each location communicate this standard presentation to all associates on all shifts each month. Encouraged to be interactive, *FIS* meetings are often a lively communication venue, complete with themes, decorations, team building activities and recognition events. These communication mechanisms are supported by other methods of making each associate aware of the Vision, Mission, Values and Core Purpose. Statements are prominently displayed in conference rooms and common areas in all locations and networked desktop computer systems greet associates with this information upon login. Associates learn about these principles during orientation and receive laminated badge cards that are worn as a constant reminder. As a learning organization Clarke American wants to appreciate the *past.* They endeavor to capture significant events and lessons learned from the journey as information integral to the longer-term communications.

The KLT drives an environment of empowerment, associate involvement, innovation, and organizational agility and learning through FIS and personal role modeling of FIS Behaviors. The ring encompassing the entire leadership system articulates the behaviors expected of each leader at Clarke American. Through his personal involvement and behaviors, the CEO is the role model for **Demonstrate Commitment and Passion**, continuously **Develop Associates and Teams**, and generously **Reward and Recognize** the associates and teams. The CEO and the entire KLT hold every leader accountable for demonstrating these same behaviors. Leaders are evaluated, rewarded and recognized based not only upon their abilities to perform the *tasks* of leadership but also on the ability to *behave* as a leader.

Passionate leadership is one of the key strengths. In his book, *The Passion Plan at Work,* organizational excellence authority Richard Chang cites Clarke American, along with companies such as Disney, GTE Directories, Ben and Jerry's, Wainwright Industries and Southwest Airlines, as examples of companies who successfully integrate passion into their day-to-day operations to improve performance in both the workplace and the marketplace. Demonstrate this passion through systematic processes, communication, inspiration, involvement of associates and inclusion of partners and suppliers in shaping the future. This passion creates an environment to successfully **Perform to Plan**. The ability to achieve consistently strong results is facilitated by an involved and empowered team of associates. Through the Baldrige-based **FIS** business model, provide a culture, tools and disciplines to actively engage associates and develop a learning, agile company. **FIS** incorporates a common language and the tools to drive continuous improvement, as well as the team structure and methodology used to execute projects. **FIS** disciplines moved from a functional structure to a division and process orientation, removing the organizational blockages to becoming truly partner and customer-driven. Examples of **FIS** processes that directly address empowerment and innovation include:

- The Suggestions, Teams, Actions, Results (*S.T.A.R.*) suggestion program through which associates propose and quantify improvements of any size.
- The commitment to individual training and organizational learning gives associates the knowledge required to make empowered decisions aligned with company goals. KLT members set the example and participate alongside (and often lead) other associates in **FIS**, product specific and safety training. Associates at all levels are empowered, through appropriate technical and professional development, to advance in their roles and initiate ideas that improve partner and customer satisfaction. This commitment to learning and development extends to all levels of associates. Provide a wide range of internal training opportunities, and constantly evaluate external learning opportunities that will further enhance individual development.
- A wide variety of recognition processes further support and encourage empowerment and innovation.
- The Open Door Policy offers associates access to leaders outside their normal reporting lines.
- The successful Career Opportunity Program (COP) provides associates the opportunity to grow and have multiple careers at Clarke American. This program supports organizational learning through sharing of best practices and ideas as associates move into various divisions or processes. Personal growth opportunities through upward and lateral movement within the company help develop "associates for life."

Common language and tools let any organization quickly assemble dedicated teams of varying sizes and duration anywhere within the company, with confidence that they can immediately become productive.

Source: Clarke (2002) pp. 6 - 8

Diagnosis

 QUESTIONS

Senior Leadership Direction 1.1a - Baldrige Criteria Questions

Set and Deploy Direction (1)

- *HOW do SENIOR LEADERS set and deploy organizational VALUES, short- and longer-term directions, and PERFORMANCE expectations?*
- *HOW do SENIOR LEADERS include a focus on creating and balancing VALUE for CUSTOMERS and other STAKEHOLDERS in their PERFORMANCE expectations?*
- *HOW do SENIOR LEADERS communicate organizational VALUES, directions, and expectations through your LEADERSHIP SYSTEM, to all employees, and to KEY suppliers and partners?*
- *HOW do SENIOR LEADERS ensure two-way communication on these topics?*

Note 1. Organizational directions (1.1a[1]) relate to creating the vision for the organization and to setting the context for strategic objectives and action plans described in Items 2.1 and 2.2.

Creating an Environment (2)

- *HOW do SENIOR LEADERS create an environment for EMPOWERMENT, INNOVATION, and organizational agility?*
- *HOW do they create an environment for organizational and employee LEARNING?*
- *HOW do they create an environment that fosters and requires legal and ETHICAL BEHAVIOR?*

NIST (2004) p. 13

 WORKSHEETS

Senior Leadership Direction 1.1a - Work Sheets

The Leadership Category examines how your organization's senior leaders address values and performance expectations, as well as focus on customers and other stakeholders, empowerment, innovation, learning, and organizational directions. Also examined is how your organization addresses its responsibilities to the public and supports its key communities.

1.1a (1) – Set, Deploy, and Communicate Values and Short- and Long-term Directions and Performance Expectations

Set Values & Expectations	Deploy Values & Expectations	Communicate Values & Expectations
Note: Expectations should be for all short- and longer-term directions and performance expectations	**Note:** This should be for customers and all stakeholders	**Note:** This should be communicated through the Leadership System

1.1a (1) – Balance Value For All Stakeholders, Communicate Direction And Performance Expectations To Partners And Ensure All Communication Is Two-Way

Balance Values for All Stakeholders	Communicate Values & Expectations to Partners (if different from above)	Ensure That the Communication to II Stakeholders is Two-Way

1.1a (2) – Create and Reinforce an Environment

Create The Environment For:	Reinforce The Environment:
Empowerment	
Innovation	
Agility	
Organizational and Employee Learning	
Legal and Ethical Behavior	

 ASSESSMENT

Senior Leadership Direction 1.1a – Diagnostic Questions

Rating Scale:

0 - **No Process** in place - We are not doing this
1 - **Reacting to Problems** - Using a Basic (Primarily Reactive) Process
2 - **Systematic Process** – We use a systematic process that has been improved
3 - **Aligned** – We use a process that aligns our activities from top to bottom
4 - **Integrated** – We use a process that is integrated with other processes across the organization
5 - **Benchmark** - We are the Benchmark!
DK - Don't Know

1. Leaders have identified the key *stakeholders*, defined their *requirements*, and used those requirements to *set the direction* of the organization.　　0　1　2　3　4　5　DK

2. Leaders role model the vision and values by consistently demonstrating, communicating, and reinforcing them on a daily basis.	0	1	2	3	4	5	DK
3. Senior Leaders are personally and visibly involved in creating an environment that promotes legal and ethical behavior.	0	1	2	3	4	5	DK
4. Senior Leaders are personally and visibly involved in creating an environment for empowerment, innovation, organizational agility, and organizational and personal learning.	0	1	2	3	4	5	DK

Design	Advanced Users

 BLUEPRINT

Senior Leadership Direction 1.1a - Blueprint

Senior leadership direction is composed of two key processes or activities. First, is how the leadership sets, deploys, and communicates the values and long-term directions and the expectations of the organization. The second area is how they create an environment that fosters empowerment, innovation, agility, learning, and legal and ethical behavior.

This setting, deploying, and communicating values is based on the needs, wants and desires that are articulated in the vision and mission values and customer and market knowledge. In addition, there are the other stakeholders' needs, wants, and desires to consider including the investors, the employees, the suppliers and partners, and the public at large. The process of setting and deploying values is connected to the performance review process, how the organization reviews progress toward the strategic objectives, analyzes data, and is communicated to the key suppliers and partners that were identified in the organization relationships area of the key factors. In addition, these values and expectations drive ethical interactions which are found in Area to Address 1.2b.

The second part of senior leadership correction is creating an environment. This environment has five characteristics: empowerment, innovation, agility, learning, and the legal and ethical behavior. These characteristics drive employee behavior which is measured in the results shown in area 7.4a.

The typical answer to this Area to Address is an integrated Leadership System which addresses both these major components.

Senior Leadership Direction 1.1a – Blueprint

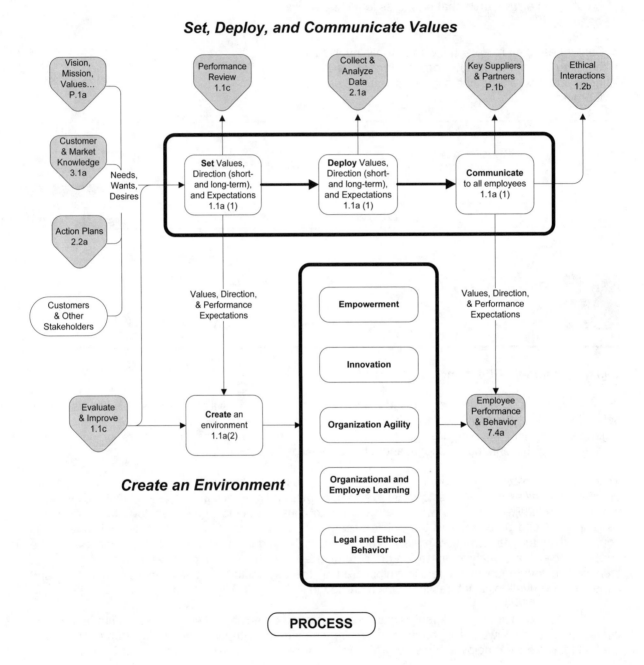

Set, Deploy, and Communicate Values

Create an Environment

PROCESS

SYSTEM INTEGRATION

Senior Leadership Direction 1.1a – Linkages

Inputs

There are four primary inputs to this area: the organization culture including vision, mission, and values; customer and market knowledge; action plans; and the evaluation and improvement process in Area to Address 1.1c.

P.1a – The first input is the organizational culture described in the Organizational Profile P.1a. The setting of values and direction including short- and long-term expectations should be consistent with and include the purpose, mission, vision, and values described in the profile.

3.1a – The setting of values, direction, and expectations should address the needs, wants, and desires of the customers and markets described in Area to Address 3.1a. While not the only stakeholder, the customers are the primary beneficiaries of the products and services. They ultimately determine if the organization is successful in their primary mission or purpose.

2.2a – Short and Long-term expectations should be consistent with and include the actions detailed in the action plans that are described in Area to Address 2.2a. If the leadership emphasizes different expectations than are in the strategic plan, or in the action plans, then the strategy remains on the shelf while employees spend their time and resources working those issues or emergencies that are important to leadership.

1.1c – The setting, deployment, and communication of values along with the creation of the desired environment are improved by the evaluation and improvement process that is described in Area to Address 1.1c. Consequently the improvement process in 1.1c should be designed in a way to include the processes in this area.

Outputs

There are five key output linkages to other processes and results from Area to Address 1.1a: the performance review process; the collection and analysis of data; the key suppliers; ethical interactions; and employee performance and behavior results.

1.1c – The values, direction, and expectations set by the leadership system should be consistent with and be an input to the agenda for the organizational performance reviews described in Area to Address 1.1c. If the leadership says one thing and then reviews other things there is a mixed message to the employees, suppliers, partners, and so forth. Reviews tend to hold people accountable and consequently people will tend to emphasize those things the leaders are asking to review.

2.1a – The values, direction, and expectations should also influence the collection and analysis of data used to develop strategies described in Area to Address 2.1a. This linkage along with the performance review linkage helps to create and send consistent messages about what is important to the organization. When the organization's strategy, values, and reviews are internally consistent, the probability of successfully implementing these throughout the organization increases.

P1.b – The communication of the values, directions, and expectations to all employees, suppliers, and partners should include the employees, suppliers and partners described in the Organizational Profile P.1b. Simply put, the communication approaches should be designed to address the same key suppliers and partners that were described in the Organizational Profile P.1b.

1.2b – One of the areas that should be consistent with the stated values, directions, and expectations are the ethical interactions of the employees described in Area to Address 1.2b. Part of the issue with ensuring ethical interactions is having clear definitions of ethics. The definitions of ethics used in Area to Address 1.2b should be consistent with and include the values of the organization as defined here in Area to Address 1.1a.

7.4a – Guidance (values, direction, expectations) is set, deployed, and communicated and an environment created in order to influence the performance and behavior of the employees in a way that will make the multiple stakeholders successful. The effectiveness of the approaches used to guide and create an environment are validated in the actual results created by the performance and behaviors. Area to Address 7.4a should explicitly include results to validate the efforts and approaches here in Area to Address 1.1a.

Transformation	**Leaders**

THOUGHTS FOR LEADERS

When people say the Baldrige process really restricts the movement (and improvement) of the organization, it sounds like they have never used the Baldrige Framework and do not understand it. Some individuals want to use complexity as an excuse for not doing something. What really high performing organizations do is define the processes, define the decision criteria and use these as a tool to move very quickly.

Organizations that understand their processes can move quickly because they know how to change those processes. While you may be quick to react if you are a leader who leads though intuition, the problem with that is, it is difficult to repeat the same performance. There is a famous cartoon of two little boys in the kitchen making a cake. The kitchen is a complete mess. One of the little boys says to the other "the problem with this is that if it comes out really good we'll never be able to make it again." Leadership without processes is not repeatable.

Smart, high–performing organizations are using processes, using leadership criteria, and using decision criteria to move very rapidly. They can even move much more rapidly than they can by using gut instinct alone.

1.1b	Organizational Governance

 FOUNDATION

Organizational Governance 1.1b - Introduction

As with Area to Address 1.1a, this is a continuation of clearly defining the areas which senior leaders cannot delegate. Senior leaders must ensure governance throughout the organization, with every stakeholder and every employee transaction. Without this level of compliance, mistakes by a few can penalize the entire company.

Area to Address 1.1b is part of the Baldrige reaction to some of the instances of companies with senior executives involved in wrong doing which have been widely publicized.

It is not enough to have slogans on the wall or policies or procedures which extol the importance of integrity, ethics, values, and governance unless those are implemented down to each and every employee and each and every transaction.

While you can't eliminate the possibility of someone doing something wrong, you can reduce the likelihood!

 EXAMPLE

Organizational Governance 1.1b - Example Practices

This is a relatively new area of the criteria. We are in the process of developing examples for this are and they will be available on the web site at: www.baldrigeusersguide.com

QUESTIONS

Organizational Governance 1.1b - Baldrige Criteria Questions

HOW does your organization address the following KEY factors in your GOVERNANCE system?

- *management accountability for the organization's actions*
- *fiscal accountability*
- *independence in internal and external audits*
- *protection of stockholder and STAKEHOLDER interests, as appropriate*

NIST (2004) p. 13

WORKSHEETS

Organizational Governance 1.1b - Work Sheets

1.1b – Organizational Governance - How does your organization address the following aspects of the Governance System?

Requirement	Process Description
Management Accountability	
Fiscal Accountability	
Independence in Internal and External Audits	
Protection of Stockholder Interests	
Protection of other Stakeholder Interests	

1.1b – *Organizational Governance* - A framework for thinking about the governance process is as follows:

Who	What	Where	How	Why						Results
Group Responsible	Our Intent	Area to Address 1.1b	Audits Performed (coded for internal & external)	Primary Stakeholder Impacted *						Item 7.6 Figure #s
				C	S	CO	E	SH		
Board of Directors Senior Leaders All: • Employees • Suppliers • Partners	Comply with all: • International Laws & Regulations • National Laws & Regulations • Local Laws & Regulations • Local Ordinances	Management Accountability								
		Fiscal Accountability								
		Audit Independence								
		Protection of Stockholders and Stakeholders								

* **Stakeholder Codes:**

Customers = C   Suppliers = S   Community = CO   Employees = E   Stockholder = SH

 ASSESSMENT

Organizational Governance 1.1b - Diagnostic Questions

Rating Scale:

0 - **No Process** in place - We are not doing this
1 - **Reacting to Problems** - Using a Basic (Primarily Reactive) Process
2 - **Systematic Process** – We use a systematic process that has been improved
3 - **Aligned** – We use a process that aligns our activities from top to bottom
4 - **Integrated** – We use a process that is integrated with other processes across the organization
5 - **Benchmark** - We are the Benchmark!
DK - Don't Know

1.	Governance Processes are Clearly Defined.	0	1	2	3	4	5	DK
2.	Governance processes are lead by all of the most senior leaders in the organization.	0	1	2	3	4	5	DK
3.	Governance processes are deployed consistently throughout the entire organization.	0	1	2	3	4	5	DK

1. All employees are trained in the governance processes,   0   1   2   3   4   5   DK
   and are clear on their personal responsibilities and what
   are acceptable and non-acceptable actions.

2. We have measures to track governance for all   0   1   2   3   4   5   DK
   employees and all transactions.

Design	**Advanced Users**

BLUEPRINT

Organizational Governance 1.1b – Blueprint

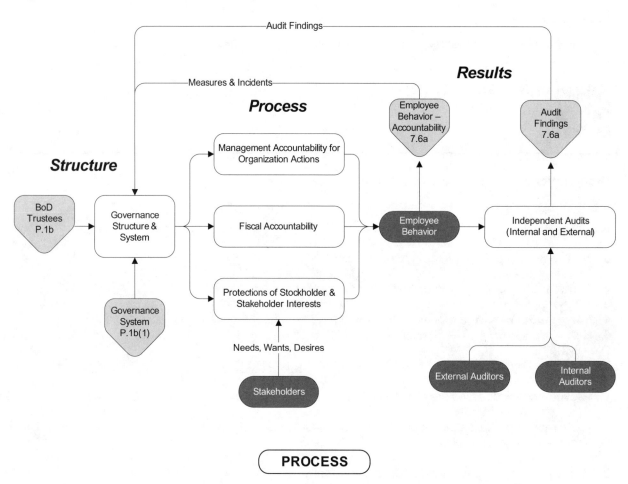

The governance process is composed of three major components: the structure, the processes, and ultimately the results. The structure is influenced by the board of directors identified in the Organizational Profile and the governance system described in the Organizational Profile. The system guides and integrates three major processes: management accountability, fiscal accountability, and the protection of stockholders' and other stakeholder interests. These processes, in particular the protection of stockholders' and other stakeholder interests process, are fed by the needs, wants and desires of the stockholders and stakeholders.

The effectiveness of the structures, system, and processes is measured through independent audits both internal and external and other measures of accountability all of which are reported in results Area to Address 7.6a.

This is a relatively new Area to Address and the examples and approaches to this area are in the early stages of evolution.

 SYSTEM INTEGRATION

Organizational Governance 1.1b – Linkages

Inputs

There are two key inputs to the governance area: the Board of Directors and the Governance System described in the Organizational Profile P.1b.

P1.b – There are two key factors to consider when evaluating or designing a governance system or process – first the structure and governance system and second the reporting relationships among the board of directors which are both described in the Organizational Profile P.1b. The approach to governance should be consistent with and appropriate for the specific situation described in the profile. This will vary widely depending on the history of the organization, the ownership model, and the legal status of the organization (incorporated, 501c(3) etc.).

Input/Outputs

In some instance other processes and results are both inputs to the process and outputs. In this case there are two results areas that are both validation measures of the approaches and also inputs to the governance structure and system.

7.6a – Employee behavior and accountability measures are included in Area to Address 7.6a and should measure the effectiveness of the governance processes that address management accountability, fiscal accountability, and ultimately protect the interests of the stockholders and stakeholders. In addition, Area to Address 7.6a includes the audit findings from both internal and external audits which also validate the effectiveness of the preventive approaches. As inputs these results are used to make governance decisions and also to evaluate and improve the governance structure, system, and processes.

1.1c	**Organizational Performance Review**

Orientation	**New Users**

FOUNDATION

Organizational Performance Review 1.1c - Introduction

In Area to Address 1.1a the leaders established what is important in the organization and the overall direction, and established the culture which will foster high performance. In 1.1b leaders established an organizational governance structure which turned governance from a plaque on the wall into a systematic process to ensure governance in all transactions of the organization. 1.1c follows these by describing the leaders' roles and responsibilities in reviewing organizational performance.

As with the earlier Areas to Address of Item 1.1, 1.1c discusses those responsibilities which a leader cannot delegate. Not only do senior leaders need to review performance, but leaders at all levels need to review performance within their span of influence. The Baldrige criteria ask how leaders review performance, how they use these reviews to assess where they are, and how they decide what actions need to be taken on a short-and longer-term basis.

One of the reasons leaders cannot delegate reviewing performance is that based on those reviews, course corrections must be made. This is true if an organization is not meeting its objectives, and is also true even if it is meeting the planned objectives, measures, and goals. To this end, Baldrige specifically asks how leaders use performance reviews to assess the organizations' ability to change, and how they drive change from those reviews.

In looking at the leaders' review of organizational performance, Baldrige basically asks what are the measures they regularly review and what are some of the findings they have recently achieved.

Once leaders have reviewed performance and assessed the organization's ability to meet some of the changing challenges or needs, Baldrige seeks to understand the process they use to translate findings into new priorities for improvement. Baldrige breaks these improvement priorities into two basic areas - continuous improvement and breakthrough improvement.

Most organizations have not formally defined the difference between continuous improvement and breakthrough improvement. One Baldrige winner (Clarke American in 2001) formally documented the difference between these two types of improvement. At Clarke American 20% improvement or more is considered a breakthrough. Less than 20% is considered continuous improvement. Additionally, Baldrige seeks to understand how leaders use these reviews of business results to identify where and how the company needs to innovate.

Once the leader has reviewed performance, understands its impact, and has analyzed what needs to be done, the responsibility evolves to clearly communicating the new priorities and opportunities throughout the organization. This also includes effectively communicating these messages to suppliers and partners to ensure they are aligned with the new directions the company is attempting to achieve.

The final portion of 1.1c – Organizational Performance Review – talks about how the leaders review their own performance and the performance of the leaders above them. Baldrige seeks to understand how leaders evaluate their own performance, and what they do with those evaluations. Specifically, how do they improve: 1) their own leadership effectiveness; 2) the effectiveness of their board or governing body; and 3) the effectiveness of their Leadership System.

Most organizations do not view leadership as a systematic process. Baldrige, however, views most activities of an organization as a systematic process and requires a systematic approach be used. Leading is no exception, a Leadership System is required. A Leadership System is not an organization chart, not a sequence of reviews through committees, and is not what you typically think of when you think of the hierarchy of an organization. A Leadership System is something which can be systematically used by every leader at every level of an organization. It can help leaders more effectively perform the activities discussed in Item 1.1. Two examples of Leadership Systems were shown earlier.

1.1c goes on to discuss the evaluation of the performance of the members of the Board of Directors. Very few organizations can evaluate their Board of Directors (which at a minimum is one level above them and could be many levels above them). What Baldrige is trying to understand is what is the culture the Board of Directors has established and flowed-down into the company. This includes whether the Board of Directors has established a culture of: excellence; high performance; high ethics; high values; and has established an organization which can be held up as a role model.

 EXAMPLE

Organizational Performance Review 1.1c - Example Practices

*Pearl River School District - **(Baldrige Recipient 2001)***

To drive results, Pearl River School District uses a Performance Review Process which analyzes results before they decide what actions to take (if any).

If the results they planned have not been achieved, the organization performs root cause analysis to determine *why?* Based on the analysis the organization can modify their current actions so they improve their overall action deployment strategy and thereby improve their chance of success. This corrective action is then evaluated to determine whether the desired result is being achieved using the new approach.

If the goal is being achieved (from the original actions or through the new actions, as described above) the organization then evaluates the standards and can decide to:

- Adjust the baseline
- Adjust the deployment technique, or
- Modify the standard.

1.1c Pearl River School District - Performance Review Process

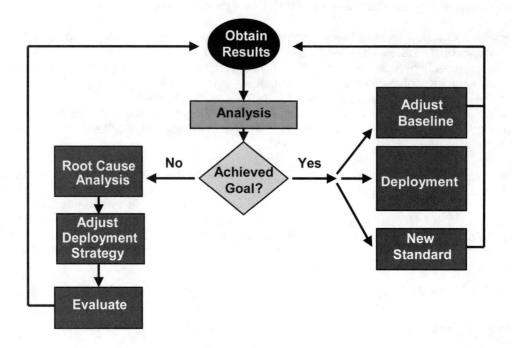

Public education is in continual fluctuation with new students in new grades each year, new mandates from state and federal authorities, and changing variables relative to the economic climate such as potential community support for a budget, private school enrollment, and the threat of vouchers and charter schools. The superintendent and the administrative council (AC - includes all district administrators) use the PRSD Performance Review Process, a data-driven system, to consistently and comprehensively review organizational performance annually at district planning and review retreats, and throughout the year as new data become available (i.e.: test scores, survey results, etc.). The process provides for leaders to adapt the organization's operations when warranted, either by adjusting minimum expectations (baselines), or by deploying new practices and/or setting new standards based upon positive results. PRSD applies this process within the structure of a balanced scorecard model, whereby aligning the district goals with strategic objectives and corresponding lag and lead goals. Senior leaders review the performance results for the lagging and leading goals.

Source: PRSD, 2002, p. 132

EXAMPLE

Organizational Performance Review 1.1c - Example Practices

SSM Healthcare - **(Baldrige Recipient 2002)**

Leadership Review Forums

Forum	Frequency	Reports Monitored	Purpose
SSMHC Board of Directors	Quarterly Annually Annually	• Financial Condition of the System • Healthy Communities Report • CRP & HIPAA	• 2 • 2, 3, 4, 5 • 5
Regional Boards	Quarterly	• Quality Report • Competency Report • CRP & HIPAA Reports	• 3, 4, 5 • 3, 4, 5 • 5
System Management	Monthly Quarterly	• SSMHC Combined Financial Statements • SSMHC PIR (16 indicators)/Quality Report • Quarterly Rankings Rpt. (Pat. Loyalty)	• 2 • 1, 2, 3, 4 • 2, 4
Operations Council	Monthly	• SSMHC PIR (16 Indicators) • Network/Entity Comb Financial Stmts • Entity Variance Report • Hospital PIR (49 indicators) • Corrective Action Plans: PIR/Qlty Rpt	• 1, 2, 3, 4 • 2 • 2 • 1, 2, 3, 4 • 2, 5
Innsbrook Group	Twice a Year	• Combined Financial Statements	• 1, 2, 3, 4
Network Leadership/Entity AC	Monthly Quarterly	• Network/Entity Comb Financial Stmts • Hospital PIR (49 indicators) • Entity Quality Report • Corrective Action Plans: PIR/Quality Report • Complaint Reports	• 2 • 1, 2, 3, 4 • 3, 4, 5 • 2, 5 • 3, 4

Purpose Codes: 1 = Competitive Performance; 2 = Performance Plan Review; 3 = Changing Needs Evaluation; 4 = Organizational Success; 5 = Regulatory Compliance

Source: SSM, 2003, p. 4

QUESTIONS

Organizational Performance Review 1.1c - Baldrige Criteria Questions

Organizational Performance Review Process (1)

- *HOW do SENIOR LEADERS review organizational PERFORMANCE and capabilities?*
- *HOW do they use these reviews to assess organizational success, competitive PERFORMANCE, and progress relative to short- and longer-term GOALS?*
- *HOW do they use these reviews to assess your organizational ability to address changing organizational needs?*

Note 2: Senior leaders' organizational performance reviews (1.1c) should be informed by organizational performance analyses described in 4.1b and guided by strategic objectives and action plans described in Items 2.1 and 2.2. Senior leaders' organizational performance reviews also might be informed by internal or external Baldrige assessments.

Key Performance Measures (2)

- *What are the KEY PERFORMANCE MEASURES regularly reviewed by your SENIOR LEADERS?*
- *What are your KEY recent PERFORMANCE review findings?*

Translation of Findings to Priorities (3)

- *HOW do SENIOR LEADERS translate organizational PERFORMANCE review findings into priorities for continuous and breakthrough improvement of KEY business RESULTS and into opportunities for INNOVATION?*
- *HOW are these priorities and opportunities deployed throughout your organization?*
- *When appropriate, HOW are they deployed to your suppliers and partners to ensure organizational ALIGNMENT?*

Senior Leader Performance Evaluation (4)

- *HOW do you evaluate the PERFORMANCE of your SENIOR LEADERS, including the chief executive?*
- *HOW do you evaluate the PERFORMANCE of members of the board of directors, as appropriate?*
- *HOW do SENIOR LEADERS use organizational PERFORMANCE review findings to improve both their own leadership effectiveness and that of your board and LEADERSHIP SYSTEM, as appropriate?*

Note 3: Leadership performance evaluation (1.1c[4]) might be supported by peer reviews, formal performance management reviews (5.1b), and formal and/or informal employee and other stakeholder feedback and surveys.

> *Note 4: Your organizational performance results should be reported in Items 7.1–7.6.*
>
> NIST (2004) p. 13

 WORKSHEETS

Organizational Performance Review 1.1c - Work Sheets

1.1c (1) - Review Process

Focus of the Review	Process Used To Review
Organizational Success	
Competitive Performance	
Progress Toward Short- and Longer-term Goals	
Ability to Address Changing Organizational Needs	

1.1c (2) - Measures and Findings

Measures Regularly Reviewed By Key Leaders	Recent Performance Review Findings
Organizational Success	
Competitive Performance	
Progress Toward Short- and Longer-term Goals	
Ability to Address Changing Organizational Needs	
Customer Results	
Product and Service Results	
Financial Results	
Human Resource Results	
Organization Effectiveness & Efficiency Results	
Governance & Social Responsibility Results	

1.1c (3) - Translate Findings into Priorities

Requirement	Process Description
Priorities for Continuous Improvement	
Priorities for Breakthrough Improvement	
Opportunities for Innovation	
Priorities and Opportunities Deployed to Supplier and Partners to Ensure Alignment	

1.1c (4) - Leader and Director Evaluation and Improvement

Requirement	Senior Leader Team	Board of Directors
Evaluate Performance		
Use Performance Review Findings to Improve Effectiveness of Leaders		
Use Performance Review Findings to Improve Effectiveness of Leadership System		
Use Performance Review Findings to Improve Effectiveness of Board of Directors		

 ASSESSMENT

Organizational Performance Review 1.1c – Diagnostic Questions

Rating Scale:

0 - **No Process** in place - We are not doing this
1 - **Reacting to Problems** - Using a Basic (Primarily Reactive) Process
2 - **Systematic Process** – We use a systematic process that has been improved
3 - **Aligned** – We use a process that aligns our activities from top to bottom
4 - **Integrated** – We use a process that is integrated with other processes across the organization
5 - **Benchmark** - We are the Benchmark!
DK - Don't Know

1. The organization has a systematic process for reviewing organizational performance and translating those findings into priorities for improvement.
   0   1   2   3   4   5   DK

2. Leaders throughout the organization are involved in the organizational performance review processes and work together to translate findings into priorities for improvement.
   0   1   2   3   4   5   DK

3. The organization performance review process is integrated with the strategic planning process.
   0   1   2   3   4   5   DK

4. The performance of all leaders is evaluated and these reviews are used to improve those leaders and the Leadership System.
   0   1   2   3   4   5   DK

BLUEPRINT

Organizational Performance Review 1.1c – Blueprint

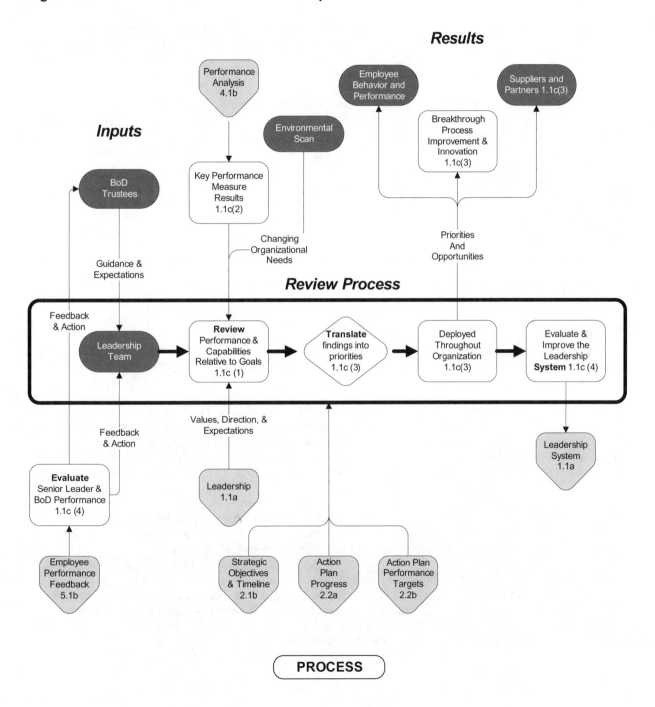

After the leadership has: 1) set and deployed values; 2) created an environment including the governance guidance required to lead the organization, the third responsibility is oversight of the organization's performance and progress toward the strategy.

The organization's performance review process begins with the involvement of the leadership team in the review and analysis of the key performance measurement results. The first step is a review of their performance capabilities relative to the vision of the organization. The findings from this review are then translated into priorities. Prioritization requires a clear decision model or decision criteria. This priority setting structure is then deployed throughout the organization. Finally, the organization establishes a review process. This review process must be values based and drive organizational improvement, leader improvement and improvement of the Leadership System.

The review process is typically connected to several other points in the criteria including leadership, the strategic objectives and timeline, action plans, and the action plan performance targets. In addition, the review process is connected to the performance analysis processes described in Areas to Address 4.1b.

The review process is just one way senior leaders can demonstrate what is important to the organization. If it is not important enough for leaders to spend time reviewing and discussing, it is likely that their direct reports will also find it is not important.

SYSTEM INTEGRATION

Organizational Performance Review 1.1c – Linkages

Inputs

There are four key inputs from other areas: values, directions, and expectations; strategy components including objectives, timelines, action plans, and performance targets; performance analysis; and employee performance feedback.

1.1a - The values, direction, and expectations that are set by the leadership system should be consistent with and be an input to the agenda for the organizational performance reviews described here in Area to Address 1.1c. If the leadership says one thing and then reviews other things there is a mixed message to the employees, suppliers, partners, and so forth. Reviews tend to hold people accountable and consequently people will tend to emphasize those things that the leaders are asking to review.

2.1b – The output of the strategy development process are objectives and a timeline as described in 2.1b. These objectives and the timeline should be incorporated into the organizational performance review process to ensure the progress being made supports the overall strategy.

2.2a – In addition to the overall objectives and timeline the specific action plans described in Area to Address 2.2a should also drive the agenda for the review process. Part of the organizational review ideally includes progress measures that allow leaders to track the schedule, scope, cost, and quality of the individual action plan projects, to ensure they are on track and provide an opportunity to identify and address issues early before they are really big problems.

2.2b – The targets that are identified in Area to Address 2.2b should also drive the agenda for the performance reviews. This allows the leaders to track the progress from the perspective of changes in the performance of the organization.

4.1b – The performance analysis process described in Area to Address 4.1b should directly feed the review process. Area 4.1b specifically calls for the analysis performed to support the organizational review process.

5.1b – The evaluation and improvement aspect of this area includes the evaluation of senior leader and board of director performance. These evaluations should be consistent with the employee performance feedback processes described in Area to Address 5.1b.

Outputs

1.1a – The evaluation and improvement process also connects with and supports the evaluation and improvement of the process to set, deploy, and communicate the values, directions, expectations and approaches to creating an environment for empowerment, innovation, organizational agility, organizational and employee learning, and legal and ethical behavior.

Transformation	**Leaders**

THOUGHTS FOR LEADERS

Leaders who suppress bad news, do not change reality. The circumstances, the problems, and the people who should have reported the bad news to them still exist. The only thing that happens is the organization does not respond to reality quickly.

There is almost no news you can bring to a leader that they cannot do something about.

Even if it is a catastrophic situation, the leader can at least prepare the organization and do some damage control. In many cases, if bad news travels up very quickly in an organization, leaders can actually subvert the consequences. What often happens is that leaders can either overtly or subliminally let it be known that you should not bring them bad news.

A great example was Lyndon Johnson during the Vietnam War. His staff could see that he was depressed by the public opinion of the war. His staff started gradually shielding him so the only place he could find any touch of reality was television. In the Oval Office he had three televisions, one on each of the major television networks so he could find out what was going on. His organization had isolated him.

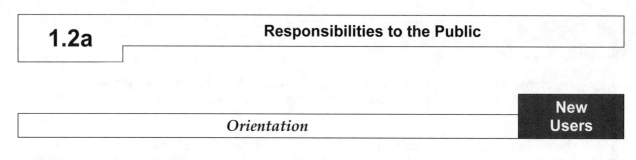

1.2a

Responsibilities to the Public

Orientation

**New
Users**

FOUNDATION

Responsibilities to the Public 1.2a – Introduction

Item 1.2 identifies whether the organization is kind to and supported by the environment in which it operates.

Does it take care of the public, does it take care of all transactions through ethics, and does it support its communities? In addition, does it ensure that all transactions of the organization meet the appropriate ethical standards?

The first part of Area to Address 1.2a assesses whether or not the organization understands the "footprint" it leaves on the world it operates within. This includes understanding its impact on the public and society from:

- The products it produces

- The services it renders and provides

- Its internal operations used

In recent years, Baldrige has turned its focus from meeting regulatory and legal requirements to surpassing regulatory and legal requirements. This is probably based on the belief that the regulatory and legal requirements will not diminish over time, but, quite possibly, will continue to become more stringent.

Baldrige expects the organization to not only be able to identify its key compliance processes, how these processes are measured, and what goals have currently been set for the measurements to achieve, but they also expect the organization to understand these processes, measures, and goals and how they are used for assessing risks. Risks need to be assessed for products, services, and operations.

Moving from the current products, services, and operations to what could happen in the future, Baldrige wants to understand the process the organization uses to anticipate what could happen. The specific question starts with "how do you anticipate public concerns..." Basically they are requesting not only to understand how you anticipate the concerns but what you are doing to prepare for those concerns (if they occur) in a proactive manner, rather than being behind the regulatory power curve and trying to catch up once public concerns drive regulation.

EXAMPLE

Responsibilities to the Public 1.2a - Example Practices

Motorola CGISS – **(Baldrige Recipient 2002)**

Impact of Products, Services and Operations

	Practices	Measures	Targets
Regulatory Requirements and Standards	• On staff knowledgeable professionals • Consult with legal department • Functional Orgs/GRO shaping regulatory standards • Industry Group participation, lobbying (NAM, AEA, IEA, ACGIH, IERG, NAEM, etc), & standard-setting • Formal processes and procedures established (e.g., M-Gates) • Mandatory topical training • ISO 14001, ISO 17025 • EHS Management System	• Regulatory Compliance & Audits • OSHA, ISO, ADA, UL, FM, CSA, CENELEC, EPA • Corporate Standards & Audits • Standards of Internal Control • EHS Management System Standards • EHS Metrics • EHS Goals	• Full regulatory Compliance • ISO 14001 Registration for all facilities • Customer EHS requirements identified and addressed • Conformance to Motorola EHS Standard A2000 • ISO 17025 certification • Agency certifications and approvals
Legal Requirements	• On staff knowledgeable professionals • Consult with legal department • Formal processes established • Design for the Environment Training • Contract Book • Ship Acceptance 2000 • Corporate EHS Document A2000	• Obtain legal counsel opinion or approval • Regulatory Approvals & Audits • Corporate Standards & Audits • Product Environmental Template	• Full legal compliance • Regulatory or agency approvals and certifications
Risks Related to Products (Hardware, Software, and Systems)	• Internal Testing • Formal processes established • M-Gates/Ship Accept 2000 • Customer Safety Inquiring Procedure, GCC/GTS • Failure Review Board (FRB) • Stop Ship procedure	• Performance Metrics • Risk Mitigation Plans established • Standards Compliance • Product Safety Design Reviews	• Full compliance with applicable laws, regulations, industry and internal standards • All risks mitigated
Risks Related to Services	• Formal processes established • Internal testing • R56 Site Installation Manual • Service EHS Management System	• Performance Metrics • Risk Mitigation Plans established	• Full compliance with applicable laws, regulations, industry and internal standards • All risks mitigated
Risks Related to Operations	• Maintain compliance with OSHA & EPA requirements • Formal processes in place for plant operations • Crisis Management • Business Recovery Plans	• OSHA/EPA regulations • Quarterly report • Corporate Audit • SIC Audit • Annual Self Assessments • Equipment Preventative Maintenance Plans and Metrics	• Full compliance applicable laws and regulations (No Citations or fines) • Satisfactory Corporate and self-assessments • Best-in-class Injury and Illness rates • Continuous improvement in EHS Impact measures • No downtime due to equipment failure

Source: Motorola, 2003, p. 15

EXAMPLE

Responsibilities to the Public 1.2a - Example Practices

University of Wisconsin Stout – (Baldrige Recipient 2001)

Key Practices and Measures of Societal Responsibility

Risks	Practices	Measures	Target	Fig. Ref.
Legal and Safety	• Safety Reviews • Community partnerships	• Campus safety/security indicators • Energy Efficiency • Injury and accident rates	• Continuous improvement • Best in UW System • Continuous Improvement	7.5-9 7.5-17 7.4-13
Risk Management	• Worker Compensation	• Work compensation claims filed • Worker compensation premiums paid	• UW Comprehensive Leader • UW Comprehensive Leader	7.4-14a 7.4-14b
Ethics and Equity	• Audits • Affirmative Action • Ethics Policy	• Number of non-conformance issues • Percent of females and minorities • Conflict of interest issues	• Zero findings • Best among peers • Zero	7.5-7 7.4-5a, b N/A
Accreditation	• NCA accreditation • Program specific accreditations	• Specific audit criteria • Accreditation approval following review process	• Ten-year accreditation • Maximum accreditation period	O-3

Source: UW-Stout, 2002, p. 194

Diagnosis

Assessors

QUESTIONS

Responsibilities to the Public 1.2a – Baldrige Criteria Questions

Compliance Processes, Measures, Goals (1)

- *HOW do you address the impacts on society of your products, services, and operations?*
- *What are your KEY compliance PROCESSES, MEASURES, and GOALS for achieving and surpassing regulatory and legal requirements, as appropriate?*
- *What are your KEY PROCESSES, MEASURES, and GOALS for addressing risks associated with your products, services, and operations?*

Anticipate Public Concerns (2)

- *HOW do you anticipate public concerns with current and future products, services, and operations?*
- *HOW do you prepare for these concerns in a proactive manner?*

Note 1: Societal responsibilities in areas critical to your business also should be addressed in Strategy Development (Item 2.1) and in Process Management (Category 6). Key results, such as results of regulatory and legal compliance or environmental improvements through use of "green" technology or other means, should be reported as Governance and Social Responsibility Results (in Item 7.6).

NIST (2004) p. 14

WORKSHEETS

Responsibilities to the Public 1.2a - Work Sheets

1.2a (1) - Regulatory and Legal Imapct

Regulatory Requirements	Key Compliance Processes	Measures	Goals/Targets	Category 7 Results Figures
For Products:				
For Services:				
For Operations:				
For Other Factors of Our Operations:				

1.2a (1) - Risks

Risks to be Addressed	Processes	Measures	Goals/Targets	Category 7 Results Figures
For Products:				
For Services:				
For Operations:				
For Other Factors of Our Operations:				

1.2a (2) - Public Concerns

Process to Anticipate Current Public Concerns:	Process to Anticipate Future Public Concerns:	Measures*	Goals/Targets*	Category 7 Results Figures
For Products:	For Products:			
For Services:	For Services:			
For Operations:	For Operations:			
For Other Factors of Our Operations:	For Other Factors of Our Operations:			

* Not explicitly called for in the criteria but logical.

 ASSESSMENT

Responsibilities to the Public 1.2a – Diagnostic Questions

Rating Scale:

0 - **No Process** in place - We are not doing this
1 - **Reacting to Problems** - Using a Basic (Primarily Reactive) Process
2 - **Systematic Process** – We use a systematic process that has been improved
3 - **Aligned** – We use a process that aligns our activities from top to bottom
4 - **Integrated** – We use a process that is integrated with other processes across the organization
5 - **Benchmark** - We are the Benchmark!
DK - Don't Know

1. The organization addresses the needs of the community, and anticipates the impacts on society of our products and services.   0   1   2   3   4   5   DK

2. There are measures and goals for the impact on society.   0   1   2   3   4   5   DK

3. The organization anticipates the impact on society of our processes, products and services, and addresses those impacts proactively.   0   1   2   3   4   5   DK

Design

BLUEPRINT

Responsibilities to the Public 1.2a - Blueprint

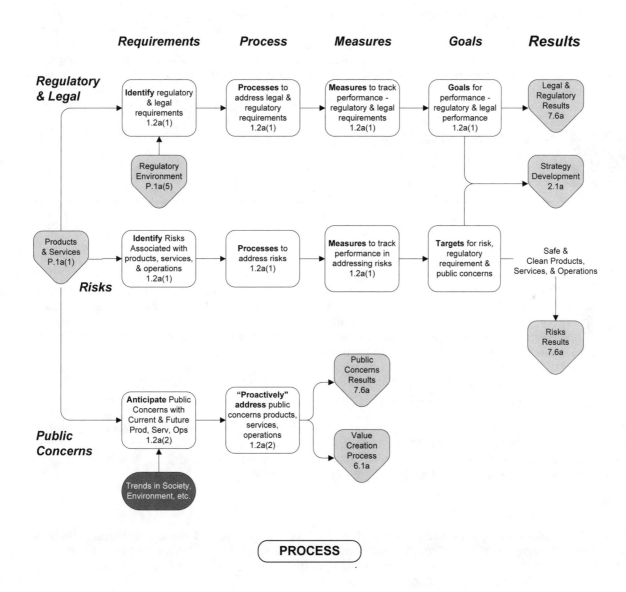

The responsibilities to the public are addressed by three processes: regulatory and legal processes; processes to address risks; and processes to address public concerns. Each of these processes follows a regular path that starts with the identification of requirements followed by a process to address those requirements and then it flows to measures to track performance. Finally goals and targets are set and the results of performance to those targets are reported in Item 7.6a.

The regulatory and legal processes begin by identifying the appropriate regulatory and legal agencies and/or requirements. The regulatory environment was described in the Organizational Profile Area P.1a. The processes that address risks of the organization begin with identifying the risks associated with products services and operations of the organization. The regulatory and legal risks, measures, goals and targets are inputs to and could be outputs from the organization's Strategic Planning Process.

Finally, the public concern requirements are actually the organization's ability to anticipate the concerns with both current and future products, services and operations. Anticipation is required in order to create processes or make decisions which proactively address these concerns. The criteria do not ask for goals and targets or the particular measures that are being used for this although the concerns that are identified would be expected to be measured and reported in Item 7.6 and considered in the value creation process.

 SYSTEM INTEGRATION

Responsibilities to the Public 1.2a – Linkages

Inputs

P.1a(1) – The most important input to this area is the description and nature of the products and services identified and described in the profile. Since this area is focused on the public concerns, risks, and regulatory and legal issues related to the organization, the type of products and services are the central driving factor that determines what is relevant and important. For example, if the products are eaten by the consumers then the FDA will be part of the regulatory environment. Some of the risks associated will be health risks to consumers, and there are public concerns to deal with such as the case of Mad Cow disease. The design of the processes to address these areas will likely be different than say for a business consulting firm or an airline.

P.1a(5) – The other key input is the description of the regulatory environment described in the profile. This environment is largely driven by the products and services, but other factors can also drive this environment including the nature of the ownership, the employees, and so forth. This is a key input to the identification of regulatory and legal requirements called for in this area.

Outputs

7.6a – Regulatory and legal results found in Area to Address 7.6a should reflect the same measures and goals described in 1.2a(1). From an assessment point of view what is identified here is fair game in the results section. From an internal improvement perspective, the results in 7.6a confirm or deny the effectiveness of the approaches described in this area.

7.6a – Risk results are also found in Area to Address 7.6a. The result in 7.6a should directly reflect the results and targets that determine the effectiveness of the processes and approaches to address the risks associated with the products, services, and operations.

7.6a – Public Concerns results found in 7.6a should directly relate to the measures identified here in 1.2a.

2.1a – The goals for regulatory and legal performance 1.2a(1) along with the performance targets for risk, regulatory and legal, and public concerns are inputs to the analysis of financial, societal, ethical, regulatory and other risks addressed in 2.1a(2). These are then used as inputs to the strategy development process. In other words Area to Address 2.1a(2) is the internal customer of Area to Address 1.2a(1).

6.1a – The public concerns that are identified in the process described in 1.2a(2) are direct inputs to the process requirements determination step described in Area to Address 6.1a(2). So, the output should be in a format that is useful for determining process requirements. In other words Area to Address 6.1a(2) is the internal customer of Area to Address 1.2a(2).

1.2b	Ethical Behavior

FOUNDATION

Ethical Behavior 1.2b – Introduction

Baldrige focuses on establishing an ethical foundation throughout an organization. This starts with understanding the organizational culture (requested in the Organizational Profile, (P1a(2)). It is further discussed in Area to Address 1.1a(1), which asks how leaders set and deploy organizational values. Ethics are specifically focused on in Area to Address 1.2b.

Baldrige basically wants to ensure that ethical behavior is deployed throughout the entire organization and at all times. The criteria focuses on not only establishing an ethical foundation, but ensuring ethical behavior in all stakeholder transactions and stakeholder interactions. As with other "how" questions, this is looking for a specific systematic process. Baldrige wants to know how the processes are used, how well they are deployed, and how they are measured. Interestingly, however, the criteria does not ask for specific goals for ethical behavior. It is probably assumed that any company would have a goal of no ethical violations. Nevertheless, actual ethical performance can be reported in Item 7.6 in the Results Category.

As with the governance structure discussed in Area to Address 1.1b, ethical behavior is to be monitored throughout the organization. It is also to be monitored with key partners (including suppliers, customers, community, and others).

In simple terms, Baldrige wants to ensure that ethical behavior is everywhere all the time. Although this is difficult for any company to guarantee, Baldrige, as usual, is looking for the processes, measures, and the checks and balances to ensure the processes have been effectively implemented.

EXAMPLE

Ethical Behavior 1.2b – Example Practices

This is a new area in the criteria and we are currently developing examples. The examples will available on the web site: www.baldrigeusersguide.com

Diagnosis

QUESTIONS

Ethical Behavior 1.2b - Baldrige Criteria Questions

Ethical Behavior

- *HOW do you ensure ETHICAL BEHAVIOR in all STAKEHOLDER transactions and interactions?*
- *What are your KEY PROCESSES and MEASURES or INDICATORS for monitoring ETHICAL BEHAVIOR throughout your organization, with KEY partners, and in your GOVERNANCE structure?*

Note 2: Measures or indicators of ethical behavior (1.2b) might include the percentage of independent board members, measures of relationships with stockholder and nonstockholder constituencies, and results of ethics reviews and audits.

NIST (2004) p. 14

WORKSHEETS

Ethical Behavior 1.2b - Work Sheets

1.2b – Ethical Behavior

Source of Ethical Requirements	Processes Used To Ensure Ethical Behavior	Measures	Results Figures
For Stakeholder_____			
For Stakeholder_____			

ASSESSMENT

Ethical Behavior 1.2b – Diagnostic Questions

Rating Scale:

0 - **No Process** in place - We are not doing this
1 - **Reacting to Problems** - Using a Basic (Primarily Reactive) Process
2 - **Systematic Process** – We use a systematic process that has been improved
3 - **Aligned** – We use a process that aligns our activities from top to bottom
4 - **Integrated** – We use a process that is integrated with other processes across the organization
5 - **Benchmark** - We are the Benchmark!
DK - Don't Know

1.	The organization has clear ethical standards and guidelines.	0	1	2	3	4	5	DK
2.	The ethical guidelines are implemented through all employees using specific measures or indicators.	0	1	2	3	4	5	DK
3.	The ethical behavior of our key partners is effectively monitored.	0	1	2	3	4	5	DK

Design	**Advanced Users**

BLUEPRINT

Ethical Behavior 1.2b – Blueprint

The processes to ensure that ethical behavior is reflected in every transaction at every level of the organization are guided by the organization's values, as described in Area to Address 1.1a.

The Organizational Profile describes the overall governance system, the stakeholders and the partners. In Area to Address 1.1b the organization is asked how they ensure that not only the "mainstream" actions of the organization are ethical, but how they ensure that ALL actions are ethical and tracked. This requires the organization understand how they have deployed the processes which drive ethics to the furthermost reaches of the organization and to all employees and all transactions.

Ethical Behavior 1.2b – Blueprint

Process *Measures* *Results*

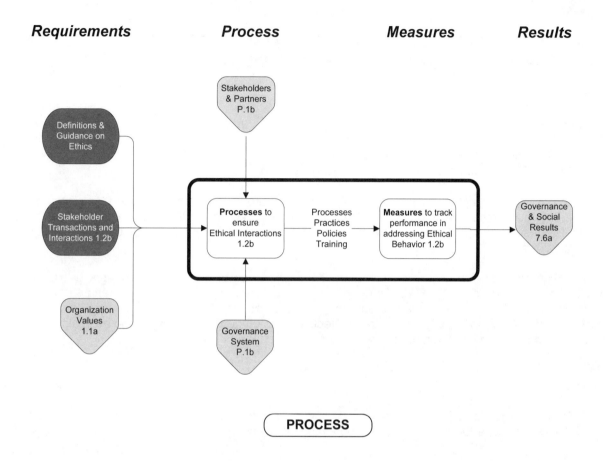

PROCESS

Organizational actions require definition or guidance on ethical limits. While this is not explicitly called for in the criteria it is a logical prerequisite for any process that is intended to ensure that all behaviors are in-control. In addition to the processes and practices, training is typically needed to ensure that the actions in the furthermost reaches reflect ethical behavior. The results of these measures are reported in Governance and Social Results in Item 7.6.

This Area to Address was recently (2003) added to the Baldrige Criteria. It addresses the concerns raised by several major companies when their ability to ensure that all transactions were ethical incurred a breakdown. Previously this issue was addressed under the broad topic of Responsibilities To The Public.

As a new Area to Address the processes, practices and approaches to address this core behavior are still in the early stages of development for some organizations using the Baldrige framework.

SYSTEM INTEGRATION

Ethical Behavior 1.2b – Linkages

Inputs

1.1a – One of the problems with ensuring ethical interactions is developing a common definition or understanding of what is and what is not ethical. One of the key inputs to the definition should be the organization's stated values as described in Area to Address 1.1a. In other words any definition of ethical should be consistent with the values of the organization.

P.1b – The second key input to ensuring ethical interactions are key players the organization interacts with including customers, stakeholders, and partners. The processes to ensure ethical interactions need to be designed to address interactions with all the categories and types of relationships the organization has.

P.1b – The processes that ensure ethical interactions also need to be designed to work within the governance system described in P.1b. All too often organizations will create processes and structures that are completely different from the main part of the organization. While this might be appropriate for processes that require "third party" status to be effective (e.g., ombudsman) they should be designed to work within and be consistent with the overall system or structure.

Outputs

7.6a – The results found in Area to Address 7.6a should include the measures identified here in 1.2b that are used to track performance in addressing ethical behavior.

| 1.2c | **Support to Key Communities** |

Orientation **New Users**

 FOUNDATION

Support to Key Communities 1.2c – Introduction

In support of key communities most organizations list all of the activities that they participate in and/or support. As impressive as these laundry lists may be, they miss the point of the criteria. The criteria is looking for a process (how?) used by the company and clear decision criteria for use within the process.

When the criteria asks, "how does your organization actively support your key communities" it is looking for a systematic set of steps that the organization follows to be proactive in their community support. Many companies, however, simply prioritize the vast list of requests they receive from their community for ongoing support. Baldrige, in seeking a process, is asking companies to be more proactive and less reactive in aligning the community support with their organizational beliefs, needs, and interests.

To establish the foundation for support of key communities, the criteria seek to understand how key communities are determined and how emphasis for organizational involvement is decided. Both of those questions require clear process and decision criteria.

Most organizations identify key communities as the predominant communities in which they do business and in which their employees live. As simple as these decision criteria are, it does meet the criterion of being clear enough to support a process. Beyond deciding what your key communities are, the criteria ask for you to list them, and then discuss how the organization decides to become involved. The simple logic flow would include questions such as:

- How does the company decide what they want to be involved in?

- How does the company decide whether or not a specific activity qualifies?

- How does the company listen to what is going on in the community to be proactive in implementing the use of their decision criteria?

- How does the company decide whether or not a specific activity warrants senior executive involvement?

Once the overall systematic process is described then the "laundry list" of community activities will make sense to the examiners. It will show how the organization has used the process and decision criteria to support the community.

1.1c is a key area where an organization needs to show a systematic process. Not only is this requested because it is a "how" question, but many organizations do not answer 1.1c using processes, but only use examples of community support activities.

 EXAMPLE

Support to Key Communities 1.2c - Example Practices

Generic Example

1.2c Generic Example – Community Support System

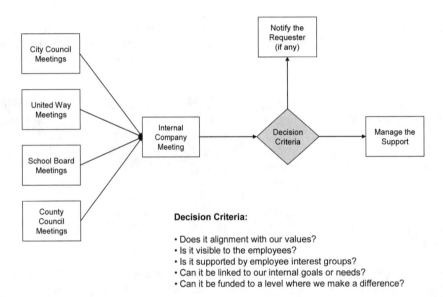

Most community support activities in organizations are reactive. This means that the organization responds to requests from the community and does not have a proactive approach to ensure that the organization is in-control of their involvement or to ensure that the involvement has a rational basis.

In the hypothetical example shown above, the organization has four listening posts in the community. The representatives involved in those listening posts occasionally meet at an Internal Company Meeting to compare what is occurring outside the organization with the company's internal decision criteria. Where the company's decision criteria matches the external need, the company approves participation.

Although not shown on this graphic, some companies have a separate set of decision criteria which help them determine whether senior leaders need to be involved in a specific community group or community support activity.

EXAMPLE

Support to Key Communities 1.2c - Example Practices

Clarke American – (Baldrige Recipient 2001)

Communities are one of the key stakeholder groups, and the Key Leadership Team (KLT) approaches the commitment to civic activities through a systematic approach. They provide support through both monetary contributions and involvement in volunteer activities. The KLT follows the process shown below to determine the investment of people and monetary resources. This approach to community involvement provides the greatest impact for the investment.

The current corporate support is focused in three key areas 1) overall community—United Way (UW) 2) education—Junior Achievement (JA); and 3) healthcare— Juvenile Diabetes Foundation (JDF). The United Way is the principal, nationwide charitable activity. Associates enjoy participating in UW fund raising and service projects in the communities where they have a manufacturing operation or contact center. Additionally, outside the corporate offices, plant or contact center managers identify two local causes to support in addition to UW. This enables the company to provide support where it is most needed.

In 1998, corporate began working with the UW of San Antonio and Bexar County to help them adopt Clarke American's **FIS** process improvement methods. In addition to training, they provided additional hours consulting with UW leadership on incorporating **FIS** techniques into their processes. At the end of the training, a business review report similar to a Baldrige feedback report was provided to the UW leadership team. This effort received "rave" reviews from the Director of the local United Way.

1.2c Clarke American – Major Project Support & Cause-Related Checks Selection Process

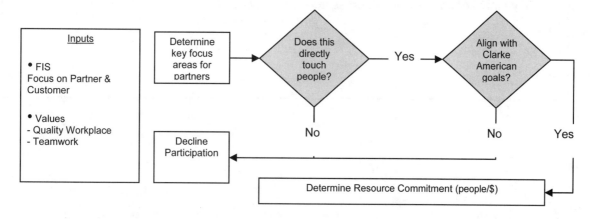

Clarke American has taken a proactive approach to many societal concerns through the creation of "cause-related checking products" in partnership with a number of national organizations. They produce checks and related merchandise with designs for eight *causes* including Save the Children, National Breast Cancer Organization, Wildlife Preservation Trust, A Better Chance and others.

Source: Clarke (2002) p. 9 - 10

QUESTIONS

Support to Key Communities 1.2c - Baldrige Criteria Questions

- *HOW does your organization actively support and strengthen your KEY communities?*

- *HOW do you identify KEY communities and determine areas of emphasis for organizational involvement and support?*

- *What are your KEY communities?*

- *HOW do your SENIOR LEADERS and your employees contribute to improving these communities?*

Note 3: Areas of community support appropriate for inclusion in 1.2c might include your efforts to strengthen local community services, education, and health; the environment; and practices of trade, business, or professional associations.

Note 4: The health and safety of employees are not addressed in Item 1.2; you should address these employee factors in Item 5.3. Item responses are assessed by considering the Criteria Item requirements; your KEY business factors presented in your Organizational Profile; and the maturity of your APPROACHES, breadth of DEPLOYMENT, and strength of your improvement

NIST (2004) p. 14

WORKSHEETS

Support to Key Communities 1.2c - Work Sheets

1.2c – Support of Key Communities

How You identify Your Key Communities:	

Key Communities	Priorities/Emphasis*	Support Given		Results
		By Employees	By Leaders	

* This should include the process to determine the areas of emphasis or priorities.

ASSESSMENT

Support to Key Communities 1.2c – Diagnostic Questions

Rating Scale:

0 - No Process in place - We are not doing this
1 - Reacting to Problems - Using a Basic (Primarily Reactive) Process
2 - Systematic Process – We use a systematic process that has been improved
3 - Aligned – We use a process that aligns our activities from top to bottom
4 - Integrated – We use a process that is integrated with other processes across the organization
5 - Benchmark - We are the Benchmark!
DK - Don't Know

1. We use clear decision criteria to determine what communities or activities should be supported.　　0　1　2　3　4　5　DK

2. There are clear guidelines for what level of the organization should be involved with a specific community group.　　0　1　2　3　4　5　DK

3. Employees have the opportunity to contribute to community activities based on their interests and beliefs.　　0　1　2　3　4　5　DK

**Advanced
Users**

BLUEPRINT

Support to Key Communities 1.2c - Blueprint

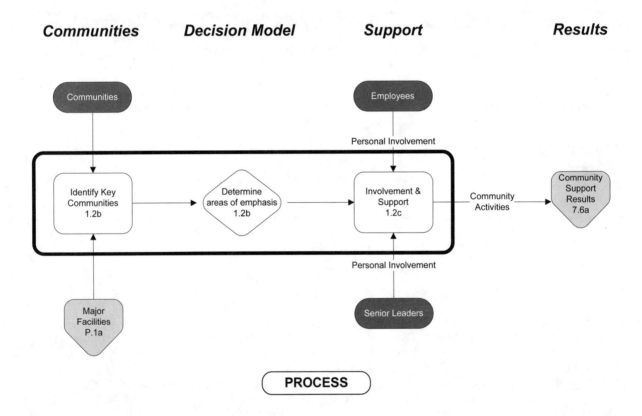

Support to key communities is really a process of identifying the key communities, determining where you are going to spend your time and effort actually supporting the key communities, and finally measuring the results of the support. Identification of key communities is typically based on the locations in which the organization operates or where their major facilities are located, as identified in the Organizational Profile.

The organization needs a systematic approach to identify the key communities. This might be easy enough for the one location "mom and pop grocery store." The identification of the key communities might be more important or more difficult for organizations that operate around the world and have small offices in literally hundreds of communities.

The determination of areas to emphasize (or to spend the time, money, and effort on) should actually be an overt decision. The organization needs some way to decide how it will spend its limited resources. Defined priorities should drive the actual time given by the employees and senior leaders and how to provide other organizational resources. These community activities produce results and those results are reported in Item 7.6.

 SYSTEM INTEGRATION

Support to Key Communities 1.2c – Linkages

The system integration for supporting key communities is not very complicated. There is only one key input or linkage to another criteria area and one key output.

Inputs

P.1a – The key input to this area is the major facilities and their locations as described in the Organizational Profile. While the criteria do not specify that an organization has to be involved in and support every community where it has an office, they do expect that the key communities will be determined from the major operating locations and possibly the locations where their products and services are used. This might be different from where the organization has facilities. The communities that are considered (by the process) for status as key communities should include those identified in P.1a.

Outputs

7.6a – The results that indicate the extent and effectiveness of the support to key communities should be located in 7.6a.

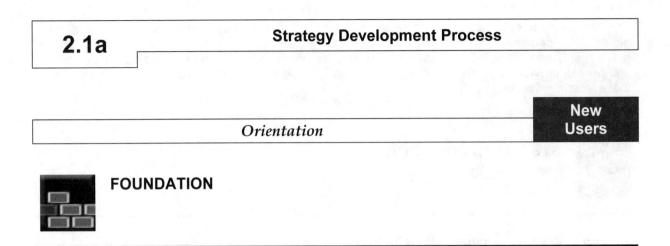

FOUNDATION

Strategy Development Process 2.1a - Introduction

Item 2.1 is where the organization officially sets its plans and starts to implement the direction the leaders set in Item 1.1. It is one of the few places in the criteria where the Baldrige framework gives users a list of issues which need to be addressed.

The criteria start by asking about the overall strategic planning process. For this, an organization should list:

- The steps in the planning process

- Who is involved in these steps

- What happens in each step

- The inputs for each step

- The outputs for each step

Additionally, the overall time horizon should be clearly defined and all of the time horizons should link back to the organization's corporate planning cycles, customer planning cycles, or other logical cycles. This should show where the organization is meeting the internal or external needs by the way they have established their planning horizons.

When addressing each of the factors to be considered during the planning process, the organization needs to do this in a manner which is clear enough for someone reading the assessment document to understand. For example, it is not sufficient to discuss customer and market needs in general terms, there should be a specific area where these are addressed at a specific point in the planning process.

The basic belief which surrounds the planning process is that several factors need to be assessed during planning. If one of these key factors is not effectively assessed (and the impact of the factor on the plan is not assessed during planning) then the implementation of the plan might be hindered by the inability of the organization to understand and/or respond to one of the factors they should have assessed during planning. For example, they may assume the workforce can support the new plan, but if they do not formally assess this, they may not realize the training and development and/or new skills required. If that happens, the development of those skills may not be a part of the overall plan and the implementation of the plan may fail.

EXAMPLE

Strategy Development Process 2.1a - Example Practices

BI - **(Baldrige Recipient 1999)**

BI's strategic planning process begins with a review of internal and external activities called Ownership Planning. This helps the organization review their overall beliefs and direction in light of both internal and external changes since the last planning cycle. The overall output of this step are BI Objectives which drive the BI strategies developed in the subsequent step. That step, Cross-Functional Leadership Planning, assesses more detailed internal and external information, which will influence the more specific approaches and strategies taken to achieve the higher level objectives. These strategies are then translated into more detailed Action Plans And Process Improvements, which are deployed down the organization to the appropriate level.

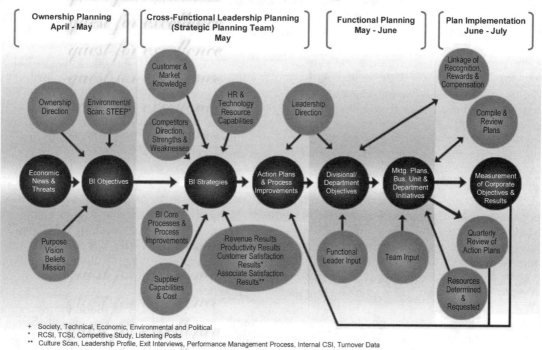

This functional planning occurs in the May-June time frame and includes input from teams and functional leaders. Additionally, detailed plans are linked to a strategy to the review performance, as well as to recognition, rewards and compensation for employees. The final step of plan implementation includes measuring performance and providing feedback in case the performance dictates a change in the action plan.

Sources: BI (2000) pp. 5 - 6 and BI Quest for Excellence Presentation 2000

EXAMPLE

Strategy Development Process 2.1a - Example Practices

University of Wisconsin Stout – (Baldrige Recipient 2001)

UW-Stout's strategic planning process begins with establishing a baseline strategy. This baseline strategy was developed over a two-year period beginning in 1996 and was further refined in 2000. In 2001, the entire strategic plan was reviewed, beginning with a Stakeholder Visioning Session. With the mission, values, Board of Regents imperatives, and state policy projections as a foundation, the Strategic Planning Committee (SPC) develops recommended goals. Business and industry input and survey data from alumni and other stakeholders were gathered to determine external factors potentially affecting UW-Stout's future. Numerous focus groups and forums were held with campus-wide groups to gather input from internal constituents regarding capabilities and needs. As information was synthesized, alternatives analyzed, and preliminary conclusions developed, the committee validated these analyses with internal and external stakeholders using the same process of forums and focus groups. This iterative process enabled the committee to refine its plans, identify issues, and develop strategic plan recommendations to meet the needs of its internal and external constituents. This collaborative approach balances priorities between the future needs of UW System and UW-Stout with its internal and external stakeholders. Recommendations were then reviewed with the governance organizations and the CAC, resulting in refinement. The final step in developing the baseline strategy was the Chancellor's approval of the long-term strategic plan goals and performance measures.

Once the goals and performance measures are developed, the SPC's role is to oversee the deployment and integration of the action plans, and to keep them updated with changing environmental conditions. The Provost, who serves as the Chair of the SPC, oversees the deployment and refinement of these plans. The process is continuous as long-term strategic goals are translated into short-term action plans through the annual budget process. Action plan owners review progress semi-annually with the SPC. During these reviews, the SPC also refines its strategies with new analysis to ensure that appropriate resources are balanced between short- and long-term actions.

To determine long-term market trends and environmental factors affecting education, the Committee uses UW System Administration studies and other industry reports such as the final report of "*The UW System in the 21st Century*" (a system-wide strategic plan). These studies and plans also provide assessments of the competitive environment and key issues affecting education. UW-Stout's own research and survey results also provide performance comparisons within the UW System, with other comparable universities, and in how UW-Stout alumni and employers compare their capabilities with other college graduate employees. Industry analyses are segmented to focus on those industries important to UW-Stout's mission, such as manufacturing and hospitality.

Student academic and service needs are obtained through the Stout Student Association (SSA), from representation on the SPC and the CAC. Student and alumni survey analysis and trends complement direct student feedback. This input has resulted in actions for increased co-op, internship and job placement; improved access to information technology; and increased support for faculty workload.

External stakeholder needs (industry, community, feeder schools, alumni, and Friends of Stout) are gathered and University of Wisconsin – Stout www.uwstout.edu aggregated through regular interaction with individuals and contact organizations. Through these contacts, UW-Stout validates and assures stakeholder expectations are clarified and understood. For external stakeholders, program quality and content, flexibility in scheduling and offering programs, skill needs, communication processes and UW-Stout image were important strategic considerations. For feeder schools, relationship processes provide information on student developmental needs, course sequencing, and use of alternative delivery methods and technology to optimize graduation success for all students, including transfer students. Partnerships with technology companies such as Ameritech, Phillips Plastics Corporation, and the Stout Technology Transfer Institute provide UW-Stout with information on technology trends and advances to plan for new internal work system capabilities and for the application of technology to enhance learning methods, broaden delivery, and to provide more flexible offerings.

2.1a UW Stout - The Planning Evolution: Strategic Planning Model

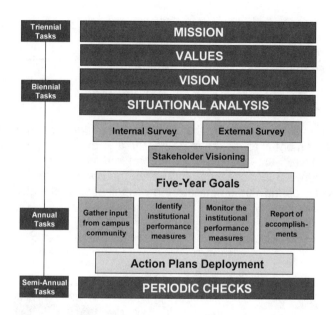

Biennially, the SPC performs a situation analysis using the SWOT (Strengths, Weaknesses, Opportunities, and Threats) analysis tool. The committee identifies organizational strengths and weaknesses from periodic action plan reviews (six-month and annual), performance indicator analysis, ad hoc surveys, environmental scan information, and other reports. The strengths and weaknesses are validated through campus-wide review at the fall budget planning forums. A stakeholder visioning session is also held biennially. This group reviews global, national, state, and local issues influencing higher education with facilitated discussion and reflection on the impact to UW-Stout and its stakeholders. This broad look forward leads to vision and mission refinement and identification of anticipated trends.

One of the significant strengths of UW-Stout's strategic planning process is its integration with the budget cycle. Applying realistic budget projections up front in planning are an integral part of the process. Annually, the budget process begins with information on progress achieved on strategic plan goals. Additionally, updates of the strategic plan from the SPC are a critical resource for developing the new annual budget priorities. This information is evaluated at the summer Chancellor's Advisory Council (CAC) planning retreats and is the origin of the initial ideas, actions, and plans developed as the campus budget priorities.

Internal stakeholders, including students, faculty, and staff, have opportunity for involvement in the strategy development process either as individuals participating in forums or committees, completing surveys, through the governance process (SSA and the Senates), or through the department organization structure. These avenues facilitate effective communication of information to improve decision quality and buy-in, increase trust in campus administration, and improve awareness and understanding of the campus direction. For faculty, input includes needs for new teaching tools, updated facilities, and developmental opportunities. For staff, work environment issues and development opportunities are primary inputs. Internal stakeholder needs related to facilities and infrastructure improvements are evaluated in conjunction with academic program development and the nature of the student population.

Source: UW-Stout (2002) p. 195 – 196

 EXAMPLE

Strategy Development Process 2.1a - Example Practices

Clarke American – **(Baldrige Recipient 2001)**

Clarke American implements their plan for the calendar year January through December. Prior to implementing the plan, four months are taken to gather the information required when initiating the plan (May – August). This "Think" time includes benchmarking other organizations, and performing a Quality Function Deployment (QFD) assessment to match the company's capabilities to the customer's requirements. Additionally, during this timeframe the organization looks inward to the needs of their associates through their Associate Survey.

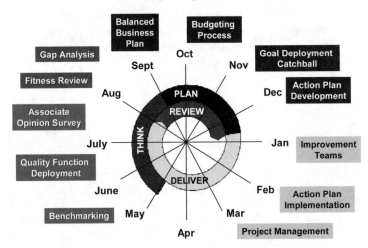

Annual Deployment Cycle

Disciplined Execution of Strategy Leads to GREAT Results

September and October are used to develop the overall business plans and budgets. November and December are used to translate the plans and budgets into detailed action plans. Once the plan is initiated in January, there is a four-month period where the company has a singular focus -- getting the year off to a good start.   Finally, in the last few months of the year, the organization performs reviews and gap analysis to assess what measures need to be taken to finish the year effectively.

Source: Clarke (2002) pp. 10 - 12

QUESTIONS

Strategy Development Process 2.1a - Baldrige Criteria Questions

Strategic Planning Process (1)

- *What is your overall strategic planning PROCESS?*
- *What are the KEY steps?*
- *Who are the KEY participants?*
- *What are your short- and longer-term planning time horizons?*
- *HOW are these time horizons set?*
- *HOW does your strategic planning PROCESS address these time horizons?*

Key Factors (2)

- *HOW do you ensure that strategic planning addresses the KEY factors listed below?*

- *HOW do you collect and analyze relevant data and information to address these factors as they relate to your strategic planning:*

  - *your CUSTOMER and market needs, expectations, and opportunities*
  - *your competitive environment and your capabilities relative to competitors*
  - *technological and other KEY INNOVATIONS or changes that might affect your products and services and HOW you operate your strengths and weaknesses, including human and other resources.*
  - *your opportunities to redirect resources to higher priority products, services, or areas*
  - *financial, societal and ethical, regulatory, and other potential risks*
  - *changes in the national or global economy*
  - *factors unique to your organization, including partner and supply chain needs, strengths, and weaknesses*

Note 1: "Strategy development" refers to your organization's approach (formal or informal) to preparing for the future. Strategy development might utilize various types of forecasts, projections, options, scenarios, and/or other approaches to envisioning the future for purposes of decision making and resource allocation.

Note 2: "Strategy" should be interpreted broadly. Strategy might be built around or lead to any or all of the following: new products, services, and markets; revenue growth via various approaches, including acquisitions; and new partnerships and alliances. Strategy might be directed toward becoming a preferred supplier, a local supplier in each of your major customers' markets, a low-cost producer, a market innovator, or a high-end or customized product or service provider.

NIST (2004) p. 15

WORKSHEETS

Strategy Development Process 2.1a - Work Sheets

Describe your organization's strategy development process to strengthen organizational performance and competitive position. Summarize your key strategic objectives.

2.1a (1) - Strategy Development Process

Planning Horizons	Number of Months or Years	Reason This Planning Horizon Was Chosen
Short-Term		
Medium-Term		
Long-Term		

Planning Process Step (In The Proper Sequence)	Description Of What Happens In The Step (Including The Decision Criteria For Key Decisions)	People Involved	Timing Of Step (Month)
1.			
n.			

2.1a (2) - Collect and Analyze Data

Key Factor	Sources of Data	Data Collection Methods	Data Analysis Performed
Customer and Market Needs, Expectations, and Opportunities.			
Competitive Environment			
Technological and other Innovations that impact products and services			
Strengths and Weaknesses – Including Human Resources			
Opportunities to Redirect Resources			
Risks – Financial			
Risks – Societal			
Risks – Ethical			
Risks – Regulatory			
National or Global Economy Changes			
Other factors unique to your organization			

ASSESSMENT

Strategy Development Process 2.1a – Diagnostic Questions

Rating Scale:

0 - **No Process** in place - We are not doing this
1 - **Reacting to Problems** - Using a Basic (Primarily Reactive) Process
2 - **Systematic Process** – We use a systematic process that has been improved
3 - **Aligned** – We use a process that aligns our activities from top to bottom
4 - **Integrated** – We use a process that is integrated with other processes across the organization
5 - **Benchmark** - We are the Benchmark!
DK - Don't Know

1. There is a systematic process in place through which senior leaders develop a strategy to achieve a competitive advantage.　　0　1　2　3　4　5　DK

2. A variety of factors are considered in developing the strategy, these include stakeholder needs, customer requirements, the environment, competitive factors, and internal capabilities (i.e., people, processes, and technology, etc.).　　0　1　2　3　4　5　DK

3. There are specific short- and longer-term planning horizons set, and clear criteria for the horizons chosen.　　0　1　2　3　4　5　DK

Design	**Advanced Users**

 BLUEPRINT

Strategy Development Process 2.1a - Blueprint

The strategy development process consists of selecting and analyzing data, making decisions about strategy, and understanding where the organization is going. This results in ultimately determining strategic objectives. All of this is based on short- and long-term time horizons. As you can see in the diagram above, the inputs to the strategy process are quite comprehensive. The complexity of the environment, the organization, and in turn, the inputs to strategy will determine or will drive the design of the strategy development process.

Strategy Development Process 2.1a – Blueprint

```
┌──────────────┐      ┌──────────────┐    ┌──────────────┐    ┌──────────────┐
│ Competitive  │      │ Competitive  │    │  Customer    │    │  Customer    │
│ Environment  │─────▶│ Environment &│    │  & Market    │    │  & Market    │
│   P.2a       │      │ Position     │    │   Needs      │    │  Results     │
└──────────────┘      │ 2.1a(2)      │    │   3.1a       │    │   7.1a       │
                      └──────────────┘    └──────────────┘    └──────────────┘
```

```
┌──────────────┐      ┌──────────────┐
│    Major     │      │  Technology  │
│ Technologies │─────▶│  Changes &   │
│    P.1a      │      │    Key       │
└──────────────┘      │ Innovations..│
                      │  2.1a(2)     │
                      └──────────────┘

                      ┌──────────────┐
                      │  Changes in  │
                      │ National &   │
                      │   Global     │
                      │  Economies   │
                      │  2.1a(2)     │
                      └──────────────┘
```

Customer & Market Needs, Expectations, and Opportunities 2.1a(2)

```
┌──────────────┐
│  Strategic   │
│ Challenges   │
│    P.2b      │
└──────────────┘
```

Analysis for Strategy 4.1b

Key Participants 2.1a(1)

Involvement

```
┌──────────────┐
│ Opportunities│
│ to redirect  │
│ resources to │
│ priorities   │
│   2.1a(2)    │
└──────────────┘
```

Deploy Values & Directions 1.1a

Financial, Societal, and Other Risks 2.1a(2) & 1.2

Collect & Analyze Data 2.1a(2)

Strategy Development Process 2.1a(1)

```
┌──────────────┐      ┌──────────────┐
│    Human     │      │Human Resource│
│  Resource    │─────▶│ Strengths &  │
│  Results     │      │ Weaknesses   │
│    7.4a      │      │  2.1a(2)     │
└──────────────┘      └──────────────┘
```

Responsibility to the Public 1.2a

Set/Determine Short- & Longer-term Time Horizons 2.1a(1)

Strategic Objectives 2.1b

```
┌──────────────┐      ┌──────────────┐
│  Supplier    │      │Supplier/     │
│ & Partner    │─────▶│Partner       │
│  Results     │      │Strengths &   │
│    7.5a      │      │weaknesses    │
└──────────────┘      │  2.1a(2)     │
                      └──────────────┘
```

Strategy Development

PROCESS

The more complex the environment and the inputs, the more complex or sophisticated the planning process needs to be. Process in this case is not intended to be a mechanism to drive only speed. Rather, it should be a framework along with a method to get the creative inputs, insight, judgment, and creativity of the key participants involved in determining creative ways to approach the future. Strategy, like people related issues, is often ubiquitous and found throughout the criteria. Consequently there are many input connections to the planning process as you will see in the next three Areas to Address. There are many linkages from the strategy to other parts of the criteria.

 SYSTEM INTEGRATION

Strategy Development Process 2.1a – Linkages

While the last Area to Address (1.2c) was relatively simple to integrate with the larger system, this Area to Address, strategy development, has 10 key inputs that are linked to other criteria areas in the focus, strategic leadership, execution excellence, and organizational learning competencies.

Inputs

P.2a – The analysis of the competitive environment is a key input to the strategy development process. This analysis should be designed to analyze the competitive environment described in the profile P.2a.

P.1a – The analysis of technology changes and key innovations is another key input to strategy development. This analysis should be designed to include or address the major technologies described in the profile P.1a.

P.2b – The strategic challenges identified in the profile P.2b are a direct input to the strategy development process. In addition, the strategic objectives that are developed as an output of this process should reflect and address these challenges.

7.4a – The analysis of human resource strengths and weaknesses is a key input to the strategy development process. This analysis helps to identify strengths to build on and leverage, areas to improve to compete, and vulnerabilities to fix to survive. In addition, this analysis helps to ensure that strategies are realistic, based on the human resource capabilities. This analysis should be based on the results (levels, trends, and comparisons) that are found in 7.4a.

7.5a - The analysis of supplier and partner strengths and weaknesses is another key input to the strategy development process for very similar reasons to the human resource analysis. Suppliers and partners can have strengths to build on and leverage, areas that need improving to compete in a particular market, and sometimes vulnerabilities that need repairing just to survive. In addition, the analysis of supplier and partner capabilities also helps to develop realistic strategies that are achievable given their capabilities. This analysis should be based on the results (levels, trends, and comparisons) that are found in 7.5a.

3.1a – The opportunities in the market and with customer groups are key inputs to market driven strategies. The process that identifies many of these opportunities is the customer and market knowledge area processes in 3.1a. The needs, wants, desires and maybe more importantly the priorities that drive purchase decisions are all key inputs to this analysis 2.1a(2).

7.1a – In addition to the opportunities identified by the customer knowledge processes in 3.1a, the actual results in key areas important to customer satisfaction, repeat business, and referrals are critical to a fact-based analysis of the opportunities, the competition, and the gaps. This analysis combined with the knowledge from 3.1a processes and the competitive environment analysis provides a comprehensive picture of the customer and market-driven opportunities.

1.1a – The development and eventual deployment of the organization's strategy is one channel or method to deploy the organization's values. The strategy should reflect not only the pragmatic analysis of the external environment, the internal environment, and the customer and market opportunities but it should also incorporate the values and expectations as described in Area to Address 1.1a.

1.2a - The goals for regulatory and legal performance in 1.2a(1) along with the performance targets for risk, regulatory and legal, and public concerns are inputs to the analysis of financial, societal, ethical, regulatory and other risks addressed in 2.1a(2). These are then used as inputs to the strategy development process. In other words 2.1a(2) is the internal customer of 1.2a(1).

4.1b – In addition to all the approaches to analysis identified above, Area to Address 4.1b also describes the analysis that is performed to support the strategic planning processes. This analysis is quite possibly redundant to the analysis described above and so each of these areas and linkages should be integrated with Area to Address 4.1a.

Outputs

2.1b – The one key output of the strategy development process is the set of strategic objectives. These objectives should have a timetable for accomplishment and clear goals. These objectives are the key input to the strategic objective deployment process described next in Area to Address 2.2a.

Transformation	**Leaders**

THOUGHTS FOR LEADERS

There is an old saying that "when you think your quality journey is over, you're right, it is". If you see two organizations and one has a lot of problems and bad news, and the other organization does not have any problems, ask yourself this question "which one is high performing, which one is low performing?"

An organization with lots of problems is **always** higher performing. All organizations have problems, so now you can divide those organizations into two categories: those who know what their problems are, and those who do not. The organizations that do not know what their problems are, obviously are not going to do anything about them.

The organizations that are very articulate and talented at identifying their problems, will fix them. It's against human nature to clearly articulate and identify a problem and then ignore it. Organizations that identify problems are going to be higher performing. This behavior, like everything else, is driven by leadership.

2.1b

Strategic Objectives

 FOUNDATION

Strategic Objectives 2.1b - Introduction

This area of the criteria is very straightforward. It simply asks for strategic objectives and when those strategic objectives will be accomplished. Under the strategic objectives the criteria ask for the goals, which the organization hopes to achieve and the timeframe when they will be achieved.

Additionally, the criteria ask the organization to link the strategic objectives back to the strategic challenges identified in P.2b in the Organizational Profile. The overall logic flow suggests that strategic challenges should drive strategic objectives which should drive strategic goals. In fact, the complete logic flow from the Organizational Profile to Item 2.1 and on to Item 2.2 is as follows:

- Strategic Challenges (P.2b)

- Strategic Objectives (2.1b(1)
  - Goals
  - Measures (not required)

- Long term action plans (2.2a(2))
  - Projected competitor performance (2.2b)
  - Timeframe (2.2b)
  - Organization performance versus competitor (2.2b)
  - Timetable (specific dates not required)
  - Changes in products and services (2.2a(2))
  - Measures or indicators (2.2a(4))
  - Goals (not required)
  - Projections (in timeframe (2.2b))

- Short term action plans
  - Projected competitor performance (2.2b)
  - Timeframe (2.2b)
  - Organization performance versus competitor (2.2b)
  - Timetable (specific dates not required)
  - Changes in products and services (2.2a(2))
  - Measures or indicators (2.2a(4))
  - Goals (not required)
  - Projections (in timeframe (2.2b))

Finally, the criteria ask several difficult questions which relate to balancing the strategic objectives, the deployment of those objectives, short- and long-term time frames, and the needs of stakeholders.

Typically organizations do not clearly address these issues. The most appropriate response is to describe how you ensure that the strategic objectives balance these factors using a systematic process (which could include specific activities during particular timeframes or planning activities) as well as clear decision criteria for how the organization decides something and/or when they decide.

 EXAMPLE

Strategic Objectives 2.1b - Example Practices

Clarke American – (Baldrige Recipient 2001)

2.1b Clarke American – Balanced Business Plan

Clarke American establishes high-level, long-term strategic objectives during development of the strategic vision.

We define shorter-term objectives, linked to the vision, during goal deployment.

	Balanced Business Plan Goals	Measures
Associates and Team	Develop, acquire, retain and motivate associates and teams to drive world class performance in core and emerging business	Retention of 2- year associates Implemented *S.T.A.R.* ideas Team huddles
Partner and Customer Value	Dramatically grow revenue through customer-preferred channels	Customer satisfaction e-Commerce revenue Customer contact center revenue
	Grow our business through partnership development and connectivity with partner service providers	Top 20 preferred service providers (PSP) Partner scorecards Branch loyalty
	Retain partnerships	Partner retention
Process and Supplier Management	Company focus to reduce waste to achieve world class manufacturing and contact center performance.	Total order cycle time Waste Reductions: Manufacturing Contact center Divisions/Processes
	Manage and improve key supplier performance to deliver increased value, cost/waste elimination, and profit improvement.	Value management workshops conducted with key suppliers New products or services developed with suppliers
Shareholder and Community Value	Drive superior financial performance to increase shareholder value	Total revenue Operating profit Return on Invested Capital
	Accelerate the **FIS** journey to achieve world class performance and recognition	Compete for TQA Compete for MBNQA
	Be recognized as a responsible contributor committed to improving the communities where we live, work, and play.	% Participation and volunteers

Clarke American establishes a range of Balanced Business Plan Goals. These are linked to how they are tracked, and their associated measures. These are aligned around the company's key stakeholders. At a higher level, these stakeholders' requirements are aligned to the associated strategic challenges. The strategic challenges are translated into strategic objectives, which are then translated into shorter-term objectives and goals. At every level the plans and goals are linked to the level above it, and are linked to the measures which will be used to track performance.

Source: Clare American Presentation – Quest for Excellence 2002

EXAMPLE

Strategic Objectives 2.1b - Example Practices

Dana Spicer Driveshaft **– (Baldrige Recipient 2000)**

2.1b Dana Spicer – TQM Control Plan

Mission Element	*KBDs*	*TQM Indicator*
We will always exceed our customers' expectations in total value.	Improve Customer Satisfaction	• On-Time Delivery • Customer Ratings • Customer Satisfaction Survey Results (NCSS) • Aftermarket Order Fill Rate
We will, on a regular basis, seek opportunities to enhance Dana's image in the marketplace.	Quality Improvement	• External PPM Rejected • Scrap
We will encourage all our people to build their future through the generation of improvement ideas.	Further Deploy the Dana Style	• Ideas Submitted • Education Hours • Quality Culture Survey Results
Our sales and profitability growth will occur through cost reductions, productivity improvement, and technological innovations.	Financial Growth	• Inventory Intensity • Working Capital • Profit Dollars • ROS • RONA • Cost Savings
We are committed to growing our business.	Business Growth	• Market Share • Sales Growth

Source: Dana Spicer Driveshaft Presentation Quest for Excellence 2001

Diagnosis	**Assessors**

 QUESTIONS

Strategic Objectives 2.1b - Baldrige Criteria Questions

Strategic Objectives and Timetable (1)

- *What are your KEY STRATEGIC OBJECTIVES and your timetable for accomplishing them?*

- *What are your most important GOALS for these STRATEGIC OBJECTIVES?*

Challenges, Opportunities, and Stakeholders (2)

- *HOW do your STRATEGIC OBJECTIVES address the challenges identified in response to P.2 in your Organizational Profile?*

- *HOW do you ensure that your STRATEGIC OBJECTIVES balance short- and longer-term challenges and opportunities?*

- *HOW do you ensure that your STRATEGIC OBJECTIVES balance the needs of all KEY STAKEHOLDERS?*

Note 3: Strategies to address key challenges (2.1b[2]) might include rapid response, customization, Lean or Virtual Manufacturing, rapid innovation, ISO 9000: 2000 registration, Web-based supplier and customer relationship management, and product and service quality. Responses to Item 2.1 should focus on your specific challenges—those most important to your business success and to strengthening your organization's overall performance.

Note 4: Item 2.1 addresses your overall organizational strategy, which might include changes in services, products, and product lines. However, the Item does not address product and service design; you should address these factors in Item 6.1, as appropriate.

NIST (2004) p. 15

 WORKSHEETS

Strategic Objectives 2.1b - Work Sheets

2.1b (1) - Strategic Objectives

Strategic Challenges*	Key Strategic Objectives	Timetable For Accomplishment	Goals	Stakeholder Impacted**
Strategic Challenge 1	L1			
	S1			
Strategic Challenge n	Ln			
	Sn			
	Sn			

L = Long-term   S = Short-term

*Strategic Challenges should be the same external Strategic Challenges identified in the Organizational Profile (P.2b).

** Stakeholder Codes:
Customers = C   Suppliers = S   Community = CO   Employees = E   Stockholder = SH

ASSESSMENT

Strategic Objectives 2.1b – Diagnostic Questions

Rating Scale:

0 - **No Process** in place - We are not doing this
1 - **Reacting to Problems** - Using a Basic (Primarily Reactive) Process
2 - **Systematic Process** – We use a systematic process that has been improved
3 - **Aligned** – We use a process that aligns our activities from top to bottom
4 - **Integrated** – We use a process that is integrated with other processes across the organization
5 - **Benchmark** - We are the Benchmark!
DK - Don't Know

1.	There are specific objectives and goals for 1) financial performance, 2) human resource development, 3) process improvement, and 4) customer results.	0	1	2	3	4	5	DK
2.	Stretch goals are set to exceed external customer expectations, and we use this approach to achieve a competitive advantage.	0	1	2	3	4	5	DK
3.	The strategic objectives balance the needs of all key stakeholders.	0	1	2	3	4	5	DK

BLUEPRINT

Strategic Objectives 2.1b – Blueprint

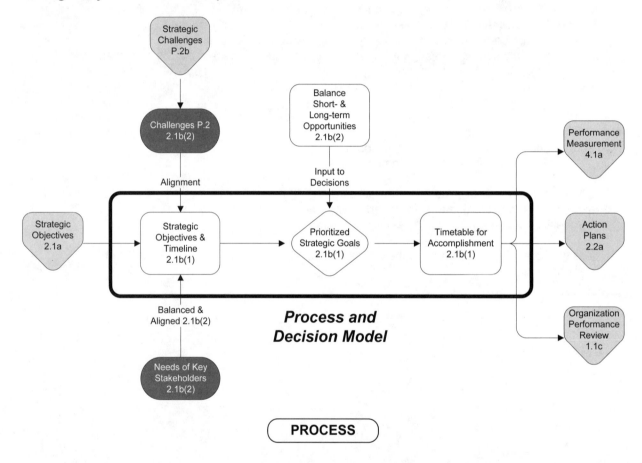

PROCESS

The strategic objectives Area to Address begins with a description of the strategic objectives developed by the strategy development process. These objectives are then placed on a timeline based on the needs of key stakeholders and how well they address the challenges of the organization.

Since most organizations have limited resources, the next step in the process is to prioritize the strategic goals. In doing so there should be a balance between short- and longer-term opportunities and objectives. The process culminates with a timetable for accomplishment. This timetable then drives several other actions and is linked to several other criteria Items including: the performance measurement, the organization performance review process, and the action planning process.

SYSTEM INTEGRATION

Strategic Objectives 2.1b – Linkages

Inputs

2.1a - The one key output of the strategy development process is the set of strategic objectives. These objectives are the key input to the strategic objectives process described next in Area to Address 2.2b.

P.2b – This criteria area asks how the strategic objectives address the strategic challenges identified in the profile P.2b. There should be an explicit linkage and alignment between the challenges and the objectives.

Outputs

4.1a – The objectives, goals, and their timetable for accomplishment drive the identification of measures to track the performance improvement. The identification of these measures should be part of the performance measurement process described in 4.1a.

1.1c - The output of the strategy development process are objectives and a timeline as described here in 2.1b. These objectives and the timeline should be incorporated into the organizational performance review process to ensure that the progress being made supports the overall strategy.

2.2a – The primary output of the strategic objectives process is the main input to the action planning process described next in 2.2a.

Transformation | **Leaders**

 THOUGHTS FOR LEADERS

Innovation starts with leadership. If leadership does not expect breakthroughs, if leadership does not understand the nature of risk, then an organization cannot innovate.

If leaders always have safe goals, if they always have a 'ten percent growth goal,' always try to achieve that goal, always have ten percent development of new product goals, and are always trying to achieve those goals, then the organization is not thinking about true opportunities.

By aiming at a ten percent change, organizations do not make behavioral changes. A forty percent change is dramatic and requires a behavioral change.

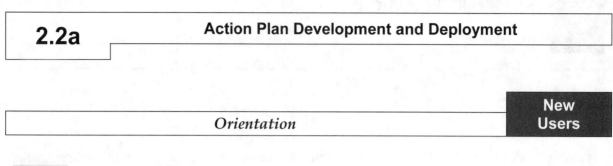

2.2a   **Action Plan Development and Deployment**

| *Orientation* | **New Users** |

 FOUNDATION

Action Plan Development and Deployment 2.2a – Introduction

Item 2.2 allows the organization to describe how they deploy the strategic plan down to the level where "somebody actually does something." This lowest level is described as the "action" level by Baldrige. Specifically, the criteria asks "how" you develop and deploy action plans to achieve your strategic objectives. This typically involves the organization describing how they take the highest level strategy and deploy it through each organizational level down to individual goals, or (at a minimum) team goals for small teams throughout the organization. This ability to directly link the top strategies (plans) to the bottom actions has been described by many Baldrige winners as the most important thing they have accomplished.

In recent years, several Baldrige winners were asked "if you could go back and go through the journey again what would you do differently?" A predominance of these winners indicated they would align the organization (top to bottom as being discussed in Item 2.2) more quickly.

After the criteria address the flowing of the strategic objectives down to the action level, and the development of the action plans, they then seek to understand how the organization ensures the changes which result from these action plans can be sustained over the longer-term. Once again, this needs to be a description of a process rather than detailed activities and/or best intentions.

This Area to Address seeks to understand what the key human resource plans are to support the overall strategy of the organization. While many organizations are reluctant to develop a human resource plan it does not have to be overly complex. Basically, it should be a plan which considers factors such as, skills needed, turnover, development of technical skills, development of managerial and leadership skills, development of ethics/social value skills, and others.

The human resource plan should describe how those skills are going to be trained/developed into the organization. Without the ability to develop people during the course of the year, the organization will not be able to achieve its strategic plan.

Finally, this Area to Address asks how the organization aligns the overall action plans up to the strategic plan. Simply stated, the criteria are asking you to check the validity of the action plans and their ability to drive the achievement of the organizational strategy.

EXAMPLE

Action Plan Development and Deployment 2.2a - Example Practices

University of Wisconsin Stout – **(Baldrige Recipient 2001)**

UW-Stout's strategy is systematically deployed through the process depicted in the table on the following page.

In this process, the owners of long-term organizational strategies within divisions and units develop annual deployment plans, align resources, review progress, and synchronize their priorities as part of the annual budget planning process. Where these actions require major resource allocations, key units within the institution will develop their own strategic plans that align with, and support, the institution's strategic plan. Examples of these strategies include the Information Technology Plan, the Academic Plan, and the Diversity Plan. The Strategic Planning Committee (SPC) developed a set of resource principles to provide deployment guidance and successful implementation of strategic objectives. One of these resource principles is to maintain budget flexibility at all levels of the organization through the use of reserves to fund unanticipated changes or emergency needs.

At UW-Stout, departments are empowered to operate within their budget allocation or to request additional resources or reallocation of funds. This "exception" management process eliminates review meetings and delegates authority and accountability to multiple levels of the organization. Budget, Planning and Analysis continually improves the budgeting process. Methods such as the American Productivity and Quality Center (APQC) benchmarking are used to learn best practices. The budget process inputs also link back into the next year's strategic plan review and update. The budget cycle begins with two Chancellor's Advisory Council (CAC) retreats to propose budget priorities to which the campus community can respond during the fall participatory sessions. At these sessions, process refinements and the addition of other improvements are identified. Improvements made to the planning process include the inclusion of capital budget issues, participation by the Foundation, and stronger emphasis on academic planning issues. The success of this empowered process is demonstrated by the budget variance performance. The SPC and CAC reviews progress on long-term objectives semi-annually.

Like the strategic planning process, UW-Stout's annual budget process is also highly participative.

Key short- and longer-term action plans are defined in the academic plan, enrollment management plan, diversity plan, information technology plan, division plans, and capital plan. These plans identify key changes anticipated. The academic plan identifies new programs and concentrations to be implemented in response to student and stakeholder needs. The current enrollment management plan indicates marginal increases in residential student populations and an increased emphasis on adult and distance learners.

University of Wisconsin Stout

University-wide level	Divisions/Units	Description
June		
Review Academic and Strategic Plan • Five-year goals • SWOT analysis • Performance Measures • Reviews/Action Plans	Annual deployment plans created to: Align resources to strategic objectives at the unit level	1) The process begins with the CAC reviewing the academic and strategic plan; its five-year goals; the current situation analysis; progress towards action plans; and performance measures, analyses, and projections.
Summer Retreats		
CAC Identification of short-term planning priorities		2) CAC holds two summer retreats to draft short-term planning priorities.
Facilitated groups discuss priorities/identify gaps		3) Early fall, facilitated groups discuss short-term planning priorities and identify gaps. This process facilitates meaningful input and participation by faculty, staff and students; involves governance and administrative groups in setting campus priorities; and increases communication at all levels during the budget development process.
November		
CAC budget planning sessions	Review of progress: Modify strategies as needed	4) Subsequently, two CAC budget planning sessions are held to review feedback from the facilitated sessions, complete the strategies to implement short-term planning priorities, establish key measures of performance and review resource needs. As the first of five feedback loops within this process, this information is shared with the campus. Group feedback is considered in finalizing the short-term planning priorities at the second CAC planning meeting and
Decision on: planning priorities, resource allocations, budget targets, performance measures.		5) The Chancellor then approves the short-term planning priorities, resource allocations, budget targets, and key measures of performance. These decisions are communicated to the campus at-large through two forum sessions.
College unit & departmental targets set by Provost/VC		6) At this point in the process, targets are deployed through a cascading approach from the Provost/VC to Deans, Chairs, and other Directors.
February		
3rd feedback – Deans, PDs, Chairs, Directors	Mid-year review of progress: • Modify strategies as needed • Budget decisions for next fiscal year.	7) There is an additional feedback University of Wisconsin – Stout 9 www.uwstout.edu process to discuss division budget priorities, gain understanding and consensus at this level, and again,
Deans, Directors deploy budgets to departments		8) as the Deans and Directors deploy budget objectives to their departments. Once consensus is achieved, budgets are submitted.
Submit budgets	Review of progress • Modify strategies as needed	
Chancellor communicates the plan university-wide		9) UW-Stout broadly communicates its strategic goals and plans internally through the CAC, in open university-wide forums, updates to the Senates, and written communication. The strategies are also documented on UW-Stout's web site for internal and external dissemination to all stakeholders as well as shared by the Chancellor with the community and legislators. Any significant feedback from this external communication is reviewed with the CAC and Senates before integration into the strategy.
Review the budget process	• Review achievement • Identify unmet needs • Refine strategic objectives/actions	

Source: UW-Stout (2002) pp. 197 - 198

EXAMPLE

Action Plan Development and Deployment 2.2a - Example Practices

Motorola CGISS – **(Baldrige Recipient 2002)**

Motorola CGISS' managers and employees develop action plans at the Sector, Group and Department levels that support the business strategies. The action plans are developed from the business cases that are prepared through the M-Gate process (for each core business) and through the growth strategy meetings (for new business).

The plans incorporate:
- Objectives
- Competitive data
- Financial analysis
- Business modeling
- Shareholder value analysis, and
- Resource requirements.

2.2a Motorola
Deployment Process Allocates Resources to Ensure Accomplishment of Action Plans

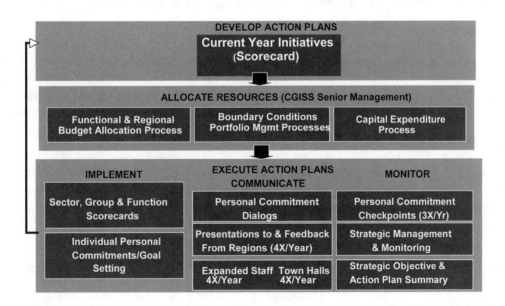

The strategic deployment approaches are specifically called out by opportunity. The action plans are included in the Performance Excellence Scorecards at each level. The Scorecards are structured to illustrate the alignment between action plans and strategies and include performance measurement. The Scorecards are fully deployed worldwide and are aligned with employees' Personal Commitment plans. Personal Commitment ensures that each employee is responsible for accomplishment of specific plans, and bonuses are determined based on performance. In this way, strategies can be driven down from deployment to the individual level and ensure dialogue between managers and their employees. The Strategic Objective Action Plan Summary indicates the key short- and long-term action plans, the key changes in product/service offerings for their customers/markets and the way they will operate to meet those changes.

The CGISS Sector Staff (senior management), is responsible for allocating resources to ensure achievement of the overall action plans. A formal cost/benefit analysis (Capital Expenditure Process) is used. There is also a formal Board of Directors meeting held quarterly to review the allocation of key business personnel (e.g. Engineers). The decision process is based on business cases developed through the M-Gate process. The communications program rollout is worldwide and includes all employees.

Sources: Motorola Presentation Quest for Excellence 2003 and Motorola (2003) pp. 18 - 20

Diagnosis	**Assessors**

QUESTIONS

Action Plan Development and Deployment 2.2a - Baldrige Criteria Questions

Action Plan Development (1)

- *HOW do you develop and deploy ACTION PLANS to achieve your KEY STRATEGIC OBJECTIVES?*
- *HOW do you allocate resources to ensure accomplishment of your ACTION PLANS?*
- *HOW do you ensure that the KEY changes resulting from ACTION PLANS can be sustained?*

Action Plans (2)

- *What are your KEY short- and longer-term ACTION PLANS?*
- *What are the KEY changes, if any, in your products and services, your CUSTOMERS and markets, and HOW you will operate?*

Human Resource Plans (3)

- *What are your KEY human resource plans that derive from your short- and longer-term STRATEGIC OBJECTIVES and ACTION PLANS?*

Performance Measures (4)

- *What are your KEY PERFORMANCE MEASURES or INDICATORS for tracking progress on your ACTION PLANS?*
- *HOW do you ensure that your overall ACTION PLAN measurement system reinforces organizational ALIGNMENT?*
- *HOW do you ensure that the measurement system covers all KEY DEPLOYMENT areas and STAKEHOLDERS?*

Note 1: *Strategy and action plan development and deployment are closely linked to other Items in the Criteria.*

Note 2: *Measures and indicators of projected performance (2.2b) might include changes resulting from new business ventures; business acquisitions or mergers; new value creation; market entry and shifts; and significant anticipated innovations in products, services, and technology.*

NIST (2004) p. 16

 WORKSHEETS

Action Plan Development and Deployment 2.2a - Work Sheets

Describe how your organization converts strategic objectives into action plans. Summarize your organization's action plans and related key performance measures or indicators. Project your organization's future performance on these key performance measures or indicators.

2.2a(1) - Action Planning Process

Steps For Action Plan Development	Criteria Or Steps For Resource Allocation	Step For Action Plan Deployment	Methods Or Steps To Sustain Improvements

2.2a(2) - Action Plans

Key Strategic Objectives *	Action Plans	Changes**	Stakeholder Impacted***	Progress Measures Area to Address 2.2a(4)	Performance Measures Area to Address 2.2a(4)

* See the Short- and Long-Term Strategic Objectives in 2.1b(1)
** Changes in this case are the changes to products, services, customers, market, operations, etc.
*** Stakeholder Codes:
  Customers = C   Suppliers = S   Community = CO   Employees = E   Stockholder = SH

2.2a(3) - Human Resource Plans

Key Strategic Objectives or Action Plans *	Human Resource Plans	Changes	Balanced Scorecard Measure** Area to Address 2.2a(4)	Category 7 Results Reported

*   See the Short- and Long-Term Strategic Objectives in 2.1b(1) or the Action Plans in 2.2a(2)
** Not required by the criteria, but many organizations report a Balanced Scorecard. If using a Balanced Scorecard the metrics in it must link with other plans and measures

 ASSESSMENT

Action Plan Development and Deployment 2.2a – Diagnostic Questions

> **Rating Scale:**
>
> 0 - **No Process** in place - We are not doing this
> 1 - **Reacting to Problems** - Using a Basic (Primarily Reactive) Process
> 2 - **Systematic Process** – We use a systematic process that has been improved
> 3 - **Aligned** – We use a process that aligns our activities from top to bottom
> 4 - **Integrated** – We use a process that is integrated with other processes across the organization
> 5 - **Benchmark** - We are the Benchmark!
> **DK** - Don't Know

1. I know my role in achieving this year's plan, and I have a way to track my progress at least monthly.	0	1	2	3	4	5	DK
2. The strategy is deployed at every level of the organization. This is through goals and objectives which link from the organizational level all the way down to every individual contributor.	0	1	2	3	4	5	DK
3. We have a documented human resource plan that is derived from the short- and longer-term strategic objectives and plans.	0	1	2	3	4	5	DK

Design

BLUEPRINT

Action Plan Development and Deployment 2.2a - Blueprint

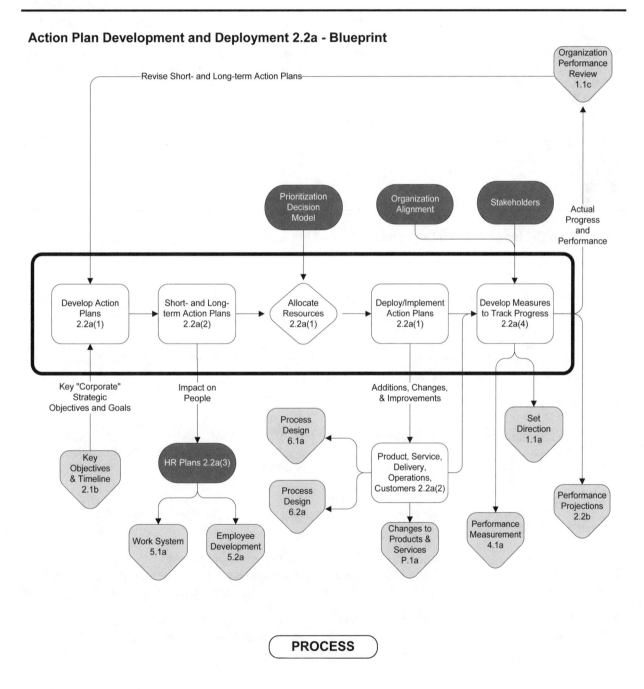

PROCESS

The action planning process converts the objectives from a timeline into a practical plan to actually accomplish the objectives. The first step is to develop both short- and long-term action plans and then allocate adequate resources to actually deploy or implement the action plans. These action plans are based on the key objectives and timeline that were documented in 2.1b. The short- and long-term action plans developed will also drive the human resource plans and ultimately affect changes in the work systems and employee development.

The allocation of resources is basically a decision model. Most organizations have limited resources (both time and people) and consequently have to make decisions and set priorities. How this is done and the model that is used is the question in the diamond in the diagram above. The deployment and implementation of action plans will affect the products, services, and delivery operations and ultimately both the value creation and support processes. Finally action plans need measures to track the progress and the performance. These measures are integrated as part of the overall performance management system. They are ultimately used to help set direction and as input to the organizational performance review process. This seeks to ensure action plans stay on schedule, within the budget, within the intended scope and produce the desired outcome. The next phase or connection is the setting of actual performance projections and 2.2b.

 SYSTEM INTEGRATION

Action Plan Development and Deployment 2.2a – Linkages

Inputs

2.1b - The primary output of the strategic objectives process is the main input to the action planning process described next in 2.2a.

1.1c – The organizational performance review process will often result in refinements to action plans to keep them on track, within budget, and on schedule. These refinements then find their way to the other plans including human resource plans as appropriate.

Outputs

5.1a – The human resource plans developed as part of the action planning process impact the design/redesign of the work system described in 5.1a. Change in the work system might be required to achieve the performance desired and necessary to accomplish the overall strategy.

5.2a – The strategy and action plans also drive the employee development efforts. The overall strategies are balanced with the needs of the individual to drive the development of both course content and the delivery methods.

6.1a – Action plans often call for additions, changes, and improvement to products, services, and the processes that created them. In this case the value creation processes are refined or changed to assist in accomplishing the strategic objectives.

6.2a – Action plans also often call for additions, changes, and improvements to support processes. Action plans can directly impact change to support processes and they can also indirectly impact support processes through changes in the value creation processes.

4.1a – A key element of the action plans are measures to track progress. The actions plans are direct inputs to the selection and alignment of measures for daily operations and overall organizational performance described in 4.1a.

1.1a – The short- and long-term expectations described in Area to Address 1.1a should be consistent with and include the actions detailed in the action plans that are described here in Area to Address 2.2a. If the leadership emphasizes different expectations than are in the strategic plan or action plans then the strategy remains on the shelf while employees spend their time and resources working those issues that are important to leadership.

1.1c - In addition to the overall objectives and timeline the specific action plans described here in Area to Address 2.2a should also drive the agenda for the review process. Part of the organizational review ideally includes progress measures that allow leaders to track the schedule, scope, cost, and quality of the individual action plan projects to ensure that they are on track and provide an opportunity to identify and address issues early before they are really big problems.

2.2b – The main output of this area – action plans – are used to determine performance projections described in the next Area to Address 2.2b.

Transformation	**Leaders**

THOUGHTS FOR LEADERS

There is only one sustainable competitive advantage, and that is the rate of your improvement. You can look at really lousy companies that have improved rapidly enough that they were a success.

Some world-class companies (look at the top ten, one hundred years ago) quit improving and they died. There is an old saying in the southern part of the United States, "If you're not rowing upstream, you're drifting down." There is no such thing as status quo.

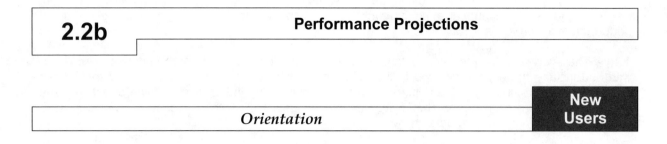

2.2b	**Performance Projections**

Orientation	**New Users**

FOUNDATION

Performance Projections 2.2b - Introduction

Area to Address 2.2b is the only place in the criteria where an organization can get credit for something they have not yet achieved. It asks for projections of performance from the action plans (which are driven by the strategy). Additionally, the criteria ask how the organization will know how its performance will compare versus competitors during those same time frames. This requires the organization to project their own performance, project the performance of competitors, and assess the comparison between the two at some point in the future (presumably at the end of each planning time frame).

Typically organizations cannot get direct competitive comparisons. These comparisons may have to come from industry knowledge or from data points which are infrequently gathered. It is important in 2.2b to describe the process used to achieve the projections and/or the assumptions which have been made in determining the projections.

EXAMPLE

Performance Projections 2.2b – Example Practices

Motorola CGISS – (Baldrige Recipient 2002)

Motorola CGISS' short- and long-term action plans are depicted in Scorecards starting with the Sector Scorecard and cascading through the organization.

The Strategic Management and Monitoring Framework provides detailed information related to any key changes in their products/services and customers/markets and manages and monitors the action plans and deliverables related to those strategic objectives.

2.2b Motorola – Strategy Deployment – Results & Projections

	Past Levels	Target Levels	3-Year Projections
Financial			
• Sales Growth %	Benchmark	8 – 10%	8 - 10%
• Gross Margin %	←	Benchmark	→
• Operating Earnings %	8 - 10%	10%	12 - 15%+
Customer			
• Satisfaction (Top 2 Box)	89%	90%	90%+
• Market Share (Relative)	2X	2X	2X
Operational			
• Sales/Employee	←	Benchmark	→

Source: Motorola Presentation Quest for Excellence 2003

EXAMPLE

Performance Projections 2.2b – Example Practices

Chugach School District (CSD) – (Baldrige Recipient 2001)

Chugach's key stretch goals and targets are based upon competitive comparisons, state standards and Baldrige Winners best practices. The indicators show key measure projections aligned to strategic objectives. Dues to innovative, visionary goals, it is difficult to make comparisons to other organizations. Changes resulting from Chugach Instructional Model (CIM) delivery, standards-based reporting, Carnegie waiver, Student Learning Profile (SLP), and other innovations have proven resoundingly successful for the students. CSD's Key Performance Indicators (KPIs) are, at times, solely established by CSD, thus creating a lack of benchmarking opportunities.

	2001	2002	2003	2004	2005	KPI
Longer-term Goal:	- Benchmark Continuous Improvement System	- PDER overlay Shared Action Plan Consistent Deployment Accurate Evaluation Proactive Refinement				7.1-7.5
Basic Skills	- Increase reading comprehension - Math Training	- Refine reading & math - Refine writing targets	- Refine targets & assessments - Peer mentoring	- Web format for data collecting - Refine reporting documents	- Evaluate web format student performance	7.1
Transition Skills	- Refine transition program - Communication plan	- Mentor other districts in transition - Refine AH phases	- Create business certification for students	- Secure additional resources - Increase partnerships	- Follow-up longitudinal study - Communications system	7.2
Character Development	- Support local plans - Refine P/S/H	- Refine Plans Community meetings	- Provide teacher training - Update P/S/H	- Community/ parent training	- Refine P/S/H standards & assessments	7.4
Individual Needs	- SLP Training - Database Tracking	- Refine SLP & Diploma	- Benchmark testing waiver	- Refine ILP process	- Independent opportunities	7.1
Technology	- Wireless - Internet Access	- Increase bandwidth - Implement CASTS	- Web CASTS - Video conferencing	- Online training	- Web based learning tools implemented	7.5

Source: Chugach, 2002, p. 90

Diagnosis

QUESTIONS

Performance Projections 2.2b - Baldrige Criteria Questions

- *For the KEY PERFORMANCE MEASURES or INDICATORS identified in 2.2a(4), what are your PERFORMANCE PROJECTIONS for both your short- and longer-term planning time horizons?*

- *HOW does your projected PERFORMANCE compare with competitors' projected PERFORMANCE?*

- *HOW does it compare with KEY BENCHMARKS, GOALS, and past PERFORMANCE, as appropriate?*

NIST (2004) p. 16

WORKSHEETS

Performance Projections 2.2b - Work Sheets

2.2b – Performance Projections and Comparisons

Performance Measure (from 2.2a worksheets)	Short-term Projection	Long-term Projection	Comparison to Competitors	Comparison to Benchmarks, Goals, or Past Performance

ASSESSMENT

Performance Projections 2.2b – Diagnostic Questions

Rating Scale:

0 - **No Process** in place - We are not doing this
1 - **Reacting to Problems** - Using a Basic (Primarily Reactive) Process
2 - **Systematic Process** – We use a systematic process that has been improved
3 - **Aligned** – We use a process that aligns our activities from top to bottom
4 - **Integrated** – We use a process that is integrated with other processes across the organization
5 - **Benchmark** - We are the Benchmark!
DK - Don't Know

1.	In setting our long-term strategy, the competitors' performance is projected to ensure that we stay ahead of them.	0	1	2	3	4	5	DK
2.	In setting our direction key benchmarks, goals and past performance are analyzed and used.	0	1	2	3	4	5	DK
3.	The strategy is used as a road map for the business to guide decisions throughout the year.	0	1	2	3	4	5	DK

Design   **Advanced Users**

BLUEPRINT

Performance Projections 2.2b – Blueprint

Performance projections both short and long are set based on the action plans identified and described in the previous Area to Address (2.2a). These projections are the logical conclusions or predicted performance based on the change as described in the action plans.

The projections also include comparisons to goals, past performance, and benchmarks and competitive comparisons. These projections are inputs to the organizational performance review process. This is so leadership can track and understand the expected performance gain from the action plans and how that compares to the projected performance of the competitors. Alternately these projections should also be reported as forecasts and the results in Items 7.1 through 7.6.

Performance Projections 2.2b - Blueprint

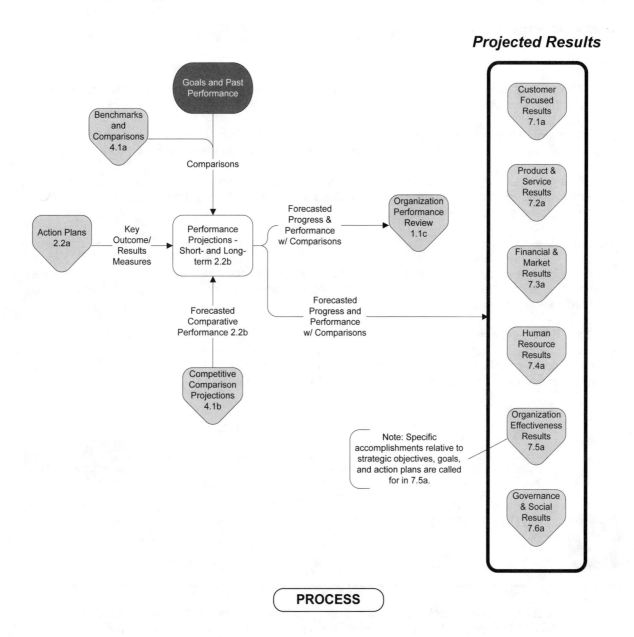

SYSTEM INTEGRATION

Performance Projections 2.2b – Linkages

Inputs

2.2a – The primary input to this area are the action plans that were developed in 2.2a. They are used to determine the performance projections.

4.1a – Benchmarks and comparisons are selected in Area to Address 4.1a(2). The benchmarks and comparisons used here for projections should be consistent with those identified by 4.1a(2).

4.1b - Part of the analysis provided by 4.1b(1) to support strategic planning includes comparisons (e.g., competitive, benchmark, industry). The analysis along with the comparisons provided by 4.1b(1) should drive the projections described here in 2.2b.

Outputs

1.1c – The targets identified in Area to Address 2.2b should also drive the agenda for the performance reviews. This allows the leaders to track the progress from the perspective of changes in the performance of the organization.

7.1a thru 7.6a – The forecasted performance (projections) along with the projected comparison performance should be reflected in the results charts depicted in Areas to Address 7.1a through 7.6a. While the criteria specifically asks for strategic plan accomplishments in Area to Address 7.5a, the ideal strategic plan will have projections for measures in all six results areas.

Transformation	**Leaders**

THOUGHTS FOR LEADERS

A Baldrige score may or may not indicate a culture. For example, two 400-point companies may be very different. One 400-point company may have a solid culture, have an established framework, have solid values, take care of its people, be customer focused and be really poised for greatness. It is a 400-point company that soon will be 500, soon afterward will be 600 and beyond. There can also be a 400-point company that gets there through forcing processes onto people, forcing the integration of its business or its customers. It is never going to go much beyond 400-points unless there are some real fundamentals changes. It is disappointing to see an organization halfway through the performance excellence journey without having laid a proper foundation. They can not get any further and are stuck year after year. Is a Baldrige organization at 650 points an indication of a very solid culture? Absolutely! It is an organization that really has taken care of customers, employees, and processes.

3.1a	Customer and Market Knowledge

 FOUNDATION

Customer and Market Knowledge 3.1a – Introduction

In the Organizational Profile (P.1b(2)) the criteria ask who the customer groups are and their requirements. These requirements should be segmented by customer group, target customer segment, or market segment, as appropriate. Item 3.1 asks how the organization determines those segments or the appropriate groupings.

Typically Baldrige expects to see the requirements of customers drive how the customers are segmented. This is the opposite of the customers being segmented by industry, type of product purchased, or other factors which do not correlate to those requirements which customers expect to be met. Additionally, Baldrige expects the organization to have a very wide view of customers. This includes customers of competitors, other potential customers, and previous customers of the organization.

Once the organization describes how they segment customers into various groups, the criteria ask for the listening and learning techniques used by the organization to understand the customer requirements and expectations. These listening and learning techniques may, however, be different for each one of the market groups or segments. They should be applied to current customers, former customers, customers of competitors, or any other place the organization can gain knowledge about customers' requirements, needs, expectations, or behavior drivers.

The basic understanding that Baldrige is trying to achieve is "does the organization understand what drives their customers' purchase behaviors?" Simply stated, if the organization really understands what drives customers' purchase behaviors then they can compete more effectively in the marketplace than if they do not have that understanding.

Finally, Item 3.1 seeks to understand how the organization identifies that their listening and learning methods need to be updated and the process used to update those methods.

EXAMPLE

Customer and Market Knowledge 3.1a - Example Practices

How do you determine or target customers, customer groups, and/or market segments? How do you consider customers of competitors and other potential customers and/or markets in this determination?

ST Microelectronics – **(Baldrige Recipient 1999)**

    3.1a ST Microelectronics – Customer Tier-Segment Matrix

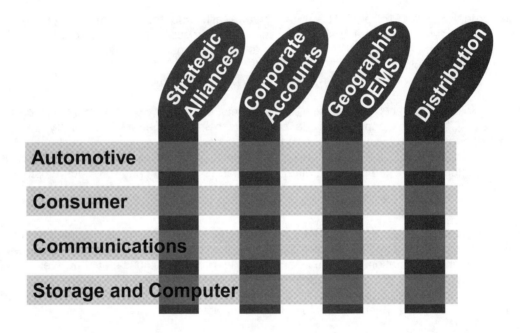

Source: ST Microelectronics Presentation Quest for Excellence 2000

EXAMPLE

Customer and Market Knowledge 3.1a - Example Practices

KARLEE – **(Baldrige Recipient 2000)**

KARLEE's approach to strategic partnerships allows continual contact with each of their primary customers. The Figure below shows their business acquisition process which illustrates KARLEE's listening and learning methods for prospective and current customers.

KARLEE's ability to anticipate and exceed customers' requirements has been a key factor in maintaining its rapid growth since 1990. Senior executives and KARLEE Steering Committee (KSC) members work with each prospect or customer to establish current requirements and future needs. Listening and learning sources include:

- Customers' Meetings
- Senior Executive Meetings with Customers
- Customers' Competitive Reports
- Customer Service Team Meetings
- Customer Satisfaction Surveys
- Problem History Report
- Internal Quality Reports
- Internal Performance Measures

Business Acquisition Process

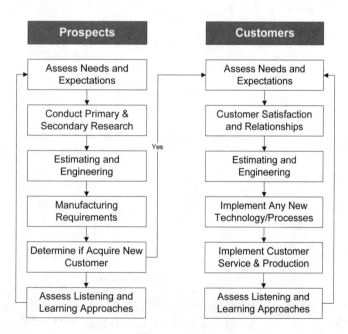

In considering changes to production processes, they look for innovations and improvements that will benefit all customers, as well as those for a single customer. New services for a single customer must be cost-effective and fit within KARLEE's overall strategic plans. The Customer Service

Representatives play an important role in aggregating key inputs including sales, customer retention, won/lost quotes to help evaluate new services.

The Senior Executive Leaders (SEL) and KSC teams evaluate the effectiveness of their "listening and learning" system annually during strategic planning and quarterly during KSC reviews. They evaluate the effectiveness of the type and frequency of information they gain. They also search for additional methods to gain and analyze information about customer requirements, expectations and preferences.

Source: KARLEE (2001) p. 13

 EXAMPLE

Customer and Market Knowledge 3.1a - Example Practices

BI – **(Baldrige Recipient 1999)**

Each Business Unit manager is responsible for analyzing Customer and Market Listening Post data to better understand customer needs and changing customer requirements. This information is systematically reviewed by the External Customer Satisfaction Team, Business Team, Customer Delight Process (CDP) Process Improvement Team (PIT), and Sales Management Team. These teams combine information gathered from all of the listening posts to form generalizations about service features, relative importance and value across BI's markets.

Listening and Learning Posts		Outcomes
CDP Account Strategy Process Strategy Grid Transactional CSI Relationship CSI Customer Complaints Customer Partnership Interviews Lost Business Reviews Account Reviews Letters to the Chief Quality Officer Customer Visits Competitive Study Customer Requirements Study Regional Competitive Revenue Analysis	Strategic Planning Process Customer Delight Process Process Improvement Teams Quality Improvement Teams External Action Teams Account Strategy Process	Overall company direction and strategy New products Product improvements New services Service improvements Improved customer relations Understand special needs of market segments and individual customers Improved customers satisfaction, repurchase, referral, loyalty and retention Understanding customers of competitors

Another group that uses listening post data to identify service products and their features and values is BI's Innovative Resources group. This group is also dedicated to the development of new concepts and branded products. By utilizing information gained through BI's listening posts, as well as media and personal interviews with customers and technical experts, Innovative Resources obtains the information necessary to determine and project the needs and requirements for future products and services.

Source: BI (2000) pp. 7 - 8

Diagnosis	**Assessors**

QUESTIONS

Customer and Market Knowledge 3.1a - Baldrige Criteria Questions

Customer Segmentation (1)

- *HOW do you determine or target CUSTOMERS, CUSTOMER groups, and market SEGMENTS?*
- *HOW do you include CUSTOMERS of competitors and other potential CUSTOMERS and markets in this determination?*

Listening and Learning (2)

- *HOW do you listen and learn to determine KEY CUSTOMER requirements and expectations (including product and service features) and their relative importance to CUSTOMERS' purchasing decisions?*
- *HOW do determination methods vary for different CUSTOMERS or CUSTOMER groups?*
- *HOW do you use relevant information from current and former CUSTOMERS, including marketing and sales information, CUSTOMER loyalty and retention data, win/loss ANALYSIS, and complaints?*
- *HOW do you use this information for PURPOSES of product and service planning, marketing, PROCESS improvements, and other business development?*

Keeping Current (3)

- *HOW do you keep your listening and LEARNING methods current with business needs and directions?*

Note 1: Your responses to this Item should include the customer groups and market segments identified in P.1b(2).
Note 2: If your products and services are sold to or delivered to end-use customers via other businesses such as retail stores or dealers, customer groups (3.1a[1]) should include both the end users and these intermediate businesses.
Note 3: "Product and service features" (3.1a[2]) refers to all the important characteristics of products and services and to their performance throughout their full life cycle and the full "consumption chain." This includes all customers' purchase experiences and other interactions with your organization that influence purchase decisions. The focus should be on features that affect customer preference and repeat business— for example, those features that differentiate your products and services from competing offerings. Those features might include price, reliability, value, delivery, requirements for hazardous materials use and disposal, customer or technical support, and the sales relationship. Key product and service features and purchasing decisions (3.1a[2]) might take into account how transactions occur and factors such as confidentiality and security.
Note 4: Listening and learning (3.1a[2]) might include gathering and integrating surveys, focus group findings, and Web-based and other data and information that bear upon customers' purchasing decisions. Keeping your listening and learning methods current with business needs and directions (3.1a[3]) also might include use of newer technology, such as Web-based data gathering.

NIST (2004) p. 17

WORKSHEETS

Customer and Market Knowledge 3.1a - Work Sheets

Describe how your organization determines requirements, expectations, and preferences of customers and markets to ensure the continuing relevance of current products/services and to develop new opportunities.

3.1a (1) - Determine Customer Groups and Market Segments

Process Step to Segment Customers	Participants	Decision Criteria Used To Segment
1.		
n.		

Note: This process should identify how the external customer segmentation presented in P.1b(2) in the Organizational Profile was determined.

3.1a (1) – Target Customer Groups and Market Segments
Note: Complete this only if the information is different from the Determination of Customer segments discussed in the previous table.

Process Step to Target Customer Groups	Participants	Decision Criteria Used To Target Customers
1.		
2.		

3.1a (2) - Listening and Learning Methods

Customer Segment or Target Group	Listening/Learning Methods Used	Approaches to Keep Method Current

3.1a (2) Continued

Customer Segment or Target Group	How You Determine What Will Drive The Customer's Purchase Decisions	Approaches to Using Information From Former or Potential Customers

3.2a(1) - Relationship Building

Approach to Relationship Building

Note: This Should Be A System To Build Relationships To: 1) Acquire Customers; 2) Meet/Exceed Expectations ; 3) Increase Loyalty; 4) Increase Repeat Business; And To 5) Gain Positive Referrals.

ASSESSMENT

Customer and Market Knowledge 3.1a – Diagnostic Questions

Rating Scale:

0 - **No Process** in place - We are not doing this
1 - **Reacting to Problems** - Using a Basic (Primarily Reactive) Process
2 - **Systematic Process** – We use a systematic process that has been improved
3 - **Aligned** – We use a process that aligns our activities from top to bottom
4 - **Integrated** – We use a process that is integrated with other processes across the organization
5 - **Benchmark** - We are the Benchmark!
DK - Don't Know

1.	There is a systematic process for determining current and future customer needs/expectations.	0	1	2	3	4	5	DK
2.	The organization has targeted specific customer segments to really understand the needs of the customers in each of those segments.	0	1	2	3	4	5	DK
3.	Competitive solutions we provide to customers are designed to match targeted customer needs.	0	1	2	3	4	5	DK
4.	Performance against specific customer requirements is measured and tracked.	0	1	2	3	4	5	DK

Design	**Advanced Users**

BLUEPRINT

Customer and Market Knowledge 3.1a - Blueprint

Setting direction and determining strategy is dependent upon an intimate knowledge of the customers and the markets. The customer and market knowledge process begins with the determination of customers, market segments and groups. These segments are described in the Organizational Profile. But the question here is, "what are the method and criteria used to determine the segments and the groups?" The segments then drive the listening and learning methods or approaches. Some organizations use different methods for different segments and groups. This will depend on the nature of these groups.

Customer and Market Knowledge 3.1a – Blueprint

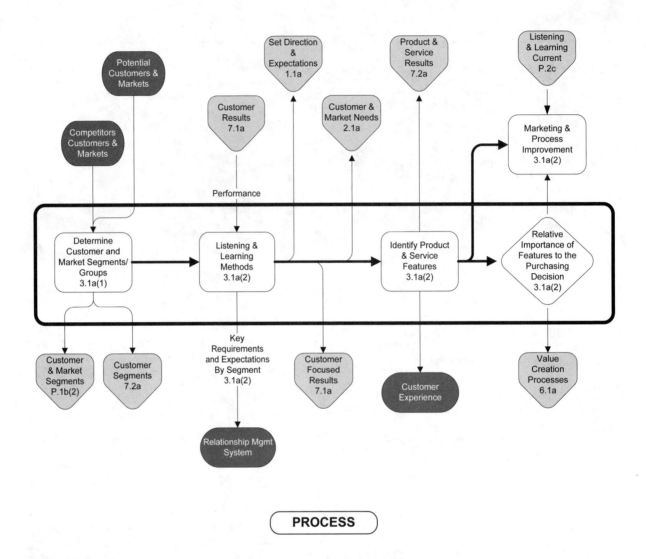

PROCESS

The listening and learning methods are used to deduce or identify the key requirements and expectations by segment or group. These are the same requirements or expectations that should be measured in the Customer Focus Results Item 7.1. These requirements and expectations drive the identification of product and service features. The final step in the process is to determine the relative importance of the product and service features in the purchasing decision of the customers. It is one thing to "want something" and it is quite another to actually pay for it.

As you can see in the diagram, this process is also linked to many other areas in the criteria. Just like people, information and strategy, the customer and market knowledge or focus runs throughout the criteria.

SYSTEM INTEGRATION

Customer and Market Knowledge 3.1a – Linkages

The customer and market knowledge processes link to processes and results in each of the competency areas including focus, strategic leadership, execution excellence, and organizational learning.

Inputs

7.1a – This area asks for how the organization determines key customer requirements and expectations (including product and service features) and their relative importance to customers' purchasing decisions. While it is very useful to survey customers and ask for their preferences it is even better to analyze their actual behavior and buying patterns along with their satisfaction results. This provides the organization with much better information for making adjustments to product and service offerings.

P.2c – The marketing and process improvement activities in 3.1a(2) should be consistent with the overall approach to performance improvement described in the profile.

Outputs

P.1b(2) – The activities to determine customer and market segments and groups described here should be consistent with the customer and market segments described in the profile. In addition, if this process modifies the customer and market segments then that should be reflected in an updated profile.

7.2a – The segments and customer groups that are identified here in 3.1a should also be the segments and groups that drive the segmentation of product and service results data. In other words, the results in 7.2a should include results requirements for each of the key customer and market segments and groups identified by the processes here in 3.1a.

1.1a - The setting of values, direction, and expectations should address the needs, wants, and desires of the customers and markets described in Area to Address 3.1a. While not the only stakeholder, the customers or primary beneficiaries of the products and services ultimately determine if the organization is successful in their primary mission or purpose.

2.1a - The opportunities in the market, and with customer groups, are key inputs to market driven strategies. The process that identifies many of these opportunities is the customer and market knowledge area processes in 3.1a. The needs, wants, desires and maybe more importantly the priorities that drive purchase decisions are all key inputs to this analysis 2.1a(2).

7.1a – The customer focused results presented in Area to Address 7.1a should include results for each key customer or market segment and/or group. In addition, the results should include results on the key requirements and expectations for each segment and group.

7.2a – Results for the product and service features that are identified in 3.1a(2) should be included in the product and service results presented in Area to Address 7.2a.

6.1a – Ultimately, the prioritized product and service features are used to determine value creation process requirements and to identify key areas of process control to ensure the value creation processes produce the desired results.

Transformation	Leaders

 THOUGHTS FOR LEADERS

An organization can not truly be agile unless bad news flows up. For example, if the customer has requirements, if the customer has a problem, if employees have a problem, if there is a problem in the marketplace, the quicker the organization can make a decision and act on these issues, the more competitive they are going to be.

It is almost impossible to think about true agility unless bad news flows up (quickly).

Execution Excellence

Part **3**

Overview

Execution Excellence is composed of the organization's approaches to process management, building customer relationships and the people that make it all happen. In other words - how the right people working together get the right stuff to the right places at the right times.

Process Management

The process management system is composed of the identification, design, measurement and control, and improvement of the organization's Value Creation Processes and Support Processes.

- How do you design your products, services, and processes?
- How do you execute and control your processes?
- How do you improve your processes?

Process Management Areas to Address:

> 6.1a – Value Creation Processes
> 6.2a – Support Processes

Building Customer Relationships

The relationship building system is composed of the access mechanisms and processes for the customer to seek information, conduct business, complain, and the methods to determine their satisfaction and dissatisfaction.

- How do you build relationships with your customers?
- How do you know how satisfied your customers are?

Customer Focus Areas to Address:

> 3.2a – Building Customer Relationships
> 3.2b – Customer Satisfaction Determination

Human Resource System

The people systems are composed of the work systems (organization and management of work, employee performance management system, and hiring and career progression); employee learning and motivation approaches (education training, and development along with motivation and career development); and employee well-being and satisfaction approaches (work environment and employee support and satisfaction).

- How do you acquire, organize and utilize your employees?
- How do you develop and motivate your employees?
- How do you ensure the well-being and satisfaction of your employees?

Human Resource Areas to Address:

> 5.1a – Organization and Management of Work
> 5.1b – Employee Performance Management System
> 5.1c – Hiring and Career Progression
> 5.2a – Employee Education, Training, and Development
> 5.2b – Motivation and Career Development
> 5.3a – Work Environment
> 5.3b – Employee Support and Satisfaction

6.1a	Value Creation Processes

| *Orientation* | New Users |

 FOUNDATION

Value Creation Processes 6.1a – Introduction

For years, Baldrige has used several different approaches to describe this Process Management Category. This has included terms such as core processes, product and services processes, supplier processes, support processes, and others. Currently, Category 6 discusses two types of processes:

- Value creation processes – these are the processes which are key in the creation of products or services that your external customers will consume.

- Support processes – these are all other processes in the organization. Sometimes Support Processes are called "enabling processes" by organizations. The feeling is that these are the processes which enable a process which produce the products and services external customers consume.

As an overview, Item 6.1 discusses the development and evaluation processes, their management and improvement. Questions include how the organization determines their process is an evaluation creation process, and requests a listing of the processes. Additionally, the criteria seek to understand why these were designated as Value Creation processes, and how they contribute to the value and success of the business.

Then the criteria seek to understand how the requirements of the Value Creation processes are determined and met. Typically the requirements of a process are determined by the user of the process. In this case, the external customers determine the requirements for product and service related processes. As the processes are designed to create products and services, the criteria ask how the organization ensures the performance levels expected will actually be achieved. This may require concurrent design (involving both designers and users or manufacturing).

Although the criteria never use the words "statistical process control - SPC" the language does ask how the organization knows the processes stay in-control. That is, how does the organization keep the processes from incurring so much variation that the output of the process is inconsistent enough to not meet customers' requirements or expectations, or produces inconsistencies which are considered to be unfavorable by the customer. This requires in-process measures which tell the organization what is happening in the process on a time interval short enough that the organization can take actions to change process performance before it is noticed by the external customer.

One question, which is frequently misunderstood, is "how do you minimize overall costs associated with inspections, tests, and process performance audits, as appropriate?" Sometimes organizations respond to this by saying "fire the inspectors." This misses the entire point since the criteria are aiming at increasing the control over variation to decrease variation, obtain process control, and therefore need less inspection.   Finally, Item 6. 1 refers to how the organization achieves its performance by improving the Value Creation processes.   This, as with other aspects of the criteria, needs to be a systematic process. This is what some companies call the "process to improve processes."

EXAMPLE

Value Creation Processes 6.1a - Example Practices

Motorola CGISS – **(Baldrige Recipient 2002)**

Motorola customer input drives product development. Motorola follows a robust market and product planning process known as M-Gates. The first 5 gates are focused on getting direct market and customer input to develop business cases and make fact based portfolio management decisions.

Input from these gates is then "fed" into the product development phases of the M-Gate process. This ensures that valuable engineering development resources are managed appropriately.

6.1a Motorola CGISS - Customer Needs Drive Product Development

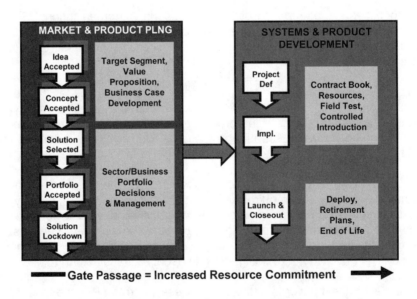

After product development, there is a focused effort for launching the product into the market or to specific customers and managing the end-of-life of a product for continued customer satisfaction.

At all phases, customer input is solicited and market conditions analyzed to ensure they remain committed to developing products that are driven from current customer requirements.

Source: Motorola Presentation - Quest for Excellence 2003

EXAMPLE

Value Creation Processes 6.1a - Example Practices

Dana Spicer Driveshaft – **(Baldrige Recipient 2000)**

Dana Spicer Driveshaft uses an Advanced Technology Process which drives ideas down a dual path in the organization. This helps the company ensure that both product and innovations are considered, proofed, tested and effectively implemented.

This dual path approach also merges the engineering and manufacturing efforts to ensure that both are ready for the changes the advanced technology represents.

As a final step before implementation both paths are merged into an integrated Advanced Quality Planning Process, which ensures that engineering, manufacturing, product and process considerations are effectively integrated.

The Advanced Product Quality Planning (APQP) process ensures that all products and services and related production and delivery processes are aligned with the needs of the customers served.

DESIGN PROCESSES

Product design begins early in the process and produces engineering drawings, specifications, and any special processing or customer requirements. Production and delivery process design begin only slightly later, allowing them to simultaneously develop or modify production process flowcharts, work instructions, process control plans, and delivery requirements and standards, including packaging, labeling, and shipping instructions.

Customers and selected suppliers are an integral part of the APQP process. Customer-driven product development programs are based on a customer's particular needs for a vehicle or platform, and customers typically participate as active team members. Dana employs a variety of other methods to solicit customer input and communicate requirements to the APQP team.

Dana tracks supplier activities as part of the overall project plan to assure timely delivery of newly developed products. They also review and respond to changing customer and market requirements at specific steps in the process, although they can also be addressed at any time. Changes are implemented through specific engineering change procedures, and result in drawing and specification updates. Changes in production or delivery requirements are implemented through modifications to purchase orders, process control plans, SOP's, work instructions, and packaging and shipping instructions.

New technology is continually incorporated into products, services, and production/delivery systems. Inputs include trade shows, benchmarking, competitive product analysis, customer and supplier inputs and developmental programs with universities. Outputs include improved products and processes, as well as production and delivery requirements. Specific groups and task forces present and recommend implementation yearly in Hellweek plans and on an ongoing basis to the Strategic Business Council for approval.

PRODUCTION AND DELIVERY PROCESSES

QUALITY AND PRODUCT PERFORMANCE REQUIREMENTS

Dana employs Design Failure Modes and Effects Analysis (DFMEA) and Process Failure Mode and Effects Analysis (PFMEA), to ensure that all appropriate specifications and performance requirements are incorporated into the manufacturing, production and assembly processes. Significant Characteristics (SC) identify special processing requirements or controls where required. These requirements are deployed through procedures, work instructions, FMEA's, control plans, inspection instructions, process control sheets, and similar methods.

DELIVERY PERFORMANCE REQUIREMENTS

Delivery performance requirements and expectations are communicated to production facilities through direct customer contact, contract review procedures, APQP team meetings, and/or sales personnel. Requirements are deployed through purchase orders or contracts, customer packaging and shipping specifications, written or electronic work instructions, and other media based upon customer needs.

PERFORMANCE REQUIREMENTS

Sales personnel and direct customer input provide projected volumes, daily scheduling requirements, target costs, and other related information that production facilities use to establish productivity and other efficiency-related requirements. These inputs are balanced with capacity and production capabilities, desired profit margins, and manufacturing costs. Facility management then establishes performance standards and associated measurements necessary to meet performance targets.

COORDINATION AND TESTING

Design Verification Plan and Report process helps to coordinate and document testing activity and ensure timely, trouble-free introduction of products. The APQP team also develops the test plan that includes design and production process validation testing.

Once Design Validation (DV) testing verifies the integrity of the product design, Engineering releases the details needed for prototype parts to be built. Parts are evaluated using applicable industry, or regulatory required tests, as well as internal lab testing according to the Joint Testing Specifications and Joint Testing Procedures. DV testing is performed on lab samples, as well as pre-production prototypes, and is often followed by field-testing the product in the intended application.

Production Trial Runs (PTR's) assure that product designs can be produced at the required volumes and to the required level of process capability. Customers are often involved in PTR planning and are often present on site during the actual process.

During the PTR, production-ready processes are used to produce a predetermined quantity of parts, and process capability is assessed, including packaging and labeling requirements. Parts are measured for conformance to all specifications as part of the Production Part Approval Process, and samples are sent to the engineering lab for Production Validation (PV) testing.

EVALUATING AND IMPROVING PROCESSES

The overall APQP process is evaluated during annual internal audits and formal third-party assessments of quality systems. At the end of a major program launch, they hold "lessons learned" sessions with customers and APQP teams. Any ideas for improvement are then shared at Dana's Best Processes Day, Technology Roundtable sessions, corporate quality councils, and various methods of sharing with team members, including the program management database on the division intranet.

To monitor and maintain process integrity, facilities develop process control plans, Standard Operating Procedures (SOP's), work instructions, inspection instructions, and packaging/shipping instructions. Control plans indicate those characteristics that contribute to form, function, and fit and are derived from FMEA's. Where appropriate, engineering identifies potential Key Control Characteristics (KCC's) or SC's for products.

Measurement system reliability is ensured through traceability to recognized international standards, and through the performance of measurement system variation studies (GR&R's). SPC or other approved control methods are used in facilities to monitor quality characteristics. Operators and cell technicians are empowered to correct out of control conditions or to shut down an operation if necessary. In addition, a production planning system is available in all production locations to address scheduling and inventory management.

INCORPORATING FEEDBACK AND IMPROVEMENTS

Customer input is continually solicited from all customer disciplines in the form of verbal requests, CAR's, performance ratings, or, more commonly now, through APQP meetings. The customers' performance requirement rating feedback is tracked locally and reported monthly. Every quarter, each operating unit's performance is reviewed in corporate Continuous Improvement Meetings where general managers are held accountable for customers' perceptions of their operating unit's performance.

In addition, QS-9000 registration and semi-annual surveillance audits have also proven to be beneficial in the evaluation and improvement of Spicer Driveshaft product and service processes.

Part of the process improvement cycle is evaluating the effectiveness of the business process implementation. This information is received through various means, including customer feedback and customer satisfaction surveys (primarily the NCSS).

Processes are systematically evaluated and improved to achieve better performance. Evaluation is accomplished through TQM and other measurements previously discussed. Improvement is accomplished through a variety of activities. Some of these include Process Improvement team and Blitz team activities, benchmarking, alternative technology, process analysis, and information sharing. Teams are active in process simplification, waste reduction, research and development, and exploration of alternative materials and technologies.

Source: Dana (2001) pp. 29 - 31

EXAMPLE

Value Creation Processes 6.1a - Example Practices

KARLEE – (Baldrige Recipient 2000) - Process Improvement Process

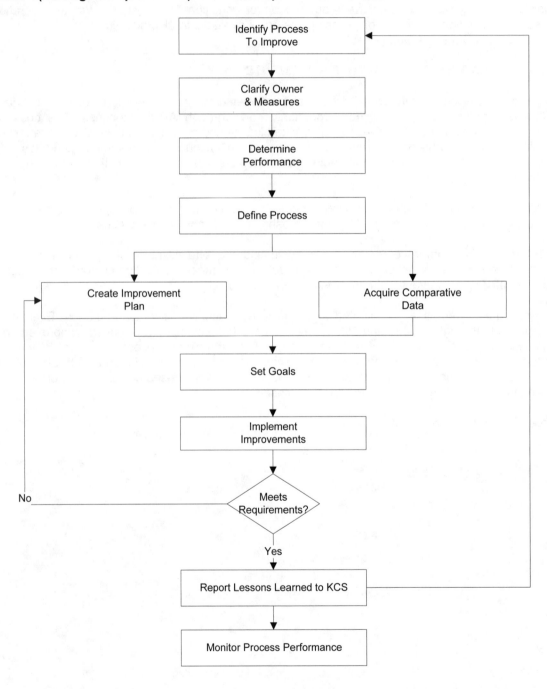

Source: KARLEE (2001) p. 27

Diagnosis	

 QUESTIONS

Value Creation Processes 6.1a - Baldrige Criteria Questions

Identify Key Value Creation Processes (1)

- *HOW does your organization determine its KEY VALUE CREATION PROCESSES?*
- *What are your organization's KEY product, service, and business PROCESSES for creating or adding VALUE?*
- *HOW do these PROCESSES create VALUE for the organization, your CUSTOMERS, and your other KEY STAKEHOLDERS?*
- *HOW do they contribute to profitability and business success?*

Note 1: Your key Value Creation processes are those most important to "running your business" and maintaining or achieving a sustainable competitive advantage. They are the processes that involve the majority of your organization's employees and produce customer, stockholder, and other key stakeholder value. They include the processes through which your organization adds greatest value to its products and services. They also include the business processes most critical to adding value to the business itself, resulting in success and growth.

Note 2: Key Value Creation processes differ greatly among organizations, depending on many factors. These factors include the nature of your products and services, how they are produced and delivered, technology requirements, customer and supplier relationships and involvement, outsourcing, importance of research and development, role of technology acquisition, information and knowledge management, supply chain management, mergers and acquisitions, global expansion, and sales and marketing. Responses to Item 6.1 should be based upon the most critical requirements and processes for your products, services, and business.

Determine Requirements (2)

- *HOW do you determine KEY VALUE CREATION PROCESS requirements, incorporating input from CUSTOMERS, suppliers, and partners, as appropriate?*
- *What are the KEY requirements for these PROCESSES?*

Process Design (3)

- *HOW do you design these PROCESSES to meet all the KEY requirements?*
- *HOW do you incorporate new technology and organizational knowledge into the design of these PROCESSES?*
- *HOW do you incorporate CYCLE TIME, PRODUCTIVITY, cost control, and other efficiency and effectiveness factors into the design of these PROCESSES?*
- *HOW do you implement these PROCESSES to ensure they meet design requirements?*

Performance Measures (4)

- *What are your KEY PERFORMANCE MEASURES or INDICATORS used for the control and improvement of your VALUE CREATION PROCESSES?*
- *HOW does your day-to-day operation of these PROCESSES ensure meeting KEY PROCESS requirements?*
- *HOW are in-process MEASURES used in managing these PROCESSES?*
- *HOW is CUSTOMER, supplier, and partner input used in managing these PROCESSES, as appropriate?*

Minimize Costs (5)

- *HOW do you minimize overall costs associated with inspections, tests, and PROCESS or PERFORMANCE audits, as appropriate?*
- *HOW do you prevent defects and rework, and minimize warranty costs, as appropriate?*

Process Improvement (6)

- *HOW do you improve your VALUE CREATION PROCESSES to achieve better PERFORMANCE, to reduce variability, to improve products and services, and to keep the PROCESSES current with business needs and directions?*
- *HOW are improvements shared with other organizational units and PROCESSES?*

Note 3: To achieve better process performance and reduce variability, you might implement approaches such as a Lean Enterprise System, Six Sigma methodology, use of ISO 9000:2000 standards, or other process improvement tools.

Note 4: To provide as complete and concise a response as possible for your key Value Creation processes, you might want to use a tabular format identifying the key processes and the attributes of each as called for in questions 6.1a(1)–6.1a(6).

NIST (2004) p. 24

WORKSHEETS

Value Creation Processes 6.1a - Work Sheets

Describe how your organization identifies and manages its key processes for creating customer value and achieving business success and growth.

6.1a(various) - Value Creation Processes – Key Components

Value Creation Process (6.1a(1))	Process To Determine Requirements (6.1a(2))	Requirements (6.1a(2))	Measures (6.1a(4))	Outputs	Customers and Markets
1.					
n.					

6.1a (various) - Value Creation Processes – Design to Improvement

Question	Approach Description
1. *Process To Determine Key Value Creation Processes (6.1a (1))*	
2. *Design Process (6.1a (3))*	
3. *Incorporate new technology and organizational knowledge (6.1a (3))*	
4. *Incorporate cycle time, productivity, cost controls, etc. (6.1a (3))*	
5. *Implementation process (6.1a (3))*	
6. *Use of in-process measure to ensure the process meets requirements (6.1a (4))*	
7. *Minimize overall costs with inspections, tests, etc. (6.1a (5))*	
8. *Process improvement (6.1a (6))*	
9. *Sharing of knowledge gained from improvement activities (6.1a (6))*	

ASSESSMENT

Value Creation Processes 6.1a – Diagnostic Questions

Rating Scale:

0 - **No Process** in place - We are not doing this
1 - **Reacting to Problems** - Using a Basic (Primarily Reactive) Process
2 - **Systematic Process** – We use a systematic process that has been improved
3 - **Aligned** – We use a process that aligns our activities from top to bottom
4 - **Integrated** – We use a process that is integrated with other processes across the organization
5 - **Benchmark** - We are the Benchmark!
DK - Don't Know

		0	1	2	3	4	5	DK
1.	The core (i.e., operations) processes through which products and services are delivered to our external and internal customers have been defined.	0	1	2	3	4	5	DK
2.	There are measures to track the performance of the core processes through which products and services are delivered.	0	1	2	3	4	5	DK
3.	Core processes are continuously reviewed and improved to reduce cycle time, increase effectiveness, reduce cost & improve performance.	0	1	2	3	4	5	DK
4.	The organization has a systematic process for designing and launching new products and services.	0	1	2	3	4	5	DK
5.	We have a process / methodology through which we manage product & service processes	0	1	2	3	4	5	DK
6.	The organization has a defined, systematic process for improving processes.	0	1	2	3	4	5	DK

Design

BLUEPRINT

Value Creation Processes 6.1a – Blueprint

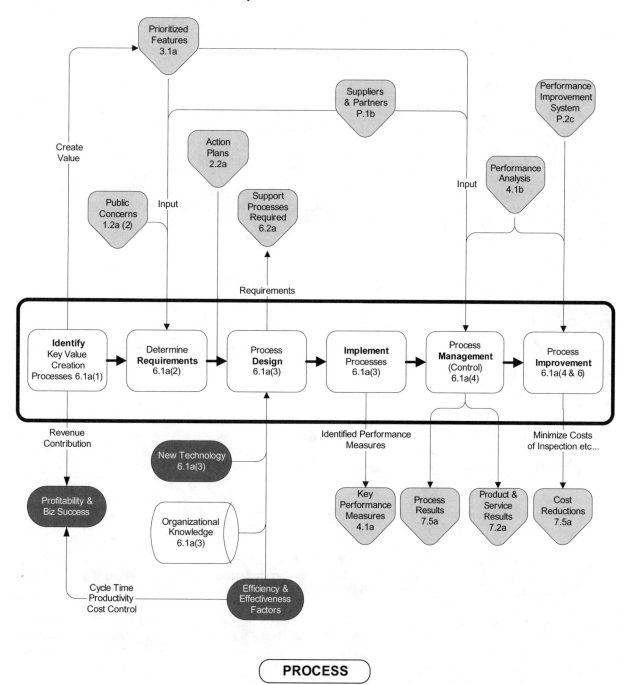

The Value Creation processes are the core of the organization. They are the central idea of what creates value for the primary benefit of external customers. The design, implementation and eventual improvement of these processes is broken down to six key components. First is the definition of the key processes themselves. What processes in the organization are the key 'supply chain' processes that deliver value to the primary beneficiaries?

After the key Value Creation processes are identified the next step is to determine the requirements for the processes. These requirements are formed by the customer. This is the knowledge gained from the processes in Area to Address 3.1a. In addition to the customers' requirements there are other requirements from groups such as the investors, the employees, the suppliers and partners, and of course the public.

With the requirements in hand, the next step is to design the processes which will develop the products and services to meet those requirements. After the processes are designed the next step is to actually implement processes and then manage or control their performance.

Next are the steps required for measuring performance, analyzing the performance and using those results to make adjustments to achieve the desired performance. Finally, how the organization actually improves the processes is addressed. There is a direct link between the continuous improvement of processes and the performance improvement system described in P.2c(1).

The design of a Value Creation process is sometimes more art than science. The synthesis and integration of the multiple stakeholders' needs, wants, and desires is not a simple task. This is because these needs, wants, and desires, are often at odds with one another. The idea here is to design and improve the processes to create sustainable results for these multiple stakeholders. Of course the Value Creation processes cannot perform without a solid base of enablement from the Support Processes (Item 6.2).

 SYSTEM INTEGRATION

Value Creation Processes 6.1a – Linkages

Inputs

1.2a - The public concerns identified in the process described in 1.2a(2) are direct inputs to the process requirements determination step described in 6.1a(2). The output should be in a format that is useful to determining process requirements. In other words 6.a(2) is the internal customer of 1.2a(2).

3.1a - The prioritized product and service features identified in 3.1a are used to determine value creation process requirements and to identify key areas of process control to ensure the value creation processes produce the desired results.

2.2a – The action plans identified in 2.2a often call for additions, changes, and improvement to products, services, and the processes that create them. In this case the value creation processes are refined or changed to assist in accomplishing the strategic objectives.

P.1b – The suppliers and partners are key inputs to both the requirements determination process 6.1a(2) and the process management activities 6.1a(4). First, the suppliers' and partners' capabilities and needs should be part of the requirements process to ensure the supply chain works as an integrated system. Second, since suppliers and partners are sometimes working side-by-side or even doing key tasks in the value chain by themselves, they may also need to be part of the process management design and execution activities.

P.2c – The process improvement methods described in 6.1a(4 & 6) should be consistent with and based on the overall approach to performance improvement described in the profile.

4.1b – The performance analysis described in 4.1b directly supports both process management (control) and process improvement. The analysis described here in 6.1a should be consistent with the description of analysis in 4.b.

Outputs

6.2a – The identification of the key support processes and their requirements is driven by the needs of the value creation processes and their requirements. There is an internal customer-supplier relationship between support processes and value creation processes.

4.1a – The selection and alignment of performance measures for daily operations 4.1a(1) is driven by the key process requirements and the in-process control requirements.

7.5a – The results (levels, trends, comparisons) for key in-process and control measures should be included in the results displayed in area 7.5a.

7.2a – The output or key final product and service results (levels, trends, comparisons) should be presented in area 7.2a.

7.5a – Process improvement results (levels, trends, comparisons) including cost reductions should be included in the results presented in 7.5a.

| *Transformation* | **Leaders** |

 ## THOUGHTS FOR LEADERS

Some organizations have documented seven hundred processes in their organization, and they do not try to be world-class in all processes.

A small number of those processes may interface with their external customers. Those are the processes which need to be world-class.

In fact, some organizations sit down with their customers every year and redefine the key customer-facing processes.

They feel that improvement is based on what the customer cares about. Customer-focused processes may have to be re-certified because they are the processes the customer says the organization needs to "be really good at."

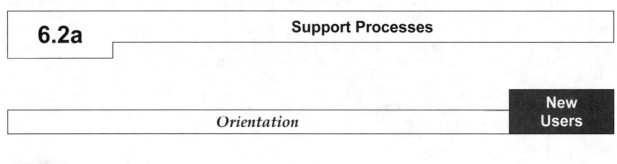

6.2a | **Support Processes**

Orientation | **New Users**

FOUNDATION

Support Processes 6.2a – Introduction

For years, Baldrige has had several different ways to describe the Process Management Category. This includes processes such as core processes, product and services processes, supplier processes, support processes, and others. Currently, Category 6 discusses two types of processes:

Value Creation Processes – Processes that end up in products or services that your external customers will consume.

Support processes – All other processes in the organization. Sometimes Support Processes are called "enabling processes" by organizations. The feeling is that these are the processes which enable a process which produces the products and services external customers consume. As an overview, Item 6.2 discusses the development evaluation processes, their management, and their improvement. Questions include how the organization determines their process is a Support Process, and requests a listing of the Support Processes. Additionally, the criteria seek to understand why these were designated as Support Processes, and how they contribute to the value and success of the business.

The criteria seek to understand how the requirements of the Support Processes are determined. Typically the requirements of a process are determined by the user of a process. In this case, the *internal* customers determine the requirements, and the processes design the internally focused product and service related processes. As the processes are designed to create products and services, the criteria ask how the organization ensures the performance levels expected will actually be achieved. This may require concurrent design (involving both designers and users).

Although the criteria never use the words "statistical process control - SPC" the language does ask how the organization knows the processes stay in-control. That is, how does the organization keep the processes from incurring so much variation that the output of the process is inconsistent enough to not meet internal customers' requirements or expectations, or producing inconsistencies which are considered to be unfavorable by the customer? This requires in-process measures which tell the organization what is happening in the process on a time interval short enough that the organization can take actions to change process performance before it is noticed by the external customer.

One question, which is frequently misunderstood is "how do you minimize overall costs associated with inspections, tests, and process performance audits, as appropriate?" Sometimes organizations respond to this by saying "fire the inspectors." This misses the entire point since the criteria are aiming at increasing the control over variation to decrease variation, obtain process control, and therefore need less inspection. Finally, Item 6.2 refers to how the organization achieves its performance by improving the Support Processes. This, as with other aspects of the criteria, needs to be a systematic process. Some companies refer to this as the "process to improve processes."

EXAMPLE

Support Processes 6.2a - Example Practices

KARLEE – (Baldrige Recipient 2000)

The table below shows the support team processes with their process requirements. Support process owners determine their requirements by analyzing input received from the key stakeholders of their processes. Input is gathered internally through satisfaction surveys and at meetings such as KSC meetings, Leaders meetings, and Safety Committee meetings.

Process owners work with the other members of their own team to determine key requirements internal to the department or cell.

The need for new support services or upgrades to services is determined by the SEL and KSC teams during strategic planning and at quarterly reviews. New support services required for manufacturing processes are defined and designed as part of the new service design process.

For internal support services, the department establishes a team to design or improve the service. For company-wide projects, such as the implementation of the new computer system, a cross-functional team is formed by the SEL/KSC to determine requirements and design the process. After determining requirements, process owners collaborate with members of their support area to design the processes associated with the area. This includes determining and implementing the appropriate process and output measures necessary to evaluate support process performance.

The support teams maintain the performance of support processes by monitoring and improving key process measures. Each team has process goals and measures tied to corporate goals and to external/internal customer requirements. All teams have goals to achieve training hours per team member and leader, to minimize safety incidents, and to reduce cycle time. The table below shows representative process measures for each support process.

Support teams conduct surveys of internal customers to gain feedback on service levels and satisfaction. The materials team tracks problems with the procurement process, including problems with upstream processes. All support teams receive the results of external customer surveys.

Support process owners work with the KSC to assess and improve their process performance using the Process Improvement methodology shown in the previous area to address.

SEL and KSC members assist support teams in identifying opportunities and targets for benchmarking to achieve breakthrough improvements. Support team members are encouraged to research alternative technologies to help streamline tasks and improve customer support.

KARLEE Support Processes

Support Team	Processes	Requirements	Measures
Materials	Procedure, track, and expedites materials and services Maintain inventory accuracy	Purchase request response time Accurate reporting of supplier delivery performance Accurate inventory measurements	Inventory accuracy Scheduling performance Supplier delivery & quality ratings
Maintenance	Establish and maintain service schedules for all KARLEE vehicles, machinery, buildings	Reduced equipment down-time and reduced number of accidents resulting in injury	Maintenance cycle time Machine down time # Accidents resulting in injury
Accounting	All accounting processes	Month-end cycle time A/P cycle time A/R cycle time Payroll accuracy	A/p cycle time A/R cycle time Payroll Accuracy Month-end cycle time
Information Systems	System installation Computer training System support	System and data availability Ease and speed of data access	Computer down time Data access time
Team Resources	Recruiting Orientation and training Team member surveys Maintain benefit programs Maintain team member records	Accurate match of new team members to job requirements Response time for data	Team member turn-over & absenteeism rates Cycle time for data distribution
Training	Maintain and publish in-house training schedule Coordinate resources to meet training schedules Maintain records of community service Develop and maintain training materials Assist in classroom training	Types and number of classes provided Accurate records of team member training and community support	Accurate training records by department Class attendee evaluations Accurate community service records

Source: KARLEE (2001) pp. 27 – 29

EXAMPLE

Support Processes 6.2a - Example Practices

ST Microelectronics

Each year *ST Microelectronics* creates/updates the "Supplier Quality Business Plan" in which they highlight past year achievements and goals for the future. The plan for coming-year audits, improvements, and objectives are outlined as a roadmap for supplier management process.

Partnership with suppliers is a key strategic element in their Total Quality Management philosophy. They consider suppliers as a part of the company; a partner with whom they have a common goal to succeed. It is this approach that has born partnership with suppliers in openness of information and shoulder-to-shoulder approach to solving problems. The supplier lifecycle is a repeating cycle that includes:

- Specification
- Supplier Selection
- Qualification
- Agreements
- Contract
- Production
- Performance Monitoring
- Supplier Benchmarking
- Improvement Programs

All key suppliers must have a quality system designed to ensure products and services perform to, and exceed expected results. The fundamental grading system for suppliers is the Materials Suppliers Quality Assurance (MSQA). Each type of supplier is given an attribute specification for materials, equipment performance requirements for manufacturing equipment, and service agreement contract for services.

Each type of supplier is judged by application-specific methods. Material suppliers are judged first through material qualification for needs, and then assessed for their quality system using the MSQA questionnaire. Equipment suppliers are selected based on equipment performance and ability to respond. Their requirements are outlined in a very extensive set of performance, delivery, and support requirements. Partnership with service suppliers is driven through service agreement contracts and standard approach.

Their systematic approach to supplier management is built around providing ongoing assistance to improve suppliers' products and services through joint problem solving, providing training, and awareness. Through the technology roadmap, they work with suppliers in determining future technical needs. Each supplier then develops their roadmap based on their customer's future needs.

All points of material influence on products are evaluated through measures and benchmarking for continuous improvement. In effect, this is a constant and continuous cycle of establishing higher goals, evaluating methods of achieving the goals, and adjusting systems to improve probability for success.

Source: STM (2000) p. 14

QUESTIONS

Support Processes 6.2a - Baldrige Criteria Questions

Identify Key Support Processes (1)

- *HOW does your organization determine its KEY support PROCESSES?*
- *What are your KEY PROCESSES for supporting your VALUE CREATION PROCESSES?*

Note 1: Your key Support Processes are those that are considered most important for support of your organization's Value Creation processes, employees, and daily operations. These might include finance and accounting, facilities management, legal, human resource, project management, and administration processes.

Requirements (2)

- *HOW do you determine KEY support PROCESS requirements, incorporating input from internal and external CUSTOMERS, and suppliers and partners, as appropriate?*
- *What are the KEY requirements for these PROCESSES?*

Process Design (3)

- *HOW do you design these PROCESSES to meet all the KEY requirements?*
- *HOW do you incorporate new technology and organizational knowledge into the design of these PROCESSES?*
- *HOW do you incorporate CYCLE TIME, PRODUCTIVITY, cost control, and other efficiency and effectiveness factors into the design of the PROCESSES?*
- *HOW do you implement these PROCESSES to ensure they meet design requirements?*

Performance Measures (4)

- *What are your KEY PERFORMANCE MEASURES or INDICATORS used for the control and improvement of your support PROCESSES?*
- *HOW does your day-to-day operation of KEY support PROCESSES ensure meeting KEY PERFORMANCE requirements?*
- *HOW are in-process MEASURES used in managing these PROCESSES?*
- *HOW is CUSTOMER, supplier, and partner input used in managing these PROCESSES, as appropriate?*

Minimize Costs (5)

- *HOW do you minimize overall costs associated with inspections, tests, and PROCESS or PERFORMANCE audits, as appropriate?*
- *HOW do you prevent defects and rework?*

Process Improvement (6)

- *HOW do you improve your support PROCESSES to achieve better PERFORMANCE, to reduce variability, and to keep the PROCESSES current with business needs and directions?*
- *HOW are improvements shared with other organizational units and PROCESSES?*

Note 2: The results of improvements in your key Support Processes and key Support Process performance results should be reported in Item 7.5.

NIST (2004) p. 25

 WORKSHEETS

Support Processes 6.2a - Work Sheets

Describe how your organization identifies and manages its key processes for creating customer value and achieving business success and growth.

6.2a (various) – Support Processes – Key Components

Support Process (6.2a(1))	Process To Determine Requirements (6.2a(2))	Requirements (6.2a(2))	Measures (6.2a(4))	Outputs	Customers and Markets
1.					
n.					

6.2a (various) – Support Processes – Design to Improvement

Question	Approach Description
1. Process To Determine Key Value Creation Processes (6.2a (1))	
2. Design Process (6.2a (3))	
3. Incorporate new technology and organizational knowledge (6.2a (3))	
4. Incorporate cycle time, productivity, cost controls, etc. (6.2a (3))	
5. Implementation process (6.2a (3))	
6. Use of in-process measure to ensure the process meets requirements (6.2a (4))	
7. Minimize overall costs with inspections, tests, etc. (6.2a (5))	
8. Process improvement (6.2a (6))	
9. Sharing of knowledge gained from improvement activities (6.2a (6))	

ASSESSMENT

Support Processes 6.2a – Diagnostic Questions

Rating Scale:

0 - **No Process** in place - We are not doing this
1 - **Reacting to Problems** - Using a Basic (Primarily Reactive) Process
2 - **Systematic Process** – We use a systematic process that has been improved
3 - **Aligned** – We use a process that aligns our activities from top to bottom
4 - **Integrated** – We use a process that is integrated with other processes across the organization
5 - **Benchmark** - We are the Benchmark!
DK - Don't Know

1. The core (i.e., operations) and support (i.e., HR & Legal) processes through which products and services are delivered to our external and internal customers have been defined.	0	1	2	3	4	5	DK
2. There are measures to track the performance of critical support processes.	0	1	2	3	4	5	DK
3. Core & support processes are continuously reviewed and improved to reduce cycle time, increase effectiveness, reduce cost & improve performance.	0	1	2	3	4	5	DK
4. On-going cross-functional management (different groups working together) is in place and is effective.	0	1	2	3	4	5	DK
5. We have a process / methodology through which we manage: 1) product & service processes, 2) support processes and 3) other non-product service processes.	0	1	2	3	4	5	DK
6. One department or group cannot be a winner (in our metrics tracking) at the expense of other departments or groups.	0	1	2	3	4	5	DK

BLUEPRINT

Support Processes 6.2a – Blueprint

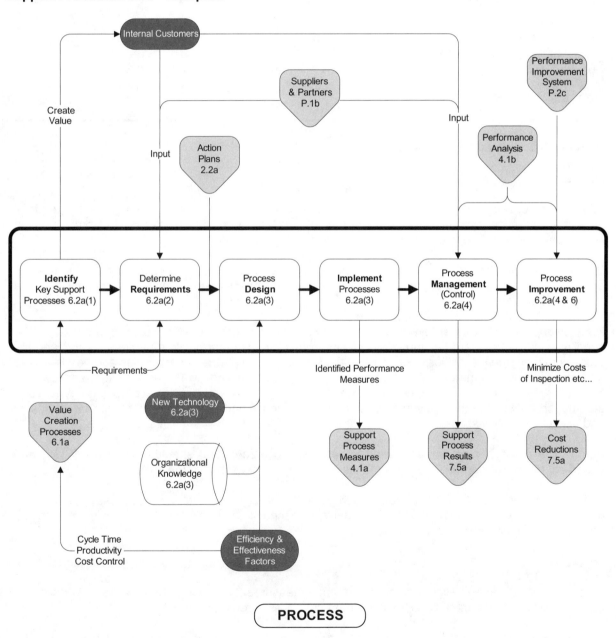

The Support Processes are very similar to the Value Creation processes. The first step is to actually identify the Support Processes that support the Value Creation processes. The fact that they are labeled 'support' does not mean that they are not essential. It is not a question of which processes are more important. It is a question, however, of which processes drive products and services that serve the customer and which ones serve the processes that serve the customer.

The Support Process customers are the Value Creation processes and other Support Processes. Consequently, the requirements for the Support Processes are derived from the needs of the Value Creation processes and other Support Processes. This is probably the only key difference between Value Creation processes and Support Processes - where the requirements are from and who is a customer. From that point on, the design, implementation, management and control, and improvement of the support processes look remarkably like those of the Value Creation processes.

 SYSTEM INTEGRATION

Support Processes 6.2a - Linkages

Inputs

6.1a – The identification of the key support processes and their requirements is driven by the needs of the value creation processes and their requirements. There is an internal customer-supplier relationship between support processes and value creation processes.

2.2a – The action plans identified in 2.2a often call for additions, changes, and improvement to support processes. In this case the support processes are refined or changed to assist in accomplishing the strategic objectives.

P.1b – Suppliers and partners are often engaged in and an integral part of the support processes. The suppliers and partners are key inputs to both the requirements determination process 6.2a(2) and the process management activities 6.2a(4). First, the suppliers' and partners' capabilities and needs should be part of the requirements process to ensure the support network works as an integrated system. Second, since suppliers and partners are sometimes working side-by-side or even doing key tasks in the support network by themselves they may also need to be part of the process management design and execution activities.

P.2c – The process improvement methods described in 6.2a(4 & 6) should be consistent with and based on the overall approach to performance improvement described in the profile.

4.1b – The performance analysis described in 4.1b directly supports both process management (control) and process improvement. The analysis described in 6.2a should be consistent with the description of analysis in 4.1b.

Outputs

4.1a – The selection and alignment of performance measures for daily operations 4.1a(1) is driven by the key process requirements and the in-process control requirements.

7.5a – The results (levels, trends, comparisons) for key in-process and control measures should be included in the results displayed in area 7.5a.

7.5a – Process improvement results (levels, trends, comparisons) including cost reductions should be included in the results presented in 7.5a.

Transformation	**Leaders**

 THOUGHTS FOR LEADERS

If leaders allow systems to be rigid, it is the precursor for going out of business. If an organism doesn't grow, it dies. Organizations are very similar. When I hear the argument that says, "systems require you to be very rigid and very inflexible," I think, "That is only true if the leaders really do not understand the power of processes."

Flexible organizations, are like a school of fish. If you see fish in a school and they are swimming, somehow instantly they all seem to be able to change direction in unison. How do they know when to do that? Flexible, agile organizations using processes can do this.

You cannot change direction quickly within a large organization unless you have processes. When everyone knows how to use the process, you can define a change and let everyone know about the change. The organizations that can change more quickly, sooner or later win in the marketplace. They are able to focus more quickly on customer requirements and implement any changes in their own processes more quickly. More importantly, they are going to beat their competitors to the customer.

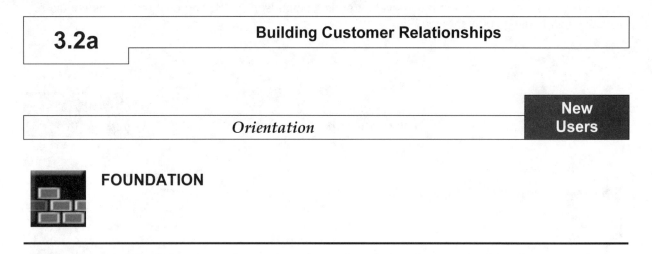

3.2a

Building Customer Relationships

Orientation

New Users

FOUNDATION

Building Customer Relationships (3.2a) – Introduction

Area to Address 3.2a describes the overall relationship with the customer. This is the umbrella relationship that organizations have with the customers and describes how they find customers, develop them, support them, and describes the activities which will drive customer satisfaction and subsequently customer loyalty.

Customer relationship building starts with acquiring customers and the process used to meet customers, understand their requirements and expectations, and align the organization to meet and exceed those requirements and expectations. The ultimate objective, as noted in Area to Address 3.2a(1) is to "increase loyalty and repeat business and to gain positive referrals." In the overall relationship with the external customer, the criteria ask how the organization establishes access mechanisms for customers so they can reach the organization whenever they need to seek information, conduct business, or complain. Many organizations set up 800 numbers, 24/7 hotlines, or give customer contact employees home numbers to customers. The first step in this process is to determine what key customers' contact requirements are. Baldrige recognizes that each customer and/or customer group may have different contact requirements and/or different contact preferences. Some customers may wish to be contacted routinely, while others may wish to be left alone. How does the organization know each of these and how do they ensure that all customer contact employees know?

Another inherent part of Area to Address 3.2a is how do key customer employees get the training they need? Although the criteria are not clear on this, it is difficult for the examiners to understand how an organization will support customer contact employees if those employees do not receive the necessary training. In many organizations, when training the customer contact employees, the two groups who are frequently excluded are executives and support staff. Executives, by virtue of their position, often feel as though they already have the customer skills and/or knowledge required. Support staff, even though they may spend a great deal of time in direct contact with customers, are not always viewed as critical to the customer response chain.

Finally, in customer relationship building there are processes which must go into play if the customer is not happy. Area to Address 3.2a(3) clearly indicates that a complaint management process is required. The criteria ask about the process itself, as well as how the process ensures that complaints are solved effectively and promptly.

Some notes about complaints which should not be missed:

- All complaints both formal and informal (possibly a customer mentioning a complaint but unwilling to fill out a complaint form) are collected.

- All complaints which are collected are logged and tracked.
- All complaints which are logged are quickly and effectively administered and closed.
- All complaints closed are closed to the satisfaction of the customer and/or the customer clearly understands what they are complaining about cannot be achieved (and why).
- All complaints are aggregated so they can be analyzed for action. For example, there may be several small complaints which (when added up) constitute an overall concern the company should address. Unless formal and informal complaints are both collected, aggregated and analyzed, the smaller complaints may not reach the attention of the leaders who can initiate action.

As with many other sections of Baldrige, the criteria seek to understand how the approaches to building relationships are kept current. Simply stated, how do you know the steps being taken to develop customer relationships need to be updated? A key indicator might be when expected customer actions are not the actions customers are taking and you are unable to anticipate customer decisions or actions.

EXAMPLE

Building Customer Relationships (3.2a) – Example Practices

BI **– (Baldrige Recipient 1999)**

BI's Service Recovery Process

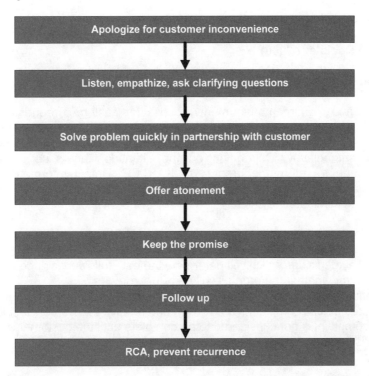

All customer complaints received by BI, regardless of where they came from, are forwarded directly to the Business Unit manager related to the complaint. The Business Unit manager, following the Service Recovery Process, contacts the customer directly for clarification of the issue and additional information. Findings are then communicated to the Account Executive, sales manager, account manager, and all involved Business Unit Associates via an e-mail communication.

BI's Service Recovery Process (cont.)

This process enables the BI team to work in conjunction with the customer to address the failure and provide a solution that meets the customer's needs. A written follow-up of the resolution is shared with all BI team members working with the customer.

Customer complaints from BI's Transactional Customer Satisfaction Index (TCSI) survey are aggregated by the Business Team members. Any overall TCSI score of 7 or less is assigned to a Business Team member who personally contacts the customer and works with them to improve performance. The PIT and QIT process is used to deal with complaints as appropriate.

BI builds loyalty with its customers through open communications and strong relationships with BI's senior leaders, the Account Executive and the Account Team. This is evidenced in the high retention of BI's Top 50 customers – 70% have been with BI for more than five years and of that group, nearly half have been with BI for more than ten years.

Source: BI (2000) pp. 7 - 9

 EXAMPLE

Building Customer Relationships (3.2a) – Example Practices

KARLEE **– (Baldrige Recipient 2000)**

Problem Resolution Process

The figure shows Karlee's return management process for customer requested upgrades/ design changes or repair of defective product. The customer is always kept informed of status and resolution throughout the process. If a problem exists at the customer site, the QA Customer Service Specialist visits the customer immediately. Depending on the situation, the issue is resolved on-site or arrangements are made to return the product to KARLEE. Defect information is entered into a Corrective Action database. The teams use this information to identify process problems and initiate improvement projects to eliminate the cause.

- Karlee's customer problem resolution process, as with many companies, has multiple paths for resolution.
- Some of the key decisions which will determine the path followed include whether field support is required and/or whether the product will be returned.
- As with all effective customer problem resolution (or complaint resolution) processes, their system ensures that all complaints are logged and resolved in a timely fashion.
- Finally, the complaint is not considered to be complete until the customer acknowledges the complaint has been effectively closed.

3.2 KARLEE - Problem Resolution

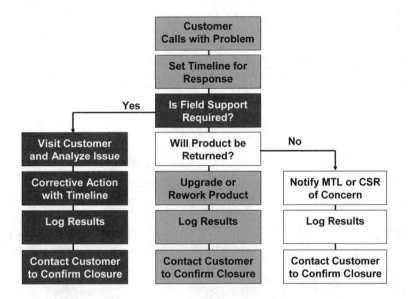

Source: KARLEE (2001) pp. 14 - 15

 EXAMPLE

Building Customer Relationships (3.2a) – Example Practices

Dana Spicer Driveshaft – **(Baldrige Recipient 2000)**

At Dana Spicer Driveshaft, both the Customer Focus Process and program management techniques provide clear direction regarding customer expectations and current product planning development. Members of customer platform teams also use quality system requirements such as QS-9000, customer quality award criteria, feedback from customer, engineering and design meetings, Quality Council, and facilities to fully understand customers' expectations.

They obtain input from current customers and non-customers (former, potential, and competitors' customers) through SD's annual National Customer Satisfaction Survey. This process assists business development and product planning by providing candid, unfiltered comments from customers about their experiences with SD, as well as key requirements they consider to be indicators of their satisfaction or dissatisfaction.

The Account Team Overview Process (ATOP) includes quarterly meetings for all major customers. The team, including CPT members and support personnel, reviews numerous aspects of the relationship, including customer requirements, trends, concerns, and gains or losses of business. With a direct focus on the customer, each group takes a personal interest not only in maintaining the quality of products and services customers receive, but also in improving processes for all involved.

Their DQLP Category 3 team evaluates listening and learning processes, and helps to implement suggestions for improvement. Customer contact requirements include responsiveness and follow-up, ease of access, product knowledge, and knowledge of customer requirements and expectations. They are deployed in several ways, including staff meetings, job descriptions, work instructions, and employee performance reviews for customer contact personnel. The Sales Department uses a system of training new customer contact people, including visits with experienced customer contact people, to become familiar with each customers' own personnel, policies, procedures, and expectations. Contact management performance measures include response to problems, sales representation and engineering support.

3.1 & 3.2 Dana Spicer – Customer Management Process

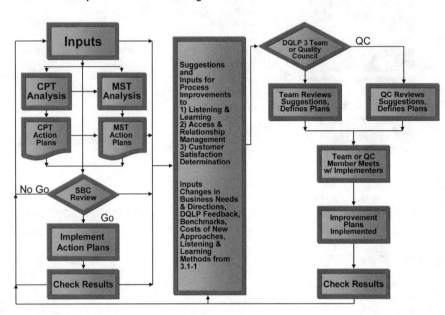

CORRECTIVE ACTION PROCESS - A standardized Corrective Action Report (CAR) process communicates customer complaints throughout the operating unit and ensures prompt follow-up. Complaints are logged into the system, which automatically assigns due dates and monitors resolution time. A built-in escalation mechanism notifies the affected parties of outstanding CAR's, reassuring the customer the problem is being addressed, while incentivizing SD people to resolve the problem.

The CAR system is a closed loop corrective action system, meaning the person who initiates the CAR is the only person who can close it out. Whenever possible, the first contact person receiving the complaint documents the concern and then communicates the complaint and resolution to pertinent parties. The system models customer-preferred problem-solving methods that place heavy emphasis on root cause analysis. Short and long-term corrective and preventive actions are implemented and verified. CAR's are reviewed at weekly quality reviews, quarterly CI meetings and quarterly ATOP meetings to ensure that they have been addressed appropriately. The CAR process itself is evaluated, improved and reviewed for effectiveness via management reviews as required by the Management Responsibility procedure.

ENSURING CUSTOMER ACCESS - SD's customer-focused platform structure provides an efficient vehicle for generating repeat business and positive referral. The MST's maintain focus on each key market, while the CPT's within them maintain an even narrower focus on particular customers. This approach allows team members to develop a one-to-one business relationship with their counterparts at the customer's various locations.

Source: Dana (2001) pp. 15 - 18

QUESTIONS

Customer Relationship Building 3.2a - Baldrige Criteria Questions

Build Relationships (1)

- *HOW do you build relationships to acquire CUSTOMERS, to meet and exceed their expectations, to increase loyalty and repeat business, and to gain positive referrals?*

Note 1. Customer relationship building (3.2a) might include the development of partnerships or alliances with customers.

Access Mechanisms (2)

- *What are your KEY access mechanisms for CUSTOMERS to seek information, conduct business, and make complaints?*
- *HOW do you determine KEY CUSTOMER contact requirements for each mode of CUSTOMER access?*
- *HOW do you ensure that these contact requirements are deployed to all people and PROCESSES involved in the CUSTOMER response chain?*

Complaint Management Process (3)

- *What is your complaint management PROCESS?*
- *HOW do you ensure that complaints are resolved effectively and promptly?*
- *HOW are complaints aggregated and analyzed for use in improvement throughout your organization and by your partners?*

Keeping Current (4)

- *HOW do you keep your APPROACHES to building relationships and providing CUSTOMER access current with business needs and directions?*

NIST (2004) p. 18

WORKSHEETS

Customer Relationship Building 3.2a - Work Sheets

Describe how your organization builds relationships to acquire, satisfy, and retain customers, to increase customer loyalty, and to develop new opportunities. Describe also how your organization determines customer satisfaction.

3.2a (1) - Relationship Building

Approach to Relationship Building

Note: This Should Be A System To Build Relationships To: 1) Acquire Customers; 2) Meet/Exceed Expectations ; 3) Increase Loyalty; 4) Increase Repeat Business; And To 5) Gain Positive Referrals.

3.2a (2) - Key Access Mechanisms

Access Mechanisms	How Your Determine Customer Contact Requirements	How You Deploy To All Customer Contact Personnel	How You Verify Deployment To All Appropriate People And Processes
Seek Information			
Conduct Business			
Complain			

3.2a (3) - Complaint Management

Complaint Management Process		
Complaint Process Step (In Sequence)	Who Is Involved	How The Step Is Measured
Complaint Aggregation and Analysis		

3.2a (4) - Keeping Current

Keeping Relationship Building Approaches Current with Changing Needs		
Relationship Building Process Step (In Sequence)	Who Is Involved	How The Step Is Measured

ASSESSMENT

Customer Relationship Building 3.2a – Diagnostic Questions

Rating Scale:

0 - **No Process** in place - We are not doing this
1 - **Reacting to Problems** - Using a Basic (Primarily Reactive) Process
2 - **Systematic Process** – We use a systematic process that has been improved
3 - **Aligned** – We use a process that aligns our activities from top to bottom
4 - **Integrated** – We use a process that is integrated with other processes across the organization
5 - **Benchmark** - We are the Benchmark!
DK - Don't Know

1.	There is clear information and easy access for customers who seek assistance, have complaints, concerns, suggestions, etc.	0 1 2 3 4 5 DK

2.	There is a systematic complaint resolution process in place which ensures rapid and effective handling of all complaints and problems.	0 1 2 3 4 5 DK

3.	The complaint resolution process ensures aggregation and analysis of all complaint data to identify and eliminate root causes of problems.	0 1 2 3 4 5 DK

Design | **Advanced Users**

BLUEPRINT

Customer Relationship Building 3.2a – Blueprint

While it is important to execute Value Creation and Support Processes to achieve high levels of quality and performance, at the same time it is critical to build a relationship with the customers. The customer relationship building processes consist of three key paths: 1) seeking information, 2) conducting business, and 3) complaining when things do not go right. Each of these three paths follows a fairly similar sequence of activities.

The first step is the identification of the access mechanism for the path. The second step is to identify the contact requirements for that specific path and access method mechanism. The third step for each access mechanism and contact requirement are the requirements for the people and processes to implement those requirements. Finally, how the organization evaluates and improves the mechanisms, the requirements, and the people and processes for each path should be based on the performance improvement system described in the profile.

Customer Relationship Building 3.2a – Blueprint

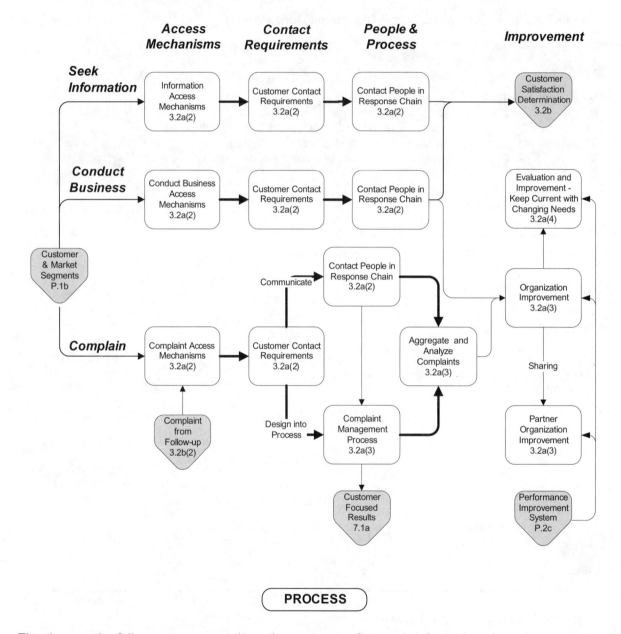

The three paths follow a sequence where the customers first seek information about the products and services, then actually conduct their business by ordering and receiving the products and services, and finally if things are not exactly the way they would like them to be, they complain.

The experience of doing business with the organization, the ease of the access mechanisms, the way in which the customers are dealt with by the customer contact employees, and the ease with which the processes meet the customer's needs all go into determining the overall customer experience with the organization.

This experience and the degree to which it meets the customer's needs will impact the motivation for the customer to do business again (repeat business) and will also impact the motivation for the customer to tell their friends (referral business).

 SYSTEM INTEGRATION

Customer Relationship Building 3.2a – Linkages

Inputs

P.1b – The customer relationship building process – seek information, conduct business, and complain – should be designed to serve the key customer and market segments and groups identified in the profile.

3.2b(2) – Occasionally, the customer follow-up activities after a transaction 3.2b(2) will generate a complaint. The system should be designed to "trigger" the complaint process here in 3.2a when that happens.

P.2c – The three improvement activities included here in 3.2a(3 and 4) should be consistent with and based on the performance improvement approaches described in the profile.

Outputs

3.2b – Customer satisfaction with their experience using the access mechanisms to seek information, conduct business, and complain, are key elements in the overall customer experience and should therefore be included in the customer satisfaction determination processes.

7.1a – Complaints that are captured, aggregated and analyzed are part of customer dissatisfaction and should be included in the results in area 7.1a.

THOUGHTS FOR LEADERS

One of the areas where Baldrige addresses approaches which can be both "formal and informal," is in external customer complaints. Typically, in that situation, formal complaints are received when a customer uses the formal complaint process. Informal complaints might be received by your organization in a different way, such as a customer walking by and mentioning a concern to an employee.

High-performing organizations get customer input (complaints or complements) any way they can: both formal and informal. If anybody in the organization hears a comment from a customer, everybody in the organization has access to that information. That means taking informal complaints and putting them into your database so they are accessible by all appropriate employees.

When Baldrige refers to formal and informal, for some organizations that translates to what is documented or not documented. Many high performing organizations feel if you can take some of the informal characteristics of the business and effectively translate them into the organizational documentation, you become more competitive.

3.2b	**Customer Satisfaction Determination**

 FOUNDATION

Customer Satisfaction Determination 3.2b – Introduction

Once the organization has developed its overall relationship with the customer (Item 3.2a), has segmented customers, and determined their needs and expectations (Item 3.1), Baldrige asks how you know customers are satisfied and/or loyal. There is an understanding in the Performance Excellence community that satisfied customers may or may not return to buy your products and services. Loyal customers, however, do return to repurchase your products and services (hence the term loyalty). In the final analysis, the criteria are trying to understand whether the organization can correlate its actions to the customers' behavior.

Customer satisfaction determination starts by asking how you determine customer satisfaction or dissatisfaction. These determination methods can be different for different customers and/or different customer groups since those customer groups may have different businesses and at a minimum may have different requirements. The criteria go on to ask how you know if you are exceeding customer requirements (another way to drive customer loyalty) and if you are able to "secure their future business."

Another part of the criteria asks what your relationship is with the customer after providing products, services, or transactions. The classic example of this is to call the customer after the product or service is delivered to understand their satisfaction with the overall transaction as well as their initial satisfaction with the product or service.

Baldrige stretches what most organizations can achieve by asking how they obtain or use information about their customer satisfaction, relative to the customer satisfaction of competitors or with industry benchmarks. In some industries, this is very difficult if not impossible to achieve. In some governmental relationships it is illegal to obtain and/or to have this information.

Baldrige is not expecting organizations to do anything that is not 100% honest, ethical, and above board. Nevertheless, there are sources that some organizations have not considered which can help them compare their performance to other high performing groups. These can include asking customers how your organization ranks with their other suppliers. Even if they will not tell you which suppliers perform at which levels, they still may tell you where you rank in the pack.

Finally, Baldrige asks how you keep the survey methods, contact methods, or customer satisfactions/dissatisfaction methods current. How do you know when the customer is tired of your surveys and/or how do you update your customer satisfaction processes?

EXAMPLE

Customer Satisfaction Determination 3.2b - Example Practices

Motorola CGISS **– (Baldrige Recipient 2002)**

Motorola uses a robust process for determining and using Customer Satisfaction which includes setting scorecard goals based on survey results and then:

Developing specific regional action plans for resolving critical actions and setting follow-up/monitoring plans.

Identifying lessons learned and benchmarking competition and comparable industries for comparisons and trend analysis.

3.2b Motorola – Customer Satisfaction Renewal Process

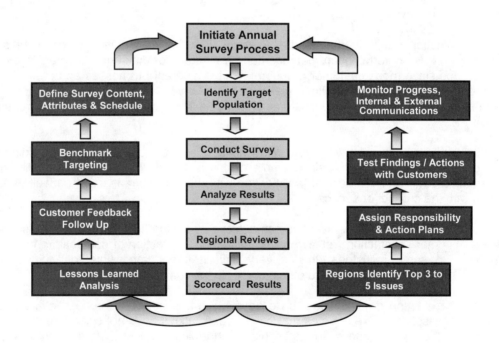

Source: Motorola Presentation – Quest for Excellence 2003

EXAMPLE

Customer Satisfaction Determination 3.2b - Example Practices

Texas Nameplate – (Baldrige Recipient 1998)

TNP uses four types of customer satisfaction determination mechanisms: 1) Perceptive, 2) Behavioral, 3) Contributory, and 4) Direct measures.

Perceptive: Perceptive measures are those that allow customers to tell them how they are doing from their point of view. The company uses an annual customer satisfaction survey as its primary perceptive measure, along with on-site visit results, Quick Response Cards, and formal recognition.

Behavioral: These are measures of customer's actions reflecting their satisfaction. These measures include customer referrals, complaints, nonconformances, and Partners for Success.

Contributory: These are measures of actions that can directly influence customer satisfaction and relationship building. Their primary measures are customer contact employee retention, customer visits, and customer follow-up.

Direct: These are measures of their performance to customer requirements. They include nonconformances, reliability returns, on-time delivery, complaints, cycle time, cost, and quote response times.

Customer dissatisfaction is measured specifically through customer surveys, complaints, lost opportunities, and low scores received on customer scorecards. The Sales team follows up with the customer to correct the cause of the dissatisfaction. Lost opportunities are tracked by the DOIT for trends and corrective actions, if required.

Source: TNP (1999) p. 8

EXAMPLE

Customer Satisfaction Determination 3.2b - Example Practices

Dana Spicer Driveshaft **– (Baldrige Recipient 2000)**

SD's approaches for determining customer satisfaction and dissatisfaction are determined by listening and responding to customer feedback (including complaint data), monitoring customer-generated ratings of performance, studying both internal and external sales figures, in addition to market share numbers, and surveys. These methods provide valid and reliable feedback on customer expectations and on satisfaction with products and services.

SD's annual NCSS gathers data from a statistically significant sample of decision-makers involved in the specification, procurement, and quality certification of driveshaft products at existing and potential customers across all market segments. The survey questions are designed to meet the following objectives:

- Identify customer satisfaction, attribute importance by market
- Provide highly reliable data and information to be used in planning and decision making
- Measure customer satisfaction and dissatisfaction with SD products and services
- Measure customer satisfaction and dissatisfaction with competitors
- Identify customer re-purchase intentions for SD products and services

Validity and reliability are ensured through strict confidentiality, as well as the use of a third party to conduct the survey and tabulate the results. Customers rate eight common attributes in terms of importance, SD performance, and SD's competitors' performance.

The results are statistically analyzed to assess the need for improvement and to initiate the continuous improvement cycle.

An additional customer survey, the Bi-Annual Brand Survey, focuses on brand loyalty and satisfaction levels with the individuals responsible for specifying which driveshaft is used in a particular vehicle. The survey is segregated by market and provides additional information on customer satisfaction with SD and their competitors.

Many customers also employ their own performance rating systems. These Customer Ratings measure SD performance according to various quality and delivery indices, as well as cost savings submissions, and other criteria. They carefully monitor each of these, as well as their delivery performance to their service customers, tracking performance and initiating improvement plans as necessary. These ratings are the key metrics reviewed at the quarterly CI meetings with executive leadership.

In addition to measuring customer satisfaction, they utilize several measurement tools that offer an early warning of potential dissatisfaction. These tools enable SD to take a proactive approach to resolving customer complaints rather than waiting for them to surface through other channels.

Source: Dana (2001) pp. 18 - 19

QUESTIONS

Customer Satisfaction Determination 3.2b - Baldrige Criteria Questions

Determining Customer Satisfaction (1)

- *HOW do you determine CUSTOMER satisfaction and dissatisfaction?*
- *HOW do these determination methods differ among CUSTOMER groups?*
- *HOW do you ensure that your measurements capture actionable information for use in exceeding your CUSTOMERS' expectations, securing their future business, and gaining positive referrals?*
- *HOW do you use CUSTOMER satisfaction and dissatisfaction information for improvement?*

Note 2: Determining customer satisfaction and dissatisfaction (3.2b) might include use of any or all of the following: surveys, formal and informal feedback, customer account histories, complaints, win/loss analysis, and transaction completion rates. Information might be gathered on the Internet, through personal contact or a third party, or by mail.

Note 3: Customer satisfaction measurements might include both a numerical rating scale and descriptors for each unit in the scale. Actionable customer satisfaction measurements provide useful information about specific product and service features, delivery, relationships, and transactions that bear upon the customers' future actions—repeat business and positive referral.

Post Transaction Follow-up (2)

- *HOW do you follow up with CUSTOMERS on products, services, and transaction quality to receive prompt and actionable feedback?*

Comparisons (3)

- *HOW do you obtain and use information on your CUSTOMERS' satisfaction relative to CUSTOMERS' satisfaction with your competitors and/or industry BENCHMARKS?*

Keeping Current (4)

- *HOW do you keep your APPROACHES to determining satisfaction current with business needs and directions?*

Note 4: Your customer satisfaction and dissatisfaction results should be reported in Item 7.1.

NIST (2004) p. 18

WORKSHEETS

Customer Satisfaction Determination 3.2b - Work Sheets

3.2b (1) - Customer Satisfaction and Dissatisfaction

Customer Group	Satisfaction/Dissatisfaction Measurement Methods	Measurement Data Tracked	Action Taken With These Data (Including Improvements)

3.2b (2) - Post Transaction Follow-up

Process for Post Transaction Follow-up For Products, Services And Transaction Quality			
Post Transaction Follow-up Process Step (In Sequence)	Who Is Involved	How The Step Is Measured	Actions Taken Based On The Feedback

3.2b (3) - Competitive Comparisons

Customer Group	Process To Obtain Comparative Data On Your Customer Satisfaction vs. Their Satisfaction With Competitors or Industry Benchmarks	Competitive Comparisons Gathered

3.2b (4) - Keeping Current

Customer Group	Method For Determining Whether Approach To Determining Customer Satisfaction Is Current	Method for Changing Approach Used	Method For Measuring Whether Approach Is Current

ASSESSMENT

Customer Satisfaction Determination 3.2b – Diagnostic Questions

Rating Scale:

0 - **No Process** in place - We are not doing this
1 - **Reacting to Problems** - Using a Basic (Primarily Reactive) Process
2 - **Systematic Process** – We use a systematic process that has been improved
3 - **Aligned** – We use a process that aligns our activities from top to bottom
4 - **Integrated** – We use a process that is integrated with other processes across the organization
5 - **Benchmark** - We are the Benchmark!
DK - Don't Know

1. Follow-up with customers is consistently provided to help build lasting relationships and to seek feedback for process improvement.　　0　1　2　3　4　5　DK

2. All employees who deal directly with customers have been trained in 'customer contact' skills.　　0　1　2　3　4　5　DK

3. There are clearly communicated service standards that define reliability, responsiveness, and effectiveness of customer contact personnel.　　0　1　2　3　4　5　DK

4. There is a systematic process for determining elements critical to customer satisfaction, and the information is used to exceed expectations.　　0　1　2　3　4　5　DK

Design	**Advanced Users**

BLUEPRINT

Customer Satisfaction Determination 3.2b - Blueprint

The customer satisfaction determination process provides fact based information to determine just how well the organization is performing in the customers' eyes. The main process consists of determining and developing measurement methods for satisfaction and dissatisfaction, then implementing those methods and evaluating them to ensure they deliver actionable information for decision making or organizational improvement. The use of this information to improve the organization so that it can exceed customer expectations can be key to ensuring repeat business and encouraging referrals.

Part of the customer satisfaction determination process is that of comparisons to competitors. It is one thing to have 80% of the customers respond that they are satisfied or very satisfied with the products and services, but is quite another if the competitors' customers respond that they are 95% satisfied or very satisfied. The comparisons may be key to the meaning of the raw data from the customers. An addition to comparisons is to follow up after transactions.

Customer Satisfaction Determination 3.2b - Blueprint

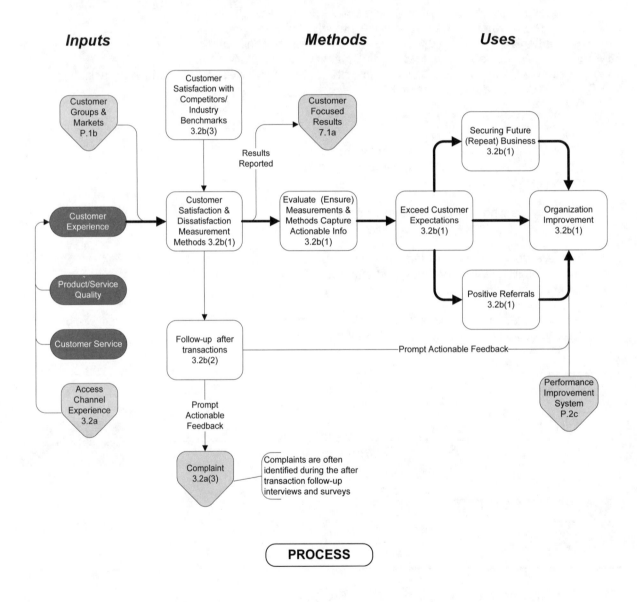

SYSTEM INTEGRATION

Customer Satisfaction Determination 3.2b – Linkages

Inputs

P.1b – The customer satisfaction determination processes should be designed to capture the satisfaction of the key customer and market segments and groups identified in the profile.

3.2a(3) – Occasionally, the customer follow-up activities after a transaction 3.2b(2) will generate a complaint. The system should be designed to "trigger" the complaint process here in 3.2a when that happens.

P.2c – The three improvement activities included in 3.2b(1) should be consistent with and based on the performance improvement approaches described in the profile.

Outputs

3.2a – Customer satisfaction with their experience using the access mechanisms to seek information, conduct business, and complain, are key elements in the overall customer experience and should therefore be included in the customer satisfaction determination processes.

7.1a – The customer satisfaction and dissatisfaction measurement methods 3.2b(1) determine the results that should be displayed in area 7.1a. In other words the results by segment as determined in 3.2b should be the same results (levels, trends, comparisons) that are displayed in 7.1a.

Transformation	**Leaders**

THOUGHTS FOR LEADERS

An important Baldrige message is that organizations really need to understand what makes their customers successful. In simple terms, if you have a product or service that makes your customer successful, then you will be a success. There is just no other part of the equation that can get in the way....if you continually make your customer a success, you will succeed.

Great leaders know this, and have a very clear focus on what goes on inside their organization to drive the necessary products and services to make their customers successful.

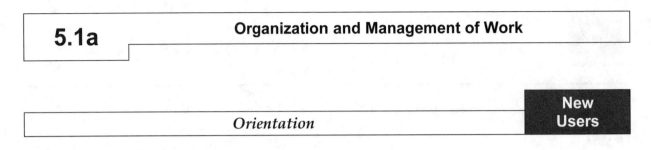

5.1a

Organization and Management of Work

Orientation

New Users

FOUNDATION

Organization and Management of Work 5.1a – Introduction

Item 5.1a describes the organization and management of work. Basically, the organization has work to be done, and describes that work in the form of job description. They then must match an individual and his/her experience and background to the job description. Baldrige asks how this process works. Work and jobs must be linked and they must be linked in a way to promote:

- Cooperation
- Initiative
- Empowerment
- Innovation
- Organizational culture

Each of the above bulleted Items needs to be addressed individually. The organization should describe how it not only matches jobs to work but how it organizes them to achieve agility so the organization can keep current as its business changes.

Once the work is linked to the jobs and people, the criteria ask how the work systems capitalize on the following factors:

- Diverse ideas
- Cultures
- Thinking of your employees
- The communities with which you interact

Basically Baldrige has the belief that your customers have a wide range of experiences, needs, and expectations. Unless you have a workforce with the same breadth and depth you may not be able to understand your customers' requirements and/or be able to meet their needs in a way which will drive long-term loyalty.

When the organization achieves alignment between work and jobs, it effectively structures the jobs so that employees have the tools, flexibility, and support they need to do their best. The criteria also ask how you communicate. This includes not only communication vertically (up and down) the organization, but horizontally, to share skills across or between work units. The basics of Knowledge Sharing are discussed in more detail in Area to Address 4.2b.

EXAMPLE

Organization and Management of Work 5.1a - Example Practices

Dana Spicer Driveshaft – **(Baldrige Recipient 2000)**

Dana Style	
People	**Leadership**
• People are our most important asset • Finding a better way • Business is 90% people/10% money • Education – 40 hours per person per year • Productive • Annual performance appraisal • Strengthened by diversity • Identify with Dana • Dana University • Two ideas per person per month – 80% implementation • Cross fertilization – cross training – across regions – across business units • Commitment • Certified Dana Supervisor • Encourage all Dana people to be shareholders • Dana people set their own goals and judge their performance – manage by objectives • Healthy and safe • Experts – 25 square feet/3 square meters • Dana people take ownership of their actions • Responsible for your own career • Pride in Dana people	• Dana Quality Leadership Process with Six Sigma objective • Vision of the future • Ability to change • Sense of urgency • Productivity improves every year • Promote from within based on performance • Teamwork • Lead by example • Four magic words – "What do you think?" • Trust • Respect for people – recognition • Support the growth of people • Freedom to fail • Recognize and reward success • High integrity and ethical standards • Listen • Do what's best for Dana

Dana Spicer Driveshaft focuses its approach to work and people on their fundamental organizational beliefs. These are captured in four documents one of, which is called "The Dana Style."

In The Dana Style it is clearly identified that employees are experts in their own work area and are best qualified to identify the most effective work methods. This is expressed as "experts – 25 square feet/3 square meters." This is translated throughout the organization to mean that employees are empowered and have the responsibility to effectively design their work, how the work flows and how it is integrated into the organization. This would be anecdotal, however, if the organization was not also prepared to supply each employee with the appropriate tools to design their work and to integrate their work into the organization.

Source: Dana Presentation – Quest for Excellence 2001

Diagnosis

QUESTIONS

Organization and Management of Work 5.1a - Baldrige Criteria Questions

Organization of Work (1)

- *HOW do you organize and manage work and jobs to promote cooperation, initiative, EMPOWERMENT, INNOVATION, and your organizational culture?*
- *HOW do you organize and manage work and jobs to achieve the agility to keep current with business needs?*

Note 1: "Employees" refers to your organization's permanent, temporary, and part-time personnel, as well as any contract employees supervised by your organization. Employees include team leaders, supervisors, and managers at all levels. Contract employees supervised by a contractor should be addressed in Category 6.

Note 2: "Your organization's work" refers to how your employees are organized or organize themselves in formal and informal, temporary, or longer-term units. This might include work teams, process teams, project teams, customer action teams, problem solving teams, centers of excellence, functional units, remote (e.g., at-home) workers, cross-functional teams, and departments—self-managed or managed by supervisors. "Jobs" refers to responsibilities, authorities, and tasks of individuals. In some work systems, jobs might be shared by a team.

Capitalizing on Diversity (2)

- *HOW do your WORK SYSTEMS capitalize on the diverse ideas, cultures, and thinking of your employees and the communities with which you interact (your employee hiring and your CUSTOMER communities)?*

Communication and Sharing (3)

- *HOW do you achieve EFFECTIVE communication and skill sharing across work units, jobs, and locations?*

NIST (2004) p. 21

WORKSHEETS

Organization and Management of Work 5.1a - Work Sheets

Describe how your organization's work and jobs enable employees and the organization to achieve high performance. Describe how compensation, career progression, and related workforce practices enable the employees and the organization to achieve high performance.

5.1a (1) - Organize and Manage Work

Area to Promote	Organize And Define Work	Define Jobs	Match Work And Jobs	Manage Work And Jobs (On An Ongoing Basis)
Cooperation				
Initiative				
Empowerment				
Innovation				
Organizational Culture				
Agility To Keep Current With Business Needs				

5.1a (2) - Capitalizing on Diversity

How Do Your Work Systems Capitalize On Diversity:		
Diverse Ideas:	**Diverse Cultures:**	**Thinking Of Your Employees:**

Role of Employee Hiring:	
Role of Customer Communities:	

5.1a (3) - Communication and Skill Sharing

Effective Communication For Skill Sharing:	Practices Of Sharing	Technology Support For Sharing
1. Between Work Units		
2. Between Functions and Jobs		
3. Between Locations		

ASSESSMENT

Organization and Management of Work 5.1a – Diagnostic Questions

Rating Scale:

0 - **No Process** in place - We are not doing this
1 - **Reacting to Problems** - Using a Basic (Primarily Reactive) Process
2 - **Systematic Process** – We use a systematic process that has been improved
3 - **Aligned** – We use a process that aligns our activities from top to bottom
4 - **Integrated** – We use a process that is integrated with other processes across the organization
5 - **Benchmark** - We are the Benchmark!
DK - Don't Know

1. The personal and professional development of employees is recognized as a vital responsibility of the organization and all of the leaders.   0   1   2   3   4   5   DK

2. Employees are encouraged to be involved in decision-making and problem solving.   0   1   2   3   4   5   DK

3. The organization looks for ways to increase employee empowerment and responsibility.   0   1   2   3   4   5   DK

Design   **Advanced Users**

BLUEPRINT

Organization and Management of Work 5.1a - Blueprint

Once the Value Creation, Support, and Customer Relationship Building processes are designed, the next step is to organize and manage the work. The organization and management of work should be designed to capitalize on the diverse ideas, cultures and thinking of the workforce in addition to being designed to accomplish the short and long-term strategies of the organization.

There are two key outputs of the organization and management of work. The first is to organize and manage work in a way that promotes cooperation, initiative, empowerment, innovation, and the desired culture. In other words to create and promote an environment consistent with the one described in the Organizational Profile P.1a(2) and Area to Address 1.1a. A second output, a result of the organization management of work, is to ensure or encourage communication and skill sharing across the work units, jobs, and locations. Given the nature of the employees in the organization, the management of work (and the approaches used) cannot be overly mechanistic or bureaucratic. Similar to the design of Value Creation processes, the organization and management of work must meet the needs of multiple stakeholders. This is often more art than science.

Organization and Management of Work 5.1a – Blueprint

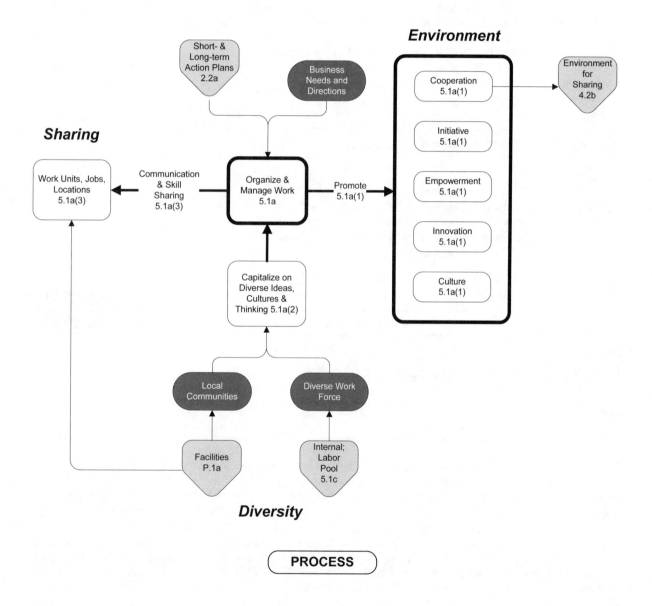

SYSTEM INTEGRATION

Organization and Management of Work 5.1a – Linkages

Inputs

2.2a – The human resource plans developed as part of the action planning process impact the design/redesign of the work system described in 5.1a. Change in the work system might be required to achieve the performance desired and necessary to accomplish the overall strategy.

P.1a – The location of the facilities as described in the profile will determine the nature and make up of the local communities. This make up, in turn, influences the approaches to capitalize on the diverse ideas, cultures, and thinking of the local communities.

5.1c – The recruiting, hiring, and retention processes described in 5.1c will determine the nature and make-up (diversity) of the internal workforce. This workforce will impact the design of the processes and approaches to capitalize on diverse ideas, cultures, and thinking.

Outputs

4.2b – The organizational knowledge area 4.2b calls for the sharing of information and knowledge. There is no process in the world that can make sharing happen if the environment is not right. The cooperative environment promoted by the organization and management of work has a big impact on the degree to which the employees share information and knowledge.

Transformation	**Leaders**

THOUGHTS FOR LEADERS

One of the things senior leaders have to do is to make the environment safe. We have all seen many instances where there is a *high risk, high probability of failure project* that needs to be staffed. Who do you want to run that project? Clearly, you want one of your best people to run it. You pick your best person and he/she does a fine job of running the project. The fact is, the original assessment was right - it was high risk, high probability of failure and the project does indeed fail. Organizations either fire the person or leave him/her inside. Everybody knows the person failed, which is really worse than being fired. Stigma is attached. Next, along comes another high risk, high probability of failure project. When you turn to the organization and ask, "Who wants to take this one?" No one volunteers and leaders are surprised. One of the things organizations have to do is to really understand both successes and failures. Why did you succeed? In failures, why did you not succeed? In both instances, if the failure was not a personal shortcoming of the person given the project, why did leadership not succeed in making the environment safe?

5.1b	**Employee Performance Management System**

Orientation	**New Users**

FOUNDATION

Employee Performance Management System 5.1b - Introduction

Once the organization has matched work and jobs (5.1a), giving employees the opportunity and support required to perform at a high level, the employee performance management system evaluates their performance. This starts with giving feedback to employees regarding their current performance, and offering opportunity areas where they can improve.

The criteria specifically seek to understand how the organization's Performance Management System supports a customer focus and supports the overall performance of the organization (a business focus).

Not only does the Performance Management System need to be linked to the goals (as discussed in Item 2.2) but it must be linked to the overall development and growth of employees (discussed in Item 5.2). Once employees clearly understand their goals and objectives, have the tools to perform, and have the leadership support, the Performance Management System should link compensation, recognition, and related rewards and incentive practices to the individual's and/or the team's performance.

Reward and recognition is an area where most organizations have a tremendous opportunity for improvement. Even high performing organizations can still improve further by more effectively aligning reward and recognition with the performance of the individual, and aligning the performance of the individual with the objectives, goals, and direction of the organization.

Most organizations have some form of non-monetary reward and recognition, but this too is, typically, an area of significant opportunity for improvement. As organizations increase their reward and recognition (including increases in non-monetary recognition) the impact can be significant in its favorable effect on overall organizational performance.

Clearly the organization must align every employee's efforts with the efforts of the overall company. The Performance Management System is one of the major tools used to achieve that alignment.

EXAMPLE

Employee Performance Management System 5.1b – Example Practices

Motorola CGISS – **(Baldrige Recipient 2002)**

In ensuring each employee's personal commitment, Motorola plans in a manner which helps each person see their impact on the organization, and gives each person input over their training plans and other areas which impact them personally.

Employees have checkpoints along the way where they can discuss their own situation, their performance, and match their own thoughts to those of their supervisor and others.

This planning and review process helps all employees have a degree of control over their career development, and understand their progress. This also helps them make course corrections during the year and improves the overall results and employee satisfaction.

5.1b Motorola CGISS – Personal Commitment

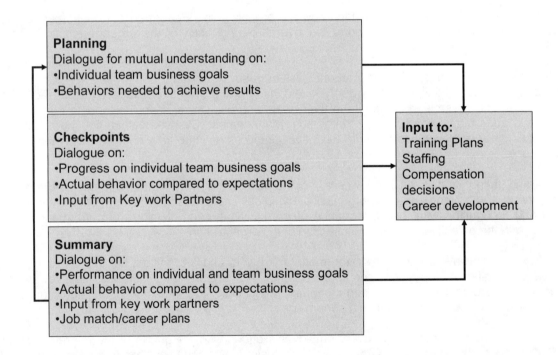

CGISS' performance management supports high performance through the PE Scorecard process, which is tied to each employee's Personal Commitment. Personal Commitment is a business improvement, performance management and employee development process created by Motorola. This process, consisting of quarterly dialogues and tools, helps employees maximize the contributions they make to the business and their own job fulfillment. Through the Personal Commitment process, managers, teams, and individuals focus on the actions needed to satisfy customers, meet business goals and achieve professional satisfaction.

The Personal Commitment process rewards individuals for meeting personal performance goals. Employees receive feedback and develop plans for the next year and beyond. The Global Rewards Team manages CGISS' compensation, recognition and incentive systems. Specific approaches include: the Motorola Incentive Plan, Personal Commitment, a pay-for-performance merit program, Stock Option Program and individual performance awards.

The Rewards organization has developed clear metrics to target and evaluate the differentiation of rewards for both executives and non-executives. Benchmark data supports the position that organizations that differentiate their reward programs, demonstrate better business performance than those who do not. The Relative Performance Assessment (RPA) system, which ranks employees relative to others in similar grade bands and functions, has been integrated with Personal Commitment. In the executive grade bands, CGISS achieved differential investment between the Most Effective (ME) and Solidly Effective (SE) and between the Most Effective and Least Effective (LE). CGISS also demonstrated increased differential investment in the areas of Stock Option awards and salary planning for 2002 executive participation. The Incentive Pay Plan (IPP) has been re-designed to focus on business results and individual performance.

CGISS' approaches to compensation, reward and recognition are evaluated and improved during quarterly operations reviews, and Category 5 Performance Excellence reviews. The specific inputs related to compensation, reward and recognition include alignment of these approaches with CGISS' strategies, PULSE results related input, benchmarks both internal and external to Motorola (including compensation rates in specific geographic locations and regions), specific input from Motorola's Global Rewards Organization, and the deployment status of Personal Commitment. On an annual basis, the Category 5 Performance Excellence Team is joined by Senior Management to review and analyze the results of the annual Performance Excellence Assessment. Succession planning is also evaluated and improved in this annual forum, with specific inputs analyzed related to retention of top candidates, the status of the Leadership Supply process, the diversity of high potential candidates, etc.

Source: Motorola (2003) pp. 35 – 36

 EXAMPLE

Employee Performance Management System 5.1b – Example Practices

Pearl River School District – (Baldrige Recipient 2001)

The figure below portrays how managers evaluate staff. All individual goals stem from district short-term goals and projects. In addition to the formal evaluation process based upon clearly defined goals, administrators provide support through their daily management practices – in feedback following class visitations, at staff and department meetings, during employee conferences, in memos and notes, and through daily management by walking around. The leader visits each building every week where he meets with the principal and visits classrooms. He also meets with the director of operations and director of facilities weekly. The focus on continuous improvement and high performance aligned with district goals is constant. They conduct formal reviews quarterly. The BOE ultimately holds the AC accountable for high performance results based upon positive faculty and staff performance.

5.1b Pearl River – Performance Evaluation Process

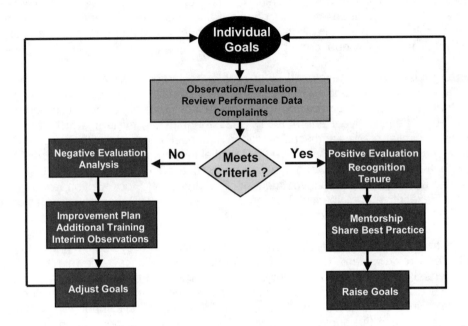

Pearl River School District gives each person the ability to know how they are performing compared to the expectations for them. This starts with individual goals, and cycles through a review of performance, and development of improvement plans.

Where performance meets the criteria, the organization has developed the ability to help the person improve further based on sharing best practices and/or providing a mentor to help the person learn from the experience of others.

Source: PRSD (2002) pp. 152 - 153

| Diagnosis | |

QUESTIONS

Employee Performance Management System 5.1b - Baldrige Criteria Questions

- *HOW does your employee PERFORMANCE management system, including feedback to employees, support HIGH-PERFORMANCE WORK?*

- *HOW does your employee PERFORMANCE management system support a CUSTOMER and business focus?*

- *HOW do your compensation, recognition, and related reward and incentive practices reinforce HIGH-PERFORMANCE WORK and a CUSTOMER and business focus?*

NIST (2004) p. 21

WORKSHEETS

Employee Performance Management System (EPMS) 5.1b - Work Sheets

5.1b – Employee Performance Management System

Factor	Process Used To Achieve This Factor:
Feedback To Employees Supports High Performance Work	
Employee Performance System Supports A Customer Focus	
Employee Performance System Supports A Business Focus	
Compensation, Recognition, And Reward And Incentive Practices Reinforce High Performance Work	

ASSESSMENT

Employee Performance Management System 5.1b – Diagnostic Questions

Rating Scale:

0 - **No Process** in place - We are not doing this
1 - **Reacting to Problems** - Using a Basic (Primarily Reactive) Process
2 - **Systematic Process** – We use a systematic process that has been improved
3 - **Aligned** – We use a process that aligns our activities from top to bottom
4 - **Integrated** – We use a process that is integrated with other processes across the organization
5 - **Benchmark** - We are the Benchmark!
DK - Don't Know

1. Employees are formally and informally rewarded and recognized for demonstrating the desired behaviors and levels of performance.	0	1	2	3	4	5	DK
2. Employee performance is fairly evaluated and feedback is provided to the employee through a systematic process that is followed by all leaders.	0	1	2	3	4	5	DK
3. The organization has a systematic process for: 1) identifying need for, 2) delivering, and 3) evaluating the effectiveness of training.	0	1	2	3	4	5	DK

Design	**Advanced Users**

BLUEPRINT

Employee Performance Management System 5.1b - Blueprint

The second element of the work system is the employee performance management system. The system is composed of two major areas: performance management and the reinforcement of the desired behaviors.

Employee Performance Management System 5.1b – Blueprint

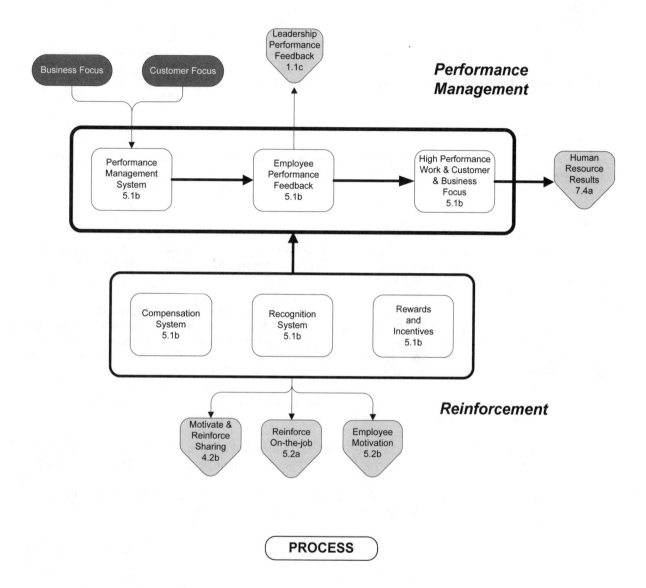

The performance management system drives employee performance feedback which is used to refine and improve high performance work and a customer and business focus. This performance or behavior is reinforced by three components: 1) the compensation system, 2) the recognition system, and 3) the rewards and incentives that are used throughout the organization. These reinforcement mechanisms are also used to reinforce the use of new skills on the job and to motivate employees.

While this diagram does not show interconnections throughout other parts of the criteria, it shows that the behavior systematically encouraged and reinforced aligns with the other characteristics of the organization. Many organizations have found that not having these systems or processes can undermine the desired results or behaviors throughout the organization.

Of all the areas that are critical to sustaining organizational change this one is among the very top.

SYSTEM INTEGRATION

Employee Performance Management System 5.1b – Linkages

Inputs

Although there are no key inputs for this item, the employee profile is always a key factor to consider when designing any of the human resource processes and approaches.

Outputs

1.1c - The evaluation and improvement aspect of this area includes the evaluation of senior leader and board of director performance. These evaluations should be consistent with the employee performance feedback processes described in area 1.1c.

4.2b – Knowledge sharing benefits from systems that capture and disseminate knowledge, however, the systems by themselves are never enough to ensure sharing throughout the organization. The environment for sharing is influenced by the design of the performance management and reinforcement systems. If the incentives in the organization pit one employee against another for limited recognition, rewards, and compensation, then the environment for sharing will suffer.

5.2a – The rewards, recognition, and compensation system should be designed to reinforce the use of the newly developed knowledge and skills on the job as described in area 5.2a.

5.2b – To help motivate employees to develop and utilize their full potential, the rewards, recognition, and compensation system should be designed to encourage the employees and not de-motivate them.

7.4a – The results that indicate the level of performance management system effectiveness should be included in the results (levels, trends, comparisons) depicted in 7.4a.

5.1c	Hiring and Career Progression

	New
Orientation	Users

 FOUNDATION

Hiring and Career Progression 5.1c - Introduction

The hiring and career progression criteria ask for a description of how you identify what skills employees need to have, how you find those employees, how you attract them, how you hire them, how you ensure the employees represent diverse viewpoints, and then how you help them develop their careers.

This begins with how you identify the characteristic skills needed by potential employees. This is directly linked to Item 5.1(1) which discussed work and jobs. There must be a link between the employees' skills, the work to be done and the skills needed to do that work. The criteria go on to ask how you find, recruit, hire, and keep the employees. The employee base should represent a wide range of experiences and ideas matching that same breadth in your customer base.

The Baldrige criteria in the past few years have asked about succession planning at all levels of the organization. Very few organizations truly succession plan for anything except top leaders. The criteria now ask for how you accomplish effective succession planning for leadership and management positions. Nevertheless, the organization has the responsibility to ensure all employees have the opportunity to progress in their careers.

Because of this, the criteria ask how you manage effective career progression for all employees throughout the organization. This is typically achieved by posting jobs so that all eligible candidates have the opportunity to apply for all positions for which they are qualified and for which they have an interest.

 EXAMPLE

Hiring and Career Progression 5.1c - Example Practices

SSM Healthcare – (Baldrige Recipient 2002)

Employee retention is critical in any organization. It is even more critical for organizations like SSM who are facing nationwide shortages in nurses over the next decade. To combat this condition, SSM instituted a Nursing Recruitment and Retention Steering Team which goes beyond merely educating, measuring, and compensating nurses, as was done in 2000.

SSMHC uses a wide variety of recruitment methods. The recruitment efforts focus on SSMHC's commitment to quality and culture of teamwork to interest candidates who have the potential to be valued employees. SSMHC screens advertising outlets and sources of job candidates based on the SSMHC valued employee profile. The system also recruits electronically, both on its external Web site and from all SSMHC intranet pages. Openings are also posted on wall bulletin boards at the entities. During 2001, SSMHC recruited 2,459 employees via the web. An online application is available. Information about all applicants, including online applicants, is tracked electronically. This tracking program helps HR staff to better focus their recruiting efforts. SSMHC has addressed the industry's critical nursing shortage by bringing together nurse and human resources executives to develop innovative recruitment and retention strategies. System Management is taking the following actions based upon the recommendations of the five systemwide nursing recruitment and retention teams: (1) implementing nursing shared accountability models at the entities, (2) improving nursing education and orientation programs offered within the system, (3) improving nursing access to technology, (4) developing programs to foster collaborative relationships between nurses and physicians, (5) offering a variety of benefits such as improved tuition reimbursement and bonuses for employees who recruit a peer.

Other recruiting strategies are student nurse internships and post-graduate clinical teaching site experiences. These programs are designed to give student nurses and postgraduate nurses an opportunity to work side-by-side with experienced nurses. As an example, in 2001, 84 percent of the student nurses stayed on as SSMHC St. Louis employees. SSMHC's entities celebrate their diversity in many ways, including events that feature ethnic foods, observances of ethnic holidays and other events celebrating racial, ethnic, and religious significance.

Source: SSM (2003) pp. 25 - 26

 EXAMPLE

Hiring and Career Progression 5.1c - Example Practices

Pearl River School District **– (Baldrige Recipient 2001)**

All organizations have a process to bring in new employees. In many organizations, however, it is informal. At Pearl River School District the selection process is integrated with the design of the work,

and the candidates are screened based on the ability to link their interests and backgrounds to the job, work, and actual success factors for the position.

AC members develop job descriptions using many of the inputs delineated in 5.1(a). The process begins with a draft description by the immediate manager with input from the stakeholders to be impacted by the position. Labor representatives review for contract compliance. The assistant superintendent and/or director of operations review for compliance with personnel and civil service regulations. Legal counsel may be invited for additional review if necessary. The superintendent gives final review and approval and affirms the salary parameters. PRSD maintains a highly structured recruitment and hiring process.

With a shrinking available pool of certain subject area teacher candidates (high level math, science, foreign language, music) and school administrator candidates, PRSD has responded with more innovative approaches to recruitment. Early anticipation of needs is crucial to capitalize on the available pool. Relationships have been strengthened with well-respected teacher colleges, such as Columbia, Fordham, and NYU, to recruit candidates prior to graduation. Relationships are also being maintained with PRHS alumni in teacher programs and encouraging current students to consider the teaching profession. Candidates must meet predetermined criteria to be considered for first-round interviews, criteria which link to action plans. For example, a teacher vacancy position may require that the candidate be trained to teach an AP level exam because that is a new course offering or a retirement or resignation was experienced in that area.

5.1c Pearl River – Recruitment and Hiring Process

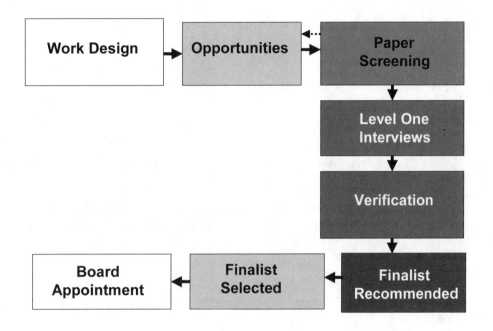

With a limited candidate pool, retention takes higher priority. Part of the retention strategy is to provide a strong orientation program to acclimate newcomers to the district's culture. PRSD maintains a supportive environment for new teachers and staff, beginning with a two day orientation before they begin and continuing with a new teacher symposium throughout the first two years. Curriculum focuses on acclimating to the PRSD culture and fostering success. Teachers and labor leaders provide input into the curriculum and evaluations are ongoing. For example, a session was added because of a need for more assistance with classroom management. Managers provide other additional support through personal meetings and printed and electronic correspondence. The PRSD community is not ethnically diverse. Approximately 92% of the students are Caucasian. Some religious diversity does exist. All candidates for employment are considered equally according to the criteria determined. When candidates of similar capabilities reach finalist status, hiring will support diversity across gender, religious, racial, age, and other backgrounds, whenever possible.

Source: PRSD (2002) p. 153

QUESTIONS

Hiring and Career Progression 5.1c - Baldrige Criteria Questions

Needs Assessment (1)

- *HOW do you identify characteristics and skills needed by potential employees?*

Recruit, Hire, Retain (2)

- *HOW do you recruit, hire, and retain new employees?*
- *HOW do you ensure that the employees represent the diverse ideas, cultures, and thinking of your employee hiring community?*

Note 3: Compensation and recognition (5.1b) include promotions and bonuses that might be based upon performance, skills acquired, and other factors. Recognition includes monetary and nonmonetary, formal and informal, and individual and group mechanisms.

Succession Planning (3)

HOW do you accomplish EFFECTIVE succession planning for leadership and management positions, including senior leadership?
HOW do you manage EFFECTIVE career progression for all employees throughout the organization?

NIST (2004) p. 21

WORKSHEETS

Hiring and Career Progression 5.1c - Work Sheets

5.1c (1) - Identifying Characteristics and Skills Needed

Factor	Process Used To Support This Factor:
Identify characteristics and skills needed by potential employees	

5.1c (2) - Recruiting, Hiring, and Retaining Employees

Process Used:	Process To Ensure Employees Represent The Diversity of the Community in:		
	Ideas	Cultures	Thinking
To Recruit:			
To Hire:			
To Retain New Employees:			

5.1c (3) - Succession Planning

Factor	Process Used:
Succession Planning For Leadership And Management Positions Including Senior Leadership	
Effective Career Progression For All Employees Throughout The Organization	

 ## ASSESSMENT

Hiring and Career Progression 5.1c – Diagnostic Questions

Rating Scale:

0 - **No Process** in place - We are not doing this
1 - **Reacting to Problems** - Using a Basic (Primarily Reactive) Process
2 - **Systematic Process** – We use a systematic process that has been improved
3 - **Aligned** – We use a process that aligns our activities from top to bottom
4 - **Integrated** – We use a process that is integrated with other processes across the organization
5 - **Benchmark** - We are the Benchmark!
DK - Don't Know

1. There is a systematic process used to identify the characteristics and skills needed by potential employees   0   1   2   3   4   5   DK

2. Rewards and recognition are linked to performance and attainment of organizational goals and objectives.   0   1   2   3   4   5   DK

3. The organization has a systematic process for succession planning for leaders and advancing the careers of other employees   0   1   2   3   4   5   DK

BLUEPRINT

Hiring and Career Progression 5.1c - Blueprint

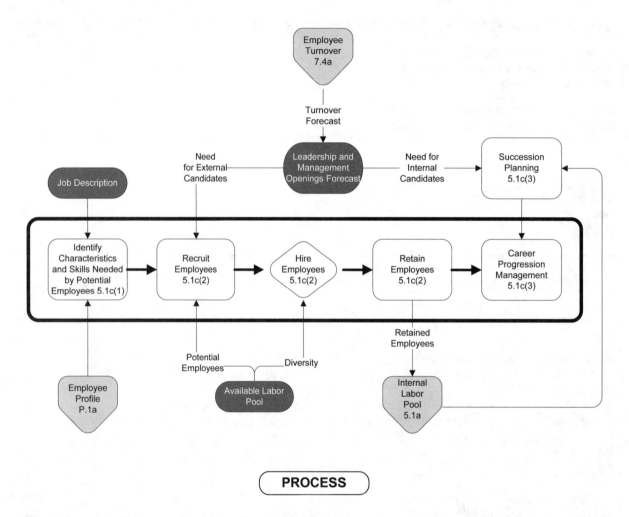

The hiring and career performance Area to Address is composed primarily of attracting, recruiting, hiring, retaining, and developing employees as they progress through the organization. The first step is the identification of the characteristics and skills needed by potential employees. Using these characteristics and skills, the next step is to recruit a group of potential employees to meet those requirements.

The center of the diagram is the hiring process which is primarily a decision process which should be driven by clear decision criteria. The question here is 'what criteria are used to make a hiring decision.' Once the employees are on board how does the organization ensure they stay? Part of the answer to this is a proactive employee progression management system.

While this process might be implemented for individual positions it is also part of a larger system to ensure the right people are in the right positions and are ready to take the place of those who move up or leave the organization.

 SYSTEM INTEGRATION

Hiring and Career Progression 5.1c – Linkages

Inputs

P.1a – The employee segments identified in the profile, together with the organization's requirements, determine the gaps that need to be filled with new employees. These gaps can be gaps in technical skills, diversity, education and so forth.

7.4a – The actual turnover of employees will influence the employee openings forecast and drive the need for hiring.

Outputs

5.1a - The recruiting, hiring, and retention processes described in 5.1c will determine the nature and make-up (diversity) of the internal workforce. This workforce will impact the design of the processes and approaches to capitalize on diverse ideas, cultures, and thinking.

5.2a	Employee Education, Training, and Development

Orientation	New Users

FOUNDATION

Employee Education, Training, and Development 5.2a - Introduction

Employee education, training, and development link the overall Strategic Plan of the organization to the development of people. The impact of people and employee capabilities were considered in the early stages of developing the Strategic Plan (Item 2.1). The human resource plan was considered during the deployment of the strategy down to action plans (Item 2.2) leaving this portion of the criteria to address the specific development and training of people to implement those plans. This begins with aggregating the training requirements at the highest levels in the organization so the organization can directly link education and training to the achievement of action plans. The overall macro training and development plans must be deployed down through the organization to get to every single employee who has personal actions linked to the short-term and longer-term organizational objectives.

The beginning of an employee's education and training starts with new employee orientation. This should typically address the culture of the organization, the values and beliefs, and what employees have to do to grow into productive members of the organization. This includes the skills and tools that all other employees understand so the new employee can use those skills and tools productively to solve problems or to progress within the culture, or improve organizational performance.

This Area to Address also focuses on the overall training process. This includes the design of the training processes and the delivery of training. The modes of training, feedback from employees and supervisors, and sharing knowledge and skills on the job (once the training has been completed) are also addressed.

One of the most difficult questions in the criteria is "how do you reinforce the use of new knowledge and skills on the job?" This clearly indicates that the organization should have specific activities which can be used to ensure that employees retain the knowledge and can apply it to their job responsibilities. Another difficult question to answer for organizations is how training effectiveness is evaluated. This can be a basic evaluation such as the evaluations which are handed out at the end of a course, ranging to evaluations which directly link the training to organizational performance.

EXAMPLE

Employee Education, Training, and Development 5.2a - Example Practices

Dana Spicer Driveshaft **– (Baldrige Recipient 2000)**

5.2 Dana Spicer – Education and Training

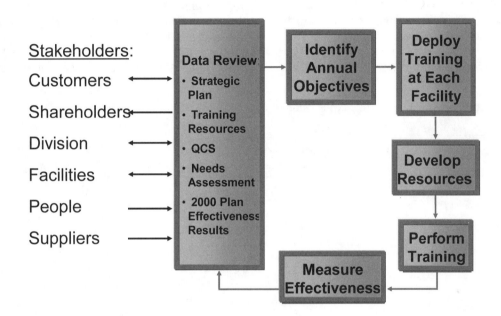

Corporate office and plant human resource managers, in conjunction with the Training and Education Council (TEC), are responsible for the assessment of education and training needs. They use inputs from individual, departmental, and organizational assessments, performance appraisal feedback, the QCS, and strategic objectives to design and implement training and education plans.

A diversity awareness program was conducted with an outside source as a pilot program for the Strategic Business Council and office supervisory staff. A diversity plan has been approved that includes a diversity training program, which will be deployed to all Spicer Driveshaft people by the end of the second quarter of 2002.

The Spicer Driveshaft training approach also supports employee development, learning and career progression.

They use several approaches to address performance excellence in education and training in the areas of performance and skill standards, quality control and benchmarking.

Source: Dana (2001) pp. 26 - 27

EXAMPLE

Employee Education, Training, and Development 5.2a - Example Practices

Ritz Carlton

Education and training is designed to keep individuals up to date with business needs. The Corporate Director of Training and Development and the Hotel Directors of Training and Development have the responsibility to make sure that training stays current with business needs. To do this, they work with Human Resource and Quality Executives who input organization and job performance training requirements or revise existing ones. The flow of this process is shown below. Key development training needs are addressed through a core of courses that all employees receive. All employees (regardless of their level in the company) receive the same mandatory two day orientation process, which includes classroom type training on The Gold Standards and their GreenBook of improvement tools.

5.2 Ritz Carlton – Course Design Process

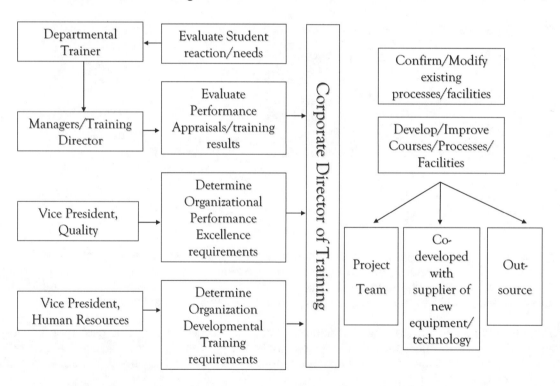

As shown in the figure above, they use input from employees and their supervisors in determining education needs primarily via a review and analysis of performance appraisal documents. The Hotel Director of Training and Development and the Quality Trainers also receive and consider direct feedback from Ritz-Carlton personnel. When training is designed, it is piloted and approved in a fashion similar to the new product and service development process described in Category 3. Participants in the pilot provide direct, candid feedback to the designers and instructors.

Although job induction training is classroom delivered by the Director of Training and Development and the General Manager, most training delivery is on-the-job. This consists of: (1) daily line-up (2) self-study documents (3) developmental assignment and (4) training certification. Most training is evaluated through examinations, while other methods include audits, performance reviews and appraisals.

Approximately 80% of the training received by The Ritz-Carlton Ladies and Gentlemen is from in-house sources which allows Ritz-Carlton to have direct control over the method of training delivery and evaluation. To gain real-life developmental experiences, they make extensive use of developmental assignments in which people choose to expand their knowledge and experience through requesting new assignments within and across hotels and functions. Since most executives came up the ranks this way, this is a widely accepted and expected process for people who would like to be promoted.

Source: Ritz-Carlton (2000) pp. 14 - 15

Diagnosis	**Assessors**

QUESTIONS

Employee Education, Training, and Development 5.2a – Baldrige Criteria Questions

Needs Assessment (1)

- *HOW do employee education and training contribute to the achievement of your ACTION PLANS?*
- *HOW do your employee education, training, and development address your KEY needs associated with organizational PERFORMANCE measurement, PERFORMANCE improvement, and technological change?*
- *HOW does your education and training APPROACH balance short- and longer-term organizational objectives with employee needs for development, LEARNING, and career progression?*

Training Offerings (2)

- *HOW do employee education, training, and development address your KEY organizational needs associated with new employee orientation, diversity, ethical business practices, and management and leadership development?*
- *HOW do employee education, training, and development address your KEY organizational needs associated with employee, workplace, and environmental safety?*

Inputs to Training (3)

- *HOW do you seek and use input from employees and their supervisors and managers on education and training needs?*
- *HOW do you incorporate your organizational LEARNING and KNOWLEDGE ASSETS into your education and training?*

Delivery of Education and Training (4)

- *HOW do you deliver education and training?*
- *HOW do you seek and use input from employees and their supervisors and managers on options for the delivery of education and training?*
- *HOW do you use both formal and informal delivery APPROACHES, including mentoring and other APPROACHES, as appropriate?*

Reinforcement (5)

- *HOW do you reinforce the use of new knowledge and skills on the job?*

Evaluate and Improve (6)

- *HOW do you evaluate the effectiveness of education and training, taking into account individual and organizational PERFORMANCE?*

Education and training delivery (5.2a[4]) might occur inside or outside your organization and involve on-the-job, classroom, computer-based, distance learning, and other types of delivery (formal or informal).

NIST (2004) p. 22

 WORKSHEETS

Employee Education, Training, and Development 5.2a - Work Sheets

Describe how your organization's employee education, training, and career development support the achievement of your overall objectives, and contribute to high performance. Describe how your organization's education, training, and career development build employee knowledge, skills, and capabilities.

5.2a (1) – Training Support of Action Plans

Types Of Action Plans	Process Used To Link Education and Training Support To The Action Plans:

Process to Balance Organizational and Employee Needs		
Education	Training	Development
Process To Link To Performance Measurement:		
Process To Link To Performance Improvement:		
Process To Link to Technological Change:		

5.2a (1) – Training Support of Action Plans (cont)

Describe Processes	
Process To Link To Balancing Education, Training and Development To Short- and Longer-Term Organizational Objectives	
Process To Link To Balancing Education, Training and Development To Employee Needs For Development, Learning And Career Progression	

5.2a (2) - *Support for Key Organizational Needs*

Need	Process For Education and Training Support Of This Need:
Employee Orientation	
Diversity	
Ethical Business Practices	
Management And Leadership Development	
Employee, Workplace, And Environmental Safety	

5.2a (3) - *Inputs – Content and Delivery Mechanisms*

Process To Seek Input And Use From:		Process To Take These Inputs And Incorporate Into Education and Training
Employees	**Managers and Supervisors**	

5.2a (4) – *Mechanisms Used To Deliver Education And Training*

Formal Approaches Used	Informal Approaches Used (Including Mentoring)
1	1
n	n

Note: Include how you seek input from managers and supervisors on options for delivery of training.

5.2a (5) - *Reinforcement On New Knowledge And Skills On The Job*

Processes Used To Reinforce New Knowledge And Skills On The Job

5.2a (6) - Evaluate Effectiveness Of Education and Training

Requirement	Process Used To Meet The Requirement:
Evaluate Education And Training Effectiveness	
Take Into Account Individual Performance	
Take Into Account Organizational Performance	

 ## ASSESSMENT

Employee Education, Training, and Development 5.2a – Diagnostic Questions

Rating Scale:

0 - **No Process** in place - We are not doing this
1 - **Reacting to Problems** - Using a Basic (Primarily Reactive) Process
2 - **Systematic Process** – We use a systematic process that has been improved
3 - **Aligned** – We use a process that aligns our activities from top to bottom
4 - **Integrated** – We use a process that is integrated with other processes across the organization
5 - **Benchmark** - We are the Benchmark!
DK - Don't Know

1. The organization has a systematic process for: 1) identifying need for, 2) delivering, and 3) evaluating the effectiveness of training.   0 1 2 3 4 5 DK

2. Employees and managers have the ability to provide input on their education and training needs.   0 1 2 3 4 5 DK

3. New knowledge and skills are reinforced on the job.   0 1 2 3 4 5 DK

4. Training plans for the organization are integrated with the strategic plan.   0 1 2 3 4 5 DK

Design

BLUEPRINT

Employee Education, Training, and Development 5.2a - Blueprint

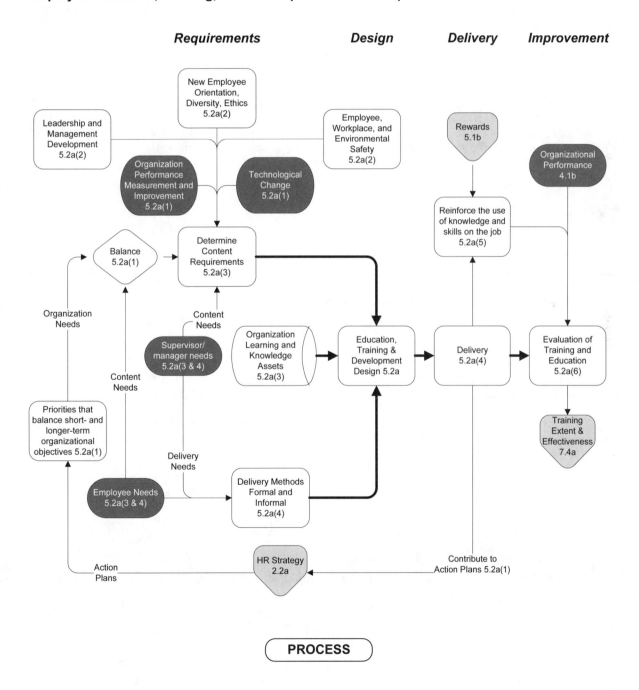

PROCESS

Employee education, training, and development is a four phase process of determining the requirements, designing the content and the delivery, actually delivering the education training, and finally evaluating and improving the education training.

The requirements for education and training tend to be a little more complicated than your typical process. First there are at least three perspectives on needs: 1) the organization and its strategy, 2) the individual supervisors or managers, and 3) the individual employees. It is a balancing act to develop content which meets all of these needs. In addition different employees and managers need different delivery approaches. For example insurance agents spread throughout the nation may need more online education courses than an organization where the employees are all in one building and work one shift.

After the education training is delivered, on-the-job reinforcement of the new knowledge and skills is critical to actually achieving the desired value from the education training. There is an old saying, "You use it or you lose it."

Linkage between the rewards and recognition are described in Area to Address 5.1b and the reinforcement and use of knowledge and skills on the job.

In the end, there are two major issues with education training and development of employees. First, there are the overall requirements of the organization and the overall training and education development plan. Second, there is the design of the individual education and training activities to meet the needs of specific individuals and managers and the overall organization.

 SYSTEM INTEGRATION

Employee Education, Training, and Development 5.2a – Linkages

Inputs

5.1b - The rewards, recognition, and compensation system should be designed to reinforce the use of the newly developed knowledge and skills on the job as described in area 5.2a.

2.2a - The strategy and action plans drive the employee development efforts. The overall strategies are balanced with the needs of the individual to drive the development of course content as well as delivery methods.

Outputs

2.2a – The criteria explicitly ask for how the education and training efforts contribute to the achievement of the action plans.

7.4a – The results from the evaluation of training and education should be part of the human resources results depicted in area 7.4a.

THOUGHTS FOR LEADERS

An organization is not going to move any faster than the leaders can learn and improve. I remember one time, assessing an organization where the leader told me, "I do not read books, everything I need to know, I have in my gut." I remember thinking to myself, "the site visit may as well end now, because this organization will never be great as long as it is lead by somebody who does not learn." Some of the greatest leaders I have ever known are lifelong learners, for example I will use: N.R. Narayana Murthy, Chairman & CEO of Infosys. When you walk into his office, the walls are lined with books and believe me, he has read them.

One of the impressions I have had with great leaders, is that they try to learn all the time. Leaders have three responsibilities to learn. First, they have a responsibility to learn themselves, because if the leader is not learning and not stretching capability and the leader is not pressing himself, then why should anybody else learn? The second responsibility of learning is that leaders have to make sure everyone else in their organization stretches themselves to learn as well. If the leader does not budget for learning, if he does not require the learning, then no one else in the organization will learn. The third part is that leaders have to make sure their processes in the organization learn. It is tragic to go through several years or cycles of a process and find that the process does not get any better. Leaders must role model everything they want the organization to do, and if the organization is not learning, it points back to the fact that the leaders are not learning.

5.2b	Motivation and Career Development

FOUNDATION

Motivation and Career Development 5.2b - Introduction

Motivation and career development starts with the needs and expectations of the employees and focuses on how the organization helps employees achieve (through both formal and informal techniques) their development objectives.

Once employee career desires are known, the criteria ask how the organization aligns the job and career development to help employees maximize their learning. Learning then needs to be applied to improve the organizational performance. The criteria also ask how employees, managers, and supervisors help employees obtain their job and career related developmental learning objectives by supporting the learning and how they ensure that employees directly apply the learning on the job. Baldrige does not necessarily embrace learning for the sake of learning. Item 5.2 clearly aligns the learning (and the skills which are gathered through learning) to improve the overall performance.

EXAMPLE

Motivation and Career Development 5.2b - Example Practices

Pearl River School District – (Baldrige Recipient 2001)

Professional development for all staff at all levels is integral to the human resource function at PRSD and manifested in the core value that district employees are highly valued resources. **5.2a(1)** Staff development activities exist at all buildings and in all departments and are organized by the Professional Development Committee (PDC) in the district's Professional Development Plan (PDP) for certificated staff, and the Support Development Plan for non-certificated staff. The PDC is comprised of administrators, staff, parents, and representatives from higher education. In response to Baldrige feedback and new NYSED requirements, the committee revised the comprehensive plans last year to follow the plan-deploy evaluate framework. Both plans are linked directly to the district's lag and lead goals, and annual projects. The committee uses student and staff performance data to outline specific staff development programs. They determine the skills needed, assess whether those skills exist among the current staff, and design and deliver training programs accordingly. They then evaluate the effectiveness of the training and re-train or adapt training programs if necessary. Professional development is management-driven and viewed as a responsibility for all staff.

5.2 Pearl River – Professional Development and Staff Evaluation System

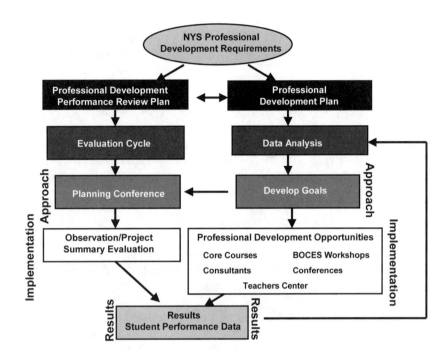

Managers include professional development in their annual goal setting with each employee. Staff use this opportunity to share their personal career goals. Managers review individual staff performance data. Together, they develop training priorities based upon both individual and organizational needs. The personnel officer tracks certification and licensure compliance and informs staff of gaps and/or requirements. Staff have input into the design and delivery of programs through other formal structures including representation on the PDC, collective bargaining, LMC, and the conference request process. Informally, as needs arise, staff and staff groups communicate those needs to their manager and a resolution is developed. These same techniques are used for input into both the content and delivery of professional development programs.

With the increasing prevalence of technology for instruction and support, PRSD employs a full-time director of technology education who coordinates technology training. The director runs a full schedule of technology workshops three times each year (fall, spring, summer), relying on input from faculty and staff, as well as the future technology plans of the district, for the design and content. They also partner with the BOCES for specialized trainings and locations. Leadership training is accomplished through study circles prior to AC meetings, external conferences, programs at the Principal's Center, and participation in professional organizations.

All new staff attend a two-day employee orientation in August where they are oriented to the PRSD quality culture, district goals, district procedures, basic instructional philosophies, and human resources and benefits. They also meet key stakeholders. Certificated staff also attend a weeklong summer symposium with further detail on instructional design, use of data, curriculum standards, and classroom management. This symposium continues once a month for two years. Staff hired during the school year are given a shortened version but must attend the full symposium the following summer. Staff not certificated continue their training through sessions in department meetings, workshops, and in-service offerings. Training in quality performance excellence is not treated as a separate entity. Quality is the "how" of district operations and not a content area unto itself. After over a decade of integrating data, performance assessments, benchmarks, and quality tools into district operations, staff learn performance excellence as the way of their professional life at PRSD. The director of facilities coordinates safety training with input from the Safety Committee. Delivery comes through BOCES, OSHA, and by training department heads and key staff who then come in and train the rest of the staff. Diversity training at PRSD is limited because of limited diversity. Key staff attend programs relevant to population and needs and integrate the information into the delivery programs described above.

PRSD increased the professional development budget by 25% to cover the increased requirement of 21 hours per certificated employee. This covers all in-service programs, consultant trainers, Superintendent's Conference Days, and approved external conferences. All faculty and staff are financially rewarded through a variety of mechanisms (stipends, reimbursements, salary adjustments) to continue their education and training. PRSD uses the Professional Performance Review Plan for program evaluation. This plan follows a quality-based approach and has as its goals:

- To provide direction for professional growth
- To promote the achievement of students' academic and social potential
- To attain district, school curriculum and/or program objectives
- To provide each staff member with a regular assessment of his/her performance
- To obtain data for administrative decisions regarding retention, tenure, and assignment

The review plan outlines cycles for supervisor and peer observation, supervision, peer collaboration, and formal reviews. Staff remain in the program until they receive a satisfactory annual summary review. The review plan also outlines an entirely new structure for evaluation of staff development programs. Participants complete Part One of the evaluation immediately following the session indicating whether the program met their purpose for attending and how they plan to integrate what they learned. Two months later, they complete Part Two where they indicate what aspects of the training they actually did integrate and any measured improvement results. The level of improvement is rated on a 5-step scale from nonexistent/anecdotal to significant/sustained over time. The PDC analyzes the evaluations and adjusts the plans accordingly.

PRSD managers and fellow employees alike reinforce skills and knowledge. In addition, they recognize individuals with outstanding performance through an annual recognition program during the September conference day, a staff accomplishment column in the employee newsletter, sending press releases and arranging for press coverage, announcing accomplishments in faculty, staff, and department meetings, and providing opportunities for staff to share best practices and mentor other staff.

Source: PRSD (2002) pp. 154 - 155

Diagnosis

QUESTIONS

Motivation and Career Development 5.2b - Baldrige Criteria Questions

- *HOW do you motivate employees to develop and utilize their full potential?*
- *HOW does your organization use formal and informal mechanisms to help employees attain job- and career-related development and LEARNING objectives?*
- *HOW do managers and supervisors help employees attain job- and career-related development and LEARNING objectives?*

NIST (2004) p. 22

WORKSHEETS

Motivation and Career Development 5.2b - Work Sheets

5.2b - Motivation and Career Development

Requirement	Process Used To Meet The Requirement:
Motivate Employees To Develop And Utilize Their Full Potential	
Formal Mechanisms To Help Employees Achieve Development Objectives	
Informal Mechanisms To Help Employees Achieve Development Objectives	
Managers And Supervisors Help Employees Achieve Development Objectives	

ASSESSMENT

Motivation and Career Development 5.2b – Diagnostic Questions

Rating Scale:

0 - No Process in place - We are not doing this
1 - Reacting to Problems - Using a Basic (Primarily Reactive) Process
2 - Systematic Process – We use a systematic process that has been improved
3 - Aligned – We use a process that aligns our activities from top to bottom
4 - Integrated – We use a process that is integrated with other processes across the organization
5 - Benchmark - We are the Benchmark!
DK - Don't Know

		0	1	2	3	4	5	DK
1.	Employees are effectively motivated to develop and utilize their full potential.	0	1	2	3	4	5	DK
2.	Employees can use both formal and informal mechanisms to attain job- and career-related development and learning.	0	1	2	3	4	5	DK
3.	Managers and supervisors help employees attain job- and career-related development and learning objectives.	0	1	2	3	4	5	DK

Design	**Advanced Users**

BLUEPRINT

Motivation and Career Development 5.2b - Blueprint

The central motivation behind the job and career related development in this Area to Address is the development and the utilization of the full potential of all the employees.

Two key inputs to the development of the employees' full potential are the mechanisms (formal and informal) and the support of managers and supervisors. The individual employee's motivation is also linked to the rewards, compensation, and recognition approaches described in Area to Address 5.1b.

Motivation and Career Development 5.2b - Blueprint

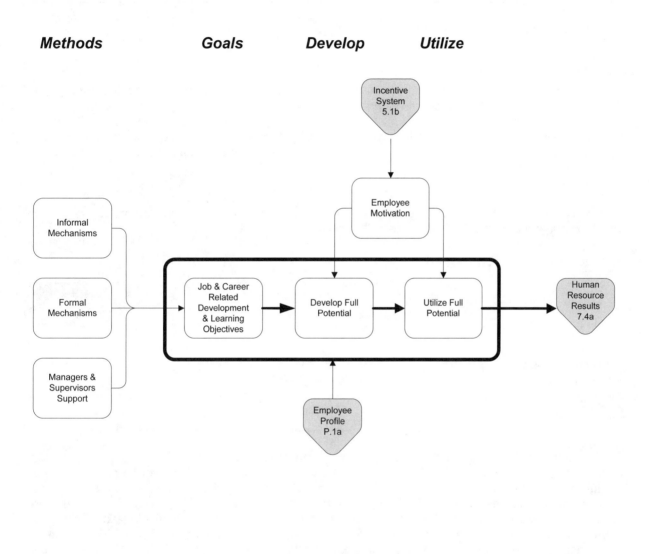

SYSTEM INTEGRATION

Motivation and Career Development 5.2b – Linkages

Inputs

P.1a – The employee profile (number, type, characteristics of employees) influences the appropriate design of the motivation and career development approaches.

5.1b – To help motivate employees to develop and utilize their full potential the rewards, recognition, and compensation system should be designed to encourage the employees and not de-motivate them.

Outputs

7.4a – The human resource results (levels, trends, comparisons) should include indicators of the development and utilization of employees' full potential.

Transformation	**Leaders**

THOUGHTS FOR LEADERS

Approximately ten years ago a large aerospace company CEO went out to a remote location and held a management club meeting of 1,500 managers. He was passionate. He spoke for an hour and a half on the leader's responsibility in supporting innovation and supporting the innovators. The example he used in his speech was of Thomas Edison. Edison did 4,500 experiments before he found Tungsten as the filament for the light bulb. A lady asked him, "Mr. Edison, don't you feel like a failure? I mean, you had 4,500 failures." Edison replied, "No ma'am, you do not understand. I had 4,500 successful experiments, and each one proved what would not work for the filament of a light bulb." The speaker's whole point was for leaders to support the innovator. This division made spacecraft so they had to have innovators.

What was so dramatic was what happened the next day. In one of the director's offices someone poked their head in the door and said, "What did you think of the boss's speech last night?" The director replied, "Not in this company. C.Y.A., be very safe."

It is striking because there is no question the CEO was setting direction. The problem was the processes and the measurements were not genuine in the minds of the leaders at other levels in the organization. People do not behave in the manner they will be incentivized, they behave the way they think they are going to be incentivised. If those two are not the same, then behavior and incentives are not aligned. It may take a couple of years for people to really understand the measurement system has changed before their behavior changes.

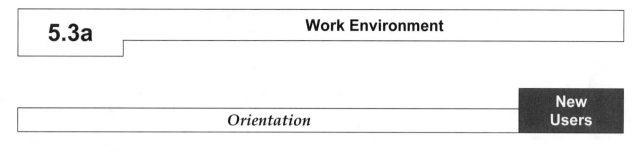

5.3a | **Work Environment**

Orientation | **New Users**

FOUNDATION

Work Environment 5.3a - Introduction

Areas to Address 5.3a focuses on the work environment an organization gives its employees. Is it safe, secure, and is the organization prepared for short and/or long term emergencies or disasters? Baldrige applications frequently discuss tracking of safety issues on a reactive basis rather than the proactive steps to prevent the safety issues. Proactive steps can include safety or ergonomics audits, security audits, health assessments, and particularly tracking near misses. Near misses are where no one was hurt but if the same circumstance occurs again someone might be hurt.

Another aspect of work environment protection is how employees participate in improving the work environment and how the organization measures their performance. Additionally, the criteria ask for not only performance measures but what levels (or targets) the organization is attempting to achieve. In the Organizational Profile the employee profile was requested. Where there are differences in different employees' groups' needs these should be addressed in this area. For example, if one group of employees is required to drive to customer locations, and another group is not, they may have very different work place environment needs. Those differences should be described in 5.3a(1).

The second part of work environment criteria addresses how the organization prepares for emergencies or disasters. This is not only focused on how the organization protects its assets and employees, but also on how they plan to stay in business. This could be a response to business continuity to ensure the customers are still supported and the employees still have a place to work.

EXAMPLE

Work Environment 5.3a - Example Practices

Branch Smith Printing – (Baldrige Recipient 2002)

To provide a safe and healthy work environment, they utilize safety consultants, OSHCON, and the Safety Committee to continually strive for improvement. They perform inspections of facilities and safety programs to identify deficiencies. Safety issues include industry related OSHA regulations for printers such as lockout/tag-out, machine guarding, personal protective equipment, hazard communications, emergency procedures, and driving of industrial trucks. The goal in all of these areas is 100% compliance and zero accidents.

Policies described within the employee manual outline rules for safety. These are based on types of positions and work environment, such as job-specific procedures for lock-out/tag-out and forklift safety. General safety rules and the evacuation plan are also included, as are requirements for new hire drug screening and drug and alcohol testing following an injury or accident on the job.

Supervisors assess their department to determine if potential hazards exist that would require use of Personal Protective Equipment (PPE). Each employee receives PPE training that coordinates with his or her work. The Safety Coordinator (SC) works with the HRM to facilitate the Safety Program and related training. The SC and a safety committee establish goals and objectives for employee safety and health. Members of the safety committee conduct quarterly safety and health self inspections for the entire facility. A comprehensive inspection checklist is used to perform inspections and is evaluated and updated with hazards identified during the inspections. The inspection report is used in trend analysis and record keeping. By maintaining effective record keeping, they identify trends and deficiencies in the safety program.

When these inspections reveal a need for training or a change in work instructions, the team recommends these changes to the QRT. Employees are also encouraged to complete a Safety Hazard Concern and Correction form if they identify an area that needs attention. The follow-up is completed and reviewed in the monthly Division or department meetings with appropriate training.

The workers' compensation insurance carrier provides a comprehensive safety and health audit on an annual basis, with a specific emphasis on ergonomics. These audits identify existing and potential hazards and noncompliance issues. The findings and recommendations for corrective actions are discussed with the HRM.

Branch-Smith (2003) p. 24

 EXAMPLE

Work Environment 5.3a - Example Practices

Motorola CGISS – **(Baldrige Recipient 2002)**

CGISS' practices related to health, safety and ergonomics include safety councils, an Ergonomics Task Force, EHS systems audits, use of the Voluntary Protection Program (proactively inviting OSHA to inspect), health fairs, on-line ergonomics classes, safety awards and recognition and emergency/non-emergency numbers at each facility.

The Environmental, Health and Safety (EHS) Teams at each CGISS site worldwide continually assess the impact of each facility's processes, products and services on the environment, health and safety of employees and work to reduce the Environmental, Health and Safety risks associated with site activities. Several CGISS facilities have either qualified or re-certified for the prestigious Occupational Safety and Health Administration's Voluntary Protection Program STAR Award. CGISS is exploring possibilities for expanding OSHA VPP globally, starting with the Penang, Malaysia site. CGISS is also proud to participate in the Motorola Assist Program, which includes Immunization services, up-to-date travel advisories, 24-hour medical advice/referrals, emergency care and emergency medical evacuation/repatriations.

Category	Practices	Measures	Targets
Health	1) Wellness Programs (W)	Utilization	____ % of HAP Participants
	2) Fitness Center Activities	Utilization	Exceed National Average
	3) Health Fair (W)	Participation	____ % of population
	4) Health and Safety Depot	Utilization	____ usages per day
	5) Customer Sat. Survey	Results	____ % in customer satisfaction
	6) AED	Globally Implement	End of first half 2002
Safety	1) 6-2222 Medical Emergency Phone Line (W)	Response Time	____ minutes for EMS
	2) 6-safe Safety & Environmental Concerns	Utilization & turn round time	____ % follow through and closure
	3) Compliance	Audit Scores	Pass
	*ADA Accessible	Out Side Consultant/Facility Changes	Compliant
	*Corporate Global EGS Audits 1993-1997 & 1999 (W)	Pass/Fail	Pass
	*Medical OSHA Surveillance Programs (W)	No Citations	____ % Compliant
	4) OSHA VPP Star Award	Qualified in 1995 Recert. In 1998	All US. CGISS Manufacturing sites
	5) MERT – Motorola Emergency Response Team (W)	Emergency Response	____ % training compliant
	6) Air and Noise level checks (W)	OSHA Recordable Incidents	No Incidents
	7) Automatic External Defibrillator (W)	Global Implementation	All Qualified Sites (MERT)
Ergonomics	Safety and Ergonomics Fairs	Participation	____ % of population
	1) Hazard Communication Training (W)	Participation	____ % Manufacturing Pop
	2) Injury and Illness Investigation (W)	OSHA Rate	Rate less than ____
	3) Job Analysis (W)	Identify Workplace Hazards	Eliminate All Workplace Hazards
	4) ESIH Champions	Employee Participation	____ % of building zones covered
	5) ISO 14001 Certification (W)	Audit	Entire Corporation Certified

In an effort to trend employee activities, EHS established metrics, which allow site managers to prioritize and redesign process. The EHS team is responsible for implementation of the corrective action reporting system for accidents, ergonomic hand tool safety, back safety awareness fairs, accident report escalation process, personal ergonomic assessments, current enhancements to facility office equipment, investigating and identifying common vendors for office furniture, and ESIH Champion development. EHS is constantly striving to lower injury/illness rates and lost time associated with these OSHA recordable incidents. Employees are able to identify health and safety concerns in the workplace using several channels: hot line numbers, ESIH Champions, attending Health Fairs, resources in OHR, web site access and awareness programs.

CGISS' approaches to employee well being and satisfaction are evaluated and improved during quarterly operations reviews, and Category 5 Performance Excellence reviews. On an annual basis, the Category 5 Performance Excellence Team is joined by Senior Management to review and analyze the results of the annual Performance Excellence Assessment. Improvements are standardized through changes in processes and practices. They are institutionalized across CGISS through sharing and communication. The Team utilizes the model presented in Item P.2.c in the Organizational Profile. These inputs include injury analysis, benchmarks, health safety ergonomics reports, corporate results, EHS Management System audit results, and specific measures outlined. Occupational Health is presently being benchmarked for the Automatic External Defibrillator program.

Source: Motorola (2003) pp. 39 - 40

	Diagnosis	**Assessors**

QUESTIONS

Work Environment 5.3a - Baldrige Criteria Questions

Improving the Workplace (1)

- *HOW do you improve workplace health, safety, security, and ergonomics?*
- *HOW do employees take part in improving them? What are your PERFORMANCE MEASURES or targets for each of these KEY workplace factors?*
- *What are the significant differences in workplace factors and PERFORMANCE MEASURES or targets if different employee groups and work units have different work environments?*

Emergency Preparedness (2)

- *HOW do you ensure workplace preparedness for emergencies or disasters?*
- *HOW do you seek to ensure business continuity for the benefit of your employees and CUSTOMERS?*

NIST (2004) p. 23

WORKSHEETS

Work Environment 5.3a - Work Sheets

Describe how your organization maintains a work environment and an employee support climate that contribute to the well-being, satisfaction, and motivation of all employees.

5.3a (1) – Improve Workplace

Process Used To Improve The Workplace For :	Process Used For Employees To Take Part In The Improvement	Measures Or Targets For Each Of The Processes	Differences In The Workplace For Different Employee Groups
Health			
Safety			
Security			
Ergonomics			

5.3a (2) - Disaster Preparedness

Requirement:	Process Used To Meet The Requirement For Protecting:			
	Employees	Facilities	Data	Other Property
Prepare for Disasters				
Ensure Business Continuity				

ASSESSMENT

Work Environment 5.3a – Diagnostic Questions

Rating Scale:

0 - **No Process** in place - We are not doing this
1 - **Reacting to Problems** - Using a Basic (Primarily Reactive) Process
2 - **Systematic Process** – We use a systematic process that has been improved
3 - **Aligned** – We use a process that aligns our activities from top to bottom
4 - **Integrated** – We use a process that is integrated with other processes across the organization
5 - **Benchmark** - We are the Benchmark!
DK - Don't Know

1.	The organization cares for the safety, well-being and morale of all employees.	0	1	2	3	4	5	DK
2.	The quality of work life is high.	0	1	2	3	4	5	DK
3.	The organization ensures workplace preparedness for emergencies and disasters in a manner which ensures business continuity.	0	1	2	3	4	5	DK

BLUEPRINT

Work Environment 5.3a - Blueprint

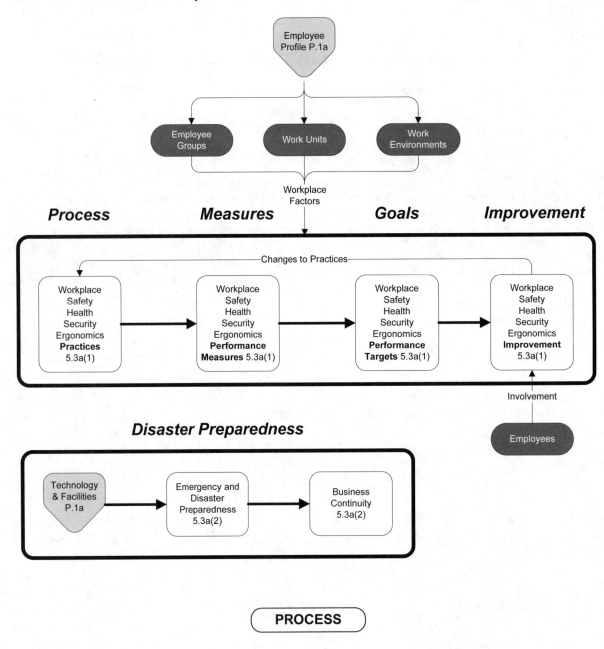

Workplace safety, health, and security is a four step process of: 1) process, 2) measures, 3) goals, and 4) improvement. This central process is influenced by the employee profile, the workgroups, and the various work environments found or described in the profile.

The workplace practices are then measured and performance targets are set for the employees involved in the improvement. These are designed to measure the practices used to meet the performance targets.

In addition to workplace safety, health, security, and ergonomics environments there is also the issue of disaster preparedness. Disaster preparedness is influenced by the type of technology and facilities and the locations of these facilities. Two issues are central to disaster preparedness. The first issue regarding the emergency and disaster preparedness processes is the approach and practices which will ensure safety and ultimately ensure business continuity. The second issue is to effectively implement these practices.

Workplace preparedness for emergencies and disasters should take into account the actions and preventative measures necessary to protect employees, facilities, other property, and data. All of these may have to be protected if the organization is to continue operations.

 SYSTEM INTEGRATION

Work Environment 5.3a – Linkages

Inputs

P.1a – Employee profile is a key input to the nature of employee groups, work units, and work environments which, in turn, influence the design of the processes, measures, and goals to create the desired work environment.

P.1a – The location and type of facilities and the nature of the technology used in the facilities is a direct input to the emergency and disaster preparedness approaches. In other words, the disaster threat differs depending on location and the nature of the technology.

Outputs

There are no significant output linkages to other criteria areas.

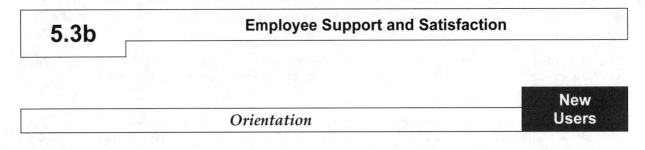

5.3b

Employee Support and Satisfaction

Orientation

New Users

FOUNDATION

Employee Support and Satisfaction 5.3b – Introduction

Employee support and satisfaction addresses two fundamental areas. The first area is how the organization knows what benefits or support employees need and gives it to them. The second area is how the organization assesses employee well-being and satisfaction and uses this information to drive priorities for improvement.

In determining the key factors which affect employee well-being, most companies do this informally and do not have a specific process with clearly defined decision criteria. Since this is a "how" question, it is necessary for the response to describe a systematic process. Additionally, differences in the workforce (as discussed in Area to Address 5.3a) may need to be addressed. Different segments of the workforce may have different requirements.

Once the organization has assessed the needs of their workforce (including the full range of diversity of the workforce and different job requirements) the criteria ask how the organization supports those needs. What many companies fail to realize is that a number of benefits can be tailored by the employees themselves to meet their specific and unique requirements. This is not achieved by the company "tailoring" the specific benefits, it is achieved by the employees' tailoring the benefits to their own needs.

The second portion of employee support and satisfaction is determination of employee satisfaction, well-being and motivation. Companies assess employee satisfaction a number of different ways, but the most common is an employee satisfaction survey. Many companies survey employees routinely, and then do not take action on the information from those surveys. In this sense, companies essentially have two responsibilities: 1) effectively understand employees feelings and needs, and; 2) do something to address those feelings and needs. If either of these factors is not addressed, the company should see their indicators (such as employee retention, absenteeism or grievances, safety, and productivity) unfavorably impacted.

The final portion of employee support and satisfaction is to link the assessment findings to business results. Do happy employees drive better organizational performance? That is the basic question Baldrige asks companies to address. Once a company understands the correlation, then how do they identify priorities for making changes which will favorably impact organizational performance.

EXAMPLE

Employee Support and Satisfaction 5.3b - Example Practices

Branch-Smith Printing – **(Baldrige Recipient 2002)**

Factors affecting employee satisfaction were originally determined through benchmarking with other quality oriented companies within the quality peer group. Over time, open-ended questions and focus group results following annual employee surveys have led the PLT to select indicators for satisfaction measurements that are based on areas of key concern by employees. In 2001, they added an importance ranking by question to the annual employee survey to allow employees to identify key areas of concern. They also added the ability to collect demographic data, allowing them to analyze importance and satisfaction by diverse category of employee.

Importance of work factors to employee satisfaction is also determined through numerous meetings and communications. They emphasize the "open door" policy in orientations and monthly meetings to give employees the opportunity to speak with their supervisors, managers, or HRM about any issue. The HRM is a resource for problem solving and general policy guidance. Monthly Division meetings are used to share information pertaining to new opportunities for company and individual growth as well as a "report card" on how the company is doing. A question and answer session gives employees the opportunity to express opinions about what is important to them. They also make suggestions through the OFI program, which is an additional opportunity for input on the importance of issues in improving the environment and satisfaction.

Company Support of Employees

Employees' satisfaction is supported through many benefits and services. They have a strong benefit program by sharing in the cost of the health insurance premiums and by offering short-term disability, life, and dental insurance. They encourage participation in physical fitness activities by sharing 50% of membership dues to the YMCA. They offer a flexible spending account that creates a tax-advantaged way to assist employees with benefits.

The 401(k) plan has an on-line service for employees to view their account balance, make changes in their investment options, and gain access to fund performance reports. In response to the employee survey, the plan is documented in English and Spanish. Another important benefit is the "open book" management approach, which gives employees a sense of ownership and allows them see how their work affects the bottom line.

Benefits are regularly evaluated and improved through input from the employee survey and the annual PIA benefit survey, which allow them to benchmark to others in the industry. The HRM works with employee volunteers to review the benefits and make recommendations for health insurance, short-term disability, and life insurance programs, all in the best interests of the diverse workforce.

The annual United Way campaign provides a way for employees to participate in community activities with the option of visiting an agency or participating in projects to support community efforts. A team of employee volunteers arranges an event to educate and encourage employee support of the community. Materials are provided in English and Spanish.

The primary objective of the newsletter is to improve communication by covering information about the service to external and internal customers, safety training, benefit utilization, and departmental spotlights. They also use the quarterly newsletter to recognize employees on a personal level, celebrating such things as the birth of child or grandchild, graduations, awards, or special trips.

Amenities enhance the satisfaction of employees such as free parking, free coffee, an attractive lunchroom, and a landscaped patio to enjoy during breaks. Other special opportunities involve several celebrations and a holiday luncheon that includes family members. The quarterly corporate meetings involve recreation and teamwork through random grouping of trivia teams to develop rapport among employees and management. Prizes provide recognition and satisfaction among the group. Teams of volunteers from both divisions work with the HRM to plan and orchestrate the quarterly meetings with communication and satisfaction as key goals.

To support the diverse workforce, they provide training in work instructions through interpreters in each department. They provide safety instruction in Spanish. They have also initiated an English as a Second Language course. Due to different national holidays and traditions in the workforce, they accommodate employees in allowing them to use their vacation or have additional time off to celebrate or be with their families. This flexibility increases employees' satisfaction.

Satisfaction Assessment Methods

The primary formal method of determining employee satisfaction is through the employee satisfaction survey. The survey addresses communication, management, customer focus, quality, job responsibility and training, procedures and processes, teamwork, and overall satisfaction. Employees rate their agreement with 50 statements in these categories as Strongly Agree, Agree, Disagree, or Strongly Disagree. Statement ratings of less than 60% agreement are given particular focus for improvement. Results are broken out by department to provide feedback to specific supervisors and to senior management for their performance. This provides upward feedback to leaders in conjunction with their normal performance evaluation. The data is shared with all employees in department and Division meetings.

Demographic information is gathered as part of the survey to determine well-being and satisfaction among the diverse workforce and to ensure no major gaps between ethnic, age, gender, or tenure groups exist. Employees also rate the importance of each issue to determine level of concerns. Focus groups, which allow employees to express concerns, ask questions, or make suggestions, provide more specific responses about problem areas. Results are used to create QIPs and as input into the SPP.

The second major approach to determine employee satisfaction is voluntary employee turnover. Reducing turnover is a Division goal and is measured for each department. The established goal is reducing voluntary turnover to 10%, which is below the average of the Fortune 100 Best Places to Work for in America. Employees that leave voluntarily are given exit interviews to provide feedback in job satisfaction and dissatisfaction.

Monthly Division meetings are an open forum to express specific concerns as well as the "open door" style of management. Concerns that affect all employees are reviewed in the monthly CLT meeting. Concerns that affect the Division are reviewed in the monthly PLT. QIPs are used to review and follow up on areas as necessary.

Assessment Finding Relative to Business Results

Through analysis of cause and affect of the relationship between customer satisfaction, employee satisfaction, and business results, they determine key priorities for improvement as part of the SPP. Positive results from the customer survey reveal quality products and services from employees, indicative of a highly satisfied and well trained, empowered employee base. Customer satisfaction results show that commitment to employee satisfaction and training affects customer satisfaction directly. Employee survey results continue to indicate that employees know who their customers are and understand goals for meeting their needs.

A training plan is developed for each employee to improve skills and grow within the company. This plan, along with reduced turnover and increased satisfaction, is related to the positive growth in Value Added Sales, etc.

Several important QIP improvements have impacted the bottom line. Due to low scores in communication on the 1999 employee survey, a QIP implemented a solution that involved better department schedules, monthly department meetings, and bulletin boards tracking performance and goals. Better communication has helped reduce PONC and brought satisfaction to employees by connecting them personally to the goals. QIP teams continue to enhance the quality focus and improve the processes, hence creating the business results desired.

The most compelling evidence of effectiveness of the HR approach is the impact of the appraisal and training method on employee satisfaction and productivity. In early 2001, the full system of roll-up reviews was implemented, linking individual employee performance goals to the goals for their work group, department, and the Division. The employee establishes performance goals in his/her annual review activity along with required training for the year. Performance to those goals is reviewed weekly and adjustments are made to the training plan. Aggregate results are reviewed quarterly as a department. Roll-ups continue through the organization on these measures. Results of satisfaction scores in many areas reflect the improved satisfaction of employees with their work as a result of the improved communication with supervisors, and satisfaction with training and the performance review. These improvements correlate closely with the accelerated improvements in 2001 results for individual process effectiveness.

Source: Branch-Smith (2003) pp. 24 – 26

 EXAMPLE

Employee Support and Satisfaction 5.3b - Example Practices

Motorola CGISS **– (Baldrige Recipient 2002)**

Motorola's PULSE employee survey was designed in 2000 as an organizational diagnostic and employee satisfaction/well-being/motivation assessment tool, and is administered every other year. Global focus groups are used to develop survey content, and determine the key factors that affect well being, satisfaction, and motivation. In 2002, an extensive redesign of PULSE was done to identify those factors that are most critical for employee satisfaction and organizational performance (i.e. factor analysis, key drivers, norms, trends, variance). The survey is conducted every other year as a census and is offered in 11 languages

CGISS provides employees with a wide array of benefits and services to enhance the work climate. The philosophy of the Global Rewards and Compensation team is: "To provide world-class reward strategies and programs that attract, retain and motivate the best people, producing outstanding business performance and shareholder value."

They provide a total compensation package that is competitive with the prevailing practices for each industry and country in which they operate, allowing for above average total compensation when market and business justifies. The Global Rewards Team routinely surveys competitors, conducts employee feedback sessions, and polls Human Resources Managers to ensure that the total rewards program provides a competitive package of benefits and services.

The Motorola policies that govern human resource activities are developed at a corporate level and are the overriding structure for managing employees with site-specific policies identified as needed to effectively manage the local workforce.

5.3b Motorola CGISS – Employee Satisfaction Survey

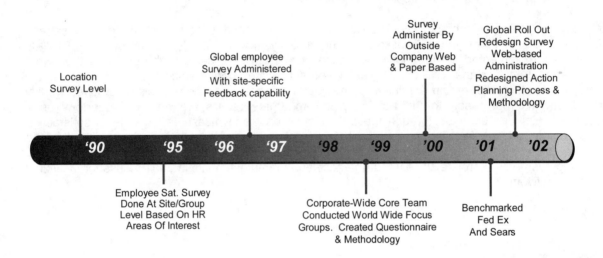

Motorola provides its employees with a number of benefits including comprehensive medical benefits, recreational and social clubs, day care options, diversity business councils, an employee award and recognition resource and referral program, call care, retirement benefits, wellness initiatives, and expanded healthy quality of life programs. Employees are made aware of these programs through various methods - newsletters, flyers, table tent cards, intranet websites, mailings to the employee's home, employee information centers, call centers, Town Hall meetings and bulletin board displays. Recent enhancements to the Motorola Employee Benefits package, specifically profit sharing and pension accounts, as well as fitness center reimbursements, were made based on employee feedback.

The importance of consistent, well-reasoned policies cannot be overstated. They ensure the fair treatment of employees and help lay the foundation for a positive/productive work environment. As the competition to attract and retain the best and the brightest intensifies, a positive work environment becomes an important differentiator. All Motorola businesses in the U.S. have accepted and implemented a consistent set of policies to ensure Motorola maintains its long-standing position as a premiere employer in the high tech field.

Specific policies include the following: Job Sharing and Flexible Work Schedules, Family Illness Leave of Absence, Bereavement Time Off and Pay, Community Service, Education Assistance, Open Door Process, Parental Leave of Absence, Personal Leave of Absence, Senior Service, Drug Free Workforce, Safe and Respectful Workplace, Motorola's Employee Assistance Program, Ambassador Program, Wellness Initiatives, Global Employee Consultation System (GECS), ONCALL, Food Service Initiatives.

5.3b Motorola CGISS – Pulse: Key Factors

PULSE Dimensions	Satisfaction	Motivation	Well-Being
Company Image and Satisfaction	x	x	
Job Satisfaction	x	x	x
Pay and Benefits	x	x	x
Employee Treatment	x	x	x
Employee Development and Advancement	x	x	
Rewards and Recognition	x	x	
Senior Management	x	x	x
Strategic Focus		x	
Enablement	x	x	
Immediate Supervisor	x	x	x
Personal Performance Goals	x	x	
Original Focus Groups			
What created a satisfying and rewarding relationship with Motorola?	x	x	x
What helped get the job done?		x	
What got in the way of ability to get the job done?		x	

CGISS' PULSE survey is used to determine employee well being, satisfaction and motivation of employees worldwide. The data from the survey was compared to over three-dozen companies similar to Motorola. The normative data indicated results were above the industry norms in many benchmarked categories. The next PULSE survey will be administered in July 2002.

The formal and informal assessment methods and measures used to determine well being, satisfaction and motivation are clearly defined. The key factors that affect employee well-being, satisfaction, and motivation are determined through methods such as employee focus groups, reviewing employee productivity, retention metrics through information exchange with employee business councils, the Office of Leadership, and through information via chat sessions with employees. These results are included in the strategic planning process, and are also included in the evaluation and improvement of leadership effectiveness.

In 2000, CGISS performed extensive linkage analysis between PULSE results and real business results (financials, customer satisfaction data, human resource outcomes, and productivity data). CGISS found a direct relationship between employee's overall satisfaction and actual turnover in business. This relationship drove the evolution of the retention team and its efforts and the extensive retention analysis on a monthly basis. PULSE also demonstrated a relationship between customer awareness, as measured by PULSE, and actual customer satisfaction.

Motorola CGISS Presentation – Quest for Excellence 2003

QUESTIONS

Employee Support and Satisfaction 5.3b – Baldrige Criteria Questions

Key Factors of Well-Being, Satisfaction, and Motivation (1)

- *HOW do you determine the KEY factors that affect employee well-being, satisfaction, and motivation?*
- *HOW are these factors SEGMENTED for a diverse workforce and for different categories and types of employees?*

Support Services (2)

- *HOW do you support your employees via services, benefits, and policies?*
- *HOW are these tailored to the needs of a diverse workforce and different categories and types of employees?*

Measures (3)

- *What formal and informal assessment methods and MEASURES do you use to determine employee well-being, satisfaction, and motivation?*
- *HOW do these methods and MEASURES differ across a diverse workforce and different categories and types of employees?*
- *HOW do you use other INDICATORS, such as employee retention, absenteeism, grievances, safety, and PRODUCTIVITY, to assess and improve employee well-being, satisfaction, and motivation?*

Correlation to Key Business Results (4)

- *HOW do you relate assessment findings to KEY business RESULTS to identify priorities for improving the work environment and employee support climate?*

Note 1: Specific factors that might affect your employees' well-being, satisfaction, and motivation (5.3b[1]) include effective employee problem or grievance resolution; safety factors; employees' views of management; employee training, development, and career opportunities; employee preparation for changes in technology or the work organization; the work environment and other work conditions; management's empowerment of employees; information sharing by management; workload; cooperation and teamwork; recognition; services and benefits; communications; job security; compensation; and equal opportunity.

Note 2: Approaches for employee support (5.3b[2]) might include providing counseling, career development and employability services, recreational or cultural activities, nonwork-related education, day care, job rotation or sharing, special leave for family responsibilities or community service, home safety training, flexible work hours and location, outplacement, and retirement benefits (including extended health care).

Note 3: *Measures and indicators of well-being, satisfaction, and motivation (5.3b[3]) might include data on safety and absenteeism, the overall turnover rate, the turnover rate for customer contact employees, employees' charitable contributions, grievances, strikes, other job actions, insurance costs, workers' compensation claims, and results of surveys. Survey indicators of satisfaction might include employee knowledge of job roles, employee knowledge of organizational direction, and employee perception of empowerment and information sharing. Your results relative to such measures and indicators should be reported in Item 7.4.*

Note 4: *Setting priorities (5.3b[4]) might draw upon your human resource results presented in Item 7.4 and might involve addressing employee problems based on their impact on your business results.*

NIST (2004) p. 23

 WORKSHEETS

Employee Support and Satisfaction 5.3b - Work Sheets

Assessment Methods include formal and informal
Measures include retention, absenteeism, grievances, safety, and productivity.

5.3b (1) - Determining Key Factors To Employee Well-Being

Process to Determine Key Factors For Employee Well-Being:	What Are The Key Factors?	Process To Tailor The Key Factors by Employee Segment:

5.3b (2) – Employee Services, Benefits, Policies

	Services	Benefits	Policies
What Are They?			
Process To Tailor These To Meet The Needs Of A Diverse Workforce:			

5.3b (3) - Determine Employee Satisfaction

Employee Segment/Group	Employee Satisfaction, Motivation And Well-Being Assessment Methods		Measures
	Formal	**Informal**	

Measures should include factors such as retention, absenteeism, grievances, safety, and productivity.

5.3b (4) - Business Results and Priorities

Methods to relate key business results to identify priorities for improvement of environment and support climate:		
Process To Link Key Business Results To Employee Assessment Findings:	**Process To Identify Priorities For Improving The Work Environment:**	**Process To Identify Priorities For Improving The Employee Support Climate:**
Employee Group_____		
Employee Group_____		

 ## ASSESSMENT

Employee Support and Satisfaction 5.3b – Diagnostic Questions

Rating Scale:

0 - **No Process** in place - We are not doing this
1 - **Reacting to Problems** - Using a Basic (Primarily Reactive) Process
2 - **Systematic Process** – We use a systematic process that has been improved
3 - **Aligned** – We use a process that aligns our activities from top to bottom
4 - **Integrated** – We use a process that is integrated with other processes across the organization
5 - **Benchmark** - We are the Benchmark!
DK - Don't Know

1. The organization assesses the key factors which adversely affect employee well-being, satisfaction and motivation.　　　0　1　2　3　4　5　DK

2. Employee benefits are tailored to meet the needs of individual groups of employees.　　　0　1　2　3　4　5　DK

3. There is a systematic process to evaluate employee satisfaction, and action is taken on the areas needing improvement.　　　0　1　2　3　4　5　DK

Design

BLUEPRINT

Employee Support and Satisfaction 5.3b - Blueprint

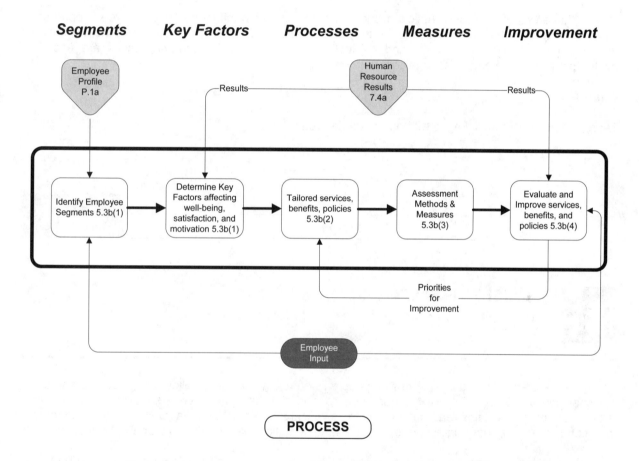

The employee support and satisfaction process is composed of five major components. The first component is the identification of employee segments. These are based on the employee profile found in P.1a. Employees' segments should be based on different requirements, needs, wants, desires. The next step is to determine the key factors that affect the employee well-being, satisfaction, and motivation. These key factors drive the customization of the services, benefits, and policies which affect employee support and satisfaction. The effectiveness of the services, the benefits, and the policies is determined by assessment methods and measures which are used to evaluate and improve the service benefits and policies.

SYSTEM INTEGRATION

Employee Support and Satisfaction 5.3b – Linkages

Inputs

P.1a – The employee profile identifies the number, type, and characteristics of key employee segments. The description of the employees in the profile should correspond to the segments used to determine key factors, processes, and measures for employee support and satisfaction approaches.

7.4a – Human resource results (levels, trends, and comparisons) influence the employee support and satisfaction approaches in two ways. First, they can be analyzed and used to determine the key factors that affect well-being, satisfaction, and motivation. Second, human resource results are used to evaluate and improve employee services, benefits, and policies.

Outputs

There are no significant linkages with other criteria areas.

Transformation	**Leaders**

THOUGHTS FOR LEADERS

Senior leaders ask, "How do I ensure that people listen to my coaching, follow my guidance, and take my coaching to heart?" One of the questions to ask is "When you have a session where you are coaching someone, what is really important?" The typical answer is: "What is really important is that my direction to them be clear and accurate, my coaching be actionable and they understand it is correct."

If in their hearts employees know you care about them, you can be brutal with your feedback. They will listen and will try to make changes. But if they have a little doubt about where you are coming from, they can be pretty thin-skinned. If people don't think the leaders care about them, why would they follow those leaders?

Organizational Learning

Overview

The organizational learning system is composed of the measurement and analysis of organization performance, information and knowledge management, and a comprehensive performance scorecard. Learning requires measurement and analysis to identify and diagnose areas for improvement and to determine the effectiveness of changes made to the systems. This knowledge is then captured and made available for others throughout the organization and those who join the organization. Finally, a comprehensive set of measures is needed to provide the systems perspective and understand the cause-and-effect relationships of the pieces and parts.

Measurement and Analysis

This system is composed of measurement selection, collection, and analysis for strategic planning, front-line decision making, and senior leader organization performance reviews. The system facilitates the critical review, creative design, construction, and continuous improvement of the strategic leadership and execution excellence systems.

- How do you measure overall organizational performance?
- How do you measure and track progress toward the strategy?
- How do you know how well your processes are doing?

Measurement and Analysis Areas to Address:

    4.1a – Performance Measurement
    4.1b – Performance Analysis

Information and Knowledge Management

This system consists of the methods and mechanisms to capture and share knowledge throughout the organization. In addition, this system includes the methods and mechanisms to ensure the integrity, timeliness, reliability, security, accuracy, and confidentiality of the data, information, and Organizational Knowledge.

- How do you capture and share best practices and Organizational Knowledge?
- How do you ensure the integrity, reliability, and accuracy of your information?
- How do you ensure the security and confidentiality of your information?

Information and Knowledge Management Areas to Address:

    4.2a – Data and Information Availability
    4.2b – Organizational Knowledge

Performance Scorecard

The third component of the organizational learning system is a comprehensive set of performance measures that include results from multiple perspectives in the organization system and stakeholders.

- How satisfied are your customers?
- How good are your products and services?
- How effective and efficient is your organization and your suppliers and partners?
- How satisfied, developed, and effective are your people?
- How healthy are your finances?
- How good a corporate citizen are you?

Performance Scorecard Area to Address:

7.1a – Customer-Focused Results
7.2a – Product and Service Results
7.3a – Financial and Market Results
7.4a – Human Resource Results
7.5a – Organizational Effectiveness Results
7.6a – Governance and Social Responsibility Results

4.1a	Performance Measurement

 FOUNDATION

Performance Measurement 4.1a – Introduction

Performance measurement begins with an organization determining the criteria they wish to use to select data. The most basic criteria include:

- **The data are required** – This could be required by regulatory agencies, governmental groups, higher level authority, company policies, industry standards, or others. Simply stated, if I am required to collect the data then I will collect the data.

- **The data are actionable** – Using the data, the organization can understand what actions need to be taken.

Other more complex data selection criteria can include:

- The data can be collected with integrity
- The data are easy to collect
- Data are meaningful
- The data are available at the source of the data/area to be monitored
- And others

Although the data selection criteria are not specifically requested by the Baldrige criteria, by answering this question organizations can more easily understand why they are collecting data and integrate that collection process with actually using the data.

The criteria ask how data are collected and what the organization does with those data. The way that Area to Address 4.1a is written needs to be integrated and aligned with how Item 2.2 describes the deployment of goals down the organization. The tracking system and measurement systems described in Area to Address 4.1a need to be compatible with each other.

Once data are selected, collected, aligned, and integrated, leaders and employees throughout the organization need to use the data and information to support decisions. The core value of **management by fact** is driven by Item 4.1. It is the ability of the organization to not only collect data but to perform analysis which drive decisions.

Another area addressed in Area to Address 4.1a(2) is how the organization collects, selects, and uses key comparative data. Most organizations are attempting to drive a comparative mindset throughout the organization and use comparisons not only at the highest level to make organizational-level decisions but to use data to make decisions at all levels.

Frequently applications discuss the organization's "benchmarking" processes. Few applications, however, describe the following logic flow:

- How the organization decides a comparison is needed.
- How the organization decides what data need to be compared.
- How the organization decides what other groups or organizations to compare with.
- The process the organization uses to collect comparative data.
- How comparative data are analyzed once they are gathered.
- How the analysis is turned into an action plan.
- How the action plan is implemented.
- How performance metrics are monitored to ensure that the changes which were desired are achieved.
- How corrective actions are taken if the performance levels do not improve.

The fundamental question in the above logic flow is – "Does data drive action?"

Once data have been gathered, analyzed, and have driven improvement, the criteria ask how the performance measurement system is kept current with changing business needs. This, once again, needs to be a systematic process which can ensure that the company's data collection, tracking, and decision processes can move at least as quickly as the external changes which influence the organization.

 EXAMPLE

Performance Measurement 4.1a - Example Practices

Clarke American **- (Baldrige Recipient 2001)**

Clarke American's systematic process for selecting, gathering, analyzing and deploying information is linked from strategic planning to daily operations. They gather and integrate data and information through a system of organizational performance metrics to continually set goals, analyze performance and achieve deployment to the individual associate.

This process helps them reflect the company values of Knowledge Sharing, Measurement, and Integrity and Mutual Respect. Performance metrics are defined for both change the business and run the business perspectives.

Change the business. In 1999, they incorporated the balanced stakeholder approach into the Balanced Business Plan (BBP) and Balanced Scorecard (BSC). They refined these tools with emphasis on changing the business.

Run the business. The Key Process Indicators (KPIs) reflect the process view of the business and are used to constantly track the efficiency and effectiveness of the processes relative to the customer requirements, based upon their targets. A Key Leadership Team (KLT) member owns each metric. The leader is responsible for formally and systematically ensuring the relevance of the metric, as well as evaluating and improving the processes for gathering and reporting the information. These metrics are defined and deployed through all levels of the organization, providing for consistent and reliable analysis and decision making. The KLT reviews key metrics for continued relevance and integrity during goal deployment. Targets are established to achieve increasing performance levels. Metrics are further reviewed for *change the business* and *run the business* items. Using both predictive and diagnostic indicators provides the continual ability to test and understand the correlation between the various metrics.

Clarke American Leading and Lagging Indicators

Change the Business	Run the Business

Predictive Indicators (Leading)

- Customer Satisfaction
- Branch Loyalty
- Value Management workshops/symposiums
- Implemented S.T.A.R. ideas
- Total order cycle time

- Plant cycle time
- 24-hour service
- Utilization of Avenue
- Partner reporting satisfaction/on-time
- Associates hired in 60 days
- 401k participation
- % APS units
- % spend co-sourced

Diagnostic Indicators (Lagging)

- Revenue growth
- Customer contact center total revenue
- Total contact center revenue
- Revenue per call
- E-Commerce revenue
- Retention of 2-year associates
- Operating profit growth

- Branch telephone survey
- Waste (voids and spoilage)
- Total errors
- Credits/reprints
- PSPs integrated
- ROIC
- Cash flow
- Revenue per associate
- Total profit improvement and contribution

Selection and alignment of balanced organizational measures and indicators begins with and is driven through the strategic goal deployment process. This integrated approach ensures that metrics are systematically chosen, deployed and aligned with all company objectives. Metrics are evaluated for alignment with daily operations, as well as overall organizational performance and needs, based on a leadership review.

Change the business: The KLT agrees on appropriate measures, targets and impacts for each strategic goal within the four quadrants of the BBP as part of goal deployment. BBP measures are the primary tool used by the KLT to evaluate organizational performance and support attainment of change the business breakthrough goals. Measures are used to support division BBP and BSC objectives. Run the business: KPIs are the measures they associate with running the business "day-to-day." Each KPI is championed by a KLT member and reviewed at least monthly at the KLT level. Each division and process also defines KPIs, directly aligned with the company KPIs, to assess ongoing performance. These KPIs include measures of accuracy, responsiveness and timeliness for deliverables to internal or external customers.

Clarke American's drive to achieve world class manufacturing and servicing processes leads them to select and effectively use a variety of comparative data to assess relative performance and establish targets. During annual goal deployment, they determine the type of comparative information needed (what they compare). This is based on three factors: 1) strategic importance, 2) degree of improvement, and 3) new measure definition. The gap analysis process identifies key areas requiring breakthrough improvement, and they often set performance measures with comparative indicators when establishing appropriate targets. The Process Champion identifies the appropriate comparative measure, both within and outside the industry, and is responsible for the effective use of that information.

4.1a Clarke American – Performance Measurement Selection Process and Criteria

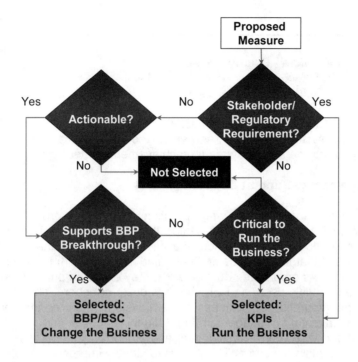

Clarke American seeks competitive comparisons from various sources (with whom they compare). Benchmarking has played a key role in improvement at Clarke American for many years. The CEO and other KLT members have been personally involved in "study tours" from which numerous best practices have been adopted. A cycle of improvement is a move to a more systematic 10-step approach to process benchmarking.

Clarke American's performance measurement system is kept current with business needs and directions through a variety of reviews and processes, including the Business Excellence Assessment and the "evaluate and improve" step in Goal Deployment. The measurement process has undergone numerous cycles of improvement. Each year during Goal Deployment, the KLT assesses business risks and identifies key measures for the upcoming year. Each KPI is owned by a KLT member who leads the formal assessment of the KPI through the review of its value and its match with business requirements. The BBP and BSC are reviewed at this same time. A recent improvement added an "impact" element to the BBP to better understand the implications of goal achievement. The number of measures included on the BSC and tracked as company KPIs has been reduced over time to ensure focus on the critical few. Measurement systems in each division and process are evaluated during the Business Excellence Assessment. They use the strengths and opportunities identified in the assessment to create action plans for improving the measurement system. A wide range of incremental improvements to the performance measurement system also come from Suggestions, Teams, Actions, Results (S.T.A.R.) ideas submitted by associates or teams.

Source: Clarke (2002) pp. 15 – 17

EXAMPLE

Performance Measurement 4.1a - Example Practices

Branch-Smith Printing - (Baldrige Recipient 2002)

Key drivers for success in the business are reflected in the Division Objectives. This involves profit and market, performance system, customer, and employee measures and goals. Data are selected and managed in order to provide status toward the achievement of these goals.

Performance Measurement to Support Decision Making

Information management for the manufacturing operations is critical to providing excellent customer service at the lowest cost. Operations are facilitated through printing management software (PSI) designed to capture shop floor data throughout the day for process management and productivity analysis reports. Time and material for jobs are estimated in the system to design the electronic job plans to manage workflow. As employees do their work, they enter the process being performed, the quantity produced, the materials used, and whether it is customer-chargeable, PONC, or other non-chargeable activity. The integration of the measurement systems ensures that job information flows directly into invoicing, inventory management, and financial systems for cost tracking by job, customer, and cost center. Utilization by cost center and productivity by process are aggregated and analyzed during the Leadership Accountability reviews to identify improvement opportunities.

Productivity and other customer and employee data are tracked using the QID. The types of data housed in the database, are used in ongoing reviews. Customer surveys, ISO 9000:2000 internal and registrar audits, and the TAPE and Baldrige feedback reports provide external sources of data, which may be entered into the QID for tracking or used for analysis purposes. The data are entered prior to department and divisional review. The QID system automatically aggregates this data in a format for making decisions and evaluating improvement options.

All improvement options are evaluated based on cost/benefit analyses as appropriate to the project. Types of analysis are taught to every employee during quality training to allow them to participate in QIP activities. Through management review, options are balanced and resources allocated in coordination with other activities.

Information and Analysis Process

Select & align measures

Key data used for organization decision-making support key performance indicators for the Division for each strategy and action plan. These were selected to ensure complete review of organizational performance to areas of greatest importance. Measures are selected during the SPP to provide appropriate information for decision making and tracking accomplishment of directions. At the daily operational level, departments and functions establish plans and measures to support organizational direction. This ensures operational tracking is aligned between groups and to the Division for decision making.

Select and use comparative

They select comparative data as a part of the annual assessment in the SPP. For all available critical measures, they identify data and sources to compare themselves to others of similar size in the industry as well as external "best-in- class" sources. They use the Printing Industries of America (PIA) Financial Ratio Studies for average and "profit leaders" comparative data by classification of product or process. They use customer survey comparisons from the survey administrator to benchmark similar manufacturers and overall participants. They compare employee satisfaction to industry association statistics, Texas Worker's Compensation safety modifiers, and the Quality Roundtable participants.

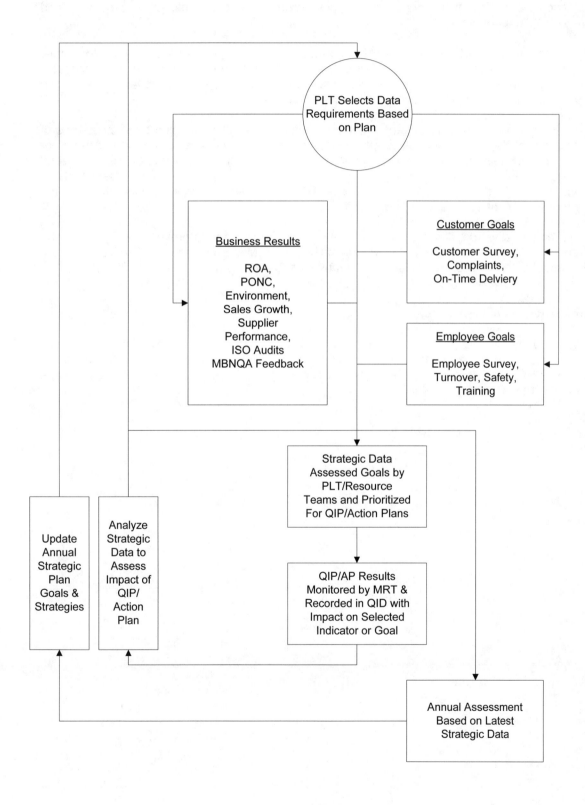

They use a "plan, do, check, act" approach to benchmarking processes and approaches. They "plan" by identifying targeted groups of companies who perform similar processes and have an outstanding performance. They are members of The Peer Group, a set of progressive companies that are active in the National Association of Printers and Lithographers (NAPL), and its Best Managed Printing Company competition. They meet three times a year with industry peers to share key industry best practices and discuss confidential matters important to closely held businesses. They attend the annual Graphic Arts Technical Foundation Continuous Improvement Conference to network and benchmark with other printers.

The "do" phase involves discussing implementation issues and analysis of the processes to identify required changes. Action plans or Quality Improvement Process (QIPs) carry out the necessary changes. The "check" activity involves tracking actions to ensure performance attains expected levels. The "act" phase is regular process tuning based on results.

The Quality Roundtable consists of various local companies that share training and discussions of issues and approaches. One member is a past Baldrige recipient and source of the benchmark for customer complaints and on-time delivery. Others include past Baldrige recipients as well as several TAPE recipients. These award winning companies provide a broad base of "best-in-class" organizations with which they benchmark practices. They also talk with suppliers about trends in the industry, pricing forecasts, competitor news, and new products.

They use comparative data in the SPP to set stretch targets for improvement. They ensure effectiveness of that data through Management Reviews (MR) meetings. Ineffective data are identified and they either seek new sources or remove that comparison.

Measurement system kept current

Evaluation and improvement of organization performance measurements occur during the Strategic Planning Process (SPP). At a more detailed level, whenever changes are required to processes based on QIPs/APs or process improvements, corresponding updates are made to ISO documents and the measurement system.

Source: Branch-Smith (2003) pp. 17 - 19

Diagnosis	

 QUESTIONS

Performance Measurement 4.1a – Baldrige Criteria Questions

Select and Collect Data (1)

- *HOW do you select, collect, align, and integrate data and information for tracking daily operations and for tracking overall organizational PERFORMANCE?*
- *HOW do you use these data and information to support organizational decision making and INNOVATION?*

Note 1: Performance measurement is used in fact-based decision making for setting and aligning organizational directions and resource use at the work unit, key process, departmental, and whole organization levels.

Comparative Data (2)

- *HOW do you select and ensure the EFFECTIVE use of KEY comparative data and information to support operational and strategic decision making and INNOVATION?*

Note 2: Comparative data and information (4.1a[2]) are obtained by benchmarking and by seeking competitive comparisons. "Benchmarking" refers to identifying processes and results that represent best practices and performance for similar activities, inside or outside your organization's industry. Competitive comparisons relate your organization's performance to that of competitors in your markets.

Keeping Current (3)

- *HOW do you keep your PERFORMANCE measurement system current with business needs and directions?*
- *HOW do you ensure that your PERFORMANCE measurement system is sensitive to rapid or unexpected organizational or external changes?*

NIST (2004) p. 19

WORKSHEETS

Performance Measurement 4.1a - Work Sheets

Describe how your organization measures, analyzes, aligns, and improves its performance data at all levels and in all parts of your organization.

4.1a (1) - Data and Information Selection, Collection, and Alignment

Use Of Data	Processes Used To:			
	*Select Data**	*Collect Data*	*Align Data*	*Integrate Data*
Track Daily Operations				
Track Overall Organizational Performance				

How Data Are Used To Support:	
Organizational decision making	
Innovation	

* This should include the use of defined data selection criteria.

4.1a (2) – Comparative Data Selection And Effective Use

Uses Of Data:	Processes Used To:	
	*Select Comparative Data**	*Ensure The Effective Use Of Key Comparative Data*
Operational Decision Making		
Strategic Decision Making		
Innovation		

* This should include the use of defined comparative data selection criteria.

4.1a (3) - Keeping Performance Measurement System Current

How Do You:				
Evaluate The Business Needs And Directions?	Evaluate Whether Your Performance Measurement System Is Current?	Identify And Document The Gaps?	Plan The Actions Needed To Fill The Gaps?	Track Whether The Actions Taken Kept The Measurement System Current?

ASSESSMENT

Performance Measurement 4.1a – Diagnostic Questions

Rating Scale:

0 - **No Process** in place - We are not doing this
1 - **Reacting to Problems** – Using a Basic (Primarily Reactive) Process
2 - **Systematic Process** – We use a systematic process that has been improved
3 - **Aligned** – We use a process that aligns our activities from top to bottom
4 - **Integrated** – We use a process that is integrated with other processes across the organization
5 - **Benchmark** - We are the Benchmark!
DK - Don't Know

1. The organization has a systematic process through which data and information are gathered and integrated from to support daily operations and organizational decision-making.

   0   1   2   3   4   5   DK

2. The functional data and information which are collected and reviewed are linked to overall organization plans, goals, and directions.

   0   1   2   3   4   5   DK

3. The organization has a process to: 1) select, 2) collect, and 3) use benchmark data or comparisons as a way of regularly looking externally to improve our own processes.

   0   1   2   3   4   5   DK

Design	**Advanced Users**

BLUEPRINT

Performance Measurement 4.1a - Blueprint

The approach to performance measurement begins with requirements and then uses the selection of measures to align daily operations and organization performance. Then the data are collected and stored in a database.

Performance Measurement 4.1a – Blueprint

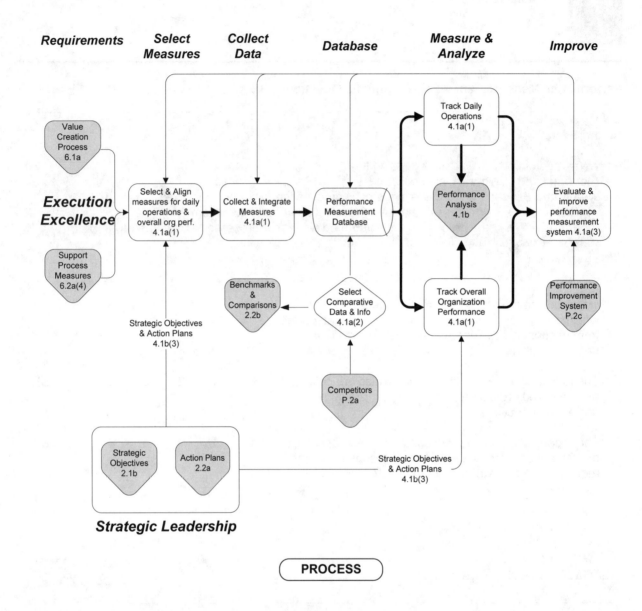

The two purposes of the data are: 1) to measure and analyze daily operations (the more tactical side); and 2) overall organization performance (the strategic side). The requirements, the selection, the data collection, and the analysis are all evaluated and improved on a regular basis. This evaluation and improvement cycle is based on the performance improvement system described in the Organizational Profile (P.2c(1)).

Part of the performance measurement system is the selection of comparative data and information. This should be based both on competitors' and industry benchmarks.

SYSTEM INTEGRATION

Performance Measurement 4.1a – Linkages

Inputs

2.1b - The objectives, goals, and their timetable described in Area to Address 2.1b drive the selection of measures to track overall organization performance and improvement.

2.2a – A key element of the strategy deployment action plans are measures to track progress. The action plans are direct inputs to the selection and alignment of measures for project management and overall organizational performance described in Areas to Address 4.1a.

6.1a – The selection and alignment of performance measures for daily operations 4.1a(1) is driven by the key value creation process requirements, in-process control requirements, and end product/service requirements.

6.2a – The selection and alignment of performance measures for daily operations 4.1a(1) is driven by the key support process requirements, in-process control requirements, and end product/service requirements.

P.2a – The selection of comparative data and information should be influenced by the key competitors described in the profile. While direct competitor performance is sometimes difficult to obtain, the process should be designed to select the most appropriate data first and then work the practicality issues as opposed to selecting the easy data then asking if it is appropriate.

P.2c – The evaluation and improvement of the performance measurement system should be consistent with and based on the improvement approaches described in the profile.

Outputs

2.2b – Benchmarks and comparisons selected here in Area to Address 4.1a(2) are used to set projections in 2.2b.

4.1b – The measures selected here in 4.1a are direct inputs to the performance analysis activities described in 4.1b. In other words, the analysis that is described in 4.1b should be based on the measures described here in 4.1a.

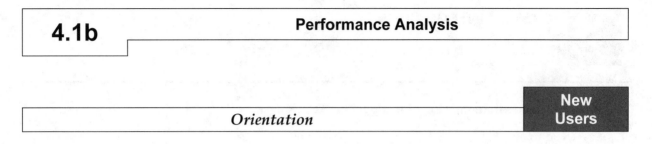

4.1b   **Performance Analysis**

Orientation   **New Users**

FOUNDATION

Performance Analysis 4.1b - Introduction

Once performance measurement (as described in 4.1a) is completed, analysis is used as the tool to translate raw data into actions. The criteria addresses this analysis at the most senior levels of the organization as the senior leaders review organizational performance and take actions which can impact the organization's strategic plans. Nevertheless, high performing organizations also have the ability to perform similar analysis at each level in the organization.

Whereas the Baldrige criteria only focus at the highest level of the organization, they do ask how the results of those analyses are communicated down to the work group and functional levels in the organization so that they can effectively support decisions which are made at the higher levels.

Performance analysis is the key tool to translate data into usable or actionable information. The organization needs to then use the information to help drive actions to improve.

EXAMPLE

Performance Analysis 4.1b - Example Practices

University of Wisconsin Stout **- (Baldrige Recipient 2001)**

UW-Stout's data driven decision-making uses a full range of analytic tools to plan and evaluate university performance.

At a macro-level, the Board of Regents, Governor, Legislature and key state agencies develop plans, incentives, disincentives and mandates to be analyzed for strategic impact. UW-Stout senior leaders participate in structured summits, task forces, and conferences discussing significant educational issues among themselves, and with national leaders brought to the state by UW System. Similarly macroenvironmental analyses of educational and non-educational trends, opportunities and challenges are performed. UW-Stout senior leaders assign offices and committees/teams to participate in this analysis and to determine potential impacts. The Chancellor consults with one or more of the leadership councils and senates to set boundaries, goals and analysis objectives for committees, offices and individuals.

The Chancellor's Advisory Council (CAC) summer retreats are the primary mechanism for addressing overall organizational health and strategic planning. Committees, councils, Senates, and units prepare correlations and projections encompassing all areas of the university to be used in planning. Managers of auxiliary units (housing, dining, intercollegiate athletics, etc.) project five year business plans addressing projected fee rate changes, revenue, expenditures, reserve levels, capital plans and debt service. Budget decisions such as allocating additional funds to a particular service (e.g. Fleet Vehicles) rely on scenarios addressing solvency projections and comparative pricing/availability data. Projections of student applicant show rates, enrollment mixes for student support service demand and tuition revenue are developed each term. Inferential statistics such as correlations, factor analysis, and regression are used to analyze surveys (student and staff satisfaction, climate, evaluation of services) and in database grounded studies such as salary equity and faculty workload.

4.1 UW Stout – Performance Measurement and Analysis

UW-Stout ensures explicit linkage of performance measurements with changing needs and direction by:

- Aligning measures and indicators
- Identifying action plans
- Identifying resource implications
- Evaluating benchmark comparisons
- Defining and tracking key measures

In addition to this top-down analysis, throughout the university, committees, teams and operational units analyze external and internal information (advisory groups, partners, students, community, stakeholders, and benchmarks) to evaluate and improve existing programs and processes. The analyses and recommendations from these planning efforts are interlocked with senior leaders, the Senates, and/or the CAC as appropriate. Key institutional entities such as the Provost's Council, Strategic Planning Council (SPC) and the Senates perform their additional analyses, and also interlock with the CAC. Senior leaders, leadership councils (CAC, Provost's Council, Administrative and Student Life Services Council), the Senates, and standing committees/teams formally review key organizational performance evaluation measures.

Directors of academic and administrative offices responsible for daily operations monitor process measures. Each of the entities (Senior Leaders, the Councils, Senates, Committees, operational offices) is responsible for analyzing performance gaps and identifying improvement opportunities. Depending on the magnitude of the issue, these entities are then responsible for performing root cause determination, gathering more information, or bringing the issue to the awareness of the appropriate senior leader, committee or council for action. In addition, these entities perform causal analysis on key performance indicators and develop richer, more direct, and more discerning causal measures, if required. This process ensures the university actually addresses the critical components of organizational health. For example, as funding rules change at the System level, UW-Stout analyzes the impact and determines the best approach to maximize resources for the organization. Several years ago funding rules changed and it was determined that earning a certain level and type of tuition revenue beyond a mandated revenue target would provide additional base funding flexibility. Identifying and generating unmarked revenue (that has not already been targeted to achieve State or System goals and mandates) is a key approach enabling the university to fund unique priorities and strategic goals. Understanding the dynamics of excess tuition revenue relies on analyses of student mix (full/part-time, graduate/undergraduate, resident, etc.); course costs; enrollment life cycle forecasts by student type; and estimates of non-payment, fee remission and other UW System rules. A small team consisting of the Provost, Vice Chancellor, Director of the Office of Budget, Planning and Analysis (BPA) and Bursar reviews and refines the goals and model semi-annually. More recently, funding rules have changed to encourage adult student access and discourage increases above enrollment targets for traditional students. As a result, the university modified freshmen and transfer student targets and focused on encouraging customized instruction targeted to adult learners. This commitment to use the data and analyses that underlie the tuition revenue key indicator has resulted in effective revenue growth.

UW-Stout values a highly collaborative structure (each person serves as a member of a unit, a governance/employee group, and several committees and teams) that encourages and empowers each employee to actively participate in assuring effective mission performance for the students and other stakeholders. Goals, actions, measures and analysis are deployed throughout the university community via the management system (administrative, governance and/or committee structures) through formal reports distributed to stakeholders, newsletters, letters from the Chancellor, on the UW-Stout website, and at forums and public meetings to facilitate two-way communication.

UW-Stout ensures that faculty/staff and educational program processes are aligned to organizational level performance analysis through: (1) broad organization-wide participation; (2) widespread deployment and access to data; and (3) review and feedback loops. Academic and administrative areas assess daily performance through direct operational and behavioral indicators and by monitoring in process, end-of-process and student and stakeholder satisfaction indicators. Performance indicators are aggregated weekly, monthly, or quarterly and compared to action plans, annual goals, and trends, and reviewed with the appropriate senior administrator or the review committee Planning and Review Committee(PRC),Educational Support Unit Review Committee (ESURC), or peer external group).

UW-Stout's CAC, cross-campus committees and open forum structures facilitate faculty and staff involvement in development of academic policy and program processes. Senior-level administrators, Program Directors, Deans, the PRC and ESURC analyze trend and comparative data to evaluate program and curricular currency, faculty performance, program and course effectiveness, and student academic achievement. The responsible offices, in conjunction with BPA, analyze information pertinent to organization-wide performance measures and action plans. Targets or ranges of expected performance, year-to-date comparisons, and projections of estimate to actual are used. UW-Stout deploys its goals, actions, indicators, and performance through its web site, providing timely access and understanding of results to all university faculty and staff.

Semi-annually the SPC reviews progress on strategic goals, related action plans, and results against expected performance levels in its key indicators. This review is an opportunity to anticipate changing governmental, regulatory, or demographic trends and to evaluate the effectiveness of academic and operational results achieved from these action plans. New studies (like salary equity and faculty workload) provide benchmarking and evaluation criteria for strategic and budget planning and goal setting, including identifying where action plans need to be altered or where stretch actions are required. As this organization-level trend analysis of key indicators identifies gaps compared to goals and benchmarks, the CAC, other senior leaders, or the Senates organize teams or committees with defined responsibility and accountability for implementing continuous or breakthrough improvement actions. This process assures that organizational analyses are aligned with annual and strategic plans, measures, and goals.

Source: UW-Stout (2002) pp. 205 - 207

 EXAMPLE

Performance Analysis 4.1b - Example Practices

Dana Spicer Driveshaft **- (Baldrige Recipient 2000)**

ANALYSIS PROCESS PERFORMANCE

Overall business unit performance is evaluated using the key measurements (TQM's) identified in SD's TQM Control Plan. These data are consolidated at the minimum frequencies specified in the plan, and are reviewed by senior management at monthly Quality Council and Manufacturing Council meetings.

Reports used for organizational performance review are typically prepared in advance for the Quality and Manufacturing Council meetings. While analysis methods vary, trend analysis is perhaps the most frequently employed. As data are consolidated at a specified frequency, year-to-date trends develop and can be compared with pre-established performance targets. Performance can also be projected by using historical data in conjunction with knowledge of how upcoming events affect particular trends. Statistical methods are also used, including correlation analysis, Statistical Process Control limits and other analysis methods to evaluate performance data.

Analysis can accurately assess overall organizational health when used within a strategically aligned measurement system. SD ensures that all measurement data are aligned with the strategic direction.

ALIGNING PERFORMANCE WITH VISION

The Vision and Mission Statements give rise to five key KBD's, which are also the drivers of the Strategic Business Plan. TQM's are aligned with each KBD. Local site and departmental indicators support each KBD. This structured method of aligning performance data with overall strategic direction ensures that analysis and review are available to the entire organization, as well as its various components. In addition, part of the measurement summit process is devoted to a review of work group or functional level measures to ensure alignment to vision, mission, and KBD's.

Various levels of SD's organization review and analyze certain types and levels of data. Data pertaining to work groups and/or functional-level operations are primarily analyzed and reviewed by plant or facility managers and departmental managers or supervisors. As illustrated in the pyramid, there is an overlap between those individuals involved at the middle level and the levels above or below. This overlap, coupled with the vertically integrated data structure, ensures that overall performance is directly linked to work group performance.

Because the total business unit data are aggregated from plant or department-level data, the measurement reporting structure can be linked to work group performance. This structure allows them to segregate and analyze customer data, quality and operational data, and employee data in a wide variety of combinations.

Designated personnel at each location report key performance data to SD to consolidate, analyze, and prepare it for review. Formal consolidated reports and charts are maintained for ongoing measurement of company performance. Many of these reports are communicated through the various electronic conferences available on the client server network.

4.1b Dana Spicer – Strategy Development Process (The Analysis Phase)

- Strategy Development

  - Methods & Techniques

  - Goals, Objectives & Action Plans

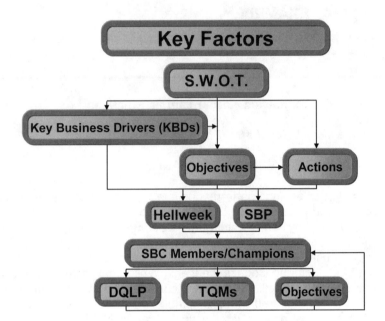

Key senior-level performance measurements and supporting data are also analyzed annually for causal connections, and those performance data with strong linear relationships are prioritized for further investigation. By analyzing data in this manner, SD is better able to understand the influence of certain indicators on key results, allowing them to further improve the usefulness of the measurement systems.

They monitor numerous additional characteristics in support of the KBD's. For instance, plant- or facility-level performance tracking is aligned with the TQM Control Plan and KBD's in support of overall performance. All data and associated action plans are consolidated, analyzed and reviewed by the individual, department, discipline or facility, as appropriate.

Additionally, analysis used at the work group level may also include other more specific techniques, including root cause analysis or 8D problem-solving, Pareto analysis, SPC or other statistical tools, measurement system analysis (Gage Repeatability & Reproducibility studies), and Weibull analysis - a statistical tool used to evaluate and predict useful life of new products during the development phase. These and other techniques are typically used in support of daily operations.

Typically, organizational-level and work group-level analysis will identify trends and conditions that require action at the operational level. For example, SD monitors all customer ratings as key indicators of customer satisfaction. If SD's overall delivery performance rating shows an unfavorable trend, additional analysis is required to understand the root cause. This will typically lead to a specific action plan required at the operational level of one or more locations to improve performance, ultimately resulting in improvement of the group's overall rating, as well as that of each facility.

SD is able to analyze performance data at any level within the organization, and by moving up or down the pyramid to the appropriate level, develop action plans to improve both organizational and operational-level performance. Because the measurement system is aligned with the KBD's and strategic objectives, data analysis at any level remains aligned with the strategic action plans.

Source: Dana (2001) pp. 22 – 24

Diagnosis	**Assessors**

 QUESTIONS

Performance Analysis 4.1b – Baldrige Criteria Questions

Analysis to Support Organizational Performance Reviews (1)

- *What ANALYSES do you perform to support your SENIOR LEADERS' organizational PERFORMANCE review?*
- *What ANALYSES do you perform to support your organization's strategic planning?*

Note 3: Analysis includes examining trends; organizational, industry, and technology projections; and comparisons, cause-effect relationships, and correlations intended to support your performance reviews, help determine root causes, and help set priorities for resource use. Accordingly, analysis draws upon all types of data: customer-related, financial and market, operational, and competitive.

Note 4: The results of organizational performance analysis should contribute to your senior leaders' organizational performance review in 1.1c and organizational strategic planning in Category 2.

Communication of Results (2)

- *HOW do you communicate the RESULTS of organizational-level ANALYSES to work group and functional-level operations to enable EFFECTIVE support for their decision making?*

Note 5: Your organizational performance results should be reported in Items 7.1–7.6.

NIST (2004) p. 19

WORKSHEETS

Performance Analysis 4.1b - Work Sheets

4.1b(1) - Organizational Performance Review Support

Type of Analysis Performed	How The Senior Leaders Use The Results Of The Analysis In The Organizational Performance Reviews

4.1b(1) – Continued

Type of Analysis Performed	Use in Strategic Planning

4.1b(2) - Communication to Work Groups and Functional Level Operations

Type Of Organizational Level Analysis	How Results Of Analysis Is Communicated To Work Groups?	How Results Of Analysis Is Communicated To Functional-Level Operations?	How The Organization Determines That The Analysis Results Are Used Effectively In Decision Making?

ASSESSMENT

Performance Analysis 4.1b – Diagnostic Questions

Rating Scale:

0 - **No Process** in place - We are not doing this
1 - **Reacting to Problems** - Using a Basic (Primarily Reactive) Process
2 - **Systematic Process** – We use a systematic process that has been improved
3 - **Aligned** – We use a process that aligns our activities from top to bottom
4 - **Integrated** – We use a process that is integrated with other processes across the organization
5 - **Benchmark** - We are the Benchmark!
DK - Don't Know

1.	Information is integrated, aggregated and analyzed to get an overall picture of the organization's performance.	0	1	2	3	4	5	DK
2.	Decisions are made based on information and analysis of data, rather than on personal preferences or "gut feel."	0	1	2	3	4	5	DK
3.	Once analysis is completed the result is made available to the appropriate work group and functional level.	0	1	2	3	4	5	DK

Design

BLUEPRINT

Performance Analysis 4.1b - Blueprint

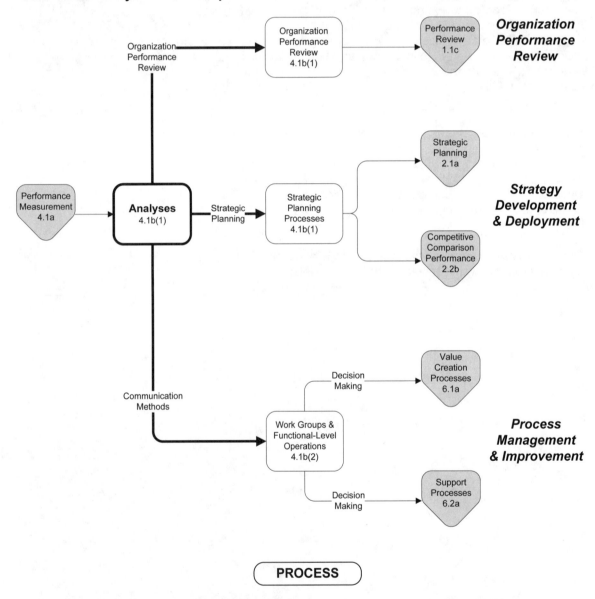

(**PROCESS**)

Once the data are collected, stored, and prepared for use, they can be analyzed for three purposes: 1) organization performance review by the leadership team; 2) strategy development and deployment; and 3) ultimately process management and improvement. The question is how is the analysis performed, what tools are used, what method is used, and how are data displayed?

SYSTEM INTEGRATION

Performance Analysis 4.1b – Linkages

Inputs

4.1a - The measures selected in 4.1a are direct inputs to the performance analysis activities described here in 4.1b. In other words, the analysis that is described here in 4.1b should be based on the measures described here in 4.1a.

Outputs

1.1c – Area to Address 4.1b specifically calls for the analysis performed to support the organizational review process. The performance analysis process described here in Area to Address 4.1b should directly feed the review process described in Area to Address 1.1c.

2.1a – In addition to all the approaches to analysis described in Area to Address 2.1a, Area to Address 4.1b also describes analysis that is performed to support the strategic planning processes. This analysis is quite possibly redundant to the analysis described in 2.1a so each of these areas and linkages should be integrated.

2.2b – Part of the analysis provided here in 4.1b(1) to support strategic planning includes comparisons (e.g., competitive, benchmark, industry). The analysis along with the comparisons provided by 4.1b(1) should drive the projections described in 2.2b.

6.1a – The performance analysis described here in 4.1b directly supports both process management (control) and process improvement. The analysis described here in 4.1b should be consistent with the description of process control and improvement in 6.1a.

6.2a – The performance analysis described here in 4.1b directly supports both process management (control) and process improvement. The analysis described here in 4.1b should be consistent with the description of process control and improvement in 6.2a.

4.2a	Data and Information Availability

Orientation	New Users

 FOUNDATION

Data and Information Availability 4.2a - Introduction

Data and information availability is the ability of the organization to put data in the hands of individuals who need it to "run the business" and "change the business." This includes both automated and mechanical ways to make sure everyone has the data they need when they need it.

Making data available to the users of the data includes making it available to suppliers, partners, and customers (although they may need less of the total company data than internal employees).

Most of Area to Address 4.2a needs to be viewed from the "user of data" point of view rather than from the IT department point of view. IT may feel the users have what they need, but the proof is whether or not the users have the right data at the right time. This culminates in the process to make hardware and software reliable, secure, and user friendly. IT may drive the processes which are the systematic approach to ensuring that hardware and software have these characteristics, but the ultimate judge of achieving the goal is the user of the hardware and software.

Finally, as with other areas, Baldrige asks how the mechanisms used to do this are kept current with the business needs and directions. These are the mechanisms for providing hardware and software systems to users as well as the mechanisms which keep the hardware and software functional during use.

 EXAMPLE

SSM Healthcare - (Baldrige Recipient 2002)

SSMHC's **Information Management Council (IMC)** determines the data and information needed by entity, network and system staff, suppliers/partners, stakeholders, and patients/customers through an **information management planning process** that is part of the overall Strategic, Financial and HR Planning Process (SFPP). The IMC is a multi-disciplinary subcommittee of System Management that represents the system, networks and entities. The IMC consists of approximately 20 System Management members, entity presidents, physicians and representatives from operations, finance, nursing, planning, and information systems. The information management (IC) plan is developed by the IMC and implemented by the SSM Information Center.

Common information systems platforms are deployed in each entity via SSMHC's network. Key clinical, financial, operational, customer and market performance data for all entities and SSMHC as a whole are provided in automated information systems that allow for significant reporting capability. Based on best practices at several entities, the ePMI (Exceptional Performance Management Initiative) Team in 2002 recommended a systemwide model for redesigning the Financial and Decision Support services within SSMHC. The new model enables improved monitoring of performance, additional decision support for executive leaders, and more rapid response to strategic opportunities.

Based on the needs of the organization, the IMC follows established criteria to classify its information systems into three categories: Required (standardized across the system and must be implemented at each facility); Standard (standardized systems that entities implement according to their needs); and Non-Standard (not standardized across the system and entities may implement according to their needs). There is a focus on standardizing information systems to ensure that standard data and information will be available for reporting at a regional and system level. The SSMIC works collaboratively with key functional areas (e.g., corporate finance) to ensure its systems meet common data definitions as, for example, with the systemwide Performance Indicator Reporting process. The required and standard information systems are deployed throughout the system by the SSMIC. The SSMIC has also implemented a sophisticated technical infrastructure that allows the physician partners to access data and information needed for their practice from any location at any time from multiple devices, including PCs, PDAs, pagers, and fax.

The SSMIC has a technology management function that monitors its information systems to ensure high availability and access of data and information. This is accomplished through the Operations Center and the use of system monitoring tools such as Spectrum and ITO. A variety of file servers are monitored for disk and CPU utilization and system uptimes. Data are used for forecasting and planning server upgrades. Additionally, network performance is monitored to ensure access to the application systems. As appropriate, the SSMIC has implemented redundancy for specific systems and within its network infrastructure for high availability.

The SSMIC's Compliance Administration Group (CAG) has developed **Security Policies and Procedures** that document the system's intentions and staff responsibilities regarding information confidentiality, privacy, and security. The policies and procedures cover all employees of SSMHC and physicians who use SSMHC information or information processing services during the course of their work. They also cover all consultants, payors, contractors, contract and resident physicians, external service providers, volunteers, and suppliers/vendors who use SSMHC information or information processing services.

To ensure data and information security and confidentiality, the SSMIC has established a department for Compliance Administration and Security, which is responsible for ensuring appropriate authorized access to its computer systems. A formal Computer Authorization process for granting access to systems and a process of routinely requiring passwords to be changed have been implemented. The department leader also is working with the project manager for HIPAA compliance and heads up the HIPAA Technical Security team to ensure that the confidentiality of electronic patient records is in compliance with federal standards.

Data integrity, reliability and accuracy is addressed through a multidimensional approach. The SSMIC's Decision Support department works with entity customers to audit the data and information loaded into its databases for accuracy. For electronic business partners, such as payors, the SSMIC has established checks and balances in the control process to validate the timely receipt and integrity of submissions for payroll direct deposit and electronic claims submissions. The SSMIC uses the **Catholic Healthcare Audit Network (CHAN)** to perform audits of information systems and processes for integrity, reliability, accuracy, timeliness, security and confidentiality. Hospitals also complete the MHA Conformance Assessment Surveys to check the accuracy and validity of clinical data and improve data reporting.

4.2a SSM Healthcare – IS Planning and Management

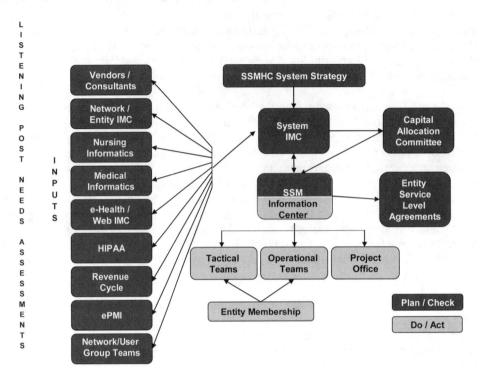

SSMHC keeps its data and information systems current through the SFPP and IS Planning & Management Process. Technology needs are assessed through the internal and external assessment step of the SFPP. The external emerging technologies analysis addresses the current situation in the industry and marketplace. The internal physical plant/technology analysis assesses the technology needs of SSMHC's entities and networks to support achievement of goals and action plans. The IMC uses the information collected through an SSMIC-sponsored IMC Education Day, and the SFPP and its own listening posts and learning tools to develop the information management (IC) plan, which incorporates network and entity information systems needs. Following approval by the IMC, the IC plan is incorporated into the system's SFP. The SSMIC communicates its goals and objectives to each entity and network through a Service Letter Agreement that details the products and services the SSMIC will provide to that entity and network during the year. A measurement system for evaluating the SSMIC's performance is a key component of the agreement.

The SSMIC also contracts with and participates in external industry research and educational groups, including the Gartner Group, Meta Group, Washington University's CAIT program, HIMMS/CHIME, and INSIGHT (participation by individual and board membership) as a way of keeping current with health care service needs and directions.

Source: SSM (2003) pp. 22 - 23

Diagnosis	**Assessors**

QUESTIONS

Data and Information Availability 4.2a – Baldrige Criteria Questions

Data Availability (1)

- *HOW do you make needed data and information available?*
- *HOW do you make them accessible to employees, suppliers and partners, and CUSTOMERS, as appropriate?*

Note 1: Data and information availability (4.2a) are of growing importance as the Internet, e-business, and e-commerce are used increasingly for business-to business and business-to-consumer interactions and as intranets become more important as a major source of organization-wide communications.

Note 2: Data and information access (4.2a[1]) might be via electronic and other means.

Reliability, Security, and User Friendly (2)

- *HOW do you ensure that hardware and software are reliable, secure, and user friendly?*

Keeping Current (3)

- *HOW do you keep your data and information availability mechanisms, including your software and hardware systems, current with business needs and directions?*

NIST (2004) p. 20

WORKSHEETS

Data and Information Availability 4.2a - Work Sheets

Describe how your organization ensures the quality and availability of needed data and information for employees, suppliers/partners, and customers. Describe how your organization builds and manages its knowledge assets.

4.2a (1) - Data and Information Availability to Key Players

Key Group:	Process To Make Data And Information Available To The Group:
Employees	
Suppliers and Partners	
Customers	

4.2a (2) - Hardware and Software Characteristics

Attribute	Process Used To Ensure That This Attribute Is Achieved For:
Reliability	Hardware:
	Software:
Security	Hardware:
	Software:
User Friendly	Hardware:
	Software:

4.2a (3) - Keeping Current

Processes to keep availability mechanisms current with business needs and directions.
For Hardware:
For Software:

 ## ASSESSMENT

Data and Information Availability 4.2a – Diagnostic Questions

Rating Scale:

0 - No Process in place - We are not doing this
1 - Reacting to Problems - Using a Basic (Primarily Reactive) Process
2 - Systematic Process – We use a systematic process that has been improved
3 - Aligned – We use a process that aligns our activities from top to bottom
4 - Integrated – We use a process that is integrated with other processes across the organization
5 - Benchmark - We are the Benchmark!
DK - Don't Know

1.	We make data readily available to our employees, customers and suppliers, as appropriate.	0	1	2	3	4	5	DK
2.	Organization-wide hardware and software are reliable and user friendly.	0	1	2	3	4	5	DK
3.	We have systematic processes to ensure that we evaluate and improve software and hardware systems as business needs and directions require.	0	1	2	3	4	5	DK

Design

 BLUEPRINT

Data and Information Availability 4.2a - Blueprint

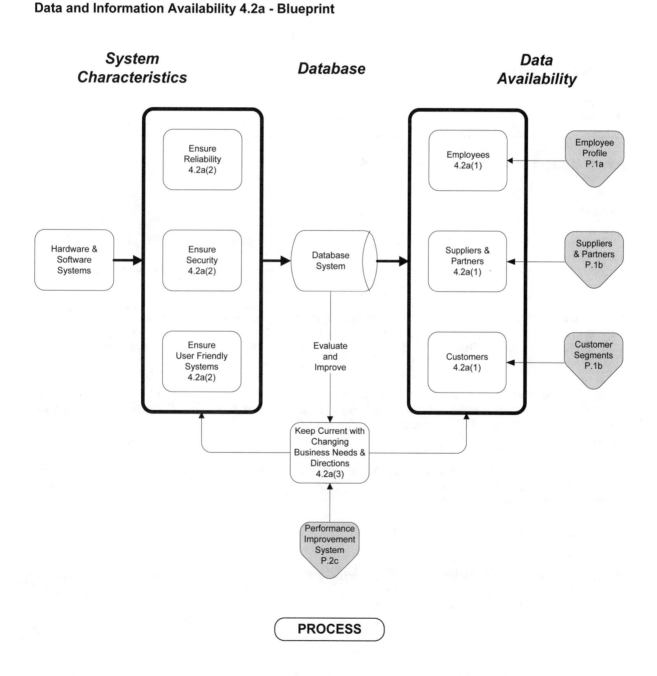

Data availability is composed of three major components: 1) the system characteristics; 2) the database or databases; and 3) the data availability to key users.

The system characteristics for the hardware and software systems are threefold: ensure reliability, ensure security, and ensure user friendly systems.

The database system stores and houses the information in a way to make it available to three key user groups. The three key user groups are the employees, the suppliers and partners, and the customers. Each of these groups may need different information. So the question is how do you determine which group gets what information and how is that delivered or made available to each group? Finally, as with many of the processes, how is the system kept current with changing business needs? These interactions are based on the overall performance improvement system described in the Organizational Profile (P.2c(1)).

 SYSTEM INTEGRATION

Data and Information Availability 4.2a – Linkages

Inputs

P.1a – The number, type, and nature of the workforce described in the employee profile is a critical input to the design of the process/system that makes the right data available to the right employees. There should be processes to ensure that the appropriate information is available for all employee groups.

P.1b – The number, type, and nature of the suppliers and partners as described in the profile is a critical input to the design of the process/system that makes the right data available to the right suppliers and partners. There should be processes to ensure that the appropriate information is available for all key suppliers and partners.

P.1b – The number, type, and nature of the customers, groups, and segments described in the profile are critical inputs to the design of the process/system that makes the right data available to the right customers. There should be processes to ensure that the appropriate information is available for all customers.

P.2c – The processes for keeping the data availability processes and systems current with changing business needs and directions should be based on the overall performance improvement system described in the profile.

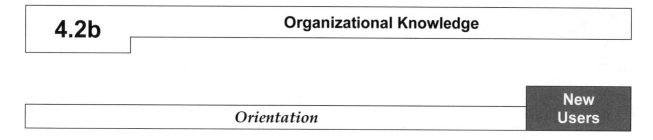

4.2b   Organizational Knowledge

FOUNDATION

Organizational Knowledge 4.2b - Introduction

After several Baldrige recipients demonstrated an ability to leverage organizational knowledge for competitive advantage, it was officially added to the criteria. Simply stated, anything that is known to one person in the company should be usable by all employees. Within that framework the criteria ask how you collect and transfer employee knowledge. The two components of this – collection and transfer – are handled separately by most companies.

Some companies have an excellent ability to collect data and develop world-class databases. In some cases, however, their ability to transfer it to the employees who need those data are insufficient. Clearly the effective use of Organizational Knowledge to accomplish increased performance requires both.

The criteria also ask how the organization transfers relevant knowledge from customers, suppliers, and partners. This is certainly more difficult across organizational (and often contractual) lines between companies. As with any process, the examiners will be looking for the process steps, the decision criteria, and the metrics to know the process is a success.

Most companies collect best practices in some form. Baldrige requires not only this identification of the best practices but effective sharing as well.

The one portion of the criteria which does relate more to the IT department is Area to Address 4.2b(2). This asks how you ensure the following properties of your data, information, and Organizational Knowledge:

- Integrity
- Timeliness
- Reliability
- Security
- Accuracy
- Confidentiality

To effectively address these, each has to be addressed independently. This is true even if there is significant overlap between these characteristics. Frequently companies try to answer this part of the criteria with an over-arching statement which does not, fundamentally, address the process used to achieve each characteristic.

EXAMPLE

Organizational Knowledge 4.2b - Example Practices

Motorola CGISS – (Baldrige Recipient 2002)

CGISS has adopted the Motorola desktop hardware and software standards to reduce costs, ensure reliability and improve ease of use by simplifying the environment that 15,000+ employees use to communicate with each other. Standards are established for hardware, software and software revision levels that can help remove barriers to communication and collaboration between internal organizations. By doing so, CGISS frees significant resources to work on external customer needs by simplifying the computing and communications environment.

Special Interest Groups (SIGs) or Technical Advisory Boards (TABS) and working groups have been formed across the corporation to involve users in establishing and updating the Desktop standards for Motorola. Working groups and SIGs exist for:

- Desktop Configuration Standards
- Desktop Hardware Standards
- Desktop Software Standards
- Ensuring business continuity
- Ensuring reliability
- Remote Access Standards
- Help Desk Standards
- Collaborative Tool Standards
- Network Infrastructure Standards
- Engineering Interoperability Standards
- Web Communities of Practice Standards

Additionally, any interested associate may submit proposals and requests directly to the working groups for consideration. All activities and proposed standards are posted for comment and review by any employee.

CGISS has also adopted an SEI (a software development capability rating) Policy to establish basic practices tl,at will ensure the quality and reliability of software, systems, services and processes. The policy of OneIT states that all IT projects will utilize an approved documented process to guide the development, acquisition, maintenance and implementation of IT products. Some products, which are a result of this effort, include the OneIT Applications Directory Password, and the Tigers purchasing system.

Individual organizations perform periodic software Capability Maturity Model (CMM) assessments designed to identify areas of strengths and weaknesses. Data are tracked over time in order to identify trends in process maturity. Action plans are developed and reviewed based on these assessments to modify existing processes or create new processes in order to improve the software and hardware reliability. Extensive software and hardware testing is performed per documented plan. Formal technical reviews are held to ensure high product integrity is in place before roll out.

The annual OneIT Strategic Planning Process includes all corporate and Sector Information Technology organizations. Steering committees, system engineering /architecture teams and software engineering process groups meet at least once a month to plan and execute process improvement activities.

The following inputs are evaluated to help keep the hardware and software current with business needs and directions:

- Business and Information Technology
- Performance Excellence Scorecards
- Board Of Director project priorities
- Strategic Plan
- Technology Roadmap
- IT/Market Trends
- Benchmarking Data
- Audit results
- Legal/Environmental/Government/DOD Requirements
- Budget Plans
- Customer Satisfaction Survey responses

In addition to CMM assessments, software and hardware councils meet on a monthly basis to monitor improvement activity, discuss issues and propose solutions in order to ensure high reliability is achieved and maintained. Individual divisions also perform Lessons-Learned activities at the conclusion of project rollouts to identify areas that represent significant reliability issues. The lessons learned material is collected, analyzed and applied to process improvement activities.

Source: Motorola (2003) pp. 33 – 34

Diagnosis	**Assessors**

 QUESTIONS

Organizational Knowledge 4.2b - Baldrige Criteria Questions

(1) HOW do you manage Organizational Knowledge to accomplish?

- *the collection and transfer of employee knowledge*
- *the transfer of relevant knowledge from CUSTOMERS, suppliers, and partners*
- *the identification and sharing of best practices*

(2) HOW do you ensure the following properties of your data, information, and Organizational Knowledge?:

- *integrity*
- *timeliness*
- *reliability*
- *security*
- *accuracy*
- *confidentiality*

NIST (2004) p. 20

WORKSHEETS

Organizational Knowledge 4.2b - Work Sheets

4.2b(1) - Collection and Transfer of Knowledge

Source	Collection Processes	Transfer Processes
Employee Knowledge		
Customer Knowledge		
Supplier and Partner Knowledge		
Best Practices		

4.2b(2) - Ensuring the Data and Information has the desirable properties

Property Of Your Data, Information, and Organizational Knowledge:	Process to Ensure This Property Is Achieved and Maintained:
Integrity	
Timeliness	
Reliability	
Security	
Accuracy	
Confidentiality	

Note: Each of these should be answered separately.

ASSESSMENT

Organizational Knowledge 4.2b – Diagnostic Questions

Rating Scale:

0 - **No Process** in place - We are not doing this
1 - **Reacting to Problems** - Using a Basic (Primarily Reactive) Process
2 - **Systematic Process** – We use a systematic process that has been improved
3 - **Aligned** – We use a process that aligns our activities from top to bottom
4 - **Integrated** – We use a process that is integrated with other processes across the organization
5 - **Benchmark** - We are the Benchmark!
DK - Don't Know

1. The organization has processes in place to ensure data integrity and reliability.	0	1	2	3	4	5	DK
2. The organization has processes in place to ensure data timeliness, security, accuracy and confidentiality.	0	1	2	3	4	5	DK
3. The organization has a formal knowledge management capability.	0	1	2	3	4	5	DK

BLUEPRINT

Organizational Knowledge 4.2b – Blueprint

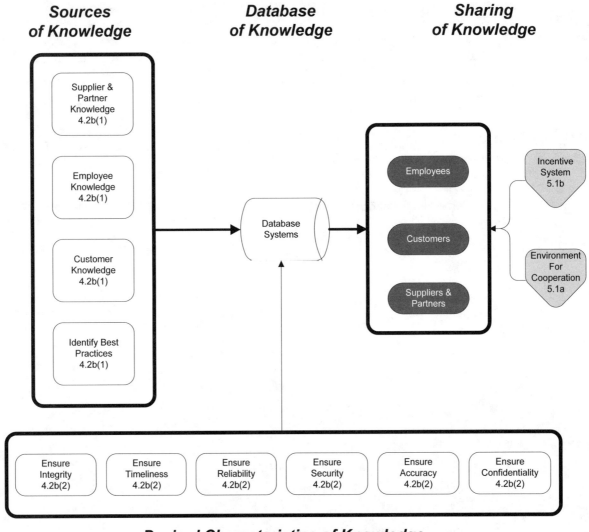

Sources of Knowledge

Database of Knowledge

Sharing of Knowledge

Supplier & Partner Knowledge 4.2b(1)

Employee Knowledge 4.2b(1)

Customer Knowledge 4.2b(1)

Identify Best Practices 4.2b(1)

Database Systems

Employees

Customers

Suppliers & Partners

Incentive System 5.1b

Environment For Cooperation 5.1a

Ensure Integrity 4.2b(2)

Ensure Timeliness 4.2b(2)

Ensure Reliability 4.2b(2)

Ensure Security 4.2b(2)

Ensure Accuracy 4.2b(2)

Ensure Confidentiality 4.2b(2)

Desired Characteristics of Knowledge

PROCESS

Organizational knowledge is an interesting and evolving concept. The criteria tend to take somewhat of a systems view of Organizational Knowledge and knowledge management. A more holistic approach, however, will include not only the systems and the processes for capturing and sharing knowledge, but also the culture and the incentives for sharing knowledge.

While the criteria are not explicit about the connection between Organizational Knowledge, knowledge sharing and incentives, there is clearly a connection between the motivations of employees, customers and suppliers and the degree to which they share information. The culture of sharing and cooperation is connected to Organizational Knowledge and the effectiveness of the systematic process used.

The Organizational Knowledge Area to Address consists of four major areas: 1) the sources of the knowledge; 2) the data base of knowledge; 3) the desired characteristics of that knowledge; and ultimately 4) the sharing of knowledge with employees, customers, and suppliers and partners.

 ## SYSTEM INTEGRATION

Organizational Knowledge 4.2b – Linkages

Inputs

5.1a – The organizational knowledge Area to Address 4.2b calls for the sharing of information and knowledge. There is no process in the world that can make sharing happen if the environment is not right. The cooperative environment that is promoted by the organization and management of work described in 5.1a has a big impact on the degree to which the employees share information and knowledge.

5.1b – Knowledge sharing benefits from systems that capture and disseminate knowledge, however, the systems by themselves are never enough to ensure sharing throughout the organization. The environment for sharing is influenced by the design of the performance management and reinforcement systems described in Area to Address 5.1b. If the incentives in the organization pit one employee against another for limited recognition, rewards, and compensation then the environment for sharing will suffer.

7	**Business Results**

 FOUNDATION

The business results presented in Category 7 give the organization the opportunity to show the tangible impact of the Approaches and Deployment described in Categories 1 through 6. Unlike those earlier Categories, Category 7 does not focus on Systematic Processes, the deployment of the processes, or the improvement of the processes. Category 7 asks for data. The more relevant the data – the higher the score.

It could be said that the score in the Category 7 Items is inversely proportional to the number of words. If you use too many words (and not enough data) the scores will be lower.

In evaluating the data presented in this Category, the examiners may consider several factors:

- Are the data aligned to the approach and deployment described in Categories 1 - 6?
- What is the absolute level of the performance?
- What is the trend?
- How long has the trend been sustained?
- How does the performance compare to 'relevant comparisons?' These can include:
  - Competitor performance
  - Industry performance
  - Best-in-class
  - Organizations recognized as having role model performance (e.g., Baldrige winners)
  - Internal company comparisons (this is typically less impactful)
- Are dips in performance explained? (This is the one time in Category 7 where a detailed explanation of the data are appropriate.) This explanation should describe: 1) what happened; 2) how the organization recovered; and 3) what checks have been put in place to ensure the dip in performance will not reoccur.

It should be noted that at higher performance levels, an improvement trend is not a reasonable expectation. For example:

- 100% Environmental Compliance
- 90+% Employee or Customer Satisfaction
- 50% Market Share where several big customers control the demand for the products or services

In those instances the 'upper limit' of performance may have already been reached. To improve further may not be reasonable to expect or may not be possible.

The Category 7 *Introductions* are different than those used for Categories 1 – 6. They are not a description of the meaning or impact of the Area to Address since this is obvious. Instead it is a listing of the types of data which should be shown in the Item.

Performance Scorecard

Performance measurement is the foundation for fact-based management and organizational learning. The Baldrige Scorecard provides organizations with a framework that serves as a performance measurement system to support the strategic management system. This framework helps organizations: (a) clarify and translate vision and strategy; (b) communicate and link strategic objectives and measures; (c) plan, set targets, and align strategic initiatives; (d) enhance strategic feedback and learning. (Kaplan and Norton, 1996, p,10). The notion here is organizations that concentrate solely on one thing - like financial aspects - do not have all the data they need to continuously improve and innovate. Rather it takes a comprehensive set of measures in order for the organization to achieve its vision and strategy.

Scorecard Generic Example

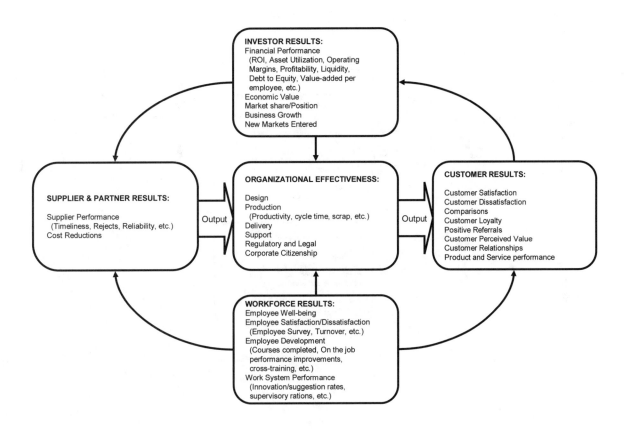

Measures should be designed to support both tactical decision making and strategy development. "Measurements should derive from business needs and strategy, and they should provide critical data and information about key processes, outputs, and results. Many types of data and information are needed for performance management. Performance measurement should include customer, product, and service performance; comparisons of operational, market, and competitive performance; and supplier, employee, and cost and financial performance." (Baldrige Core Values and Concepts).

EXAMPLE

***Boeing Airlift & Tanker* - (Baldrige Recipient 1998) - Scorecard Example**

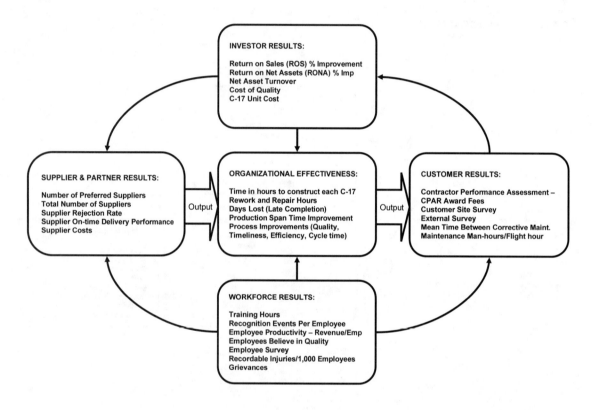

EXAMPLE

The Ideal Performance Results Graph

The ideal results graph displays the performance level, trend, and comparisons all in one view. Comprehensive charts like the one above often take several years to create.

Example:

Figure 7.3.1
% of Employees that rated company as a "good" or "great" place to work.

Sources: Annual Employee Survey and the Coolest 100 Places to Work.

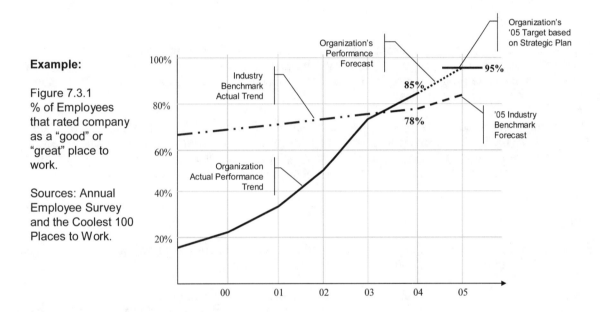

Key Elements:

1. **Trend** of actual organization performance to analyze the impact of improvement efforts over time.
2. **Trend** of **comparison** (e.g., Industry Benchmark) to analyze the changing gap between organization and relevant comparison to assess if: (a) we are closing in on the competition; (b) the competition is closing in on us; (c) the competition is leaving us behind; or (d) we are leaving the competition behind.
3. The **current levels** of performance with actual percentages for both company and the comparison to determine how large a gap exists today.
4. **Target** for future performance based on organization action plans.
5. **Forecast** of organization and comparison performance.
6. Clear label with source(s) of data.

Long-term Perspective

How do organizations develop sustained trends like those in the example? Typically, an organization will have multiple initiatives over several years. In this case the initiatives might have been: (a) leadership development to improve the relationship between management and employees; (b) policy and process changes to help employees do their job better and improve their ability to take pride in their work; and (c) initiatives to improve teamwork and camaraderie. These initiatives "play out" over time and their effects often lag behind the actual execution by several months. Long-term trends in overall employee satisfaction like the ones presented in this chart clearly show that what ever this organization is doing to influence employee satisfaction, it is working.

Further Enhancements

One technique that can be used to enhance this chart even further would be to add the completion dates for significant improvement initiatives. Even though there may be a lag between the completion dates and the contributions to the trend line, over time it does provide an impressive visual of the impact of the efforts.

Another enhancement would be additional trend lines that show **different employee segments** and/or locations. "Overall" trends are useful but can cover up problem areas. It is possible to have the trend line above and still have an entire location (e.g. plant, facility, etc.) or demographic segment (customer service, engineering, etc.) that is dissatisfied.

It is one thing to influence the results of one performance measure or indicator in isolation. It is quite another to positively influence the results of all or most of the key performance indicators. The ideal results charts are combined into a comprehensive picture that illuminates the cause-and-effect relationships and provides a comprehensive picture of organization performance.

Comparisons

There are basically four comparison situations. These four situations are based on two variables: which organization is on top and are the trend lines diverging or converging.

1. Dominant – The dominant situation is the best place to be. The dominant position is when your organization is on top and improving at a faster pace than the comparison. Life is good and getting better.

2. On Track – is the second best place to be. In this situation your organization is on bottom but it is improving at a faster rate than the comparison which means that you will soon overtake the comparison.

3. Impending Danger – is not a good place to be but there is still time. In this situation your organization is currently performing better than the comparison but the comparison is improving at a faster rate than your organization and consequently will soon overtake you if you do not change your approach to improvement.

4. Danger Worsening – is the least attractive place to be – things are bad and they are getting worse. In this situation your organization's performance is not as good as the comparison and they are improving at a faster rate. In this situation if something does not change quickly and dramatically, the situation will continue to get worse.

Comparisons (cont.)

1. Dominant

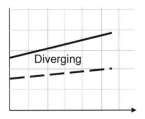

1. You're on top and leaving the comparison behind

2. On Track

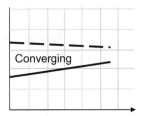

2. You're on bottom but closing in on the comparison

3. Impending Danger

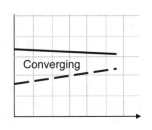

3. You're on top but the comparison is closing in!

4. Danger Worsening

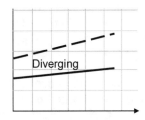

4. You're on bottom and the comparison is leaving you behind

Your Performance ─────
Comparison Performance ─ ── ▪

The results areas are interested in four things – the level of current performance, the trend of performance, the comparisons, and the importance of the results. As you continue to develop your scorecard and assess the organization's performance keep these four dimensions in mind.

Suggested Steps to Develop A Scorecard

1. Determine the Customers Satisfaction Measures.
2. Determine the "proxies" for customer satisfaction – Product and Service Quality.
3. Determine the in-process measures that will predict product and service quality.
4. Determine the key supplier and partner measures that will predict in-process performance and product and service quality.
5. Determine the people measures that will predict employee satisfaction and well-being, in-process performance, and product and service quality.
6. Determine the financial measures that indicate the overall health of the organization including expenses, income, etc.
7. Determine the governance and social responsibility measures.

7.1a	Customer-Focused Results

 FOUNDATION

Customer-Focused Results 7.1a - Introduction

The customer-focused results validate the performance of the organization from the perspective of the customer and sometimes the customer's customer. Regardless of whether the organization collects revenue for their services or provides the service free of charge or uses tax dollars – the primary beneficiaries of the value creation processes are for our purposes the customers.

Why measure the customers' perceptions and purchase behaviors? One reason is to validate the product and service measures that are used to determine the quality of the output of the value creation processes. We determine customer requirements, translate those into product and service features then measure how well the products and services meet those requirements. But how do we know that we got the requirements right or complete? We measure the satisfaction and behavior of the customer.

 EXAMPLE

SSM Healthcare – (Baldrige Recipient 2002) – Example Measures

- Patient Loyalty Index – Inpatient Satisfaction
- Emergency Department Satisfaction
- Outpatient Surgery Satisfaction
- Home Care Satisfaction
- Staff Did All Possible to Control Pain
- Did Nursing Staff Respond Quickly?
- Emergency Department Satisfaction – Total Wait Time Reasonable
- Were Adequate Directions Given About Taking Medications or Follow-up Care?

Source: SSM (2003) pp. 38 – 41

EXAMPLE

Motorola CGISS - **(Baldrige Recipient 2002) – Example Measures**

- % Top Box – CGISS
- Customer Perception of Best Overall Mobile Radio Terminal Mfg: 6/02
- Customer Satisfaction - % Top Box
- Satisfaction with Service Received - % Satisfied and % Very Satisfied
- Customer Loyalty
- Customer Recommend

Source: Motorola (2003) pp. 51 – 52

 EXAMPLE

Branch-Smith Printing - **(Baldrige Recipient 2002) – Example Measures**

- Overall Customer Satisfaction
- Weighted Customer Satisfaction
- Complaints/100 Pre Press Plates
- Value Pricing Satisfaction
- Accessibility Satisfaction
- Customer Retention and Growth
- Product Quality Satisfaction
- Added Value Satisfaction
- Reliability Satisfaction
- Meets Deadlines Satisfaction
- Responsiveness Satisfaction
- Prompt Problem Solving

Source: Branch-Smith (2003) pp. 32 – 35

QUESTIONS

Customer-Focused Results 7.1a - Baldrige Criteria Questions

Customer Satisfaction and Dissatisfaction (1)

- *What are your current LEVELS and TRENDS in KEY MEASURES or INDICATORS of CUSTOMER satisfaction and dissatisfaction?*
- *HOW do these compare with competitors' LEVELS of CUSTOMER satisfaction?*

Note 1: Customer satisfaction and dissatisfaction results reported in this Item should relate to determination methods and data described in Item 3.2.

Note 2: Measures and indicators of customers' satisfaction with your products and services relative to customers' satisfaction with competitors might include objective information and data from your customers and from independent organizations.

Customer Loyalty (2)

- *What are your current LEVELS and TRENDS in KEY MEASURES or INDICATORS of customer-perceived VALUE, including CUSTOMER loyalty and retention, positive referral, and other aspects of building relationships with CUSTOMERS, as appropriate?*

NIST (2004) p. 26

WORKSHEETS

Customer-Focused Results 7.1a - Work Sheets

Summarize your organization's key customer-focused results, including customer satisfaction and customer-perceived value. Segment your results by customer groups and market segments, as appropriate. Include appropriate comparative data.

Customer-Focused Results 7.1a - Work Sheets

Category	Measure	Level	Trend	Comparison
Customer Satisfaction	**Survey – Overall Satisfaction**			
	Survey – Perceived Value			
Customer Dissatisfaction	**Complaints**			
Customer Relationships	**Survey – Satisfaction with Relationship**			
Customer Retention	**Repeat Business (sales)**			
Customer Referrals	**Referred Business (sales)**			

 ASSESSMENT

Customer-Focused Results 7.1a – Diagnostic Questions

Rating Scale:

0 – No Business Results - We Do Not Have These Data
1 – Few Business Results – Early In Improving
2 – Improvements And/Or Good Results Reported – Early Stages Of Trends
3 – Good Trends In Most Areas – No Adverse Trends And Some Comparisons
4 – Good To Excellent In Most Areas – Most Trends Are Sustained And Several Comparisons
5 – Excellent Performance In Most Important Areas - We Are The Benchmark!
DK - Don't Know

1. The organization has measures of customer satisfaction.   0   1   2   3   4   5   DK

2. The organization has measures of customer dissatisfaction.   0   1   2   3   4   5   DK

3. The organization has measures of customer loyalty and customer retention.   0   1   2   3   4   5   DK

	Design	Advanced Users

BLUEPRINT

Customer-Focused Results 7.1a - Blueprint

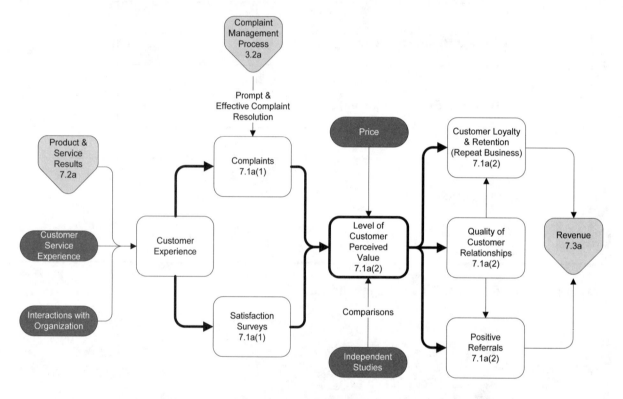

Inputs and Outputs

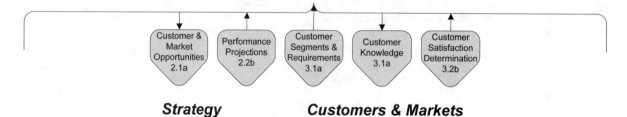

Strategy   **Customers & Markets**

RESULTS

Customer focused results are the scorecard for the external customer and their satisfaction. It begins with a customer experience, which is based on the products and services results. These can include factors such as quality and reliability, which are reported in Item 7.2. Item 7.1 reports against the impact of these factors and centers on the overall customer experience. It should be noted that this is also based on the customer service experience and all the interactions with the organization.

The organization should measure that experience based on customer satisfaction surveys, customer complaints and other objective data sources. One of the final questions is the customer's view of the overall level of customer perceived value. This perceived value affects customer loyalty, retention and repeat business or positive referrals. These, in turn, impact the revenue which is reported in 7.3a. The input to customer focused results are connections from other parts of the criteria. These are mainly found in two areas: 1) strategy (the opportunities) and the projected performance comparisons; and 2) customers and markets (both the customer and market requirements) and the customer satisfaction determination.

SYSTEM INTEGRATION

Customer-Focused Results 7.1a – Linkages

Inputs

2.2b – The forecasted performance (projections) along with the projected comparison performance described in 2.2b should be reflected in the results charts depicted in Area to Address 7.1a. While the criteria specifically ask for strategic plan accomplishments in Area to Address 7.5a, the ideal strategic plan will have projections for measures in all six results areas.

3.1a – The customer focused results presented in Area to Address 7.1a should include results for each key customer or market segment and/or group identified in Area to Address 3.1a. In addition, the results should include results on the key requirements and expectations for each segment and group.

3.2a – The customer satisfaction and dissatisfaction measurement methods identified in 3.2b(1) determine the results that should be displayed in Area to Address 7.1a. In other words the results by segment as determined here in 3.2b should be the same results (levels, trends, comparisons) that are displayed in 7.1a.

7.2a – Product and service results are "proxies" for customer satisfaction. The results in 7.2a should correlate with the results presented here in 7.1a. The analysis of this correlation will help to validate and refine the product and service measures in 7.2a.

Outputs

2.1a – In addition to the opportunities identified by the customer knowledge processes in 3.1a, the actual results in key areas important to customer satisfaction, repeat business, and referrals are critical to a fact-based analysis of the opportunities, the competition, and the gaps. This analysis combined with the knowledge from 3.1a processes and the competitive environment analysis provides a comprehensive picture of the customer and market-driven opportunities.

3.1a – The results presented here in 7.1a are a key input to the process for determining key customer requirements and expectations (including product and service features) and their relative importance to customers' purchasing decisions. While it is very useful to survey customers and ask for their preferences it is even better to analyze their actual behavior and buying patterns along with their satisfaction results. This provides the organization with much better information for making adjustments to product and service offerings.

7.3a – The revenue results depicted in Area to Address 7.3a should correlate to the customer satisfaction results presented here in Area to Address 7.1a. The notion here is that if customer satisfaction is high compared to competitors the customer will come back (repeat business) and tell their friends (referral business).

7.2a	**Product and Service Results**

Orientation	**New Users**

FOUNDATION

Product and Service Results 7.2a – Introduction

Customer satisfaction and purchase behavior are the ultimate measures of product and service quality – these measures (reported in Item 7.1) often lag behind the actual delivery of those products and services. Therefore they are often not timely enough to use to control the quality of the products and services. In other words it is often impractical to have the customer stand over your shoulder and smile or frown as you make the product or deliver the service. Consequently an organization needs "proxies" for customer satisfaction.

This Area to Address asks for how the organization performs on their measures of the quality of the products, service and customer experience. This helps them to measure in a manner which helps to control the processes to ensure they deliver the products, services, and experience that will lead to customer satisfaction, repeat business, and referrals.

EXAMPLE

SSM Healthcare - (Baldrige Recipient 2002) – Example Measures

- Unplanned Readmissions within 31 Days
- Improving the Care of CHF Patients % of Patients Rec'd Weighing Instructions
- Percent of CHF Patients on Coumadin
- CHF Patients w/ Medication Instructions
- Secondary Prevention of Ischemic Heart Disease – Patients Discharged on aspirin/antilatet meds
- Patients treated with lipid lowering agents (LLA's)
- Achieving Exceptional Safety - % of orders w/ dangerous abbreviations
- Mortality Rates
- Nursing Home (LTC) Physical Restraints

Source: SSM (2003) p. 38 - 51

EXAMPLE

Motorola CGISS - (Baldrige Recipient 2002) – Example Measures

- Product Warranty %
- Customer Issue Resolution Cycle Time
- Technical Call Center: Call Abandon Rate
- Technical Call Center: Speed of Answer
- Non-Technical Call: Abandon Rate
- Non-Tech. Call: Speed of Answer

Source: Motorola (2003) p. 51 - 60

Diagnosis	**Assessors**

QUESTIONS

Product and Service Results 7.2a – Baldrige Criteria Questions

- *What are your current LEVELS and TRENDS in KEY MEASURES or INDICATORS of product and service PERFORMANCE that are important to your CUSTOMERS?*
- *HOW do these RESULTS compare with your competitors' PERFORMANCE?*

Product and service results reported in this Item should relate to the key product and service features identified as customer requirements or expectations in P.1b(2) based on information gathered in Items 3.1 and 3.2. The measures or indicators should address factors that affect customer preference, such as those included in P.1, Note 3 and Item 3.1, Note 3.

NIST (2004) p. 26

WORKSHEETS

Product and Service Results 7.2a - Work Sheets

Summarize your organization's key product and service performance results. Segment your results by product groups, customer groups, and market segments, as appropriate. Include appropriate comparative data.

Product and Service Results 7.2a - Work Sheets

Category	Measure	Level	Trend	Comparison
Key Product and Service Features	**Defects**			
Customer Use	**Ease of Use**			
Responsiveness	**Response Times**			
3rd Party Assessments				
Key Correlations				

ASSESSMENT

Product and Service Results 7.2a – Diagnostic Questions

Rating Scale:

0 – **No Business Results** - We Do Not Have These Data
1 – **Few Business Results** – Early In Improving
2 – **Improvements And/Or Good Results Reported** – Early Stages Of Trends
3 – **Good Trends In Most Areas** – No Adverse Trends And Some Comparisons
4 – **Good To Excellent In Most Areas** – Most Trends Are Sustained And Several Comparisons
5 – **Excellent Performance In Most Important Areas** - We Are The Benchmark!
DK - Don't Know

1. The organization has measures of product and service performance against the key customer requirements.	0	1	2	3	4	5	DK
2. The organization has these product and service performance measures segmented by the customer segments.	0	1	2	3	4	5	DK
3. The organization has a comparison of these results against the competitor's performance.	0	1	2	3	4	5	DK

Design	Advanced Users

BLUEPRINT

Product and Service Results 7.2a – Blueprint

Product and service results are primarily the proxies for customer satisfaction. In most businesses it is impractical for the customer to stand over your shoulder and smile or frown as you execute the processes and produce the products and services.

Since they do not have this immediate feedback mechanism for control, output measures are proxies for customer satisfaction. The key requirements and output measures are then used to develop in-process measures that can then be used to manage the performance of processes to ensure the desired output quality and performance.

The product and service results fall into three main categories: output measures, customer use measures, and the responsiveness and third party assessment measures. Output measures are the defects in products and service quality measures that are measured at the end of the value creation processes. The customer use measures include use of customer evaluations of product and service performance.

These are different than customer satisfaction and are actually the customers' evaluation of the product and service. Finally, responsiveness and third party assessments are used as part of the overall performance that leads directly to customer satisfaction and perceived value found in Area to Address 7.1a. This correlation between product and service results and customer satisfaction results serves to validate the product and service results.

Product and Service Results 7.2a – Blueprint

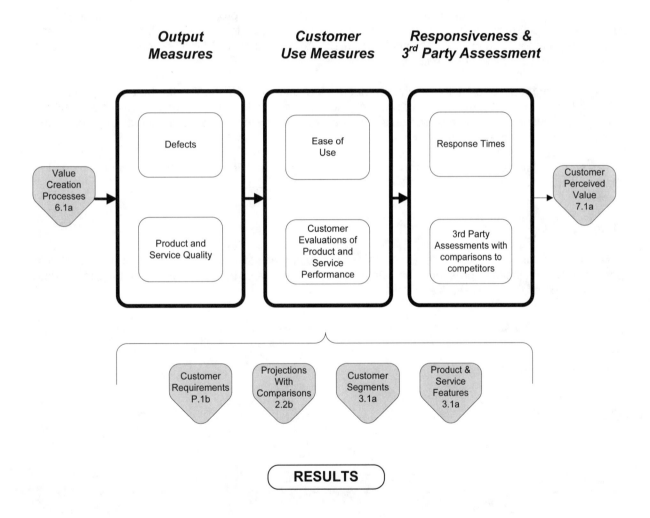

SYSTEM INTEGRATION

Product and Service Results 7.2a – Linkages

Inputs

6.1a - The output or key final product and service results (levels, trends, comparisons) should be presented here in Area to Address 7.2a.

P.1b – Customer requirements as described in the profile are key inputs to determining the key product and service results that are "proxies" for customer satisfaction.

2.2b – The forecasted performance (projections) along with the projected comparison performance should be reflected in the results charts depicted here in Area to Address 7.2a. While the criteria specifically ask for strategic plan accomplishments in Area to Address 7.5a, the ideal strategic plan will have projections for measures in all six results areas.

3.1a – The segments and customer groups that are identified in 3.1a should also be the segments and groups that drive the segmentation of product and service results data. In other words, the results in 7.2a should include results requirements for each of the key customer and market segments and groups identified by the processes in 3.1a.

3.1a - Results for the product and service features that are identified in 3.1a(2) should be included in the product and service results presented in Area to Address 7.2a.

Outputs

7.1a - Product and service results are "proxies" for customer satisfaction. The results in 7.2a should correlate with the results presented here in 7.1a. The analysis of this correlation will help to validate and refine the product and service measures in 7.2a.

7.3a	**Financial and Market Results**

Orientation	

FOUNDATION

Financial and Market Results 7.3a - Introduction

Financial and market results measure both the outcome of how well the organization produces products, delivers services, and creates a positive customer experience by measuring the customers' purchase behavior through revenues and their growth. Financial measures also measure how efficient the organization is at creating and delivering the products and services by measuring expenses.

Financial measures are the ultimate validation of both process effectiveness and efficiency. However, like customer satisfaction they are lagging measures and are often not very useful for managing the processes and people to ensure organization performance.

EXAMPLE

SSM Healthcare – (Baldrige Recipient 2002) - Example Measures

- Not-for-Profit Health Care Ratings
- Approved Capital Investment
- Overall Operating Margin Percentage
- Operating Revenue and Expense per APD (adjusted patient day)
- SSM Home Care Operating Margin Percentage
- Monthly Net Revenue per Physician
- Physician Practice Direct Operating Costs
- Days Cash on Hand
- Market Share

Source: SSM (2003) pp. 41 - 43

EXAMPLE

Motorola CGISS **- (Baldrige Recipient 2002) – Example Measures**

- Motorola Stock Performance v. Competitors
- Sales Growth
- Gross Margin %
- Cash Flow %
- ROA % with CGISS RONA Comparative
- Profit Contribution to Parent
- Subscriber Unit Global Market Share
- Region Market Size and Motorola Share

Source: Motorola, 2003, pp. 53 - 54

 EXAMPLE

Branch-Smith Printing **- (Baldrige Recipient 2002) – Example Measures**

- Total Sales % Growth
- Gross Profit on Value-Added Sales
- Value Added Asset Turnover
- Market Share

Source: Branch-Smith, 2003, pp. 35 - 36

Diagnosis	Assessors

 QUESTIONS

Financial and Market Results 7.3a – Baldrige Criteria Questions

Financial Performance (1)

- *What are your current LEVELS and TRENDS in KEY MEASURES or INDICATORS of financial PERFORMANCE, including aggregate MEASURES of financial return and economic VALUE, as appropriate?*

Marketplace Performance (2)

- *What are your current LEVELS and TRENDS in KEY MEASURES or INDICATORS of marketplace PERFORMANCE, including market share or position, business growth, and new markets entered, as appropriate?*

Responses to 7.3a(1) might include aggregate measures such as return on investment (ROI), asset utilization, operating margins, profitability, profitability by market or customer segment, liquidity, debt to equity ratio, value added per employee, and financial activity measures.

NIST (2004) p. 27

 WORKSHEETS

Financial and Market Results 7.3a -Work Sheets

Summarize your organization's key financial and marketplace performance results by market segments, as appropriate. Include appropriate comparative data.

Financial and Market Results 7.3a -Work Sheets

Category	Measure	Level	Trend	Comparison
Profitability and Return	Revenue			
	Profit			
	Return on Investment			
	Earnings per share (ROI)			
	Return on Net Assets (RONA)			
Other Financial Performance	Cash-to-cash Cycle Time			
Growth	Change in Market Share			
	New Markets Entered			
	New Products and Services			
Market Performance	Market Share			

ASSESSMENT

Financial and Market Results 7.3a – Diagnostic Questions

Rating Scale:

0 – No Business Results - We Do Not Have These Data
1 – Few Business Results – Early In Improving
2 – Improvements And/Or Good Results Reported – Early Stages Of Trends
3 – Good Trends In Most Areas – No Adverse Trends And Some Comparisons
4 – Good To Excellent In Most Areas – Most Trends Are Sustained And Several Comparisons
5 – Excellent Performance In Most Important Areas - We Are The Benchmark!
DK - Don't Know

1. The organization tracks a full range of financial measures, including aggregate measures of financial return and economic value, as appropriate. 0 1 2 3 4 5 DK

2. The organization tracks key market information, including market share or position. 0 1 2 3 4 5 DK

3. The organization tracks business growth and new markets entered. 0 1 2 3 4 5 DK

Design	**Advanced Users**

 BLUEPRINT

Financial and Market Results 7.3a -Blueprint

The financial and market results are focused on three key areas of: 1) growth; 2) markets; and 3) financial (profitability and return on investment).

The growth area includes new products and new markets entered, percentage of sales from new products, and growth in the marketplace. These impact the second focus area of markets.

Financial and Market Results 7.3a –Blueprint

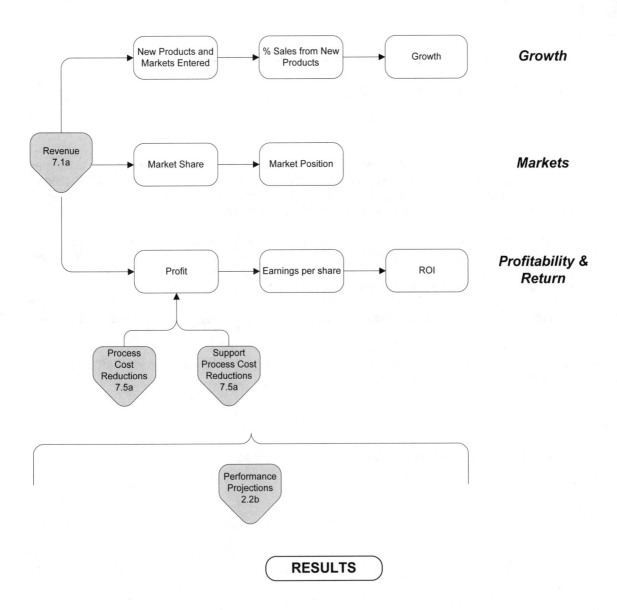

Markets include market share and the position in the markets. These markets should correspond to the customer groups and markets identified in the Organizational Profile (P.1b(2)).

The last element includes the profit, return on investment, earnings per share. In addition, other appropriate measures are tracked. Profit is affected not only by the revenue and Area to Address 7.1a, but also by the expenses incurred in the value creation processes and support processes. The financial and market results should also include projected performance with competitive comparisons as found in the data presented in Area to Address 2.2b.

SYSTEM INTEGRATION

Financial and Market Results 7.3a – Linkages

Inputs

7.1a – The revenue results depicted here in Area to Address 7.3a should correlate to the customer satisfaction results presented in Area to Address 7.1a. The notion here is that if customer satisfaction is high compared to competitors the customer will come back (repeat business) and tell their friends (referral business). Repeat and referral business mean increased revenue.

2.2b – The forecasted performance (projections) along with the projected comparison performance should be reflected in the results charts depicted in Areas to Address 7.1a through 7.6a. While the criteria specifically ask for strategic plan accomplishments in Area to Address 7.5a, the ideal strategic plan will have projections for measures in all six results areas.

7.5a – The value creation process cost reduction results depicted in Area to Address 7.5a are a direct input to the profitability of the organization.

7.5a - The support process cost reduction results depicted in Area to Address 7.5a are a direct input to the profitability of the organization.

Outputs

No significant output linkages with other criteria areas.

7.4a	Human Resource Results

Orientation **New Users**

 FOUNDATION

Human Resource Results 7.4a - Introduction

Human resource results measure the multiple aspects of the people component of the organization. Product and service quality measures are not the only "proxies" of customer satisfaction.

Heskett, Sasser, and Schlesinger (1997) link key people measures such as capability, satisfaction and loyalty, with productivity and services quality which is linked to customer satisfaction and, in turn, revenue growth. Some such as Becker, Huselid, and Ulrich (2001) have proposed that there is an HR scorecard that is aligned with and supports the overall organization strategy.

The people results should be comprehensive enough to provide a clear picture of the overall status of the workforce and should also provide insight into the various segments of the workforce.

 EXAMPLE

SSM Healthcare - **(Baldrige Recipient 2002) – Example Measures**

- Employee Satisfaction
- Total Training Hours per Employee
- Turnover
- Lost Time Injuries
- Workers Compensation Claims
- Back Incidents
- Advanced CQI Training (# of employees trained)
- Medical Staff Satisfaction Survey
- Nursing Response to Patient in Reasonable Time
- Administration Response to needs
- Training Effectiveness (employee demonstrated competences and skills)
- Clinical Collaborative Participation
- % of Minorities in Professional and Managerial Positions

Source: SSM (2003) pp. 44 - 47

EXAMPLE

***Motorola CGISS* - (Baldrige Recipient 2002) – Example Measures**

- Employee Satisfaction
- Turnover
- Training Expenditures
- Stock Option History
- Accident Rate (per 100 employees)
- Injury and Illness Rate
- Worker's Compensation (dollars/employee)
- Job Simplification

Source: Motorola (2003) pp. 55 - 56

Diagnosis	**Assessors**

 QUESTIONS

Human Resource Results 7.4a – Baldrige Criteria Questions

Work System Performance (1)

- *What are your current LEVELS and TRENDS in KEY MEASURES or INDICATORS of WORK SYSTEM PERFORMANCE and effectiveness?*

Note 1: Results reported in this Item should relate to activities described in Category 5. Your results should be responsive to key process needs described in Category 6 and to your organization's action plans and human resource plans described in Item 2.2.

Note 2: Appropriate measures and indicators of work system performance and effectiveness (7.4a[1]) might include job and job classification simplification, job rotation, work layout improvement, employee retention and internal promotion rates, and changing supervisory ratios.

Employee Learning and Development (2)

- *What are your current LEVELS and TRENDS in KEY MEASURES of employee LEARNING and development?*

Note 3: Appropriate measures and indicators of employee learning and development (7.4a[2]) might include innovation and suggestion rates, courses completed, learning, on-the-job performance improvements, and cross-training rates.

Employee Well-Being and Satisfaction (3)

- *What are your current LEVELS and TRENDS in KEY MEASURES or INDICATORS of employee well-being, satisfaction, and dissatisfaction?*

Note 4: For appropriate measures of employee well being and satisfaction (7.4a[3]), see Item 5.3

NIST (2004) p. 27

WORKSHEETS

Human Resource Results 7.4a - Work Sheets

Summarize your organization's key human resource results, including work system performance and employee learning, development, well-being, and satisfaction. Segment your results to address the diversity of your workforce and the different types and categories of employees, as appropriate. Include appropriate comparative data.

Human Resource Results 7.4a - Work Sheets

Category	Measure	Level	Trend	Comparison
Work System Performance	**Productivity**			
Learning and Development	**Extent of Training**			
	Effectiveness of Training			
	Impact of Training			
Employee Satisfaction and Dissatisfaction (soft measures)	**Survey Results**			
Employee Satisfaction and Dissatisfaction (hard measures)	**Voluntary Turnover**			
	Absenteeism			
	Complaints (Grievances)			
Employee Well-Being	**Sick days**			
	Accidents (number and severity)			

ASSESSMENT

Human Resource Results 7.4a – Diagnostic Questions

Rating Scale:

0 – No Business Results - We Do Not Have These Data
1 – Few Business Results – Early In Improving
2 – Improvements And/Or Good Results Reported – Early Stages Of Trends
3 – Good Trends In Most Areas – No Adverse Trends And Some Comparisons
4 – Good To Excellent In Most Areas – Most Trends Are Sustained And Several Comparisons
5 – Excellent Performance In Most Important Areas - We Are The Benchmark!
DK - Don't Know

1. The organization tracks trends in key measures in work system performance and effectiveness.   0   1   2   3   4   5   DK

2. The organization tracks key measures in employee learning and development.   0   1   2   3   4   5   DK

3. The organization tracks key measures or indicators of employee well-being, satisfaction, and dissatisfaction.   0   1   2   3   4   5   DK

Design	Advanced Users

BLUEPRINT

Human Resource Results 7.4a – Blueprint

Human resource results are focused on three main areas: 1) employee satisfaction; 2) work system performance; and 3) learning and development. Employee satisfaction is determined not only through surveys, exit interviews, and other qualitative 'perception delight' instruments, but it is also determined by harder (more quantitative) measures such as turnover, absenteeism, and complaints or grievances.

Work system performance (described as high performance work systems in Area to Address 5.1a) is primarily composed of productivity and safety. These are determined by the work system design and employee qualifications. Employee qualifications are driven by the extensiveness of training and the effectiveness of recruiting.

Human Resource Results 7.4a – Blueprint

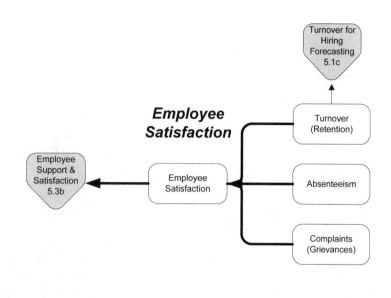

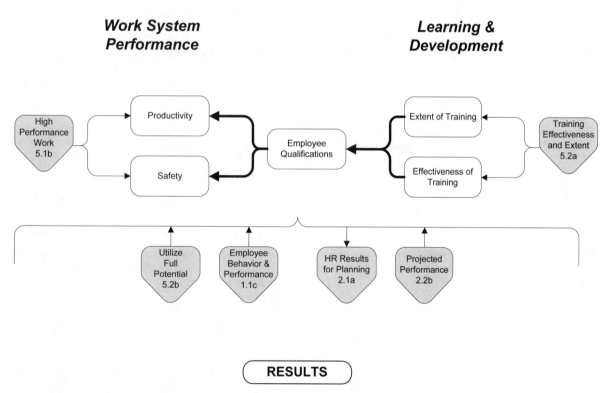

These results areas are connected to other parts of the criteria through the strategic leadership elements including HR planning, project performance, and organizational performance reviews. In addition, these results link with several areas critical to execution excellence. These include the utilization of the full potential of employees, the training and education processes, the hiring and forecasting processes, employee support and satisfaction and well-being processes, and the high performance work system.

361

SYSTEM INTEGRATION

Human Resource Results 7.4a – Linkages

Inputs

1.1a – Guidance (values, direction, expectations) is set, deployed, and communicated and an environment created in order to influence the performance and behavior of the employees in a way that will make the multiple stakeholders successful. The effectiveness of the approaches used to guide and create an environment is validated in the actual results created by the performance and behaviors. Area to Address 7.4a should explicitly include results to validate the efforts and approaches in Area to Address 1.1a.

2.2b - The forecasted human resource performance (projections) along with the projected comparison performance should be reflected in the results charts depicted here in Area to Address 7.4a. While the criteria specifically ask for strategic plan accomplishments in Area to Address 7.5a, the ideal strategic plan will have projections for measures in all six results areas.

5.1b – The results that indicate the level of performance management system effectiveness should be included in the results (levels, trends, comparisons) depicted here in 7.4a.

5.2a – The results from the evaluation of training and education should be part of the human resources results depicted here in Area to Address 7.4a.

5.2b - The human resource results (levels, trends, comparisons) should include indicators of the development and utilization of employees' full potential should be depicted here in Area to Address 7.4a.

Outputs

2.1a – The analysis of human resource strengths and weaknesses is a key input to the strategy development process. This analysis helps to identify strengths to build on and leverage, areas to improve to compete, and vulnerabilities to fix to survive. In addition, this analysis helps to ensure that strategies are realistic based on the human resource capabilities. This analysis should be based on the results (levels, trends, and comparisons) that are found here in 7.4a.

5.1c - The actual turnover of employees that is reported here in 7.4a will influence the employee openings forecast and drive the need for hiring.

5.3b – Human resource results (levels, trends, and comparisons) influence the employee support and satisfaction approaches in two ways. First, they can be analyzed and used to determine the key factors that affect well-being, satisfaction, and motivation. Second, human resource results are used to evaluate and improve employee services, benefits, and policies.

7.5a	**Organizational Effectiveness Results**

FOUNDATION

Organizational Effectiveness Results 7.5a - Introduction

The products and services provided to external customers by an organization are outputs of the organization's system of processes. These include both value creation processes and support processes.

This area to address focuses on the predictors of product and service quality including in-process measures cost, time, and waste. These measures (and others) are used to proactively manage the organization's processes and to evaluate their effectiveness and efficiency.

EXAMPLE

SSM Healthcare - (Baldrige Recipient 2002) – Example Measures

- Average Acute Length of Stay
- Paid Hours per Adjusted Patient Day
- Number of Admits and Visits
- Total Outpatient Visit Time
- Average Mammogram Reporting Turnaround (hours)
- IDN Connected Physicians (number of physicians)
- Availability of Inventory
- Invoice Error Rate
- Purchasing Savings
- Days Sales Outstanding
- Audit Results
- Information Systems Customer Satisfaction
- Insurance Cash Collections
- Net Accounts Receivable Days
- JCAHO 2000 Survey Scores
- OSHA Reportable Incidents

Source: SSM (2003) pp. 47 - 50

EXAMPLE

Motorola CGISS - (Baldrige Recipient 2002) – Example Measures

- Cost of Poor Quality
- Book to Ship (manufacturing cycle time)
- Service Repair Cycle Time (hours)
- 1st Time Yield
- Supplier Quality (PPM Defective)
- Patents Issued
- Employee Productivity
- Inventory Turns
- % Recycled

Source: Motorola (2003) pp. 57 - 59

Diagnosis	**Assessors**

QUESTIONS

Organizational Effectiveness Results 7.5a – Baldrige Criteria Questions

Value Creation Processes - Operational Performance (1)

- *What are your current LEVELS and TRENDS in KEY MEASURES or INDICATORS of the operational PERFORMANCE of your KEY VALUE CREATION PROCESSES?*
- *Include PRODUCTIVITY, CYCLE TIME, supplier and partner PERFORMANCE, and other appropriate MEASURES of effectiveness and efficiency.*

Support Processes – Operational Performance (2)

- *What are your current LEVELS and TRENDS in KEY MEASURES or INDICATORS of the operational PERFORMANCE of your KEY support PROCESSES?*
- *Include PRODUCTIVITY, CYCLE TIME, supplier and partner PERFORMANCE, and other appropriate MEASURES of effectiveness and efficiency.*

Organization Strategy and Action Plans (3)

- *What are your RESULTS for KEY MEASURES or INDICATORS of accomplishment of organizational strategy and ACTION PLANS?*

Note 1: Results reported in Item 7.5 should address your key operational requirements and progress toward accomplishment of your key organizational performance goals as presented in the Organizational Profile and in Items 1.1, 2.2, 6.1, and 6.2. Include results not reported in Items 7.1–7.4.

Note 2: Results reported in Item 7.5 should provide key information for analysis (Item 4.1) and review of your organizational performance (Item 1.1) and should provide the operational basis for customer-focused results (Item 7.1), product and service results (Item 7.2), and financial and market results (Item 7.3).

NIST (2004) p. 28

 WORKSHEETS

Organizational Effectiveness Results 7.5a - Work Sheets

Summarize your organization's key operational performance results that contribute to the achievement of organizational effectiveness. Segment your results by product groups and market segments, as appropriate. Include appropriate comparative data.

Organizational Effectiveness Results 7.5a - Work Sheets

Category	Measure	Level	Trend	Comparison
Process Performance	Productivity			
	Supplier/Partner Performance			
Costs	Inspections, Testing, Audits			
	Defect Reduction			
	Rework and Warranty			
Time	Cycle Time			
	Lead and Set up Times			
	Time to Market			
Waste	Waste			
	Emissions			
	Recycling			
Organizational Strategy and Action Plans				

ASSESSMENT

Organizational Effectiveness Results 7.5a – Diagnostic Questions

Rating Scale:

0 – No Business Results - We Do Not Have These Data
1 – Few Business Results – Early In Improving
2 – Improvements And/Or Good Results Reported – Early Stages Of Trends
3 – Good Trends In Most Areas – No Adverse Trends And Some Comparisons
4 – Good To Excellent In Most Areas – Most Trends Are Sustained And Several Comparisons
5 – Excellent Performance In Most Important Areas - We Are The Benchmark!
DK - Don't Know

1.	The organization tracks the operational performance of key value creation processes.	0	1	2	3	4	5	DK
2.	The organization tracks the operational performance of key support processes.	0	1	2	3	4	5	DK
3.	The organization has key measures or indicators which track performance toward the organizational strategy and action plans	0	1	2	3	4	5	DK

Design	**Advanced Users**

 BLUEPRINT

Organizational Effectiveness Results 7.5a - Blueprint

Organizational effectiveness results are a catchall for the underlying results that have not been included in the other areas.

These results include things like cost, time, waste and other data. In particular, supplier and partner results should be reported. Other costs include cost of inspections, cost of testing, defect reduction and so forth. Time elements include the flow times, setup times, cycle times and, of course, time to market. All of these can have a significant impact on external customer satisfaction and internal cost.

Organizational Effectiveness Results 7.5a – Blueprint

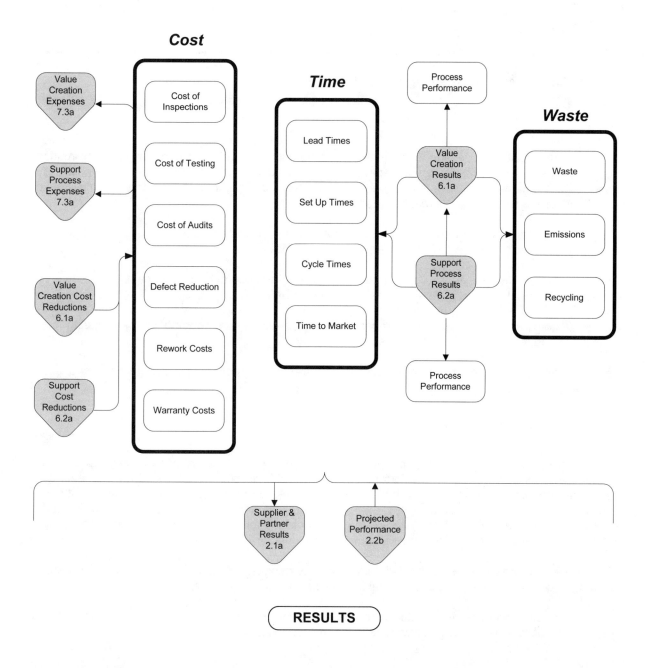

One area not addressed in detail in the criteria is the supplier and partner results. These have a different level of importance for each organization, and are the key to an effective supply chain. Another key question is "what are the measures or inputs to your value chain?"

The results and projected performances found in Category 2 should also be depicted in the charts presented in Area to Address 7.5a.

SYSTEM INTEGRATION

Organizational Effectiveness Results 7.5a – Linkages

Inputs

2.2b – The forecasted performance (projections) along with the projected comparison performance should be reflected in the results charts depicted in Area to Address 7.5a. While the criteria specifically ask for strategic plan accomplishments here in Area to Address 7.5a, the ideal strategic plan will have projections for measures in all six results areas.

6.1a – The results (levels, trends, comparisons) for key in-process and control measures should be included in the results displayed here in Area to Address 7.5a.

6.2a – The results (levels, trends, comparisons) for key in-process and control measures should be included in the results displayed here in Area to Address 7.5a.

6.1a – Value Creation process improvement results (levels, trends, comparisons) including cost reductions should be included in the results presented here in 7.5a.

6.2a – Support process improvement results (levels, trends, comparisons) including cost reductions should be included in the results presented here in 7.5a.

Outputs

2.1a – The analysis of supplier and partner strengths and weaknesses is another key input to the strategy development process. Suppliers and partners can have strengths to build on and leverage, areas that need improving to compete in a particular market, and sometimes vulnerabilities that need repairing just to survive. In addition, the analysis of supplier and partner capabilities also helps to develop realistic strategies that are achievable given their capabilities. This analysis should be based on the results (levels, trends, and comparisons) that are found in 7.5a.

7.3a – The value creation process cost reduction results depicted here in Area to Address 7.5a are a direct input to the profitability of the organization depicted in Area to Address 7.3a.

7.3a - The support process cost reduction results depicted here in Area to Address 7.5a are a direct input to the profitability of the organization depicted in Area to Address 7.3a.

7.6a	Governance and Social Responsibility Results

New Users

FOUNDATION

Governance and Social Responsibility Results 7.6a - Introduction

The last results Area to Address focuses on how well the organization ensures fiscal accountability, ethical behavior, regulatory and legal compliance, and organizational citizenship. While these things are not the central purpose of the organization they are essential aspects that determine overall success.

EXAMPLE

Motorola CGISS – **(Baldrige Recipient 2002) - Example Measures**

- Community Involvement (# of volunteers and # of contributors $)
- % Recycled
- Finance Audit Compliance
- VOM Emission Per Sales
- Water Use Normalized
- Hazardous Waste Normalized

Source: Motorola (2003) pp. 59 - 60

EXAMPLE

Branch-Smith Printing - **(Baldrige Recipient 2002) – Example Measures**

- VOC Emissions
- Annual Paper Recycling (tons)
- United Way Participation ($K)

Source: Branch-Smith (2003) p. 40

QUESTIONS

Governance and Social Responsibility Results 7.6a – Baldrige Criteria Questions

(1) What are your KEY current findings and TRENDS in KEY MEASURES or INDICATORS of fiscal accountability, both internal and external, as appropriate?

(2) What are your RESULTS for KEY MEASURES or INDICATORS of ETHICAL BEHAVIOR and of STAKEHOLDER trust in the GOVERNANCE of your organization?

(3) What are your RESULTS for KEY MEASURES or INDICATORS of regulatory and legal compliance?

(4) What are your RESULTS for KEY MEASURES or INDICATORS of organizational citizenship in support of your KEY communities?

Note 1: Responses to 7.6a(1) might include financial statement issues and risks, important internal and external auditor recommendations, and management's response to these matters.

Note 2: For examples of measures of ethical behavior and stakeholder trust (7.6a[2]), see Note 2 to Item 1.2.

Note 3: Regulatory and legal compliance results (7.6a[3]) should address requirements described in 1.2a. Organizational citizenship results (7.6a[4]) should address support for the key communities discussed in 1.2c.

NIST (2004) p. 29

WORKSHEETS

Governance and Social Responsibility Results 7.6a - Work Sheets

Summarize your organization's key governance and social responsibility results, including evidence of fiscal accountability, ethical behavior, legal compliance, and organizational citizenship. Segment your results by business units, as appropriate. Include appropriate comparative data.

7.6a - Governance and Social Responsibility Results 7.6a - Work Sheets

Category	Measure	Level	Trend	Comparison
Fiscal Accountability	Audit Findings			
Ethical Behavior	Violations Reported			
Regulatory Compliance	Environmental			
	Public Safety			
	Sanctions			
Legal Compliance	Law Suits			
Organizational Citizenship	Extent of Involvement			
	Effectiveness of Involvement			

 ASSESSMENT

Governance and Social Responsibility Results 7.6a – Diagnostic Questions

Rating Scale:

0 – No Business Results - We Do Not Have These Data
1 – Few Business Results – Early In Improving
2 – Improvements And/Or Good Results Reported – Early Stages Of Trends
3 – Good Trends In Most Areas – No Adverse Trends And Some Comparisons
4 – Good To Excellent In Most Areas – Most Trends Are Sustained And Several Comparisons
5 – Excellent Performance In Most Important Areas - We Are The Benchmark!
DK - Don't Know

1. The organization tracks key measures in fiscal accountability, and uses internal and external audits.   0   1   2   3   4   5   DK

2. The organization tracks key measures in ethical behavior and in stakeholder trust in the organizational governance.   0   1   2   3   4   5   DK

3. The organization tracks key measures for regulatory and legal compliance.   0   1   2   3   4   5   DK

4. The organization tracks key measures for organizational citizenship in support of your key communities.   0   1   2   3   4   5   DK

Design

 BLUEPRINT

Governance and Social Responsibility Results 7.6a - Blueprint

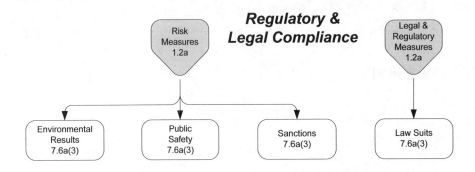

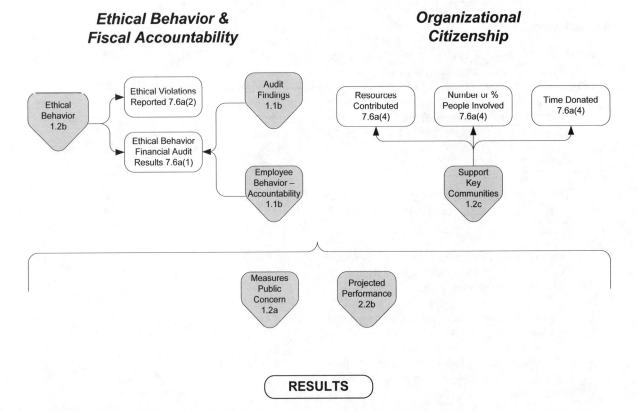

The governance and social responsibility results are divided into three areas: 1) regulatory and legal compliance; 2) ethical and fiscal accountability; and 3) organizational citizenship.

The regulatory and legal compliance area includes environmental results, public safety results, sanctions and lawsuits. Ethical and fiscal accountability include things like violations reported and the findings from financial audits.

Organizational citizenship is directly linked to the key communities and the support identified in Area to Address 1.2c. These indicators might include metrics like resources contributed, the number or percentage of people involved, and the amount of time donated. As with all the other results areas, the projected performance should also be depicted on these charts.

 SYSTEM INTEGRATION

Governance and Social Responsibility Results 7.6a – Linkages

Inputs

1.1b – Employee behavior and accountability results from 1.1b activities are included here in Area to Address 7.6a and should measure the effectiveness of the governance processes that address management accountability, fiscal accountability, and ultimately protect the interests of the stockholders and stakeholders. In addition, Area to Address 7.6a includes the audit findings from both internal and external audits which also validate the effectiveness of the preventive approaches. As inputs these results are used to make governance decisions and also to evaluate and improve the governance structure, system, and processes.

1.2a – Regulatory and legal results depicted here in Area to Address 7.6a should reflect the same measures and goals described in 1.2a(1). From an assessment point of view what is identified in Area to Address 1.1a is fair game here in the results section. From an internal improvement perspective the results in 7.6a confirm or deny the effectiveness of the approaches described in Area to Address 1.2a.

1.2a – Risk results are also found in Area to Address 7.6a. The results here in 7.6a should directly reflect the results and targets that determine the effectiveness of the processes and approaches to address the risks associated with the products, services, and operations.

1.2a – Public Concerns results that are found here in 7.6a should directly relate to the measures identified in Area to Address 1.2a.

1.2b – The results found here in 7.6a should include the measures identified in Area to Address 1.2b that are used to track performance in addressing ethical behavior.

1.2c - The results that indicate the extent and effectiveness of the support to key communities described in Area to Address 1.2c should be located here in 7.6a.

2.2b - The forecasted governance and social responsibility performance (projections) along with the projected comparison performance should be reflected in the results charts depicted here in Area to Address 7.6a. While the criteria specifically ask for strategic plan accomplishments in Area to Address 7.5a, the ideal strategic plan will have projections for measures in all six results areas.

Outputs

There are no significant output linkages between Area to Address 7.6a and other areas in the criteria.

The Journey

Part

5

Overview

The journey is a continuous process or cycle of learning consists of three components: (1) **diagnosis** which includes questions from the criteria, answers or responses for each question (a.k.a. award application), and evaluation based on the responses (a.k.a. examiner feedback); (2) **design/redesign** of the systems to improve performance and (3) **transformation,** the implementation of the new designs to transform the organization. This book supports each phase of the learning cycle. As noted earlier, using this Baldrige User's Guide can help organizations learn about their current practices, analyze those practices, compare them to world-class practices, and significantly change their overall performance and competitiveness.

The Learning Cycle

The path to performance excellence is characterized by the systematic development of three organizational competencies: strategic leadership, execution excellence, and organizational learning. Latham (1997) and Ford and Evans (2001) both found that the Baldrige self-assessment and improvement cycle was essentially an organizational learning cycle.

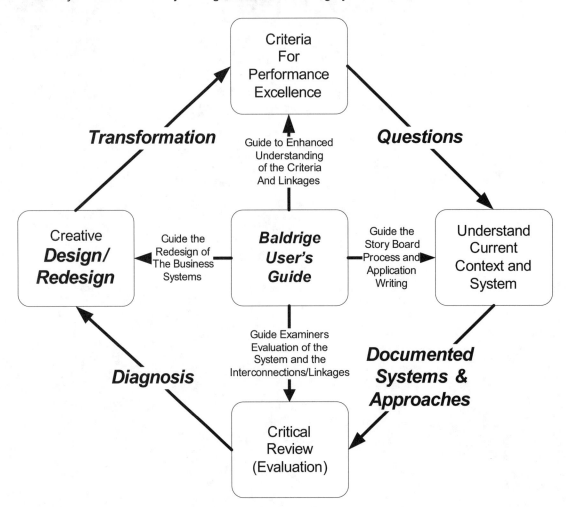

The process begins with an understanding of the questions that are found in the Baldrige criteria. Using the questions the organization's current context (key factors), current processes, and results are described and documented. This is the application in an award process. These descriptions are then evaluated and a feedback report is written that details the diagnosis. This is known as the feedback report from the examiners in an award application process. The diagnosis is then used to creatively redesign the processes to increase performance. The implementation of the new processes contributes to a transformation process that plays out over several years. This learning cycle is repeated over and over again and is the essence of the journey.

Diagnosis

How do we know where we are?

To plot a course for improvement requires two points of reference – the organization's current position and the desired position. The user of this book can diagnose where the organization has significant (or even subtle) opportunities for improvement (or what examiners call OFIs). This process will give the leaders of any organization a large supply of ideas on how to improve. It also helps the organization establish a common language with which they can communicate with other organizations, divisions, departments, functions, etc. A common language enables sharing between organizations. This sharing is one of the reasons many organizations use the Baldrige Assessment process. There are three key elements of diagnosis:

- qualitative (and sometimes quantitative) descriptions of the factors, process, and results
- evaluation of those descriptions formatted as strengths and opportunities for improvement
- identified levels on the maturity scale which is also known as scoring based on the evaluation comments

The diagnostic questions used earlier in this book, provide a starting point to assess the status of your progress. They are intended to be a relatively simple model that can be used to approximate the scoring level of an organization.

More importantly, however, the questions can be used in order to better understand where employees and leaders feel the greatest opportunities for improvement lie. This simple approach can give an organization a quick look at organization member perceptions. For a more detailed, comprehensive, and valid assessment, the organization can follow the traditional assessment and evaluation processes used by award applicants.

Helpful Steps to Conducting an Assessment

To build quality into the learning cycle we start with the deliverable and work backwards. The transformation is ultimately the deliverable of the learning cycle. It is through transformation that the organization achieves performance excellence. The quality of the transformation is dependent not only on leading change but on the quality of the design and redesign of the processes. The quality of the process design/redesign is dependent on the quality of the diagnosis which is influenced by the quality of the documented key factors, processes, and results (Latham, 1997). The quality of the description (a.k.a. award application) is determined by the writing process and the talents of the team.

The steps below are some of the lessons learned over the years working with organizations in all phases of the learning cycle and our own research into the process. This process is focused not on awards but rather on the main purpose of the criteria - organizational improvement.

1. Calibrate all of the Organization Leaders on the Baldrige Maturity (Scoring) Levels

- Discuss the scoring with the leaders, and calibrate them on what level most companies are at, based on a 1000 point scale:
  - Average Government = 80-150 points
  - Average Companies = 150-200 points
  - State winners = 450 + points
  - Baldrige Winners = 600 + points
- The Leadership Focus needs to be on improvement and not on achieving a high score
- If they focus on the score they will always be dissatisfied with the process, since it is radically different from any other scoring system in our society.
- If they focus on improvement they will always be thrilled with the process, since it will provide a limitless supply of Opportunities for Improvement (OFIs) to make the organization better.
- Focus the leaders on using the process to be more competitive in the marketplace.

2. Talk to the Boss (the Organization Leader)

- The senior leader must own this assessment process
- Describe a Systematic Process to them
- Help them to understand that:
  - A Systematic Process is repeatable, and managing a company with leadership opinion (tribal knowledge) is not repeatable.
  - The systematic processes they help to establish and perfect may be their legacy after they leave the organization.
- Discuss the Opportunities for Improvement from this Assessment Guide
- Discuss their views on the Opportunities for Improvement
- Discuss their views on using this assessment tool to improve the organization
- They must remove the barriers for the writing team (when the writing team faces barriers within the organization) which the writers cannot remove for themselves
- Develop the Rules of the Game for writing an assessment document, such as:
  - This assessment and writing process is owned by the senior leaders
  - The strengths and gaps are owned by the entire organization
  - Do not shoot the messenger
  - Leaders (and others who have not been trained in the criteria) can advise the writing team, but they do not write portions of the document
  - The writers have a fixed schedule for the various draft steps....the schedule will not change for any one leader who is not available
- The senior leaders are responsible for reviewing the various drafts – hence, they are responsible for getting on the writing team's calendar, and not vice versa
- The writers are representing the leadership team, and need access to all material requested by the criteria
- They need to get their staff and the entire organization committed

3. Enlist the Writing Team, including the following members:

- Organization Leader
- Champions (for each Category)
- Team Leaders
- Bosses of the Writers
- Writers
- Editors
- Others?

4. Finalize the Writing Team

- Two things will determine the quality of the documented systems (application) – the time available to do the writing task and the productivity of the team. The productivity of the team is driven primarily by their qualifications (Latham, 1997).
- We are not familiar with a training process that can make up for a selected team that is poorly qualified. Training can enable a talented team but it cannot create talent.
- Consequently team selection is critical. If this isn't important enough to put your best and brightest on the team then we suggest that you re-evaluate the project.

5. Train the Writing Team and Other Key Leaders

- An organization cannot write a Baldrige-based application unless they have people who have been trained in the criteria and have used it enough that they are comfortable with what the criteria means. This means that the criteria training should include (at a minimum) the following groups:
  - o Leadership – They need a basic understanding and clear guidance on their responsibilities during the writing process.
  - o Writers – They need to be comfortable with what the criteria means and how this relates to the policies, procedures, practices, systems and process of the organization.
  - o Subject Matter Experts (SMEs) – They need a basic understanding of the criteria in their area of expertise.

6. Ensure that the writing team members and their bosses understand the level of effort involved.

- One of the biggest problems faced by the individual "matrixed" team member is the dilemma of having two jobs while on the team. It is common for the part of the organization that provided the individual to expect them to continue to do their regular job while they participate on the assessment team. This often means that they are mediocre at both jobs.
- Clear agreements and commitment are necessary for the individual to have enough time to do a quality job.

7. Complete the Worksheets

- The worksheets provided in this guide and electronically on the CD are the starting point for preparing the first draft.
- These tables help collect, document, and organize the data prior to actually writing the descriptive text.

8. Define the Processes:

- Start with the Anchor Processes and get the "big picture" on paper first.
- Then expand the detail to include the 17 critical processes.
- List the processes:
  - o Agree on which processes you have
  - o Get everyone to agree on the process steps of each of the processes
  - o Agree on which ones you do not have
- Develop a plan to story-board the processes if they do not already exist

9. Story-Board the Organizational Profile

- Identify Organizational Profile Gaps
- Give each gap an owner and a due-date to 'fill the gap'
- This needs to be completed early in the writing process
- Write the Organizational Profile

- Get agreement on the definitions used in the Organizational Profile for 'key aspects' of the business, such as Customers, Customer Segments, Customer Requirements, Employee Groups, etc.
- Leaders approve the final Organizational Profile

10. Story-Board the Application

- Identify gaps in the descriptions
- Identify other barriers
- Identify linkages
- Process Items include questions that begin with the word "how." Responses should outline your key process information, such as methods, measures, deployment, and evaluation/improvement/learning factors. Responses lacking such information, or merely providing an example, are referred to in the Scoring Guidelines as "anecdotal" information (NIST, 2004, p. 30).
- Two types of questions in Process Items begin with the word "what." The first type of question requests basic information on key processes and how they work. Although it is helpful to include who performs the work, merely stating who, does not permit diagnosis or feedback. The second type of question requests information on what your key findings, plans, objectives, goals, or measures are. These questions set the context for showing alignment in your performance management system. For example, when you identify key strategic objectives, your action plans, human resource development plans, some of your results measures, and results reported in Category 7 should be expected to relate to the stated strategic objectives. (NIST, 2004, p. 60)

11. Review the Story-Boards with the Champions, including an open discussion of the:

- Gaps
- Barriers
- Their ideas as to how to remove the barriers
- Their Hot Buttons
- Their questions or concerns

12. Write 1st draft / Edit / Review with the Champions

Note: The 1st, 2nd, and 3rd (final) drafts should be 7 - 10 calendar days apart. Too much time between drafts deteriorates the quality of the document.

13. Write 2nd draft / Edit / Review with the Champions

14. Write Final document / Edit / Review with the Champions

15. Get the required number of copies printed

- Do not forget copies for internal use
- Do not forget 'modified' copies for restricted use

16. Mail the Application copies to the appropriate organization by their deadline

17. Celebrate the Completion of the Document

18. Quit Proofreading!

- Focus on improvement, not on typos in the Assessment Document

WORKSHEETS

Cross-cutting Themes

The final component of the diagnosis is a review of the Cross-Cutting Themes. The cross-cutting themes are based on an understanding of the Core Values, and knowledge of the organization. They are those issues which have an impact throughout the organization. The themes are the key things that all examiners (or outside visitors) will remember about the organization. They are those things which permeate all parts of the business, and give the organization a competitive advantage.

Cross-Cutting Themes Based On:		
	Strengths	**Core Values**
Practices		
Processes		
Linkages		
Knowledge		
Systems/Data		
Other Categories		

Design – Redesign

What should we do?

To help the design/redesign process this book includes examples of what other organizations have done to respond to the criteria. While these approaches will not perfectly fit any organization except the one for which they were designed, the generic concepts described may be creatively adapted for use in other organizations. This means the learning(s) gained from others can be revised to fit your organization. Additionally, the "common sense" descriptions of what the criteria are addressing (the first portion of each section) can be used to guide the tailoring of the benchmarked process. The output of this phase is a new process design and description. This phase also has three main steps or elements:

- learn from the examples regardless of the industry
- research new examples (e.g., from award application summaries on www.baldrigeusersguide.com)
- synthesize the various examples into a new model
- apply or custom fit the new model to your unique organization

The tools to help this process are the book blueprints and linkages along with the electronic blueprints on the CD-ROM. The creative design/redesign process is typically an iterative one that requires the involvement of different perspectives from a variety of stakeholders from inside and sometimes outside the organization.

Transformation

According to Niccolo Machiavelli, *"There is nothing more difficult to take in hand, more perilous to conduct, or more uncertain in its success, than to take the lead in the introduction of a new order of things"* (The Prince, 1532, ch. 6).

The long list of failed corporate change initiatives seems to confirm Machiavelli's nearly 500 year old "wisdom." No book on performance excellence would be complete without a section on change. This is only intended to be a very high level perspective and treatment of the topic. There are many comprehensive books written on the emotions of change and leading change. This brief introduction does, however, present a simple model for viewing change, and for understanding what drives many of the barriers to change.

The process of transformation is a process of learning. By tracking the performance trends the organization can determine whether the diagnosis and design processes were effective. The only valid reason that we can think of for using the Baldrige Criteria for Performance Excellence is to improve the performance of the organization. If this does not occur, then changes to the approaches need to be made. Each change implemented should be monitored and the approach improved if the changes which were anticipated are not achieved. One way to improve the success rate of implementation and actually get people to use the new process is to involve them in the design/redesign of the process. There are three key elements of the transformation phase:

- implementation of the new design/redesign
- measure and stabilize the performance of the new design
- evaluate and improve the new design

Beckhard and Harris (1987) propose a formula for change that proposes that the force of the dissatisfaction with the status quo combined with the forces of a compelling vision, first steps, and believability, all have to be greater than the resistance to change (D x V x FS x B > R). Robert Quinn of the University of Michigan proposes that there are three aspects to sustainable change:

- the what of change (the easy part)
- the we of change (the culture), and
- the I of change (the hard part).

When you combine the two concepts we find a comprehensive and very practical model for planning and leading change initiatives of all sizes.

The following model combines Quinn with Beckhard and Harris to help us understand the barriers and resistance to change.

The Vertical Axis (a.k.a. Beckhard and Harris Axis)

The vertical axis has five key elements which are based on the change formula proposed by Beckhard and Harris.

Dissatisfaction with Status Quo and a Compelling Vision: The first two variables combine to provide the primary forcing function for change. The dissatisfaction pushes the individuals to change but does not provide a direction. They know they are not happy but do not know how to make it better. The vision pulls the individuals to change and provides a direction for change. Will we like the current system/situation? What will the new system/situation do for us? Beckhard and Harris call this the "desirability of the end state."

First Steps: It is seldom that we know all the required steps to accomplish a transformation but it is important to have a good idea what the first steps will be. A high level project plan with the major activities, deliverables, and benefits can help increase the motivation to change. Beckhard and Harris call this the "practicality of the change."

A Model for Change

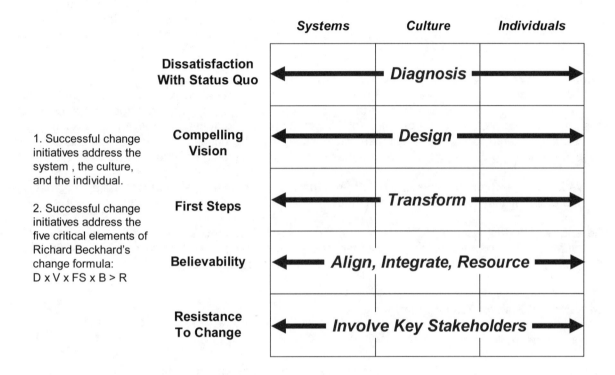

1. Successful change initiatives address the system , the culture, and the individual.

2. Successful change initiatives address the five critical elements of Richard Beckhard's change formula:
D x V x FS x B > R

Believability: The first three variables must form a believable "package" that is supported by credible leadership – both words and deeds. A vision and a plan without resources is just a fantasy. The product of these first four variables must combine and be greater than the resistance to change.

The product of these first four elements has to be greater than the resistance to change in order for change to occur and be sustained.

Resistance to Change: Few people like change, but we like change that is imposed on us the least. At the same time that organizations work on increasing the variables on the left side of the equation they also work on reducing the variable on the right. This is often accomplished by involving the people in designing and implementing the change. Beckhard and Harris call this the "cost of change."

If you are dealing with a change initiative that has stalled - chances are one or more of the variables in this formula is the problem.

The Horizontal Axis (a.k.a. Quinn Axis)

Robert Quinn proposes that sustainable change is achieved when all three dimensions of change are accomplished.

Systems – are the easiest component to change. While they may be complex, we have the technology and knowledge to redesign and change the systems to improve performance. Unfortunately, our experience suggests that often the performance improvement is not sustainable due to the resistance of the culture and individuals that push back on the new ways of doing things.

Culture – the norms, traditions, values of an organization are a powerful force in many organizations. If the new design is not compatible with these norms and values then the chance of successful implementation is reduced. When we say that we have to change the way we work together, people often think that others will have to change but not me. Consequently, we need the third component – the "I" of change.

Individuals – are the essence of any sustainable change. Sustainable change requires that the individuals change and grow. This is often the hardest part of the change process. At the core of this change is a typical learning process where the "gray matter gets grayer" and the "grooves get deeper." This is often not pleasant but it is necessary and it all starts at the top. If the leadership team isn't learning then the assessment process will not make much difference. As pointed out before, the assessment process is a learning process and as such requires that individuals change and transform.

We have found that when change initiatives are not making progress they are not adequately addressing one or more of the elements in the combined model.

In the end we find that we are just facilitators of the process. The process must be led and individuals must actually change or be transformed in order for the organization to be transformed. So, we find that leading change and the journey to performance excellence is a "contact" sport!

Recommended Plan for Transformation:

1. Prioritize the Implementation Plans

2. Assign Responsibilities For The Most Important Aspects of the Implementation Plans

3. Communicate the Implementation Plans

4. Develop a progress review process with:
   a. Metrics to track progress
   b. Accountability for the leadership and participation in each of the steps
   c. Regular reviews to track progress

5. Make Appropriate Course Corrections:
   a. Make adjustments where progress is slower or faster than anticipated
   b. Make adjustments where resources are more or less available than anticipated

Glossary

Glossary of Key Terms

This Glossary of Key Terms defines and briefly describes terms used throughout book that are important to key performance management concepts. The majority of this glossary was taken directly from the Baldrige Criteria (NIST, 2004, pp. 30 – 36). The definitions have been slightly edited and some definitions added for use with this book.

Action Plans

The term "action plans" refers to specific actions that respond to short- and longer-term strategic objectives. Action plans include details of resource commitments and time horizons for accomplishment. Action plan development represents the critical stage in planning when strategic objectives and goals are made specific so that effective, organization-wide understanding and deployment are possible. In the Criteria, deployment of action plans includes creation of aligned measures for work units. Deployment might also require specialized training for some employees or recruitment of personnel.

An example of a strategic objective for a supplier in a highly competitive industry might be to develop and maintain a price leadership position. Action plans would likely entail design of efficient processes and creation of an accounting system that tracks activity-level costs, aligned for the organization as a whole. Performance requirements might include unit and/or team training in setting priorities based upon costs and benefits. Organizational-level analysis and review would likely emphasize productivity growth, cost control, and quality.

See definition of "strategic objectives" for the description of this related term.

Alignment

The term "alignment" refers to consistency of plans, processes, information, resource decisions, actions, results, analysis, and learning to support key organization-wide goals. Effective alignment requires a common understanding of purposes and goals and use of complementary measures and information for planning, tracking, analysis, and improvement at three levels: the organizational level, the key process level, and the work unit level.

See definition of "integration" for the description of this related term.

Analysis

The term "analysis" refers to an examination of facts and data to provide a basis for effective decisions. Analysis often involves the determination of cause-effect relationships. Overall organizational analysis guides process management toward achieving key business results and toward attaining strategic objectives.

Despite their importance, individual facts and data do not usually provide an effective basis for actions or setting priorities. Actions depend on an understanding of relationships, derived from analysis of facts and data.

Anecdotal

The term "anecdotal" refers to process information that lacks specific methods, measures, deployment mechanisms, and evaluation/improvement/learning factors. Anecdotal information frequently uses examples and describes individual activities rather than systematic processes.

An anecdotal response to how senior leaders deploy performance expectations might describe a specific occasion when a senior leader visited all company facilities. On the other hand, a systematic approach might describe the communication methods used by all senior leaders to deliver performance expectations on a regular basis, the measures used to assess effectiveness of the methods, and tools and techniques used to evaluate and improve the communication methods.

Approach

The term "approach" refers to how an organization addresses the Baldrige Criteria Item requirements, i.e., the methods and processes used by the organization. Approaches are evaluated on the basis of the appropriateness of the methods/ processes to the Item requirements, the effectiveness of their use, and their alignment with organizational needs. For further description, see the Scoring System.

Basic Requirements

The term "basic requirements" refers to the most central theme of an Item. Basic requirements are the fundamental or essential requirements of that Item.

In the Criteria, the basic requirements of each Item are presented as an introductory sentence(s) printed in bold. This presentation is illustrated in the Item format.

Benchmarks

The term "benchmarks" refers to processes and results that represent best practices and performance for similar activities, inside or outside an organization's industry. Organizations engage in benchmarking activities to understand the current dimensions of world-class performance and to achieve discontinuous (non-incremental) or breakthrough improvement.

Benchmarks are one form of comparative data. Other comparative data organizations might use include industry data collected by a third party (frequently industry averages), data on competitors' performance, and comparisons with similar organizations in the same geographic area.

Cycle Time

The term "cycle time" refers to the time required to fulfill commitments or to complete tasks. Time measurements play a major role in the Criteria because of the great importance of time performance to improving competitiveness. "Cycle time" refers to all aspects of time performance. Cycle time improvement might include time to market, order fulfillment time, delivery time, changeover time, customer response times, and other key measures of time.

Deployment

The term "deployment" refers to the extent to which an organization's approach is applied to the requirements of a Baldrige Criteria Item. Deployment is evaluated on the basis of the breadth and depth of application of the approach to relevant processes and work units throughout the organization. For further description, see the Scoring System.

Effective

The term "effective" refers to how well an approach, a process, or a measure addresses its intended purpose. Determining effectiveness requires the evaluation of how well a need is met by the approach taken, its deployment, or the measure used.

Empowerment

The term "empowerment" refers to giving employees the authority and responsibility to make decisions and take actions. Empowerment results in decisions being made closest to the "front line," where work-related knowledge and understanding reside.

Empowerment is aimed at enabling employees to satisfy customers on first contact, to improve processes and increase productivity, and to better the organization's business results. Empowered employees require information to make appropriate decisions; thus, an organizational requirement is to provide that information in a timely and useful way.

Goals

The term "goals" refers to future condition or performance level that one intends to attain. Goals can be both short term and longer term. Goals are ends that guide actions. Quantitative goals, frequently referred to as "targets," include a numerical point or range. Targets might be projections based on comparative data and/or competitive data. The term "stretch goals" refers to desired major, discontinuous (nonincremental) or breakthrough improvements, usually in areas most critical to your organization's future success.

Goals can serve many purposes, including:

- clarifying strategic objectives and action plans to indicate how success will be measured
- Fostering teamwork by focusing on a common end
- encouraging "out-of-the-box" thinking to achieve a stretch goal
- providing a basis for measuring and accelerating progress

High-Performance Work

The term "high-performance work" refers to work approaches used to systematically pursue ever higher levels of overall organizational and individual performance, including quality, productivity, innovation rate, and cycle time performance. High-performance work results in improved service for customers and other stakeholders.

Approaches to high-performance work vary in form, function, and incentive systems. Effective approaches frequently include cooperation between management and the workforce, which may involve workforce bargaining units; cooperation among work units, often involving teams; self-directed responsibility/employee empowerment; employee input to planning; individual and organizational skill building and learning; learning from other organizations; flexibility in job design and work assignments; a flattened organizational structure, where decision making is decentralized and decisions are made closest to the "front line"; and effective use of performance measures, including comparisons. Many high-performance work systems use monetary and nonmonetary incentives based upon factors such as organizational performance, team and/or individual contributions, and skill building. Also, high-performance work approaches usually seek to align the organization's structure, work, jobs, employee development, and incentives.

How

The term "how" refers to the processes that an organization uses to accomplish its mission requirements. In responding to "how" questions in the Approach-Deployment Item requirements, process descriptions should include information such as methods, measures, deployment, and evaluation/improvement/learning factors.

Innovation

The term "innovation" refers to making meaningful change to improve products, services, and/or processes and create new value for stakeholders. Innovation involves the adoption of an idea, process, technology, or product that is either new or new to its proposed application.
Successful organizational innovation is a multistep process that involves development and knowledge sharing, a decision to implement, implementation, evaluation, and learning. Although innovation is often associated with technological innovation, it is applicable to all key organizational processes that would benefit from change, whether through breakthrough improvement or change in approach or outputs.

Integration

The term "integration" refers to the harmonization of plans, processes, information, resource decisions, actions, results, analysis, and learning to support key organization-wide goals. Effective integration is achieved when the individual components of a performance management system operate as a fully interconnected unit.

See the definition of "alignment" for the description on this related term.

Leadership System

The term "leadership system" refers to how leadership is exercised, formally and informally, throughout the organization–the basis for and the way key decisions are made, communicated, and carried out. It includes structures and mechanisms for decision making; selection and development of leaders and managers; and reinforcement of values, directions, and performance expectations.
An effective leadership system respects the capabilities and requirements of employees and other stakeholders, and it sets high expectations for performance and performance improvement. It builds loyalties and teamwork based on the organization's values and the pursuit of shared goals. It encourages and supports initiative and appropriate risk taking, subordinates organization to purpose and function, and avoids chains of command that require long decision paths. An effective leadership system includes mechanisms for the leaders to conduct self-examination, receive feedback, and improve.

Levels

The term "levels" refers to numerical information that places or positions an organization's results and performance on a meaningful measurement scale. Performance levels permit evaluation relative to past performance, projections, goals, and appropriate comparisons.

Measures and Indicators

The term "measures and indicators" refers to numerical information that quantifies input, output, and performance dimensions of processes, products, services, and the overall organization (outcomes). Measures and indicators might be simple (derived from one measurement) or composite.
The Criteria do not make a distinction between measures and indicators. However, some users of these terms prefer the term indicator (1) when the measurement relates to performance but is not a direct measure of such performance (e.g., the number of complaints is an indicator of dissatisfaction but not a direct measure of it) and (2) when the measurement is a predictor ("leading indicator") of some more significant performance (e.g., increased customer satisfaction might be a leading indicator of market share gain).

Mission

The term "mission" refers to overall function of an organization. The mission answers the question, "What is this organization attempting to accomplish?" The mission might define customers or markets served, distinctive competencies, or technologies used.

Multiple Requirements

The term "multiple requirements" refers to the individual questions Criteria users need to answer within each Area to Address. These questions constitute the details of an Item's requirements. They are presented in black text under each Item's Area(s) to Address. See the definition of "overall requirements" for more information on Areas to Address.

Overall Requirements

The term "overall requirements" refers to the specific Areas Criteria users need to address when responding to the central theme of an Item. Overall requirements address the most significant features of the Item requirements. In the Criteria, the overall requirements of each Item are introduced in blue text and assigned a letter designation for each Area to Address. This presentation is illustrated in the Item format.

Performance

The term "performance" refers to output results obtained from processes, products, and services that permit evaluation and comparison relative to goals, standards, past results, and other organizations. Performance might be expressed in nonfinancial and financial terms.

The Baldrige Criteria address three types of performance: (1) customer-focused, including key product and service performance; (2) financial and marketplace; and (3) operational.
"Customer-focused performance" refers to performance relative to measures and indicators of customers' perceptions, reactions, and behaviors and to measures and indicators of product and service characteristics important to customers. Examples include customer retention, complaints, customer survey results, product reliability, on-time delivery, customer-experienced defect levels, and service response time.

"Financial and marketplace performance" refers to performance relative to measures of cost, revenue, and market position, including asset utilization, asset growth, and market share. Examples include returns on investments, value added per employee, debt to equity ratio, returns on assets, operating margins, cash-to-cash cycle time, other profitability and liquidity measures, and market gains.
"Operational performance" refers to organizational, human resource, and supplier performance relative to effectiveness and efficiency measures and indicators. Examples include cycle time, productivity, waste reduction, regulatory compliance, and community involvement. Operational performance might be measured at the work unit level, key process level, and organizational level.

Performance Excellence

The term "performance excellence" refers to an integrated approach to organizational performance management that results in (1) delivery of ever-improving value to customers, contributing to marketplace success; (2) improvement of overall organizational effectiveness and capabilities; (3) organizational and personal learning. The Baldrige Criteria for Performance Excellence provide a framework as an assessment tool for understanding organizational strengths and opportunities for improvement and thus for guiding planning efforts.

Performance Projections

The term "performance projections" refers to estimates of future performance or goals for future results. Projections may be inferred from past performance, may be based on competitors' performance, or may be predicted based on changes in a dynamic marketplace. Projections integrate estimates of your organization's rate of improvement and change, and they may be used to indicate where breakthrough improvement or change is needed. Thus, performance projections serve as a key planning management tool.

Process

The term "process" refers to linked activities with the purpose of producing a product or service for a customer (user) within or outside the organization. Generally, processes involve combinations of people, machines, tools, techniques, and materials in a systematic series of steps or actions. In some situations, processes might require adherence to a specific sequence of steps, with documentation (sometimes formal) of procedures and requirements, including well-defined measurement and control steps.

In many service situations, particularly when customers are directly involved in the service, process is used in a more general way, i.e., to spell out what must be done, possibly including a preferred or expected sequence. If a sequence is critical, the service needs to include information to help customers understand and follow the sequence. Service processes involving customers also require guidance to the providers of those services on handling contingencies related to customers' likely or possible actions or behaviors.

In knowledge work such as strategic planning, research, development, and analysis, process does not necessarily imply formal sequences of steps. Rather, process implies general understandings regarding competent performance such as timing, options to be included, evaluation, and reporting. Sequences might arise as part of these understandings.

Productivity

The term "productivity" refers to measures of the efficiency of resource use.
Although the term is often applied to single factors such as staffing (labor productivity), machines, materials, energy, and capital, the productivity concept applies as well to the total resources used in producing outputs. The use of an aggregate measure of overall productivity allows a determination of whether the net effect of overall changes in a process—possibly involving resource tradeoffs—is beneficial.

Purpose

The term "purpose" refers to the fundamental reason that an organization exists. The primary role of purpose is to inspire and organization and guide its settings of values. Purpose is generally broad and enduring. Two organizations in different businesses could have similar purposes, and two organizations in the same business could have different purposes.

Results

The term "results" refers to outcomes achieved by an organization in addressing the purposes of a Baldrige Criteria Item. Results are evaluated on the basis of current performance; performance relative to appropriate comparisons; the rate, breadth, and importance of performance improvements; and the relationship of results measures to key organizational performance requirements. For further description, see the Scoring System.

Senior Leaders

The term "senior leaders" refers to an organization's senior management group or team. In many organizations, this consists of the head of the organization and his or her direct reports.

Stakeholders

The term "stakeholders" refers to all groups that are or might be affected by an organization's actions and success. Examples of key stakeholders include customers, employees, partners, stockholders, and local/professional communities.

Strategic Challenges

The term "strategic challenges" refers to those pressures that exert a decisive challenge on an organization's likelihood of future success. These challenges are frequently driven by an organization's future competitive position relative to other providers of similar products or services. While not exclusively so, strategic challenges are externally driven. However, in responding to externally driven strategic challenges, an organization may face internal strategic challenges.

External strategic challenges may relate to customer or market needs/expectations; product/service or technological changes; or financial, societal, and other risks. Internal strategic challenges may relate to an organization's capabilities or its human and other resources.

See the definition of "strategic objectives" for the relationship between strategic challenges and the strategic objectives an organization articulates to address key challenges.

Strategic Objectives

The term "strategic objectives" refers to an organization's articulated aims or responses to address major change/ improvement, competitiveness issues, and/or business advantages. Strategic objectives generally are focused externally and relate to significant customer, market, product/service, or technological opportunities and challenges (strategic challenges). Broadly stated, they are what an organization must achieve to remain or become competitive. Strategic objectives set an organization's longer-term directions and guide resource allocations and redistributions.

See the definition of "action plans" for the relationship between strategic objectives and action plans and for an example of each.

Systematic

The term "systematic" refers to approaches that are repeatable and use data and information so that improvement and learning are possible. In other words, approaches are systematic if they build in the opportunity for evaluation and learning and thereby permit a gain in maturity. For use of the term, see the Scoring Guidelines.

Systematic Process

A systematic process, typically, is a process where the steps undertaken are:
Defined (how the organization does something - the steps are defined to a level where all parties involved and/or outsiders can understand the sequence of activities, who is involved, and what happens in each step); Measured - each of the steps has measures (these can be in-process measures or end-of -process measures) - which indicate whether or not steps and/or the entire process is on track; Stable - this means that each step of the process and/or the entire process is reliable or repeatable, and can give consistent results to the organization; Improved – each of the processes has improvement and feedback cycles (where each time you go through the process there is a learning cycle which can be used at the beginning of that process the next time it is repeated).

Trends

The term "trends" refers to numerical information that shows the direction and rate of change for an organization's result. Trends provides a time sequence of organizational performance.
A minimum of three data points generally is needed to begin to ascertain a trend. The time period for a trend is determined by the cycle time of the process being measured. Shorter cycle times demand more frequent measurement, while longer cycle times might require longer periods before a meaningful trend can be determined.

Example of trends called for by the Criteria include data related to customer and employee satisfaction and dissatisfaction results, products and service performance, financial performance, marketplace performance, and operational performance, such as cycle time and productivity.

Values

The term "value" refers to the perceived worth of a product, service, process, asset, or function relative to cost and relative to possible alternatives.
Organizations frequently use value considerations to determine the benefits of various options relative to their costs, such as the value of various product and service combinations to customers.

Organizations need to understand what different stakeholder groups value and then deliver value to each group. This frequently requires balancing value for customers and other stakeholders, such as stockholders, employees, and the community.

Value

The term "values" refers to the guiding principles and /or behaviors that embody how the organization, and its people are expected to operate. Values reflect and reinforce the desired culture of the organization. Values support and guide the decision making of every employee, helping the organization to accomplish its mission and attain its vision in an appropriate manner.

Vision

The term "vision" refers to the desired future state of an organization. The vision describes where an organization is headed, what it intends to be, or how it wishes to be perceived.

Work Systems

The term "work systems" refers to how your employee is organized into formal or informal units; how job responsibilities are managed; and your processes for compensation, employee performance management, recognition, communication, hiring, and succession planning. Organizations design work systems to align their components to enable and encourage all employees to contribute effectively and to the best of their ability.

Blueprint Legend

Blueprint Legend

Approach or Process

The approach or process blocks identify key steps or activities in the business system.

——Flow——▶

The connecting arrows identify the relationships among the other five types of blocks. Often the information or items that are flowing from one block to the next are described on the line itself.

Decision Model

The decision model block identifies activities (decision models, criteria, and/or process) at key decision points in the business system

━━Flow━━▶

The connecting arrows that are thicker identify the main flow of the process.

Linkage to Organizational Learning Criteria Item

The linkage blocks identify key linkages to other criteria areas to address or organization profile areas. For each of these there is a matching block on the chart that is indicated.

Input/Output

The input/output blocks identify key inputs to the activity, decision, or database. These blocks also identify key outputs of the processes.

KEY FACTOR

PROCESS

RESULTS

There are three types of criteria areas to address – key organization factors which are in the organization profile section; process areas which are Categories 1 through 6; and results areas which are found in Category 7.

Database

The database block is used for all types of knowledge or data storage including digital and/or hard copy.

References

Bibliography

R

Becker, B. E., Huselid, M. A., & Ulrich, D. (2001). *The HR Scorecard: Linking People, Strategy, and Performance*. Boston: Harvard Business School Press.

Beckhard, R., & Harris, R. T. (1987). *Organizational Transitions: Managing Complex Change* (2nd ed.). Reading Massachusetts: Addison-Wesley.

BI. (2000). *BI 1999 Application Summary*. Paper presented at the Quest for Excellence XII, Washington, D.C.

Bossidy, L., & Charan, R. (2002). *Execution: The Discipline of Getting Things Done*. New York: Crown Business.

Branch-Smith. (2003). *Branch-Smith Printing 2002 Application Summary*. Paper presented at the Quest for Excellence XV, Washington, D.C.

Chugach. (2002). *Chugach School District 2001 Application Summary*. Paper presented at the Quest for Excellence XIV, Washington, D.C.

Clarke. (2002). *Clarke American Checks, Inc. 2001 Application Summary*. Paper presented at the Quest for Excellence XIV, Washington, D.C.

Collins, J. (2001). *Good to Great: Why Some Companies Make the Leap...and Others Don't*. (1st ed.). New York: HarperCollins.

Crosby, P. B. (1994). *Completeness: Quality for the 21st Century*. New York: Plume.

Dana. (2001). *Dana Corporation - Spicer Driveshaft Division, Inc. 2000 Application Summary*. Paper presented at the Quest for Excellence XIII, Washington, D.C.

Deming, W. E. (1994). *The New Economics: For Industry, Government, Education* (2nd ed.). Cambridge, MA: Massachusetts Institute of Technology Center for Advanced Engineering Study (MIT CAES).

Drucker, P. F. (1973). *Management: Tasks, Responsibilities, Practices*. New York: Harper & Row, Publishers.

Evans, J. R., & Ford, M. W. (1997). Value-Driven Quality. *Quality Management Journal, 4*(4), 19 - 31.

Ford, M. W., & Evans, J. R. (2001). Baldrige Assessment and Organizational Learning: The Need for Change Management. *Quality Management Journal, 8*(3), 9 - 25.

Forrester, J. W. (1975). *Collected Papers of Jay W. Forrester*. Portland: Productivity Press.

Heskett, J. L., Sasser, E., & Schlesinger, L. A. (1997). *The Service Profit Chain: How Leading Companies Link Profit and Growth to Loyalty, Satisfaction, and Value*. New York: Free Press.

Kaplan, R. S., & Norton, D. P. (1996). *The Balanced Scorecard: Translating Strategy into Action*. Boston: Harvard Business School Press.

KARLEE. (2001). *KARLEE Company, Inc. 2000 Application Summary*. Paper presented at the Quest for Excellence XIII, Washington, D.C.

Latham, J. R. (1995). Visioning: The Concept, Trilogy, and Process. *Quality Progress*, 65 - 68.

Latham, J. R. (1997). *A Qualitative and Quantitative Analysis of Organizational Self-Assessment At U.S. Air Force Wings Using Baldrige-Based Nonprescriptive Criteria.* Unpublished PhD Dissertation, Walden University, Minneapolis.

Motorola. (2003). *Motorola Commercial, Government and Industrial Solutions Sector 2002 Application Summary.* Paper presented at the Quest for Excellence XV, Washington, D.C.

Porter, M. E. (1985). *Competitive Advantage: Creating and Sustaining Superior Performance.* New York: The Free Press.

PRSD. (2002). *Pearl River School District 2001 Application Summary.* Paper presented at the Quest for Excellence XIV, Washington, D.C.

Quinn, R. E. (1996). *Deep Change: Discovering the Leader Within* (1st ed.). San Francisco: Jossey-Bass.

Ritz-Carlton. (2000). *Ritz-Carlton Hotel Company, L.L.C. 1999 Application Summary.* Paper presented at the Quest for Excellence XII, Washington, D.C.

Senge, P. M. (1990). *The Fifth Discipline: The Art & Practice of The Learning Organization.* New York: Currency Doubleday.

SSM. (2003). *SSM Health Care 2002 Application Summary.* Paper presented at the Quest for Excellence XV, Washington, D.C.

STM. (2000). *ST Microelectronics 1999 Application Summary.* Paper presented at the Quest for Excellence XII, Washington, D.C.

Tang, V., & Bauer, R. (1995). *Competitive Dominance: Beyond Strategic Advantage and Total Quality Management.* New York: Van Nostrand Reinhold.

TNP. (1999). *Texas Nameplate Company: 1998 Application Summary.* Paper presented at the Quest for Excellence, Washington D.C.

UWStout. (2002). *University of Wisconsin-Stout 2001 Application Summary.* Paper presented at the Quest for Excellence XIV, Washington, D.C.

Wu, K.-C. (1928). *Ancient Chinese Political Theories.* Shanghai, China: The Commercial Press, Limited.